The Accordion in the Americas

MUSIC IN AMERICAN LIFE

*A list of books in the series appears
at the end of this book.*

The Accordion in the Americas

Klezmer, Polka, Tango, Zydeco, and More!

Edited by

HELENA SIMONETT

UNIVERSITY OF ILLINOIS PRESS

Urbana, Chicago, and Springfield

Library of Congress Cataloging-in-Publication Data
The accordion in the Americas : klezmer, polka, tango, zydeco, and
more! / edited by Helena Simonett.
p.   cm. — (Music in American life)
Includes index.
ISBN 978-0-252-03720-7 (cloth)
ISBN 978-0-252-07871-2 (pbk.)
1. Accordion—United States—History. 2. Accordionists—United States.
3. Accordion music—United States—Social aspects.
4. Immigrants—United States—Music—History and criticism.
I. Simonett, Helena, editor.
ML1083.A23   2012
788.8'6097—dc23   2012008976

Contents

The Accordion in the Americas

Figure 0.1 Accordion traditions in the Americas. Map by Helena Simonett.

Introduction

HELENA SIMONETT

When my grandfather would reach for his button accordion, a pre–World War I Schwyzerörgeli ("little Swiss organ"), his grandchildren would gather at his feet and listen. I marveled how his calloused fingers could run so effortlessly up and down the keyboard and produce this magic sonorous tone: he made his instrument purr like a cat sleeping on the stove bench. I also remember the bellows changing color, showing beautiful wallpaper when pulled apart, and the alpine flowers that decorated the wooden frame. But I began to detest this sound of my childhood, and more generally Swiss folk music, when I entered my adolescent years. I don't think I ever knew, or wanted to know, the reason for my rejection—the music was just old-fashioned and corny. Not so with Tex-Mex or New Tango, though! I fell in love with Flaco Jiménez, with his shiny gold crown exposed by his wide smile and energetic accordion playing, after seeing the documentary film *Polka: Roots of Mexican Accordion Playing on the Borderline between South Texas and North Mexico*, produced by the Dutch anthropologist Robert Boonzajer Flaes and filmmaker Marteen Rens in 1986. Boonzajar Flaes, who taught visual anthropology at the University of Amsterdam, cunningly juxtaposes Jiménez and Austrian accordionists trying to play each other's polka styles (after listening to a tape), with the former—of course—much more successful than the latter. While I discovered an array of new "world musics" (many of which feature the accordion prominently, I have to point out), some young people from my part of the country thought Swiss folk was cool and began to fully embrace "ethnic" music—a trend that grew after the mid-1980s and in the 1990s. Yet we all came full circle: "folk accordionists" such as Pareglish's Markus Flückiger play everything from "urchig" (original Swiss) to Finnish, Irish, Chinese, and klezmer; my own Schwyzerörgeli is at arm's distance as I edit this volume. This volume is, in a way, my "coming out of the closet," a way of dealing with my own ambivalence regarding the instrument that carries so many memories.

Throughout its history, the accordion, like no other instrument, has spurred intense reactions. Why is it that this object is so dearly loved by peoples around the world and so intensely hated at the same time by others? Is it the physical object itself—that pleated cardboard contained by a square wooden box? Is it the sound—that rough tone rich in upper harmonics with a noise-to-sound ratio higher than the European (classical) norm? Is it the repertoire—the low aesthetic value of polkas and other ludicrous dance tunes associated with "beer, brats, and bellies"? Or is it the locales where the accordion found a home—the German taverns, the American dancehalls, the Argentine brothels, and all the other places of dubious moral standing?

The accordion worlds are far too complex for a plain answer to these questions, but maybe one first response can be found in a *Garfield* cartoon by Jim Davis. Jon explains to his cat: "The accordion is my life, Garfield. You know why? Because I have soul!" To which Garfield replies nonchalantly: "No, Jon. You have an accordion."

People are drawn to the sound of the accordion because it strikes a chord inside; it triggers remembrance even though there may be no actual accordion experiences to which to relate. The sounding accordion elicits "imaginary worlds of memory, tradition, and community"—or what Marion Jacobson (in chapter 14 of this volume) describes, in an allusion to Raymond Williams with regard to the contemporary accordionist William Schimmel's experimental sound work, as a "structure of feeling." But if culture indeed would be understood as a "structure of feeling" lived and experienced by the vast majority of people in a given society, and not as "high culture" and "low culture," concepts inherited by a premodern class society, one wonders why the accordion has so passionately been ridiculed and rejected. Richard March (chapter 2 of this volume) concludes that perpetuated sociological factors play an important role in the instrument's perception as "unsophisticated," "simple," and "low-class."[1]

The Marvel Box

The genius of the accordion lies in its inner workings. Accordions have thousands of miniscule pieces that must be in their proper place: metal tongues, rivets, nails, screws, washers, springs, buttons, wooden hammers, bits of felt, leather, cloth, cardboard, and so forth. Each instrument is a mechanical marvel, a small masterpiece of mechanical ingenuity developed and perfected in the nineteenth century. The instrument's very name reflects the unique and revolutionary feature by which, through the handing of one key or button, a full chord resounds—derived from the older German word *Accord* (chord). A closed system that sounds harmoniously, the accordion prevents disharmonious playing. Tuning is not necessary, and no previous musical knowledge is required to squeeze out a plain melody with some harmonizing chords.

To understand how sound is produced on the accordion, some technical information will be necessary (see also the glossary). As suggested by the instrument's widespread nickname "squeezebox," pulling and pushing the bellows generates airflow that is directed on reeds by depressing buttons or keys that raise palettes. The sound itself is produced by free reeds, steel tongues that are riveted to a metal reed plate with two slots of the same size as the reeds. One reed is attached on each side of the plate, and a leather tap covers the opposite side to each reed to prevent air from entering and actuating the reed. If the pair of reeds is identical, the same pitch will sound on either push or pull; this principle is called "uni-sonor" (used in the piano accordion and certain concertinas). If the reeds are of different size or thickness, each button actuates two different pitches, one on bellows push and the other on pull; this is called "bi-sonor" (used in diatonic accordions). Sets of reed plates are fixed on wooden reed blocks that are mounted on the palette board in alignment with the holes corresponding with the valves. The more buttons an accordion features, the more reed blocks are necessary to accommodate the palettes. Up to six reed blocks may be fitted in the treble casing, to which the right-hand fingering board is attached at a right angle. The bass side is similarly constructed. It is equipped with an air-release valve to enable the bellows to open and close silently when desired. Buttons and palettes are connected by rods and levers. Steel springs cause the buttons to return to their resting position after being released.[2] Palettes are covered with fine leather or felt to make them airtight, as are the reed blocks where they touch the casing and the casings where they connect to the bellows. Bellows are made of layers of cloth and cardboard, folded and pleated, with soft leather gussets for the flexible inside corners and shaped metal protectors for the outside corners. All accordion types work on variations of this same principle.

Three basic models with combinations of fixed chords and single notes that were either uni- or bi-sonor existed as early as 1834. Nineteenth-century instrument makers experimented intensely with timbre using different kinds of woods and metal alloys. Shifts or switches to operate registers of different-sounding reeds were introduced in the mid-1800s to create tremolo effects and changes in timbre and loudness. Such models are most prominently used by Cajun musicians today (Mark DeWitt, chapter 3 of this volume).

The (early) accordion's limited possibility to create a large range of pitches was ample reason to blame it for the loss of traditional folk music. In fact, the accordion's asset of being able to produce preset pitches with harmonious chords

Figure 0.2 Detail photographs of button mechanism (1), reed blocks (2), and single reeds (3) of a Swiss accordion. Photographs by Helena Simonett.

was also one of its downfalls. Much of the music played on diatonic accordions is diatonic in the sense of being in a major or minor key.[3] Early one-row accordions with few treble buttons constrained musicians to the use of the seven notes of a major scale—a severe limitation for those playing music outside of Western traditions. Black Creoles, for example, interested in playing the blues with its flattened seventh, particularly experienced the limits of the accordion (Jared Snyder, chapter 4 of this volume). They had to either modulate into another key or retune their factory-made instrument—a practice still common among Dominican *merengue*, Colombian *vallenato*, and Mexican *norteño* and Tejano accordionists, as explained by Sydney Hutchinson (chapter 12), Egberto Bermúdez (chapter 10), and Cathy Ragland (chapter 5), respectively.[4] Some instruments are specially modified to meet the performance needs of individual accordionists.

Despite its limitations, the diatonic button accordion is unquestionably the most popular type of accordion across the globe.[5] Virtually every culture has its favored version of accordion adapted to the requirements of its music and its sound aesthetics. According to the World of Accordions museum curator Helmi Strahl Harrington, between forty and fifty-five accordion varieties can be identified. Their predominant usage is in traditional music.[6]

Materials determine the sound quality to a great degree. The choice of wood for the frame has some influence on an instrument's resonance but is not nearly as important as the material of the reeds. The purring sound of my grandfather's accordion partly resulted from the kind of zinc alloy of which prewar reed-plates were made and partly from the unique tuning of the individual reeds. Schwyzerörgeli makers imported reeds and reed-plates from Italy until World War I, when raw materials became scarce and Italian factories were forced to redirect their production. After the war, lighter aluminum alloy replaced the sonorous-sounding zinc reed-plates. Although Swiss instrument makers strove constantly to improve the quality of their products, they also kept trying to emulate the prewar sound of the old Schwyzerörgeli that was so firmly entrenched in Swiss folk-music aesthetics. Argentine tango accordionists similarly insisted on the use of the earlier material, which had fallen out of fashion among the German concertina players who began to identify with a different sound after the war (María Susana Azzi, chapter 11 of this volume).

The tuning of the individual reeds is a crucial component of eliciting particular tone colors. The number of reeds per pitch for the right-hand buttons varies between one and four. Multiple reeds may be tuned in different combinations of the fundamental note and its upper and lower one or two octaves, and from "dry" (with reeds in unison and no acoustic beating) to various degrees of "wetness." For the latter, some of the reeds that sound together are slightly detuned relative to the other(s) to produce a "beating"—an interference between sound waves of slightly differing wavelengths that results in a tremolo or shimmering effect.

The rate of the tremolo is typically referred to as the amount of "wetness." To give an example: The three reeds that sound together on pitch A on my Swiss accordion are roughly tuned as follows: fundamental 440 Hz, first upper octave 878 Hz, second upper octave 882 Hz. Ideally, the difference in frequency between the upper octaves should be between three and five oscillations (interference, however, varies within the same instrument). This tuning is moderately "wet" compared to the wetness of, for example, the French *musette* tuning, which may differ up to ten oscillations. Variations in timbre between instruments also result from the density of the steel reeds. Swiss accordion tuners, for example, aim at a soft rate of recurrence and therefore file off material at the rear end of the reed, not at the top end. They also favor a tongue that responds quickly to minimal airflow. Hence, the position of each of the roughly 130 reeds of a standard three-reed, three-row, eighteen-bass Swiss accordion must be individually adjusted for optimal sound. A tuner, professionally equipped with an electronic tuning device and electric precision file, will spend two to four working days for this process. In the end, however, the tuner's ear will decide what sounds correct.[7]

6

While the Argentine *bandoneón* (concertina) has two reeds per pitch that are tuned in a perfect octave apart, it sounds "small" or "serious," in María Susana Azzi's translation from the Spanish language, compared to a zydeco accordion, for which a "wet" tuning is preferred with four reeds per pitch, where the two sets of the middle octave may be as much as fifteen centimeters apart. Jared Snyder believes that Creole accordionists did not retune new, factory-tuned instruments; rather, there was a natural fatigue in the metal of the reed caused by the heavy use of these instruments that made them go out of tune in a way Creole musicians found pleasing. To achieve this "Creole sound aesthetics" on a piano accordion—such as used by the zydeco musician Clifton Chenier—a "combination of bellows control and well-worn reeds amplified with an inexpensive microphone that is overloaded by either a sound system or a guitar amplifier" makes up for wet tuning.[8]

The sound of the accordion is primarily produced by pulling and pushing the bellows while pressing buttons or keys that open valves to allow airflow to vibrate the reeds. But the means of the sound production is more like that of the violin bow than the touch of piano keys. Volume, accents, intonation, varying tone intensity, and an overall expressiveness that resembles the human voice all depend on the handling of the bellows. Combined with the unvoiced sounds of the bellows, the accordion is able to express an array of human feelings. It cries, sings, screams, hisses, whispers, whines, groans, mutters, squeals, sighs, sobs, wails, whimpers, and wheezes; it breathes as it becomes alive in its player's hands. "Its physical and sonorous plasticity" is the instrument's greatest strength—"its ability to take a thousand forms let[s] the musician establish an intimate rapport with it, . . . transforming it into a living extension of the body."[9]

No wonder that the accordion and its myriad forms—from the button and piano accordion to the concertina and the *bandoneón*—has spread and taken roots across many cultures. The accordion reflected the zeitgeist of the industrial era of the late nineteenth century. In a time of technical excitement, the new, mechanically sophisticated instrument came to symbolize progress and modernity. For émigrés who were optimistically looking forward to a future on new shores and whose dreams had been shattered, it provided a strong emotional link to the world left behind. As outlined in my own contribution to this volume (chapter 1), within less than half a century of its birth in 1829, the accordion had become a most popular instrument. The accordion was a radically democratic instrument: it offered anyone and everyone a chance to participate in musical activities. At the same time, complaints about the loss of traditional folk music and the disappearance of folk instruments began to mount; allegedly responsible for this agonizing loss was the ubiquitous noisy and simple accordion. A lithograph titled "L'accordéon dit soufflet a musique" (The accordion knocked out the music) by the French

Figure 0.3 Lithograph by Honoré Daumier. Original caption: "L'accordéon, dit soufflet a musique.—On n'a pas encore le droit de tuer les gens que jouent de cet instrument, mais il faut espérer que cela viendra." Source: *Le Journal Amusant*, September 8, 1865. The Daumier Register Digital Work Catalogue.

cartoonist Honoré Daumier appeared in a newspaper in 1865, which may be the first published accordion joke: A bourgeois billiard player tells the working-class accordionist next to him, "One does not yet have the right to kill the people who play this instrument, but there is hope that one soon will have."[10]

Branded as "the little man's 'piano,'" the accordion became a medium for popular folk music in numerous regions of the world in the late nineteenth and early twentieth centuries. The accordion was thriving among the less affluent because it was a complete "one-man-band," capable of providing melody, harmony, and bass at once; it was also loud and durable and therefore ideal for outdoor performances. Since the accordion hardly ever severed from the broader popular social life that had sustained it, vernacular names emerged that reflected a bourgeois perception of the instrument as low-class: "squeezebox," "pleated piano," "piano with suspenders," "stomach Steinway," "waistline Wurlitzer," "Belly Baldwin," or "concert screamer."

The perceived "simplicity" of the accordion may have more to do with this negative popular image than the instrument itself. With the shift in the instrument's status from enormously fashionable to outdated, the accordion in the Americas became equated with immigrant, ethnic, and working-class expression—the music of the rural, poor, corny, and uneducated masses. The negative image of the accordion, primarily based on social differences, prejudices, and judgments, has been perpetuated ever since its consolidation in the 1880s. No other instrument has provoked so many scornful jokes—as Richard March details in his semischolarly essay (chapter 2 of this volume)—yet the accordion's distinctive sounds have touched millions of people, stirring up passions and soothing pain.

* * *

Accordion traditions are paradoxically both popular and little understood. Apart from a few articles here and there (and a handful of books, mostly in non-English languages[11]), academic interest in this popular instrument had been meager—until the accordion's recent comeback as world-music and "retro" instrument, that is.[12] A few recent book-length studies focus on accordion cultures in the Americas, including Mark DeWitt's *Cajun and Zydeco Dance Music in Northern California: Modern Pleasures in a Postmodern World* (2008), Cathy Ragland's *Música Norteña: Mexican Migrants Creating a Nation between Nations* (2009), and Marion Jacobson's *Squeeze This! A Cultural History of the Accordion in America* (2012). Like other European working-class cultural exports of the late nineteenth century, however, accordion music has scarcely been considered a musical form worthy of scholarly attention.[13] This kind of accordion phobia among scholars is perplexing if we consider that accordion traditions speak to the power struggles between social classes as well as to the makings, politics, and aesthetics of popular music. Alan Lomax, otherwise known for his broad interest in American folk life, called the accordion "this pestiferous instrument" that had spoiled folk music in the Old as well as the New World.[14] According to James Leary, Lomax's "anti-squeezebox stance echoed a succession of critics who, despite erstwhile solidarity with rural and working-class peoples in Old and New Worlds, imagined a golden age of unsullied folk authenticity that had been polluted by machines and mass production."[15] Intellectuals often failed to recognize their own class-based judgments and preconceptions when they ignored certain working-class cultural expressions and cherished others. Thus, Ann Hetzel Gunkel concludes in a critical essay on polka music, "It is perhaps a sad testament to our collective historical illiteracy that the accordion is widely accepted today as a popular stereotype for the old-fashioned and the corny."[16]

Thus, the twenty-first century calls for a reevaluation of the accordion and the many musicultural traditions associated with this instrument. This book is a start—but since this is a single-volume publication, only a small selection of accordion traditions could fit into this anthology. A choice had to be made at the expense of many other outstanding accordion cultures around the world[17] and even within the Americas, the geographic limits of this volume.

Like the accordion that comes in many guises, the authors of this volume—each of them an expert in one or more of the most significant accordion traditions of the Americas, and some of them amateur or professional accordionists themselves—come from a variety of intellectual fields. Together they represent ethnomusicology, musicology, music theory/composition, social and cultural anthropology, folklore, and cultural studies; each of these intellectual traditions comes with its own concerns, theoretical frameworks, and methodological approaches. Rather than being thematically streamlined essays, we believe that their particularity in approach and focus contributes to the richness of the overall volume. As such, the essays will speak to a broad academic audience as well as to the accordion enthusiast who will discover many hitherto unknown facets of this intriguing instrument.

Thus, the essays in this anthology consider the specific histories and cultural significance of a variety of accordion traditions to shed light onto the instrument's enigmatic popularity in the New World. Because power relations between the social elites and the working class—often immigrants or marginalized ethnic communities—have shaped the accordion's histories across the Americas, issues that emerge as pivotal include identity, discourses of inclusion/exclusion, marginality, and cultural agency; music's capability to engender community; sound aesthetics; and the accordion's place in mainstream and "world music." Below follows a brief overview of the individual essays and outline of the main themes. Rather than put in a strictly geographical order from north to south or vice versa, the essays follow several main threads and intersect at various points.

My own contribution, "From Old World to New Shores" (chapter 1), presents a brief history of the accordion, from its experimental beginning in the early nineteenth century to its phenomenal rise as a truly global commodity, emphasizing the social predicament that relegated this instrument to a marginal position within the (educated) musical world. Having grown up in the midst of an accordion-driven folk-music culture in Central Europe, my own ambivalent feelings toward the instrument are rather telling of the widespread and deeply ingrained apprehension (not just in the Western world) that resulted in a myriad of popular jokes about the allegedly "low" instrument. The accordion jokes collected by the folklorist Richard March (chapter 2), although transmitted in the English language, seem to be universal, but most strikingly, as March notes, they express an intense hostility toward the instrument. In December 2000, after a round of jokes—mostly accordion jokes—was exchanged on the electronic mailing list of the Society for Ethnomusicology, one of the subscribers wrote: "It was my impression that the SEM list would not be a forum for jokes or other 'spam.' I respectfully suggest we not use the SEM list for jokes." The moderator Mark DeWitt felt compelled to answer: "Jokes are a genre of folklore. They have been collected by generations of folklorists. Jokes about musical instruments and the musicians are of special interest to ethnomusicologists because they reveal cultural attitudes about music. So while we may laugh at (or be grossed out by, in the case of the drooling accordionist!) these jokes, there is a serious point to passing them along to the list."

Indeed, March points out that accordions and accordion players are mocked first and foremost because of their class status and cultural associations. However, it would be wrong to believe that the socially and culturally superior-feeling joke tellers are necessarily cultural outsiders. As becomes apparent in virtually all of the contributions to this volume, the accordion's history is a rocky one: the instrument may at one time be a most significant and unique identity marker for a whole community or group of people, and years later it may be seen by the same people as obstructing progress and integration, only to be chosen at a later time as a symbol of one's "new ethnicity"—as has happened to the Louisiana Cajun accordion. Mark DeWitt (chapter 3) is keenly aware of the need to contextualize such changes. He aptly shows how the changing politics of identity in post–civil rights America has enabled Cajuns to turn the accordion's (and their own) "chanky-chank" (low-class) stigma into a powerful symbol of ethnic identity and pride. Cajuns' renewed interest in and valuation of accordion music has spilled over to a young generation of musicians, including non-Cajun "Yankee chank" accordion players.[18] Music in contemporary America may indeed be "at once an everyday activity, an industrial commodity, a flag of resistance, a personal world, and a deeply symbolic, emotional grounding for people in every class and cranny the superculture offers,"[19] rather than simply a class marker. Yet music has not lost its significance as an identity marker and identity maker.

Black Creoles in Louisiana have created their own, distinctive accordion music adapted from French, Native American, and African cultures. While Creole musicians in the early twentieth century were often hired for Cajun dances, where they played Cajun dance music, at their own gatherings they played a uniquely Creole repertoire that drew from the African American blues—a repertoire later developed by accordionists such as Clifton Chenier and Boozoo Chavis. Zydeco, as this music eventually was labeled, has become a symbol of Louisiana Creole culture. Jared Snyder, who explores the history of the Creole accordion in chapter 4, concludes that despite the pressure on modern zydeco bands to adapt to the demands of the music industry, the traditional accordion and rubboard remain the core instruments, and zydeco accordionists keep playing in a distinctively Creole style. Creole musical practice, as well as Creole identity, fits Peter Preston's notion of identity as "a shifting balance between what is remembered and what is currently demanded."[20]

Like the Cajuns and Creoles, the Texan-Mexicans (Tejanos) and northern Mexicans (Norteños) share the same geographic space; thus, historically contested relationships between the different communities have been articulated in musical practices. Like the musicians of the Cajun and Creole traditions, Tejanos and Norteños have not only created distinctive styles but also identifiable accordion sounds that connect individual musicians to their history, place, and legacy. In chapter 5, the ethnomusicologist Cathy Ragland illustrates how the diatonic accordion symbolically embodies the Texan-Mexican community's economic struggle while also distinguishing it as the core of an "authentic" Tejano conjunto sound despite the significant change and fragmentation the music has undergone, particularly during the last fifty years. This Tejano population would also try to distinguish itself musically from the more recent waves of Mexican immigrants who tend to cling on to their own kind of accordion-based music—*música norteña*. While for the Tejano the accordion symbolizes the cultural memory of a working-class past that allows them to celebrate their role in the making of a prosperous Texan and American society, for Mexican immigrants it is a symbol of regional identity and, at the same time, of their transnational experience.

Cultural memory and identity are constituted in musical performance because the sense of being enjoined is fundamental to the musical experience. Even though the ethnomusicologist Janet Sturman stresses individual choices and taste over shared cultural practice in her essay on Tohono O'odham accordion music, she acknowledges the significance of people's communal experience and affective response to their music. The O'odham of southern Arizona similarly identify with and at the same time distinguish themselves from their surrounding musical world by creating their own popular borderland music, *waila*. While the O'odham made the accordion their own—imbuing it with their language and voice—*waila* has given them a sense of home, place, and roots, linking them to their community, their ancestors, and their traditions.

Music not only informs our sense of place, it also creates and articulates the very idea of community. Music helps people make sense of their social world and their place in it. But neither "tribes" nor "ethnic groups," "subcultures," or "communities" are stable units of contained people, defined or self-defined. Perceptions of such groups are not only discursively and historically constituted, boundaries and contents are constantly negotiated, and allegiances are shifting. Nowhere is this more noticeable than with the European immigrants to America's Upper Midwest, where communities with mixed ethnicity were as common as ethnic enclaves. The anecdote with which the folklorist James Leary begins his essay about the accordion culture along the south shore of Lake Superior is telling: to the French Canadians, Germans, Italians, Irish, Scandinavians, and Slavs who would gather in rural taverns, accordion music was a "common language" that unified the diverse audience yet nonetheless helped sustain a group's sense of being Czech or Polish or Finnish. From the late nineteenth century through the present, the accordion has reigned in the area as the most ubiquitous and emblematic folk-musical instrument. A downright working-class instrument, it fostered egalitarian social relations and interethnic alliances—a kind of alliance only possible in the New World, where the politics of ethnic identity has come to govern many social relations.

Accordion music and accordion sound have also preserved the cultural memory of Italian immigrants, encouraging them to shape a common Italian American identity beyond their original regional identity. Telling the story of two accordion pioneers from upstate New York, the folklorist Christine Zinni shows in chapter 8 how upwardly aspiring, entrepreneurial Italian American musicians managed to work themselves out of the ghetto by creating a parallel economy and a cultural space that compel us to reevaluate the "ethnic" as a driving force in America's musical life. Italian American accordionists had already proliferated in the "ethnic" recording business in the early decades of the twentieth century; in the 1930s and 1940s, a number of flamboyant Italian American piano-accordion virtuosos catapulted to fame and the concert stage, bridging the chasm between "low" and "high" culture, and "folk" and "classical." With their expressive "Italian" performance style, they triggered a nationwide accordion craze that lasted until rock 'n' roll enraptured the American youth in the early 1960s.

Similarly, Jewish accordionists at the beginning of the twentieth century carved out a space in the emerging U.S. recording business. The music theorist and composer Joshua Horowitz takes a closer look at the role of the accordion in klezmer music—an instrument overshadowed by the clarinet despite the numerous historic recordings and other evidence that prove it integral to the klezmer genre. Like the pioneering Italian American virtuoso accordionists, Jewish musicians felt equally at home playing classical and folk music. Horowitz's select analysis of early accordion playing styles and stylistic characteristics sheds light on the interaction and interplay of klezmer musicians with their surrounding worlds—Old and New. A distinctive feature of the early "klezmer sound" was the accordion's imitation of the human voice heard in liturgical, paraliturgical, and Yiddish song. But whether the accordion was seen in the United States at the time as a typical klezmer instrument or an "ethnic" instrument (of Russian, Polish, Hungarian, or Lithuanian provenance) depends on the historian's interpretation. In any case, by the late 1930s, the accordion was often used for chordal accompaniment (rather than as a solo instrument). It was an integral element of the popular Hasidic bands of the 1960s and the "klezmer ensembles" that embraced the new Israeli music as well as earlier "Palestinian" music; and although it was often deemed "an outsider," for the revivalists of the 1980s and beyond, the accordion has been characteristic of the klezmer style.

The accordion is equally emblematic for a number of genres and traditions throughout South America and the Caribbean. Based on meticulous archival research, the Colombian musicologist Egberto Bermúdez traces the accordion's history from its arrival at Colombia's Atlantic shores to its ubiquitous presence in popular *vallenato* music. Accordions and harmonicas were assimilated into local musical culture as early as the 1860s, combined with scrapers or other rhythm and percussion instruments, such as the triangle and side drum. Trading routes along the main rivers into the interior of the country allowed for the dispersion of accordions and their music during the economic boom in the tobacco-, banana-, and coffee-growing zones. With *vallenato*'s increasing national popularity in the mid-1980s, the accordion, which was firmly rooted in the lower strata, needed a new social veneer. The soap-opera actor and *vallenato* accordionist and singer Carlos Vives's international success in the mid-1990s, recognized by multiple Grammy awards, reached a level of visibility that validated the music—despite *vallenato*'s infamous and unbroken connection with the Colombian mafia. According to recent media reports, *vallenato* music is vital to money-laundering entertainment enterprises linked to megaconcerts that promote the government's political agenda. Thus, the "devil's accordion," of which we are told in a legendary Colombian folk tale, comes full circle in the modern *vallenato* accordion.

Originally associated with Buenos Aires's lower strata, the tango's emblematic instrument has been considered a "hellish" instrument too, literally and metaphorically. In the late nineteenth century, the German Bandonion, in the hands of skillful Argentine musicians, became the *bandoneón*. The Argentine anthropologist María Susana Azzi traces the history of the instrument and of the dance from their inception through the Golden Age, to conclude her chapter with an homage to the internationally acclaimed bandoneonist Astor Piazzolla, who singlehandedly redefined tango in the 1980s. Piazzolla considered the accordion "a strong instrument" because of its noisy sound—it is this "mud quality" (Piazzolla's term) that is so characteristic of his *tango nuevo* (new tango).

Sound ideals are often socially constructed and as such enter the moral discourse of music. Referring to Attali's theory on noise versus sound, the ethnomusicologist Sydney Hutchinson argues that the button accordion had been viewed by Dominican elites as a disorderly noisemaker rather than an orderly musical instrument, despised because of its German origins and its proclivity toward African-influenced sound. Still today, the accordion and its associated genre, the *merengue típico*, occupy an ambiguous position in Dominican society. What constitutes "noisiness" seems to depend on sound aesthetics shaped by class membership. For Dominican accordionists, the majority of whom belong to the lower classes, "noisiness" means liveliness, sweetness, and tenderness; new factory-made instruments must be customized according to this "noisy" preference to become alive. The retuning of factory-pretuned instruments is a prevalent practice in most of the accordion traditions discussed in this volume. It speaks to the importance of homegrown sound aesthetics developed by musicians and audiences embedded in distinct social and cultural environments.

Customization of the accordion may also take visual forms, and its tuning and outward appearance can be highly individualistic. While the study of "accordion cultures" tends to foreground shared cultural practices, several contributors stress the importance of exploring individual musical choices and tastes that have shaped those "cultures." The anthropologist Megwen Loveless centers her essay upon the fascinating life story of the Brazilian accordionist Luiz Gonzaga, while examining Brazil's national musical and political context that allowed this extraordinary musician to come forth as the creator of a new accordion-driven music and dance genre called *forró*. With his "unwieldy" instrument in his hands, the bohemian Gonzaga shaped a quintessentially Brazilian music—one that, unlike the urban *samba* and the cosmopolitan *bossa nova*, stands for the rural roots of the nation. Part of Gonzaga's success was due to his ability to create a credible onstage persona, to portray a "country bumpkin" identity (to refer to Loveless's subtitle) with a unique performance style and musical accent—the accordion undoubtedly underlined his hinterlandishness. Gonzaga's creativity and originality made him into one of Brazil's most successful recording artists.

While we find numerous "ethnic" accordion personalities around the world, fewer have attempted to reconcile the accordion with classical music. The musicologist Marion Jacobson introduces the reader to the impressive work of the contemporary composer and accordionist William Schimmel and his experimental use of the piano accordion. Schimmel's somewhat odd choice of instrument—the piano accordion is not an accepted "concert instrument," from the music academy's point of view—unshackles him from some classic compositional constraints, giving him the freedom to explore the piano accordion's unique tonalities and textures. Schimmel's interpretations not only give a new voice to classic works but release meanings hitherto concealed by strict adherence to the musical score. By opening up new possibilities for the potential of the accordion to signify "avant-garde," Schimmel clearly walks on new shores.

Schimmel regards the accordion as a "culture"—a concept picked up by Marion Jacobson for her guest-edited 2008 issue of *the world of music* titled "Accordion Culture." As the contributors of this anthology attest, the accordion is much more than a material object: people across the globe have adapted the instrument to their own aesthetics, their own places, and their own social and cultural realities. Thus, a central theme of this volume is the instrument's symbolic meaning, whether ascribed from outside or inside, and its central role as a significant identity marker for those who have adopted it—often against an elite view of the instrument as "lowly." Although for a good part dependent on social sensibilities, accordionists may also "consciously manipulate stylistically racialized or classed 'codes' to heighten musical affect."[21] Gendered meaning—accordion playing is typically coded as a masculine activity, even though the instrument has frequently been taken up by women—can be challenged too, as Sydney Hutchinson illustrates in her lucid analysis of the accordion in Dominican discourse as a dual-gendered instrument.[22] In some societies, professional female accordion players may become such a threat to their male colleagues that some men denounce their femininity, as Cathy Ragland relates in her essay on Texas-Mexican conjunto music. Despite the fact that female accordionists are all too often overshadowed by their male counterparts, many have contributed to the accordion cultures discussed in this volume. Rather than thinking about "accordion culture" in the singular, this anthology invites the reader to see beyond a single culture and to come to understand and appreciate the accordion in its many manifestations.

Notes

1. Because of its historical association with the common people, the accordion has often been considered a "simple instrument," a notion even perpetuated by authors who mean well. See, for example, Carlos Guerra, "Accordion Menace . . . Just Say Mo'!" and Ramino Burr, "The Accordion: Passion, Emotion, Musicianship," in *Puro Conjunto: An Album in Words and Pictures*, ed. Juan Tejada and Avelardo Valdez (Austin, Tex.: CMAS Books, 2001), 115 and 121.

2. Playing techniques such as Cajun "hammering" call for stiffer springs that return quickly to their original position after the buttons are released. See Mark F. DeWitt, "The Diatonic Button Accordion in Ethnic Context: Idiom and Style in Cajun Dance Music," *Popular Music and Society* 26.3 (2003): 323.

3. Diatonic notes belong to the standard major and minor scale, consisting of eight notes in an octave. The remaining semitones of the octave are called "chromatic."

4. The documentary by the Swiss filmmaker Stefan Schwietert, *El acordeón del diablo: Vallenato, Cumbia, und Son* (Berlin: Zero Film, Absolut Medien, Arte Edition, DVE 743, 2000), shows the retuning process of the new Hohner models that arrive at Colombia's northern shores to fit local aesthetics.

5. The piano accordion, introduced in the early 1900s, would eventually "complete the process of the accordion's globalization." Marion S. Jacobson, "Notes from Planet Squeezebox: The Accordion and the Process of Musical Globalization," *the world of music* 50.3 (2008): 7. But in terms of variety of models, the button accordion stands out.

6. Harrington, "Accordion," Helmi Strahl Harrington, "Accordion," in *The New Grove Dictionary of Music and Musicians*, vol. 1, ed. Stanley Sadie (London: Macmillan, 2001), 57; See also World of Accordion Museum, Superior, Wisconsin, http://museum.accordionworld.org (accessed January 7, 2012). For an acoustic comparison of the various accordion traditions, I highly recommend the compilation *Planet Squeezebox: Accordion Music from Around the World*, CD-3470 (Ellipsis Arts, 1995), 3 CDs and fifty-six-page booklet.

7. See Ernst Roth, *Schwyzerörgeli: Geschichte, Instrumentenbau, Spielpraxis* (1979; reprint, Altdorf: Gamma, 2006), 70–71.

8. Jared Snyder, personal correspondence, March 16, 2009.

9. Arturo Penón and Javier García Méndez, *The Bandonion: A Tango History*, trans. Tim Barnard (London, Ont.: Nightwood Editions, 1988), 31.

10. *Le Journal Amusant*, December 9, 1865; reproduced in François Billard and Didier Roussin, *Histoires de l'accordéon* (Castelnau-le-Lez: Climats, 1991).

11. The accordion has received more attention in Europe, particularly in Germany. The music journalist and author Christoph Wagner has published two impressive and carefully documented volumes about the instrument: *Das Akkordeon: Eine wilde Karriere* (Berlin: Transit Buchverlag, 1993) and *Das Akkordeon, oder die Erfindung der populären Musik: Eine Kulturgeschichte* (Mainz: Schott, 2001). The latter contains short contributions by Keith Chandler (Scotland), Olivier Durif (France), Joshua Horowitz (klezmer), and Stephan Meier (Finland). The chapter on "The Tropical Accordion" (the Caribbean, Latin America, and Africa) was written by Wagner himself.

12. There are two main publications in English with a similar premise: "The Accordion in All Its Guises," a special issue of the journal *Musical Performances*, was published in the United Kingdom in 2001 (Overseas Publishers Association). The journal itself is somewhat obscure, as only three volumes appeared before its publication ceased. Accordingly, this issue is hard to come by (merely a handful of libraries in the United States own it). Its title is rather bold, as a major part of the journal deals with the accordion in classical and concert music. Of the remaining nine essays, four are dedicated to European traditions and one each to Madagascar, the Dominican Republic, Texas, klezmer, and Cajun. A second compilation of five essays appeared in 2008 as a special issue of the ethnomusicological journal *the world of music* devoted to "Accordion Culture," guest edited by Marion Jacobson. Her monograph on the history of the piano accordion as a uniquely American musicultural phenomenon recently appeared in print. Marion Jacobson, *Squeeze This! A Cultural History of the Accordion in America* (Urbana: University of Illinois Press, 2012).

Interestingly, but tellingly, the only book fully devoted to the instrument in the New World is the gruesome *Accordion Crimes* (New York: Scribner, 1997) by the novelist E. Annie Proulx, which follows a button accordion's odyssey from the hands of its Sicilian maker, who immigrated to New Orleans in 1890, until it is crushed by a truck in Florida in 1996. The book's characters are connected only through the accordion, which travels from New York, to the Midwest (in the hands of Germans), Texas (Mexicans), Maine/Canada (French), Louisiana (black slaves from Nantes), and Chicago (Poles)—and through their shared American experience.

Although the three-CD set *Planet Squeezebox*, produced by Michael Shapiro, filled a void in the recorded-music market, the insufficiencies of the accompanying fifty-six-page booklet made clear that more scholarly research about the instrument in its numerous cultural contexts is dearly needed.

13. Mark F. DeWitt, *Cajun and Zydeco Dance Music in Northern California: Modern Pleasures in a Postmodern World* (Jackson: University Press of Mississippi, 2008); Cathy Rag-

land, *Música Norteña: Mexican Migrants Creating a Nation between Nations* (Philadelphia: Temple University Press, 2009), and Jacobson, *Squeeze This!* Charles Keil, Angeliki V. Keil, and Dick Blau, in *Polka Happiness* (Philadelphia: Temple University Press, 1992), chronicle the enormous popularity of polka music in nineteenth-century Europe and its enduring popularity in the United States. As its title suggests, the book is more concerned with the shared sense of belonging embodied in polka sociability than with the instrument with which this Euro-American dance music continues to be most closely associated. Published the same year, Victor Greene's *A Passion for Polka: Old-Time Ethnic Music in America* (Berkeley: University of California Press, 1992) traces the popularization of old-time ethnic dance music from the turn of the century to the 1960s, focusing on historical documents about the major recording artists of the time. The subtitle of James P. Leary's book speaks for itself: *Polkabilly: How the Goose Island Ramblers Redefined American Folk Music* (New York: Oxford University Press, 2006). On one of Europe's other significant cultural exports of the nineteenth century, the brass-band movement, see Margaret H. Hazen and Robert M. Hazen, *The Music Men: An Illustrated History of Brass Bands in America, 1800–1920* (Washington, D.C.: Smithsonian Institution Press, 1987).

14. Qtd. in James P. Leary, "Fieldwork Forgotten, or Alan Lomax Goes North," *Midwestern Folklore* 27.2 (2001): 18.

15. Leary, *Polkabilly*, 180–81.

16. Ann Hetzel Gunkel, "The Polka Alternative: Polka as Counterhegemonic Ethnic Practice," *Popular Music and Society* 27.4 (2004): 409.

17. See, for example, Yin Yee Kwan, "The Transformation of the Accordion in Twentieth-Century China," *the world of music* 50.3 (2008), 81–99, as well as the publications mentioned in notes 11 and 12 above.

18. See DeWitt, *Cajun and Zydeco Dance Music.*

19. Mark Slobin, *Subcultural Sounds: Micromusics of the West* (Hanover, N.H.: Wesleyan University Press and University Press of New England, 1993), 77.

20. Peter W. Preston, *Political/Cultural Identity: Citizens and Nations in a Global Era* (London: Sage, 1997), 49.

21. Maria Sonevytsky, "The Accordion and Ethnic Whiteness: Toward a New Critical Organology," *the world of music* 50.3 (2008): 101–18.

22. In this volume and in more detail in "Becoming the *Tíguera*: The Female Accordionist in Dominican *Merengue Típico*," *the world of music* 50.3 (2008): 37–56.

⟫ 1 ⟪

From Old World
to New Shores

HELENA SIMONETT

In his article on immigrant, folk, and regional American musics, Philip Bohlman engages the accordion for commenting on territorial transgressions. The instrument's popular appeal, he holds, was mainly due to its "adaptability and its ability to respond to a wide range of musical demands in the changing cultural contexts" of the New World.[1] Despite its malleability, the accordion remained an emblematic immigrant instrument, a symbol of the working-class people, throughout the twentieth century. Yet the accordion has challenged and transgressed its social associations many times during its relatively short history of nearly two hundred years. During the first decades after its invention in the early 1800s, the accordion was an upper- and middle-class instrument: its buyers were young, urban, affluent, ambitious, fashion conscious, and future oriented—in short, early nineteenth-century "yuppies." Each instrument was meticulously handcrafted, which made the early accordion costlier than a guitar and put it out of reach for the common people. The finest materials were used—polished ebony wood for the frame and delicate kidskin for the bellows. Labor-intense filigree carvings and spangles, inlay, rhinestone, and ivory work decorated these luxury models, created in a process involving hundreds of hours of labor. This first essay briefly traces the history of the accordion from its humble beginnings in the early 1800s to its meteoric rise and consolidation as a truly global instrument.

Although the Viennese organ and piano manufacturer Cyrill Demian was the first to have his new invention patented (1829), numerous other European inventers were cooking up their own versions of free-reed instruments at the same time. Demian's accordion, "a little box with bellows [and] five keys, each able to produce a chord"[2]—hence its name—topped an invention frenzy among instrument makers, but it inspired rather than stopped their creative zeal. Once an instrument circulated, it was subject to a restless continuation of improvements. In fact, the accordion was itself a continuation and a perfection of many late eighteenth-century experiments with free-reed aerophones: in 1770, a Bavarian musician performed in St. Petersburg, Russia, on a "sweet Chinese organ"—most likely a Chinese *sheng*. The *sheng* is an ancient free-reed instrument that consists of a wooden mouthpiece attached to a gourd equipped with bamboo pipes of varying lengths. It is believed that the early European attempts to create bellows-driven instruments based on the free-reed principle—tongues that are vibrated by an airflow—were derived from the *sheng*. In 1779, a portable free-reed organ called the Orchestrion had been developed in St. Petersburg, based on ideas for a talking machine developed by an acoustics professor in Denmark. The invention of the Pys-harmonika (Vienna, 1821) and the Äoline (Bavaria, 1822) followed. A Viennese music-box maker patented his "Harmonika in Chinese manner" in 1825, calling himself a "Certified Music Box- and Mouth-Harmonica-Maker."[3]

European countries in the nineteenth century were closely connected through travel and trade. It is no surprise, then, that Demian's accordion appeared in Paris the year after its invention. The patent protected his invention until 1834, but not in a foreign country. Thus, Parisian instrument makers immediately copied the novelty. Six years later, there were twenty accordion and harmonica makers registered in Paris. With some modifications of the Viennese model, they tried to appeal to the sophisticated Parisian ears.[4] M. Busson in Paris added a piano keyboard for the right hand, a novelty that became known as *accordéon-orgue, flûtina*, or *harmoniflûte*. With its casework made in rosewood and inlays of ivory and mother-of-pearl, it was geared "towards the ladies of the better society and advanced to a desired bourgeois object of female distraction."[5] Unencumbered by gender expectations, the novel instrument was indeed considered suitable for young women. Busson's new invention was shown at the World Exhibition in Paris in 1855. The popularity of the accordion continually increased as the number of published method books, some printed in two or even three languages (German, French, and English), indicates. "It was the accordion's uniform tone, considered novel at the time, and its breadth of nuance-rich music, as well as its portability and affordability, that endeared it to large populations."[6] The flourishing French accordion production came to a halt during the Franco-Prussian War (1870–71), after which Italian manufacturers from Stradella pushed onto the market.

The luxurious artisanal Stradella model was one of the two main Italian accordion types to succeed.[7] In the early decades of the accordion's conquest, the instrument found its way into two music-loving towns: Stradella in the northern Italian province of Pavia, a region that at the time was under the power of the Austrian

Empire, and Castelfidardo, located in the province of Ancona (Marche region) in central-eastern Italy. The latter town, marked by its old castle and surrounding walls, was the place where in 1860 a decisive battle between the Piedmontese troops and the papal army laid the groundwork for Italy's unification. Immediately after the annexation of the Marche region, "we witness the birth of the first accordions and concertinas which were probably introduced to the Italians by French troops allied to the Papal State. These instruments were soon adapted to suit Italian taste."[8]

Italians, their ears accustomed to the sound of the bagpipe (*zampogna*), a popular instrument found from Sicily to the Lombardy, quickly embraced the new instrument that allowed playing sustained notes resembling bagpipe drones and generated a similar jarring sound as the traditional double-reeded *zampogna*. The later nineteenth century saw the accordion gain unprecedented popularity: according to the director of Castelfidardo's accordion museum, Beniamino Bugiolacchi, Giuseppe Verdi put forward a proposal to the Italian conservatory for the study of the instrument in his role as president of the ministerial commission for the reform of musical conservatories during the 1870s.[9] Accordion workshops sprang up all over Italy to appease the population's craving for the new instrument. But like elsewhere around the turn of the century, the separation of leisure activities along class lines, aggravated by unremitting urbanization and modernization, had increased, and "the joyous sound of the accordion, exalted by the gaiety of country outings and barnyard dancing, soon end[ed] up hoarsened in the outdoor settings of a geography neglected by other more ancient and illustrious instruments."[10] The bagpipe's modern rival was eventually delegated to the peasantry. The instrument, with its "decidedly vulgar sound," void of any "noble phonic aspirations,"[11] nevertheless later served a fascist regime in its populist politics. Bugiolacchi writes, "[T]he propaganda of the time spoke of the accordion as a musical instrument invented in Italy, and as being 'the pride of our industriousness and delight of the Italian people.' . . . In 1941 Benito Mussolini ordered that a quantity of 1,000 accordions be distributed to the various troops fighting in the Second World War."[12]

The accordion had a similar meteoric career in northern Europe. Six weeks after Demian filed a patent for his accordion in Vienna, the Londoner Charles Wheatstone filed a patent for an invention he called "symphonium," an aerophone with a keyboard layout and bellows. This instrument served as the prototype for Wheatstone's concertina—"a hexagonal double-action, forty-eight key instrument"[13]—a patent for which he would eventually file in 1844. Because of the close musical relationship between Vienna and London at the time, it is likely that Wheatstone knew of Demian's experiments. His early concertina models combined "the twenty-four-key fingering system of the symphonium with the exposed pearl pallets and wooden levers of Demian's first accordion."[14] Neil Wayne suspects that Wheatstone's concertina models were first intended for his lectures on acoustics at the King's College in London, where he was a professor of experimental physics, and not for commercial sale. Wheatstone had also a scientific interest in Oriental free-reed instruments (the Chinese *sheng*, the Japanese *shô*, and Javanese musical instruments) and the jew's harps and German mouth harmonicas (mouth organs) that had already been circulating for several years. In 1821, Christian Friedrich Ludwig Buschmann (Berlin) constructed a small mouth-blown device with fifteen reeds as an aid for tuning, which he continued to improve.[15] A year later, Buschmann had added hand-operated bellows, valves, and fitting buttons. This became his Hand-Äoline, or Konzertina.

Like a host of others with similar experimental inclinations, Wheatstone created a number of new and improved musical instruments, including the "foot-powered concertina," "wind piano," "bellows-fiddle," and free-reed pitch devices. He was also working on typewriters, electromagnetic clocks, artificial voice devices, and the electric telegraph, for which he later would gain fame.[16] Most of Wheatstone's musical inventions seemed rather preposterous, much like "the multitude of attempts of all kinds daily made by instrument-makers, and their pretended inventions, more or less disastrous, . . . the futile specimens which they seek to introduce amidst the race of instruments."[17] This critique was expressed by an open-minded and extremely progressive composer for his time, Héctor Berlioz. The French composer liked to explore new tone colors in his orchestrations and made use of the (Wheatstone English) concertina, whose sound he found "at once penetrating and soft . . . it allies itself well with the quality of tone of the harp, and with that of the pianoforte."[18] However, he criticized the concertina's mean-tempered tuning—"conforming to the *doctrine* of the acousticians,—a doctrine entirely contrary to the *practice* of musicians"[19]—which prevented it from being useful in combination with any well-tempered instrument.[20]

Despite this limitation, the concertina quickly rose in popularity as prominent Victorian concertinists began to perform virtuoso solo works, concertos, and chamber music. Benevolent reviews from respected critics—such as the playwright George Bernard Shaw's comment that "the concertina has now been brought to so great perfection . . . [it] can perform the most difficult violin, oboe, and flute music"[21]—helped its reception among the affluent. Indeed, the main purchasers of the concertina into the 1870s were members of the aristocracy, male and female alike. Once exclusively at home on the concert stage and in the upper-class salon, the concertina was gradually adopted by the English working class and thus was eventually abandoned by the "serious" musicians of the Victorian era. Maybe that was the incentive for this widely known joke: "What is the definition of a gentleman? Somebody who knows how to play the accordion but refrains from doing so!"

The trend toward an increasing proletarization of music making in the second half of the nineteenth century was backed by the import of low-priced, mass-produced concertinas from Germany, which did their part to crumble the instrument's image as "exclusive." English concertina makers got on the bandwagon with their own "people's concertina" models, affordable for the working class. Like the earlier brass-band movement, the concertina swept the British Isles as the working class began to form thousands of clubs. The concertina was particularly suited for dance music because the pull-and-push motion gave the music a strong rhythmic bounce. The instrument was popular in the taverns and pubs of port cities, from whence it quickly traveled to and conquered the British colonies and the United States. Sailors and whalers were particularly fond of the small portable instrument.

The accordion was in many ways a revolutionary instrument, suiting the liberal ideas of the late nineteenth century and partaking in the Industrial Revolution. The invention of the accordion effactually signified the birth of popular music, in both the sense of "people's music" and "music of the masses," for it coincided with the end of the preindustrial era and became a symbol of industrialization and mass culture.[22]

Accordion (concertina and harmonica) manufacturing centers first emerged in Germany: Trossingen (Christan Messner, 1830), Magdeburg (Friedrich Gessner, 1838), Berlin (J. F. Kalbe, 1840), Gera (Heinrich Wagner, around 1850), Klingenthal (Adolph Herold, 1852), and Chemnitz (Carl Friedrich Uhlig, concertinas, 1834), but skilled workers soon went on to open their own competing workshops and factories all over Germany that quickly developed into important production centers on their own terms.

Before mass production was introduced in the 1850s, all parts of an accordion were made by hand. Instrument makers, in collaboration with metal workers, locksmiths, fitters, mechanics, and a host of other skilled workers, toiled to develop a series of machines that would make possible the industrial production of individual accordion parts. Soon the reed beds were no longer hand cut and filed but punched out using a specially made fly-press dies, a metalworking-machine tool used to cut through sheet metal in one movement by shearing it. Laborious processes were rationalized by mechanically automated routers and milling machines. With the introduction of steam power in the late 1870s, accordion-production costs could be drastically lowered as unskilled workers were hired to operate the machines. Factory owners continued to outsource the manufacturing of parts that required hand labor by relying on a well-established homework system that employed low-wage workers—men, women, and children. Overall, production output increased while maintaining the quality of the musical instruments. One factory, for example, employed around four hundred workers to produce one hun-

Figure 1.1 Photograph of production in Hohner's factory, ca. 1910. Photo courtesy German Harmonica and Accordion Museum, Trossingen.

dred thousand accordions and 750,000 mouth harmonicas in 1855, but required only 250 workers seven years later to fabricate the same number of accordions and more than a million harmonicas.[23] Accordion and harmonica making was a dynamic, fast-growing business that soon oriented itself toward export and overseas markets. Indeed, a large number of the more than half-million accordions made annually in Germany at that time were special models for export.[24]

Among the many types of diatonic accordions invented before the 1850s was the Bandonion, a concertina that eventually became most famous in Argentina as the *bandoneón*. A predecessor model with a square shape and single notes instead of chords on the bass side was developed in Chemnitz by Carl Friedrich Uhlig in the early 1830s. The musician and teacher Heinrich Band, from Krefeld near Düsseldorf, ordered a model with eighty-eight pitches, retuned some of them, and called the new instrument "Bandonion" (the name appeared in 1856). Due to his energetic instrument trading, the name soon surpassed the general "concertina." Most German concertinas were produced in Saxony, where the instrument was popular among the working class in the 1880s.

In the second half of the nineteenth century, a number of noteworthy new models appeared: at the 1854 Industrial Exhibition in Munich, the Vienna ac-

Figure 1.2 Meinel & Herold accordion advertisement for Brazil where the company competed with Italian Dallapè models and local instrument makers. Photo courtesy German Harmonica and Accordion Museum, Trossingen.

cordion builder Matthäus Bauer showed his Clavierharmonika, a prototype of the piano accordion.[25] These first chromatic button accordions soon became a favorite among the Viennese Schrammelkapellen, ensembles inspired by the Viennese chamber music of the Schrammel brothers, after whom these popular (pseudo-)folk ensembles were named.[26] The Schrammel accordion,[27] resembling a clarinet in timbre, was added to the string ensemble, likely to strengthen the overall sound volume. At home in the taverns of Vienna's suburbs, the accordion acted, in Wagner's words, "as midwife for an emerging new music style" that fused folk-dance rhythms (Ländler) and Hungarian gypsy tunes with popular waltzes.[28] Schrammel music, with its accordion virtuosos, enjoyed a high reputation among the Austrian aristocracy, and contemporary composers joined the euphoria.

Like elsewhere in Europe, rural people stranded in the cities strove to restore and maintain their traditions in new rituals, displays, and diverse forms of entertainment—constructed and, if necessary, invented. The new contexts for social life generated new traditions that were genuinely urban. Folk music no longer was used as a symbol for stability and continuity of rural traditions, but it served as an emotional crutch for people transitioning from one lifestyle to another. The accordion, above all other instruments, was part of both worlds; it was traditional yet modern. Moreover, it was able to compete with the noise of the growing industrial cities and a lifestyle increasingly dominated by machines.

The accordion also quickly gained ground in more rural areas and countries with a less export-driven economy. In central Switzerland, the production of "hand harps" began in the 1830s. Larger numbers of various regional types of Schwyzerörgeli were manufactured in small, often family-operated workshops towards the end of the century, when the mechanical instrument definitively began to displace the fiddle and the hammered dulcimer.[29] The more popular the accordion grew among the mountain dwellers, the more hardcore traditionalists vilified it. The following denunciation, printed in the yearbook of the Swiss Alpine Club in 1868, is representative of many that followed: "The so-called Handharmonika [hand harmonica] is hugely enjoyed by alpine herdsmen and dairymen, who with desperate stubbornness persevere in cultivating—that is, pushing and pulling—it; such 'handling' can not be called playing or musicking. If not already the case, very soon only few tourists will be spared such torturous sound when traveling on frequented paths to alpine cabins. Our present-day youth of the mountainous area consider it more convenient to pull at a hand harmonica or to blow a humming mouth harmonica than to strain their good and sturdy lungs for the effective alp-horn."[30]

Indifferent to such criticism, the accordion quickly became a favorite pastime instrument; and, if a photograph of my grandfather's family in 1899 is any indication, maybe also as a children's instrument or "toy."

My grandfather's interest in the accordion was more than musical. The little box he held so dearly was a mechanical marvel that attracted his curiosity. Unfortunately, he never was given the opportunity to follow his calling, for the premature death of his father forced him to become the family's caregiver. Still, his restless mind and enormous dexterous abilities and initiative set him apart from the peasants around him. Instead of laboring on the land, he began to invent all kinds of mechanical tools to make farming more bearable, such as a piping con-

Figure 1.3 Photograph of my grandfather, Theodor Bucher, at age eleven, holding a button accordion. His younger siblings display toy instruments, as well as school utensils (1899).

struction for liquid manure with an automatic shift mechanism. He would bicycle long distances to inspect the newly built hydroelectric power stations in the Alps, and he was fascinated by the mountain railways and cableways. My grandfather was a "natural engineer" but also a fine musician—although, as far as I know, he never played music for a living. Together with four of his brothers, he formed a Haus-Kapelle (house band) in 1910 (or earlier), which was one of the first of its kind in central Switzerland.

Like the great majority of folk musicians, my grandfather never learned to read music, although there existed a music notation written in tablature for the standard Schwyzerörgeli—a fingering notation system still in use today to teach and learn Swiss folk tunes for musically illiterate people. Radio broadcast was his main source for new tunes.

Because the rural and lower classes had been making music by ear for centuries, by the early 1900s, the accordion had largely taken the place of established instruments such as the fiddle and bagpipe in all of Europe. Interestingly, however, local accordion playing styles often adopted older styles that they replaced—a phenomenon that we can also observe elsewhere (see, for example, Hutchinson

Figure 1.4 Photograph of my grandfather's family ensemble in 1910, Inwil, Lucerne. My granduncle plays a standard 18-bass, three-row button Schwyzerörgeli.

in chapter 12 of this volume). Hence, sound effects, ornamentations, and timbres varied according to local aesthetics. The accordion's versatility in terms of sound production may have been one of its strongest assets in its conquest of the world. Dissemination of the instrument was further encouraged by waves of overseas migration during the height of its popularity among European working classes.

To New Shores

In the early 1830s, button accordions fabricated in Saxony were exported to the United States. Musical-instrument dealers from Saxony settled in Philadelphia, from whence the novelty instruments promptly began to conquer the New World. Minstrel shows added the squeezebox to their ensemble of banjo, fiddle, tambourine, and castanets made of bones. Figure 4.2 in Snyder's essay on zydeco in this volume is a reproduction of a studio portrait of a black man holding an accordion with twelve treble keys and two bass buttons—we can only speculate whether the man was a free Creole or the indentured servant of a Creole of color, an accordionist by profession or simply a man holding a studio prop.[31] The Louisiana State

Figure 1.5 Hohner harmonica and accordion advertisement
for the United States. Photo courtesy German Harmonica and
Accordion Museum, Trossingen.

Museum in New Orleans dates the photograph circa 1850, suggesting that the
instrument had entered black Louisiana before midcentury. References to the
popularity of the accordion in local dances became more frequent toward the
end of the century.

Equally little is known about when and how the concertina took hold in the
United States.[32] But it comes as no surprise that the burgeoning working-class
concertina-orchestra movement of the Old World would also sweep the United
States, particularly in areas of heavy German, Bohemian, and Polish immigration.

First concertina clubs sprang up in the urban centers of Chicago and Milwaukee in 1889 and 1890, respectively. James P. Leary reasons that "displaced from the old country's close-knit agrarian villages, newcomers to the urban Midwest sought community by forming countless fraternal and cultural organizations, most of which encouraged musical performance."[33] Immigrant entrepreneurs such as the one who championed the German concertina to a cosmopolitan and self-assured clientele at the 1893 Columbian Exposition in Chicago helped establish an infrastructure that allowed the concertina to thrive in the American Midwest.[34] A large number of the two hundred thousand "German harmonicas" imported annually in the early twentieth century were actually concertinas. Americans began to craft their own German concertinas mainly because of the shortage of supply caused by the First World War.

Spurred by a growing anti-German sentiment in the United States, German American performers such as Whoopee John Wilfahrt, whose Concertina Orchestra (founded in 1928) popularized the German or Dutch "oompah-beat," became targets for verbal assault and ridicule. Maintaining a "visual balance between the ethnic clown and the American sophisticate,"[35] the comic representation emulated by subsequent Dutch musicians, however self-empowering it might have been, was not freely chosen. Immigrant, folk, and regional musics, Bohlman asserts, represent the ways in which Americans use music to strengthen their group and community identities as well as their connections to U.S. history. An examination of the "musics of difference" inevitably unveils the central role of racism and ethnic prejudice in the U.S. musical landscape. Immigrant music connects to American concerns for identity, and regional musics reveal the strong yet differing approaches in the United States to the sense of place.[36] After the Second World War, the different ethnic music styles merged into pan-American popular music and became known as "polka music"—yet the concertina held on to its Germanness.

The origin of the first accordion to reach Argentine shores is controversial, as many contradictory stories circulate. The largest port city in South America, Buenos Aires harbored millions of immigrants who had come in the late nineteenth century to furnish labor for farming and urban occupations, as well as large numbers of people displaced from the countryside, uprooted by the drastic changes to the pastoral-oriented economy in the 1880s. The accordion, which may have appeared in Argentina as early as the 1850s,[37] would turn out to be an ideal instrument to express the new urban reality in which newcomers from the Pampas and from abroad found themselves. In the borderlands of northeastern Argentina and southern Brazil, German immigrants had introduced their popular social dances, polka and mazurka, as well as the inevitable accordion and Bandonion, which soon were integrated into the regional *chamamé* song form accompanied by guitar and violin. Shortly after the turn of the century, a German sailor began to sell musical instruments similar to the concertina in La Boca, a Buenos Aires neighborhood settled by Italian immigrants who worked in the warehouses and meatpacking plants in the area.[38]

Brazilian accordion music has been brought to international attention by Luiz Gonzaga, whose exceptional career Megwen Loveless analyzes in chapter 13 of this volume. Now associated with *forró* music from northeastern Brazil, the instrument was first introduced into southern Brazil by German and Italian immigrants in the mid-1800s. From there, the diatonic eight-bass accordion, known as *sanfona de oito baixos*, was carried to the Northeast by soldiers who had fought in the war against Paraguay in the 1860s. The new instrument, together with a triangle and a bass drum, soon became the favorite musical accompaniment for social celebrations and replaced the older *bandas de pífano* (fife and drum bands).[39]

The Devil's Accordion, Stefan Schwietert's seductive documentary of Colombian *vallenato* music, opens with narration by the ninety-three-year-old accordionist Francisco "Pacho" Rada: "My story begins with a shipwreck. The ship was from Germany. It was full of accordions. It was on its way to Argentina and ran aground on our shores. That's how the accordion came to our country."[40] Other legends have the accordion turn up in more remote times; but most likely the first instruments arrived on the Colombian Caribbean coast in the late 1860s, as documented by Egberto Bermúdez (chapter 10 of this volume), and became more easily available in the 1910 and 1920s.[41] From the main port cities, it quickly spread along the Magdalena River far beyond the coastal regions. A widely sought-after contraband article, the accordion began to replace the indigenous *gaita*, a duct-flute made of cane, whose characteristic sonorities it was able to reproduce. A three-row, twelve-bass button accordion was commonly used in 1945—the time *vallenato* music took off. Colombia still imports such models from Germany, although upon arrival they have to be completely retuned to fit the local sound aesthetics.

Struggle for "Image"

One of the internationally most prominent European harmonica exporters was, and remains, the Hohner Company. Founded in 1857 by Matthias Hohner in the Swabian town of Trossingen, the plant earned worldwide recognition with its quality mouth organs. It was not until 1903, however, that Hohner began its production of button accordions, with the intention to enter the export business.[42] One of the Hohner sons moved to New York to establish a branch store and an aggressive advertising campaign that also targeted Canada and prerevolutionary Mexico. By 1913, the Toronto subsidiary had secured Hohner's dominance of the Canadian harmonica market, with a share of 68.6 percent. Hohner's goal was to emulate this success in Mexico, which it saw as crucial gateway to the markets in Central and South America. A Hohner representative opened a subsidiary in Mexico in 1908. After its closure only three years later due to the outbreak of the Mexican Revolution, Hohner had to temporarily revise its expansion plan. From a violence-ridden Mexico, Hohner's representative wrote to New York in 1913: "Despite all the revolutions, this country, no doubt, will become one of the best distribution areas. . . . I only wish 'Uncle Sam' would annex the whole republic."[43] At the onset of the First World War, Hohner dominated half of the U.S. harmonica market and one third of the world market.

Back home, the Hohner family practiced harsh acquisition strategies to expand its global market share: it purchased the J. F. Kalbe plant of Berlin (because of its bestselling Imperial-Model) in 1912; the following year it acquired Friedrich Gessner of Magdeburg and in 1928–29 the Trossingen competitors Messner and Andreas Koch (the world's second-largest accordion producer), as well as another half-dozen smaller accordion plants. Hohner's accordion production increased rapidly: already in 1906, 100,000 accordions were manufactured; before the outbreak of the First World War, the number had increased to 150,000. The war forced German factories to stop their export activities due to a labor shortage, lack of raw materials, and difficulties in organizing transportation. Production after the war resumed, and by 1929, just before the Great Depression hit, half of all accordions produced in Germany were exported to the Americas: 23 percent to the United States, and 24.4 percent to Latin America (three quarters of which went to Argentina despite horrendous import taxes).[44]

After the war, Hohner began to produce piano accordions. Due to relentless marketing, offers of financial incentives for retailers, installment plans for their customers, and special deals for music teachers, Hohner's "quality" instruments gained ground again. With 4,500 employees in 1930, Hohner had become the worldwide leader in accordion manufacturing. In its own economic interest, the firm was eager to pull the instrument out of the raucous tavern and into the concert hall. In line with official ideology between the two world wars that favored the "popular arts"—instead of keeping the masses away from "high art," classic literature was arranged to make music accessible to all—Hohner was keen to improve the accordion's image. Among its market strategies were the founding of accordion clubs, with a focus on community music making, and accordion orchestras.[45] Hohner built its own music academy in Trossingen to facilitate the professional training of teachers and conductors and founded a music publishing house. The school and publishing house encouraged the composition of concert literature for the instrument. The goal was to transform the accordion into a concert instrument. Similar efforts were made in the United States, as documented by Christine Zinni in this volume (chapter 8). Hohner furthermore tried to sophisticate the chromatic piano accordion in the 1930s by distinguishing it from the diatonic Ziehharmonika ("pull harmonica" or squeezebox).

Instrument production in Germany had ceased during the war years but resumed thereafter, foremost to satisfy the great demand of popular concertina-Bandonion clubs in Germany and for export to the United States. Although the German musical organizations were initiated purely for entertainment, between the two world wars their membership sympathized with the communist workers' movement. As a result, concertina and Bandonion clubs came under scrutiny and, in 1933, were banned by the Nazi regime and their instruments confiscated.[46] Harmonica and accordion music, however, served the regime well to propagate a fascist ideology of "folk community," and the power of the Schützengrabenklavier (trench piano), as the accordion was called, to boost the German troops' morale was certainly acknowledged. Yet, the politically and ideologically motivated polemic around the instruments let to a state decree in 1938 against the formation of harmonica and accordion orchestras in any Hitler Youth organizations. Arrangements for accordion of the great works by composers such as Haydn, Mozart, Beethoven, Wagner, and others were forbidden.[47]

Caught up in the polemic around the accordion during the Nazi regime, which dismissed the instrument as "good enough for peasant dances" but not suitable to accompany the artistic songs of the Hitler Youth, Hohner and some music pedagogues argued for the instrument's educational value: the cultivation of the accordion, they claimed, would help to overcome the "gulf between art and folk music."[48] Nazis, however, believed that only "cultured instruments" were able to lead the masses to the appreciation of "high art." Curiously, the antifascist music critic Theodor W. Adorno, in his polemic book *Dissonanzen* (1956), similarly argued against the "inhumanly mechanical" and "sentimental" instrument that would "adjust the ideal to the intellectual level of the uncultured" instead of elevating the uncultured onto a higher stage.[49]

Composers and arrangers affiliated with Hohner certainly saw a place for the piano accordion in the classical orchestra. While the diatonic button accordion had already been used by classical composers—Tchaikovsky in his *Orchestral Suite No. 2* (1883), Umberto Giordano in his opera *Fedora* (1898), and Charles Ives in *Orchestral Set No. 2* (1915)—to add a burlesque flavor, Paul Hindemith composed *Kammermusik No. 1* (1921) to make full use of the novelty piano accordion manufactured by the Hohner Company.[50] Seeing beyond the accordion's "lower social status," mid-twentieth-century experimental musicians were intrigued by the instrument's sound capabilities. Despite these endeavors to pave a way for the accordion to enter the classical music world, it was ultimately the accordion's strong ties with folk music and oral traditions that hindered a smooth transition into the concert world. More than a century of oral tradition and musical practice had created many stylistic characteristics incompatible with Western classical idioms.

Conclusion

In the early nineteenth century, coexisting capitalist and precapitalist economic formations furthered the unequal distribution of commodities and marked the division between the elite and the masses, particularly in the urban centers. Modernization was carried out at the expense of the peasantry and the urban poor, who became even more marginalized. In the last decades of the nineteenth century, the speed of technological modernization increased, and the social classes began to more sharply distinguish themselves by way of cultural participation and cultural expression.

The proletarian classes also enjoyed some of the benefits of the industrial age: more leisure time, increased disposable income, and greater access to material goods due to low prices through mass production. While the accordion at first was an expensive and hence exclusive instrument in upper-class drawing rooms, by the last quarter of the nineteenth century it had spread to the middle and working classes. The accordion of the nineteenth century was a symbol of progress and modernity as well as of mass culture and industrialization. This dichotomy is one of the reasons for the elite's ambivalence towards and uneasiness with the accordion.

Accordions had proliferated in many sizes and systems since the early 1800s. Enabled by several inventions that helped to cut back on manual labor, the mass production of the instrument began in the second half of the century and made the novelty instrument available to the common people. Although the more luxurious models were out of reach for the less affluent, with only a two-days' salary a worker in 1890 could purchase the cheapest one-row button model.[51] The fact that it was a loud and durable one-man band was one of the chief advantages of the accordion. This also meant that it was more cost-effective to hire an accordion player for a private event than a traditional ensemble. Thus, "[T]he accordion, with its uncomplicated and cheerful sound, its ease of use and transportation, was the ideal instrument to adopt in opposition to the elitist and costly music of previous years."[52]

Indeed, by appropriating the accordion into their own musical practice, the popular classes began for the first time to write music history themselves. Raymond Williams points out that categories such as "aristocratic" and "folk," "educated" and "uneducated" had distinct social bases in feudal and immediately postfeudal society, but that such relations have become problematic since the period of industrial urbanization.[53] Yet, these established categories of broad cultural descriptions have influenced popular and academic discourse about the accordion. The acceptance of the tango into all of Argentine society, for example, only happened because the admired, trend-setting Parisians were fascinated by the exotic genre. Indeed, "the aversion of the patriciate to the tango was less the product of their occasional prudery than it was a smokescreen to shield a class sensibility from the phenomenon's real origin."[54]

If liberal elites thought they could use art as a means of educating and elevating the ordinary masses so that they would adapt themselves to high civilization, they certainly underestimated the power of working-class culture. The appeal of popular musicking rested in its emphasis on oral transmission, improvisation, and face-to-face communication, all of which provided participants with a strong sense of identity, community, and place.

I would like to extend what Bohlman has called for in a narrower geographical realm: returning these (immigrant, folk, and popular) musics to history leads to a new meaning of the word "Americanization," not as the homogenization of culture in a melting pot but as a celebration of difference in a postethnic world.[55]

The accordion in the New World has its own histories, and those are exquisitely unraveled on the following pages.

Notes

1. Philip V. Bohlman, "Immigrant, Folk, and Regional Musics in the Twentieth Century," in *The Cambridge History of American Music*, ed. David Nicholls (Cambridge: Cambridge University Press, 1998), 301–2.

2. From the description of the patent given to Cyrill Demian and his sons, Karl and Guido, on May 23, 1829, qtd. in Walter Maurer, *Accordion: Handbuch eines Instruments, seiner historischen Entwicklung und seiner Literatur* (Vienna: Edition Harmonia, 1983), 55–56.

3. This essay is based on information from Armin Fett, "Harmonika," in *Die Musik in Geschichte und Gegenwart*, vol. 5, ed. Friedrich Blume (Kassel: Bärenreiter Verlag, 1956), 1665–99; Maria Dunkel, "Harmonikainstrumente," in *Musik in Geschichte und Gegenwart*, vol. 4, ed. Ludwig Finscher (Kassel: Bärenreiter Verlag, 1996), 167–210; Helmi Strahl Harrington, "Accordion," in *The New Grove Dictionary of Music and Musicians*, vol. 1, ed. Stanley Sadie (London: Macmillan, 2001), 56–66.

4. Maurer, *Accordion*, 87.

5. Christoph Wagner, *Das Akkordeon, oder die Erfindung der populären Musik: Eine Kulturgeschichte* (Mainz: Schott, 2001).

6. Harrington, "Accordion," 61.

7. Davide Anzaghi, "Doremifa: Accordions at Castelfidardo," *FMR: The Magazine of Franco Maria Ricci* 79 (1996): 81–98. In 1863, Paolo Soprani founded the first accordion industry in the commune of Castelfidardo. The town features an accordion museum, the Museo Internazionale della Fisarmonica, which documents the history of the *fisarmonica* (Italian accordion). The Museo della Fisarmonica in Stradella features a collec-

tion of Mariano Dallapè's production, from the first 1876 prototype to the present day. The collection also includes Dallapè's gem, the "liturgical" accordion. Stradella would stick to their labor-intensive button-accordion manufacturing despite the increasing industrialization and popularity of piano accordions from competing Castelfidardo.

8. Beniamino Bugiolacchi, "Castelfidardo: International Centre of Accordion Production in Italy," Accordions Worldwide, http://www.accordions.com/index/his/his_it.shtml (accessed February 13, 2009).

9. Ibid.

10. Anzaghi, "Doremifa," 81.

11. Giampiero Tintori, *Gli strumenti musicali*, qtd. in ibid., 83.

12. Bugiolacchi, "Castelfidardo."

13. Double action means that each button produces the same pitch regardless of the direction of the bellows. More on the different models and playing techniques below.

14. Neil Wayne, "The Wheatstone English Concertina," *Galpin Society Journal* 44 (1991): 132.

15. Harrington, "Accordion," 61. The reeds were cut from a single piece of metal and attached to a piece of wood with chambers and blowholes. For a history of the Hohner mouth harmonica, see Martin Häffner, *Harmonicas: Die Geschichte der Branche in Bildern und Texten* (Trossingen: Hohner Verlag, 1991). Johann Buschmann, Christian Friedrich's father, was a pipe-organ builder who in 1816 developed the Terpodion, a friction instrument with a piano-like keyboard, based on the same principle as the glass harmonica. In 1821 the two traveled to London to promote the sale of the Terpodion.

16. Wayne, "Wheatstone English Concertina," 122.

17. Héctor Berlioz, *A Treatise upon Modern Instrumentation and Orchestration*, trans. Mary Cowden Clarke, 2d ed. (London: Novello, Ewer, and Co., 1858), 233. Berlioz's remarks about the concertina were first published in 1843, just a few years before some of the mainstream English composers turned their attention to it.

18. Ibid., 235.

19. Ibid.

20. These two tuning systems are in fact incompatible: "meantone tempering" was an attempt to produce as many almost pure major triads (chords like C-E-G) as possible within pure octaves. Since pure major thirds, pure fifths, and pure octaves are not really compatible, the meantone tuning scheme involved slight adjustments to the sizes of the major thirds and fifths. As a result, only about eight of the twelve major keys are usable. The "well tempering," which became popular around 1700, was an attempt to make all keys useable and none of the scales and chords bad sounding. The English concertina was tuned in the older system, with enharmonic intervals between the A flat and the G sharp, and between the E flat and the D sharp. When played together with instruments whose A flat and G sharp, and E flat and D sharp, respectively, were identical, they sounded frightfully dissonant.

21. Qtd. in Allan W. Atlas, *The Wheatstone English Concertina in Victorian England* (Oxford: Clarendon Press, 1996), 73.

22. Wagner, *Das Akkordeon*, 9. Wagner's book title boldly states: "The Accordion; or, The Invention of Popular Music."

23. Dunkel, "Harmonikainstrumente," 180.

24. Ibid., 174.

25. Maurer, *Accordion*, 75.

26. In 1877, the violinists Johann Schrammel (1850–93) and his brother Joseph (1852-95) formed the Schrammel Quartet, which also included a bass guitar and a clarinet. Popular Viennese Schrammel ensembles replaced the clarinet with the accordion.

27. Ibid., 76–86. See also Walther Soyka, "Die Schrammelharmonika,"http://schrammelharmonika.nonfoodfactory.org (accessed February 19, 2009). See also Andreas Teufel, "Die Schrammelharmonika" (Master's thesis, Universität für Musik und Darstellende Kunst Graz, 2006), accessed December 1, 2011; http://schrammelharmonika.nonfoodfactory.org/Andreas_Teufel (with sound examples).

28. Wagner, *Das Akkordeon*, 32.

29. Ernst Roth, *Schwyzerörgeli: Geschichte, Instrumentenbau, Spielpraxis* (1979; reprint, Altdorf: Gamma, 2006).

30. H. Szadrowsky, "Die Musik und die tonerzeugenden Instrumente der Alpenbewohner," qtd. in ibid., 10.

31. I would like to thank Erica Segre and Jared Snyder for sharing their comments on this portrait.

32. James P. Leary, "The German Concertina in the Upper Midwest," in *Land without Nightingales: Music in the Making of German-America*, ed. Philip V. Bohlman and Otto Holzapfel (Madison, Wisc.: Max Kade Institute for German-American Studies, 2002), 191–232. See also Victor Greene, *A Passion for Polka: Old-Time Ethnic Music in America* (Berkeley: University of California Press, 1992), 112.

33. Leary, "German Concertina," 197.

34. Ibid.

35. James P. Leary and Richard March, "Dutchman Bands: Genre, Ethnicity, and Pluralism," in *Creative Ethnicity: Symbols and Strategies of Contemporary Ethnic Life*, ed. Stephen Stern and John A. Cicala (Logan: Utah State University Press, 1991), 38.

36. Bohlman, "Immigrant, Folk, and Regional Musics," 278.

37. Rubén Pérez Bugallo, "Corrientes musicales de Corrientes, Argentina," *Latin American Music Review* 13.1 (1992): 84, dates the accordion's arrival in 1853 without giving the source of this information. Another source refers to 1863 as the first mention of an accordion-like instrument in the area. According to a log entry of a Swiss military officer aboard a ship bound for Montevideo, Uruguay, a Swiss blacksmith entertained the travelers on his squeezebox. He was en route to New Helvetia, the Swiss colony of Uruguay. Since the original source in German could not be consulted, I would be wary to specify the instrument as a concertina or Bandonion, even though the Spanish translation of the log entry refers to a *bandoneón*. Jorge Labraña qtd. in Oscar Zucchi, *El tango, el bandoneón y sus intérpretes* (Buenos Aires: Editorial Corregidor, 1998), 24.

38. A self-proclaimed historian of Buenos Aires qtd. in ibid., 25.

39. Larry Crook, *Brazilian Music: Northeastern Traditions and the Heartbeat of a Modern Nation* (Santa Barbara, Calif.: ABC-Clio, 2005), 256.

40. *El acordeón del diablo: Vallenato, Cumbia, und Son*, dir. Stefan Schwietert (Berlin: Zero Film, Absolut Medien, Arte Edition, DVE 743, 2000).

41. See also Jacques Gilard, "El vallenato: tradición, identidad, y poder en Colombia," in *Músicas, sociedades y relaciones de poder en América Latina*, ed. Gérard Borras (Guadalajara, Mex.: Universidad de Guadalajara, 2000), 67.

42. The history of the Hohner Company is analyzed in detail in Hartmut Berghoff, *Zwischen Kleinstadt und Weltmarkt: Hohner und die Harmonika 1857–1961, Unternehmensgeschichte als Gesellschaftsgeschichte* (Paderborn: Ferdinand Schöningh, 2006). See also the richly illustrated coffeetable book by Haik Wenzel, Martin Häffner, Petra Schramböhmer, and Anselm Rössler, *Ewig jung trotz vieler Falten: History Unfolds!* (Bergkirchen: PPVMedien, Edition Bochinsky, 2004). Information for this paragraph is drawn from these two sources.

43. Berghoff, *Zwischen Kleinstadt und Weltmarkt*, 157.

44. Wagner, *Das Akkordeon*, 165.

45. The company orchestra, the twenty-five-member Hohner-Harmonika Orchester, was founded in 1929. See Wenzel et al., *Ewig jung*, 42–51. Hohner's professional accordion symphony orchestra existed from 1947 to 1963. It gave 476 concerts abroad, from Europe to North Africa, Australia, New Zealand, and the United States. Accordion arrangements of works by Strauss, Liszt, Brahms, and Rossini, recorded in 1961 and 1963, are reissued on the CD *Akkordeon Symphonie Orchester: Berühmte klassische Akkordeonbearbeitungen (Das Orchester des Hauses Hohner unter der Leitung von Rudolf Würthner)* (Trossingen: Deutsches Harmonika Museum, n.d.).

46. Wagner, *Das Akkordeon*, 85–86.

47. Thomas Eickhoff, "'Harmonika—Heil': Über ein Musikinstrument und seine Ideologisierung im Nationalsozialismus," in *Die dunkle Last: Musik und Nationalsozialismus*, ed. Brunhilde Sonntag, Hans-Werner Boresch, and Detlef Gojowy (Cologne: Bela Verlag, 1999), 165, 170, 173.

48. Ibid., 175.

49. Qtd. in ibid., 149.

50. For a complete list of classical compositions that employ the accordion, see Henry Doktorski, "The Classical Accordion, Part 1" (1998), http://www.ksanti.net/free-reed/history/classic.html (accessed December 1, 2011).

51. Maurer, *Accordion*, 80–81.

52. Bugiolacchi, "Castelfidardo."

53. Raymond Williams, *The Sociology of Culture* (1958; reprint, Chicago: University of Chicago Press, 1995), 227.

54. Arturo Peñón and Javier García Méndez, *The Bandonion: A Tango History*, trans. Tim Barnard (London: Nightwood Editions, 1988), 56.

55. Bohlman, "Immigrant, Folk, and Regional Musics," 307.

⇘ **2** ⇙

Accordion Jokes

A Folklorist's View

RICHARD MARCH

How many accordions can you fit in a phone booth?
One hundred and one, if you chop them up fine enough.

What's the difference between an onion and an accordion?
People shed tears when you chop up an onion.

What's the difference between a concertina and an accordion?
An accordion takes longer to burn.

What is a bassoon good for?
Kindling for an accordion fire.

If you throw an accordion, a banjo, and a bagpipe off the Empire
    State Building, which one hits the ground first?
Who cares?

A friend of mine spent the night in a rough section of town. He had to park
    out on the street, and he left his accordion in the back seat. The next
    morning he was shocked to see the car's window was smashed. He looked
    in and discovered that now there were two accordions in the back seat.

People tell jokes almost everywhere, and as a folklorist trained in the 1970s, tape recorder in hand, I collected them at parties, at work, and in taverns. Of course, nowadays the joke tellers are more active than ever at collecting jokes themselves, using the Internet. I Googled "accordion jokes" and quickly found several versions of the preceding jokes. Jokes denigrating the accordion and a few other musical instruments seem to be widespread. The common theme of such jokes is that they express an intense hostility to the accordion—it ought to be smashed, chopped up, or burned. Owning an accordion is such a misfortune, it seems, that only having two of them could be worse!

Aside from jokes gleefully cheering the destruction of accordions, there are these that emphasize accordion music's unpopularity:

> This accordionist plays a New Year's Eve gig, and afterward the club owner says, "Great job! Can you play again next year?" The accordionist replies, "Sure. Can I leave my instrument here until then?"

> What do you call an accordionist with a beeper?
> An optimist.

> What is the accordionist's most requested song?
> Play "Far, Far Away."

> What do an accordionist and a true music lover have in common?
> Absolutely nothing!

> Why did the chicken cross the road?
> To get away from the accordion concert.

A couple of jokes combine the music's unpopularity with an extension of the gleeful destruction from the instrument to the accordionist:

> What's the difference between a road-killed skunk and a road-killed accordionist?
> The skid marks in front of the skunk.

> What do you call twenty-five accordionists buried up to their necks in sand?
> Not enough sand.

While these jokes all indicate a popular distaste for squeezeboxes and their players, the mention of bassoons, banjos, and bagpipes in some of the jokes suggests that the accordion isn't the only instrument to be the butt of this type of joke. Indeed, when I Googled "bagpipe and banjo jokes," there were even more jokes devoted to these instruments. It was not surprising that frequently there were the identical joke motifs—the chopped up and burned banjos and bagpipes and their optimistic players with a beeper. Most of the time you could fill in the blank with an instrument's name and the joke still was coherent. Only a few of the abundant jokes are instrument-specific, referring to physical characteristics such as the accordion's bellows:

What is an accordion good for?
Learning to fold a road map.

What do you call a group of topless female accordionists?
Ladies in Pain.

Why are politicians good accordion players?
They're used to playing off both ends against the middle.

I found even fewer jokes that refer to the structure or shape of the banjo or the bagpipes:

Why did the Boy Scout take up the banjo?
It makes a good canoe paddle.

An octopus came into a bar where a lot of musicians hang out and said
to the bartender, "I'll bet fifty dollars that I can play any musical
instrument in the house." So a guitarist handed him a guitar, and he
played it just like Segovia. A trumpeter handed him a trumpet, and
he played it just like Miles Davis. Finally, a Scotsman handed him
a bagpipe. The octopus started poking around at it but didn't play it.
"Aha," said the Scotsman. "You can't play it." "Play it?" retorted the
octopus. "I was trying to have sex with it, if I could figure out how to
take off its pajamas."

Though only a few jokes refer to the specific shapes of the instruments, a number of jokes are based on the notion that the sounds they produce are horrible. I found the following jokes applied to banjo, bagpipes, and/or accordion:

How is a cat like an accordion?
They both make the same sort of noises when you squeeze them.

What is the difference between an accordion and a South American
macaw?
One makes loud obnoxious squawks, and the other is a bird.

There's nothing like the sound of an accordion, unless it's the sound
of a chicken caught in a vacuum cleaner.

And there are a lot of jokes that the instruments are perpetually out of tune:

How long does it take to get a banjo in tune?
Nobody knows.

What's the difference between a bagpipe and a chainsaw?
You can tune a chainsaw.

What's the definition of a minor second?
Two bagpipers trying to play in unison.

While versions of the horrible-sound and out-of-tune jokes are also told on the accordion, they seem less credible or applicable and turn up less frequently. By and large, in all of the despised-instrument jokes the source of disdain is a combination of sonic factors, distaste for the actual sounds they produce, and sociological factors, the perception that the instruments and their players are unpopular, stupid, unskilled, or geekish. It is easier to justify the sonic factors for the bagpipes and banjo. To someone who, unlike me, has not learned to adore the sound of the bagpipe's shrill reeds or the banjo's piercing metallic plunk, just listening to the instruments might be unpleasant. The accordion, however, is a mechanical, automated music-making machine manufactured to produce a euphonious sound. Its reeds are pretuned by the maker and seldom need tuning. Pressing the left-hand buttons produces preset harmonious chords. It is difficult—nearly impossible—for a player to make the reeds squawk. There is no sound that can come from the accordion that would be inherently grating to anyone imbued with the aesthetics of Western music like, for example, the screech of the bow on the strings of the novice violin student or the blat of a beginner on trumpet.

Sociological factors must have played the dominant role in assigning the accordion to the realm of despised instruments. Indeed, from its invention in the nineteenth century, the accordion never attained the respect of the elite class. It was a clever mechanical musical gadget. The accordion fad was in tune with the later nineteenth century's fascination with mechanization. Lacking a venerable pedigree, the accordion caught on among the less well-heeled part of the emerging middle class and the more plebeian working classes, and the instrument certainly was never accepted as a peer of the established classical orchestral instruments. An editorial in the *New York Times* of August 18, 1877, asserted, "the so-called musical instrument variously known as the accordion or concertina [is the] favorite instrument of the idle and depraved."

It is noteworthy that at the time this editorial was penned, the popularity of another free-reed, keyboard-controlled, air-pumped musical instrument that sounded much like an accordion, the reed organ, was burgeoning. Dozens of companies in New England and the Midwest, such as Whitney and Holmes, Story and Clark, and the longest-lived, the Espie Organ Company of Brattleboro, Vermont, turned out millions of reed organs. Straddling the realms of sacred church music and secular parlor music for the genteel class, the "parlor" organs were elegant Victorian pieces of furniture. Many were constructed with a high back, often decorated with mirrors and bric-a-brac shelves edged by intricate turned-wood railings. The organ builders also manufactured an even more accordion-like but less ornate product, portable reed organs that folded up into a case about the size of a steamer trunk—just the thing for a missionary headed to "savage lands." And guess what? Despite the organs' similarity in sound to the accordion, I can't find any jokes about reed organs or even their successors, electric organs.

Accordions and accordion players are mocked first and foremost because of their class and cultural associations. In the United States, squeezeboxes are firmly associated with central, eastern, and southern European immigrants and their progeny, a core working-class population of late nineteenth- and early twentieth-century America. The predominantly WASP elite was not about to allow even the most financially successful members of these groups into their country clubs. When discrimination against Italians, Slavs, and Jews eased after World War II, when the definition of "white" was expanded to include these lesser European races, accordion music made a brief foray toward becoming a form of mainstream popular music, with Frankie Yankovic leading the charge. But by 1955, Yankovic and his ilk were chased back into their ethnic strongholds, castigated as uncool amid the popularization of African American blues, the music of a still more exploited culture group. As in the Jazz Age thirty years earlier, black music was repackaged, this time as rock 'n' roll, with Elvis Presley as its white standard bearer. The electric guitar has been "in" ever since, and the accordion is considered decidedly unsexy. Hence this joke:

> *What do accordion players use for contraceptives?*
> *Their personalities.*

The message was clear: "You lesser Europeans can ascend from the working to the middle class, but don't try to bring any of your ridiculous cultures with you. Leave the accordions behind!"

So just remember:

> *What do people say when a ship loaded with accordions sinks to the*
> *bottom of the ocean?*
> *Well, that's a start.*

◣ 3 ◢

From Chanky-Chank
to Yankee Chanks

*The Cajun Accordion
as Identity Symbol*

MARK F. DeWITT

The diatonic button accordion has been played by musicians the world over, but it has attained a uniquely prominent status in Louisiana Cajun culture. Over the decades, this one particular type of accordion has served as a tabula rasa onto which have been projected changing views of Cajun music and the status of Cajun ethnic identity.

When we talk about the Cajun accordion, what do we mean? We could be referring to an instrument made by a Cajun accordion maker, of which there are several, and how these instruments differ from other accordions. We might also be thinking of a certain playing style and musical repertoire for the accordion that Cajuns and Creoles have developed over the last century or so, with the idea that the Cajun accordion is used to play Cajun music. That may seem obvious, but consider also that a Cajun who owns an accordion can play any kind of music on it that he or she wishes, and in some sense the music that results still comes from a "Cajun accordion."

The word "Cajun" is a phonetic transformation of "Acadian," which aptly signifies the cultural transformation that took place when French-descended settlers in what was known as *Acadie*, now part of the Canadian maritime provinces, made a new home for themselves on the prairies and bayous of Louisiana. Many of these settlers in Acadia were not immigrants from France but rather native-born francophones who for several generations had their own community identity. These settlers refused to swear allegiance to the British crown in 1755 during a seesaw battle for control of the region with France and were deported at the hands of British colonial troops, or left a few years later under their own power after resistance to the British proved futile. Forcibly scattered along the eastern seaboard of the United States (and elsewhere), a decade later some Acadians were lured south by the Spanish, who owned Louisiana at the time and were looking to create a buffer zone of settlements against British-occupied lands to the north. Unlike in the British colonies, the Acadians found their Catholicism and French language accepted in Louisiana, and eventually nearly three thousand of the deportees from the north resettled in Louisiana on farmlands west of New Orleans.[1]

In their new home, the Acadians in Louisiana found themselves in contact with a cultural diversity that was new for them: Spanish colonial governors, African slaves, unfamiliar Native American cultures, French-speaking whites and blacks who arrived by way of St. Domingue (Haiti), and free Creoles of color. The Acadians brought their own musicality with them—scholars have found documentation of their use of violins, clarinets, and a cappella dance music in eighteenth-century Louisiana—and they did not hesitate to adapt it to their new cultural environment.[2] Influences from other cultures facilitated a gradual shift from an Acadian identity to a Cajun one. *Acadien* became '*cadien* became *Cajun* as English speakers came to power after the Spanish ceded the Louisiana Territory back to the French, who turned right around and dealt it to the United States in the same year (1803).[3]

On their farms and ranches, relatively isolated from the urban center of New Orleans by the swampy Atchafalaya Basin, French-speaking Cajuns and Creoles were not forced to learn English in the nineteenth century.[4] Schooling was practically nonexistent, and most Cajuns were illiterate. The more upwardly mobile among them did learn English but still referred to themselves as Acadians and identified with Henry Wadsworth Longfellow's epic poem *Evangeline* (1847), which told the story of two young Acadian lovers in Canada separated and deported, one of whom ends up in Louisiana.[5] The name Evangeline is still evident in southwest Louisiana, for example as the name of a parish (county) and a brand of bread. Middle-class Acadians notwithstanding, most Cajuns engaged in farming and other kinds of manual labor for their livelihoods. Intermarriage with immigrants from other places led to a proliferation of distinctly non-French-sounding Cajun surnames such as Ortego, Schexnayder, McGee, and Abshire. Male outsiders who married Cajun women found themselves learning to speak French (if they did not already) and to follow Cajun customs, in essence becoming Cajun by marriage even as they were bringing outside cultural elements into Cajun communities.[6]

Although they had been U.S. citizens since the Louisiana Purchase and affected by national events such as the Civil War and Reconstruction, the Americanization process for Cajuns really began with the completion of the railroad from New Orleans to Houston in 1880, facilitating the movement of goods and people on a whole new scale.[7] Within a few years, in predominantly Cajun towns along the rail route, German Jewish merchants began opening general stores, where the geographer Malcolm Comeaux believes Cajuns bought their first accordions.[8] The influx of more English-speaking people heightened the awareness of cultural differences between Cajuns and Anglo-Americans, stereotypes on both sides that had been developing already for decades, which James Dormon summarizes as follows: "In the eyes of Anglos and Creoles alike, Cajuns were still a fundamentally impoverished, illiterate peasant folk, mired in tradition and kinship domination and a kind of reactionary orthodoxy, beyond the pale of the burgeoning Anglo-Creole agricultural/commercial world."[9] Cajuns, for their part, viewed *les Américains* as untrustworthy and overly materialistic. The word *cadien* or Cajun itself became loaded with negative connotations to the point where many considered it an epithet. Cajuns often referred to themselves simply as "French."

Because of increased commerce coming into the region from the rest of the United States, financial pressure continually grew for Cajuns to Americanize themselves in order to do business with outsiders and newcomers—for example, to learn English and work in the oil industry after oil was discovered in the area. Learning English became imperative in 1916 when the Louisiana state legislature essentially outlawed bilingual education: all schoolchildren in the state were to be taught in English only.[10] A generation of Cajun children went through the trauma of learning to speak French from the cradle, then showing up for their first day of school expected to speak and understand a language they did not know. Speaking French in the classroom resulted in discipline, sometimes in corporal punishment.[11] This generation in turn raised its children to speak only English so that they would be ready for school and not discriminated against for speaking French. Thus did the language begin to disappear from use.[12] It was not until the late 1960s, when the civil rights movement began to spill over into a new awareness of ethnic pride among other groups, that a state-supported Council for the Development of French in Louisiana (CODOFIL) was formed with the idea of building, rather than suppressing, French instruction in the public schools. The value placed on Cajun identity came nearly full-circle in the 1980s, when the Louisiana economy plummeted along with oil prices, and government officials began promoting tourism heavily. Southwest Louisiana became known as "Cajun Country," a cultural-tourism destination known especially for its music and food. Instead of an economic liability, Cajun identity became a selling point.[13]

Several themes from the development of Cajun identity recur in the history of Cajun music and the Cajun accordion: the varied cultural influences, the perception of having to choose between an American identity and a Cajun one, the importance of cultural symbols in Cajun identity (language, food, music), and the changing nature and valuation of Cajun identity itself. For example, just as children were punished in school for speaking French, some were punished at home when they tried to play the accordion—Cajun French music was considered as backward as the language. Several prominent players such as Nathan Abshire reported the necessity of practicing surreptitiously as children until they could play well enough to prove themselves to their elders.[14]

In the eighteenth century, the British did not manage to remove all Acadians from the maritime provinces of what is now Canada. To the extent that there is an identifiably Acadian musical culture there today, it sounds almost nothing like Cajun music from Louisiana. Cultural influences not present in Canada have had over two centuries to find their way into Cajun music, especially African musical practices from slaves, free Creoles of color, and their descendants. A second reason is the eventual Cajun adoption of the accordion, invented in Europe in the 1820s, which also caught on in Québec but not in the Acadian region of French Canada.

The first recording of Cajun music was made in 1928, "Lafayette (Allons à La-fayette)," and it featured Joe Falcon on accordion and his wife Cleoma on guitar.[15] So it is tempting to think that the accordion has always been a part of Cajun music, but of course this cannot be so because the Acadians arrived in Louisiana and were making music before the accordion was even invented. So at what point did the accordion "take over" Cajun music, as most seem to agree that it has? Interest-ingly, Comeaux suggests that "fiddles remained the main instrument of choice on the prairies of southwest Louisiana until the 1920s"—in other words, in the same decade that Cajun music was recorded![16] This is surprising and perhaps debatable, given that there is evidence that the accordion arrived in the area several decades earlier. Former slaves interviewed in the 1930s by the Federal Writers' Project told of accordions in Louisiana during the slavery period.[17] Joe Falcon, the ac-cordionist on the first Cajun recording, was born in 1900 near Rayne, Louisiana, and told an interviewer that he asked for and received an accordion when he was seven years old.[18] Cleoma Falcon's father, Auguste Breaux, was also known as a "renowned accordionist" and was probably playing prior to 1900.[19]

Regardless of when the accordion came to prominence, another question remains to be answered: How did the instrument change Cajun music?[20] One hypothesis commonly ventured is that the accordion greatly affected the Cajun musical repertoire due to the instrument's design. As should be clear to readers of this volume, accordions come in many configurations, but the diatonic button accordion with a single row of buttons for the right hand was the most popular among Cajuns (see figure 3.1 for the correspondence of button layout and notes played). This type of accordion is capable of playing all of the notes of one major scale; the first note of that scale is used to name the "key" of the accordion. For example, Cajun accordions today are often tuned in the key of C, which means that they can play all of the notes within a certain range corresponding to the white keys on a piano (seven notes per octave) and none of the notes corresponding to the black keys (the other five notes per octave). In contrast to the diatonic accordion, an accordion with a piano keyboard for the right hand may be called a "chromatic accordion," because it can play all twelve notes per octave that are typically used in Western classical and vernacular music.

The diatonic accordion also differs from the piano accordion in that the same button is capable of sounding two different notes (or chords, in the case of the single-chord button) depending on whether the air is coming in (player pulling) or out of (player pushing) the bellows (figure 3.1). The tuning of the buttons and the changing of pitch with air direction are directly analogous to the configuration of the diatonic harmonica (often used by blues musicians), which uses the player's respiratory tract instead of a bellows for impelling air movement and reversing its direction.

The Hohner Company, a German firm with a long history of making harmonicas and accordions, advertises their line of diatonic accordions thus:

> *Traditional diatonic accordions—featured in all cultures worldwide.* Maybe this is the most intuitive form of music making: to pick up an instrument and simply start to play it. Where is which note? One learns this in short time by heart—with these instruments, one does not think about music, one simply plays it![21]

While it is an exaggeration to say that the diatonic accordion appears in *all* cultures, it is certainly widely distributed across the world. The notion that "one does not think about music, one simply plays it" misleadingly downplays the role of intelligence in diatonic accordion playing, but at the same time, it realistically suggests that one can teach oneself how to play the instrument. Joe Falcon recalled, "I kept banging on the accordion until I struck a tune."[22] Not surprisingly, the same instrument sounds quite different whether one hears it played in Louisiana or Québec or West Africa. The Cajun folklorist Barry Jean Ancelet's way of saying this is that the accordion "arrived in Southwest Louisiana without an operator's manual."[23] Cajuns and Creoles invented a playing technique that began with some of the musical repertoire they were already singing and playing on the fiddle. When Joe Falcon taught himself how to play, he knew when he had "struck a tune" based on the music that surrounded him, the melodies as well as the fiddle and accordion players he had heard.

As the accordion became more popular at Cajun dances, fiddle tunes that did not fit on the accordion, such as most in the minor mode or those that were otherwise more chromatically inflected, fell into disuse. The Cajun fiddler Dennis McGee (1893–1989), who recorded some of these older tunes and played them into his nineties, is usually cited as the exemplar of what Cajun music might have

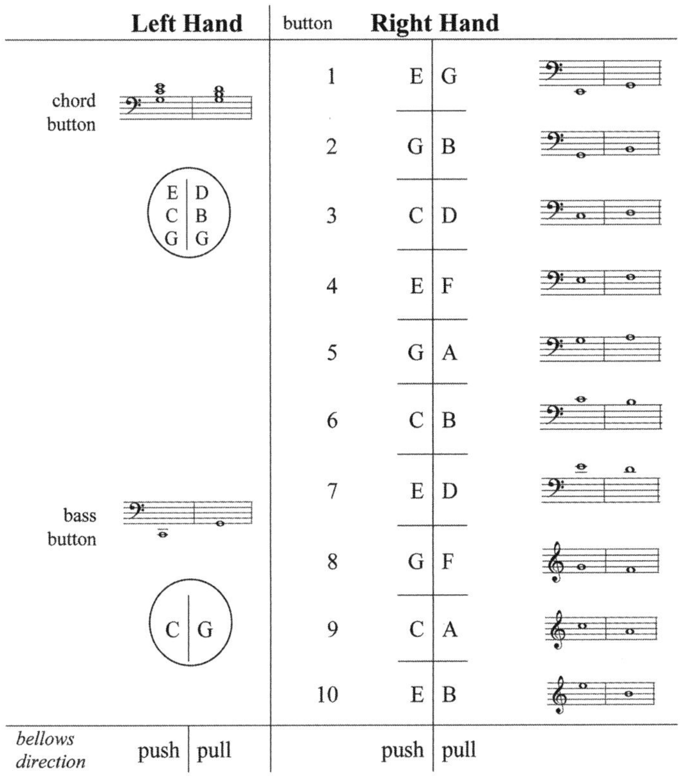

Left Hand	button	Right Hand

Figure 3.1 Button layout of the Cajun accordion.

sounded like prior to when the accordion became the primary instrument to accompany dancing.[24] Before electric amplification, other means had to be employed to ensure that dancers could hear the music or at least enough of the rhythm to keep dancing. Fiddlers developed techniques for playing as loudly as they could (playing on two strings, pressing down hard with the bow even if it led to a scratchy sound) and were sometimes accompanied by a triangle, whose metal-on-metal sound could be heard at the far end of the room when the fiddle could not.[25] The accordion, with its metal reeds, had the advantages of being much louder and staying in tune for long periods of time, so in an acoustic dance situation it was in constant demand, and the fiddler had to play what the accordion could play.

The accordion rose to great popularity in Cajun music, waned, then waxed again against the backdrop of twentieth-century American history and popular culture. Most if not all of the accordions that Cajuns played in the 1920s and 1930s were made in Europe, and when war broke out there, the supply of new instruments was essentially cut off, especially from Germany.[26] Coincidentally or not, the 1930s were a time when American popular music in the form of country music was making great inroads into southwestern Louisiana through radio and the phonograph. It is not difficult to see why Cajuns at the time were motivated to Americanize. The intense campaign for English only in the public schools had been in place for over a decade, the Great Depression was on, and seekers of salaried jobs in the oil industry and elsewhere found ways to accommodate themselves to the anglophone culture in the region. The jazzy style of country music from neighboring Texas, known as Western swing, became quite popular.[27] With its focus on the guitar, fiddle, and songs with sophisticated harmonies, there was no room for the diatonic accordion in the new style. Cajuns formed their own bands in imitation of the American hillbilly and Western swing bands they heard through the media, singing in a mixture of French and English. One such band, the Hackberry Ramblers, introduced electric amplification to dance-hall performances and thus enabled their music to be heard without need of the acoustically powerful accordion.[28] Young accordion players like Lawrence Walker and Nathan Abshire, who had already recorded in the mid-1930s, practically stopped performing in public for a decade or more. The Cajun fiddler Harry Choates recorded his hit waltz "Jolie Blonde" in 1946 with piano accompaniment and no accordion.[29]

There was a change in the public mood among Cajuns following the close of World War II in 1945. Those who had served in the military could take pride in their accomplishments, and some had actually found their French to be useful overseas, dialectical differences notwithstanding. People began to take more pride in their own cultural identity, and times were less hard economically. With more wealth to go around, the pressure may have eased somewhat to conform socially to get ahead. One result of this change in mood was a renewed interest among Cajuns in accordion music, signaled in 1948 with the enthusiastic reception to a new recording by a young accordionist named Iry Lejeune.[30] With his remarkably soulful singing in French and rapid-fire accordion playing, Lejeune left a recorded legacy of some two dozen songs before his premature death in a car accident, a repertoire that Cajun musicians are still playing today. Some of these songs he had reworked from previous recordings by the Creole accordionist Amédé Ardoin. Walker, Abshire, and other accordionists from the prewar period returned to the dance halls and recording studios. Even as the accordion returned, Cajun dance bands retained some characteristics from the Western swing period: the presence of drums, steel guitar, and amplification. It also helped, of course, that accordion production resumed in Europe to provide a fresh supply of instruments to a new generation of accordion players.

The quality of the postwar Hohner accordions from Germany left something to be desired, however. They were more difficult to play, and, according to Marc

Savoy, even the tuning did not sound right.[31] More advanced accordion players kept or sought out higher-quality prewar makes like Sterling and Monarch and had them repaired and retuned so they could keep playing them. Sidney Brown, an accordion repairman in Lake Charles, Louisiana, who had been making some of his own replacement parts, started making whole new accordions based upon the Sterling and Monarch models. He would cannibalize new Hohner accordions for the reeds, bellows, and other parts he could not readily make in his shop, and fashion the rest of the instrument himself. Marc Savoy was a teenaged accordion player who was already repairing accordions when he first played one of Sidney Brown's accordions, and within three or four years he was trying his own hand at making them. After finishing a bachelor's degree in chemical engineering, he found himself still obsessed with improving the technology of his accordions, so he opened his own shop in 1966 to become a full-time instrument maker and musician. Although his instruments were and are significantly more costly than German or Chinese imports (retailing for up to thrice as much), the difference in quality apparently more than made up for it in light of consumer demand.[32] He apprenticed other accordion makers, such as Junior Martin, in his shop because there was more than enough business to go around. By the early 1980s there were a couple of dozen accordion makers in Louisiana.[33] The Savoy Music Center in Eunice, Louisiana, has become something of a tourist destination, not only for people seeking to buy accordions but also for the Saturday-morning Cajun jam sessions that Savoy hosts in his store.

What are the basic working components of a diatonic accordion, and what have Cajun accordion makers done to distinguish themselves and their instruments? Figures 3.2 and 3.3 show photographs of two accordions owned by the author and made in the shop of Junior Martin in Scott, Louisiana. The basic diatonic accordion layout includes ten melody buttons for the right hand, and for the left hand one bass button, one chord button, and an air-release-valve button to allow the player to recover the bellows without playing a note. The bellows connect the two wooden halves of the instrument and must be airtight. Each note played by the right hand is sounded by up to four reeds; the four knobs on top of the instrument each control one bank of reeds. The banks of reeds are tuned in octaves: two in the middle octave for each note, one an octave below, and one an octave above. When a button is pressed, an air hole to a particular set of reed assemblies is exposed. As the bellows open or close, air rushes through the hole and sets the reeds vibrating. A flexible flap covers a reed on one side so that it only sounds when air is flowing in one direction and not the other. These basic facts apply to most single-row diatonic button accordions, as played in many music cultures.

Instrument makers in Louisiana have done several things to distinguish Cajun accordions from other diatonic accordions, of which some are visible and some

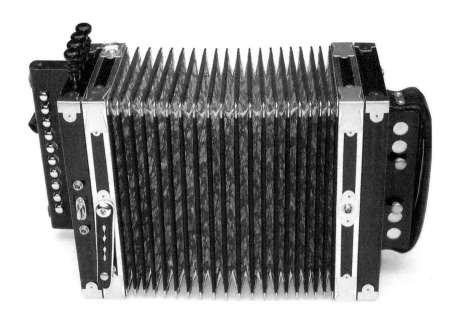

Figure 3.2 Cajun accordion painted black, bellows extended. Photograph by Mark F. DeWitt.

Figure 3.3 Cajun accordion with clear finish, front view. Photograph by Mark F. DeWitt.

are not. Figure 3.2 shows an instrument painted black, an homage to the prewar Sterling and Monarch accordions from Germany that were the prototypes for Louisiana accordion building. Also retained from those older accordions are the visible flaps on the right-hand side that expose the air holes to the reeds. When the right hand presses a button, the corresponding flap is lifted away from body of the instrument. Whereas contemporary factory-made Hohner diatonic accordions have hidden this action behind a grill, Cajun makers have chosen not only to keep the flaps open to view but also to cover them with shiny contact paper so that they flash in the light. They become part of the spectacle of watching someone play the instrument. The gaudy flaps also make it easier for other accordion players to see what notes the person on the bandstand is playing, which may play some role in the transmission of the tradition. The bass and chord buttons on the left are also a small departure from the German models, which use narrow levers instead.[34]

The accordion in figure 3.3 represents a further stylistic innovation in Louisiana accordion making introduced by Marc Savoy: the revealing of the wood grain through a clear or stained finish.[35] This particular accordion is made of bird's-eye maple with a clear finish. The number of wood pieces that make up the right-hand button board is more clearly visible due to Martin's alternation of black and natural wood material. There is additional fine inlay work in the wood pieces attached to the bellows. These touches do not enhance the sound of the instrument, only its visual appeal, which may help increase sales to tourists. The right face shows the same kind of detailing as the other instrument (they were made in the same shop), but with Mr. Martin's trademark.

Some of the most profound expressions of identity to be found in the construction of the Cajun accordion are invisible in the final product: the approaches to building and tuning the instrument. As noted above, the Cajuns as an ethnic group formed through a history of rural isolation, manual labor, and a certain aversion to materialism. Self-sufficiency was also a value, gained through ingenuity and the acquisition of a wide variety of skills. It was not unusual a century ago for a Cajun family to achieve a comfortable subsistence through a combination of farming, ranching, hunting, and fishing over the course of the year. Communal reciprocity of goods and services filled in the gaps and took place through group activities such as butcherings, harvests, and farm-construction projects. Cajuns also made their own farm implements using local materials.[36] So with a history of occupational versatility, creative use of the materials at hand, making their own tools, and a vibrant musical tradition, it is not surprising that Cajuns started making their own musical instruments and using found objects to make music.[37] They saw no reason to rely solely on instruments made by others. Washboards were taken and scrapers found to turn them into percussion instruments. Tines broken off from pitchforks were reshaped to make triangles. Violin makers tried fashioning instruments from cigar boxes, cypress planks, Formica, or interior paneling. For the fiddler who could not afford a higher-quality instrument, a homemade one was good for a start. Marc Savoy's first accordion repair was to replace a broken spring with a safety pin from his mother's sewing box.[38] In new accordions, Cajun instrument builders might make the left-hand buttons from metal glides designed for use on the bottoms of chair legs, and the right-hand buttons from plastic dowels or .45 caliber bullet jackets. The reed flaps (the parts covered with shiny contact paper) are simply made from wood dowels that have been cut in half lengthwise. The rigid metal parts that connect the buttons to the flaps might be made from electrical motor wire and a length from a bicycle spoke.[39]

Eventually, materialist values from mainstream society filtered into Louisiana instrument making, just as American country music found its way into Cajun music, and Cajun-made instruments achieved a more professional quality. The emphasis on quality over economy in Cajun accordion making—in the instrument's ease of playing, acoustic power, durability, visually attractive craftsmanship, and materials such reeds and bellows from Italy and woods from other parts of the world—reflects a substantial turn toward material values as well as an improved socioeconomic situation for Cajuns in the second half of the twentieth century. Nevertheless, significant remnants of a distinctive approach to material culture remain in Cajun accordions, which builders continue to make by hand.

What makes a diatonic accordion *sound* like a Cajun accordion has to do with its tuning and how it is played. Part of what motivated Marc Savoy to start tinkering with accordions was that the Hohner models "were stream-lined and retuned to the point where no self-respecting Cajun would play them."[40] Most players of traditional Cajun dance music prefer what they call "dry tuning," which is hardly unique among diatonic accordion traditions but also not universal. To understand the basic idea and sound of a dry tuning, recall that each note on the accordion is sounded by four banks of reeds, one each for low and high octaves plus two in the middle. In a dry tuning, the two reeds in the middle octave are tuned to the exact same pitch (as measured in vibrations per second), while the other two reeds are tuned in exact mathematical relationship: the higher octave at twice the number of vibrations per second, the lower octave at half the number. These numbers can be measured by an electronic tuner. Savoy feels that a final tuning by ear is required to improve the warmth and resonance of the tone; otherwise it may be too pure and consequently lifeless.[41] Nonetheless, the hallmark of a dry tuning is that the notes have a straight tone, in contrast to a "wet tuning," where one of the two middle reeds is intentionally tuned slightly off from its partner to produce acoustical beating, giving the effect of a vibrato. It is common to deviate from the equal-tempered tuning used for pianos by lowering the third and seventh degrees of the scale (E and B on a C accordion, for example) by as much as fifteen cents (15 percent of a semitone); some also prefer to raise the fourth degree (F on a C accordion) by about as much.[42]

Wet tuning is preferred by zydeco musicians, who sometimes also use diatonic accordions (see Jared Snyder's chapter on Creole music in chapter 4 of this volume). Zydeco players also prefer the deeper sound of an accordion tuned in B flat, as opposed to the C and D accordions that Cajuns normally play.[43] Thus accordion tuning, which is at one level a matter of individual taste, in Louisiana also becomes a group identity marker differentiating Cajun from Creole music. This is not to say that Cajuns never play wet-tuned accordions; more on that below.

Of course, the sound of a Cajun accordion is not simply determined by its tuning but also by how it is played and, to some extent, which music is played on it. In an accordion-instruction video, Marc Savoy delineates five "levels" of accomplishment in Cajun accordion playing: 1) knowing the melody by ear and being able to play it on the instrument; 2) "hammering" the melody in a staccato style; 3) playing notes above and below the melody note; 4) playing two or more notes at the same time with the right hand (octaves and chords); and 5) adding grace-note embellishments.[44] We can summarize what these levels mean for the listener to discern a Cajun style of accordion playing in terms of two factors: playing multiple notes at the same time (level 4) and ornamentation of the melody (levels 2, 3, and 5) in a rhythmic fashion that provides a nearly constant subdivision of the beat. Note that while the diatonic accordion is perfectly capable of playing two, three, or even four notes at the same time with the right hand, in many traditions this feature is seldom exploited. In Irish or Québecois music, for example, the diatonic accordion usually renders the melody one note at a time, with the addition of an occasional octave note.[45] Several have speculated, with some justification, that the Cajun preference for two-note simultaneous combinations (especially fourths and fifths) may be an attempt to echo the Cajun fiddling style of frequently playing double stops (two strings at a time).

The characteristic subdivision of the beat in Cajun accordion playing is part of the larger picture of rhythm in Cajun music. A fundamental fact of Cajun music is that it is dance music. Most Cajun dancing is done in couples, and most songs played in duple meter (two or four beats per measure) are danced as two-steps, and then there are also waltzes (three beats per measure). The two-step, which involves variations on quick-quick-slow footwork, works within a certain range of moderate tempos. Toward the faster end of this range, the beat is typically divided into two more-or-less equal parts, with triplet eighth notes (triple subdivision) or sixteenths (quadruple subdivision) used only occasionally as ornamentation (level 5). Generally, the slower the tempo, the more the rhythm is "swung" in such a way that the offbeat note gets delayed and is therefore shorter than the note on the beat.[46] A good example of a two-step that is done on the faster side is Iry Lejeune's "J'ai été au bal" (I Went to the Dance).[47] If the tempo is slow enough, then beat subdivision can become a full triplet figure, dividing the beat into three parts of equal length. As a rule, waltzes are performed at tempos that call for triplet subdivision of the beat. There are also some duple-meter songs in the standard Cajun repertoire with tempos slow enough to use triplet subdivision, often songs that draw their means of expression from other genres like the blues (Lejeune's "Grand Bosco") or country music ("Grosse Erreur"). Note that Irish accordion players can play reels, which generally follow tempos faster than would ever be used for a two-step and employ triplet subdivision of the beat, using the same type of diatonic accordion. So there is no limitation of the instrument that dictates duple subdivision at faster two-step tempos; rather, it is a stylistic choice that Cajun musicians make, at least partly in response to dancers' wishes.[48]

To summarize the discussion of musical identity thus far, while it is difficult to describe in words what makes a Cajun accordion sound like a Cajun accordion when it is played, it is possible to say something. Practices that include dry tuning, playing multiple notes simultaneously, and playing certain dance rhythms within a range of tempos while subdividing the beat in specific relationship to the tempo, together add up to a particularly Cajun style of playing the diatonic accordion.

Still, there is an elusive quality to the unmistakable sound of Cajun music that must be acknowledged, as elusive as understanding what people exactly mean by the controversial local term "chanky-chank." The folklorist Barry Jean Ancelet gives some indication of its connotations when describing public reaction in Louisiana to the announcement that a trio including Dewey Balfa on fiddle was to perform Cajun music at the 1964 Newport Folk Festival in Rhode Island:

> There alongside nationally known folk revivalists like Joan Baez, Peter, Paul, and Mary, and Bob Dylan, they performed the turn-of-the-century, unamplified music which made the Louisiana cultural establishment uneasy. These "unrefined" sounds embarrassed the upwardly mobile "genteel Acadians" who barely tolerated the more polished sounds of popular dance bands like Belton Richard and the Musical Aces. They considered the music chosen for the Newport Festival crude, "nothing but chanky chank."[49]

The phrase was apparently an equal-opportunity epithet also applied to Creole accordion music; Nicholas Spitzer relates in an ethnographic anecdote from his field research in the 1970s in which a young black man near Breaux Bridge, Louisiana, refers derogatively to zydeco as "that chank-a-chank 'cordion stuff."[50]

Others have explained that "chanky-chank" refers to "the stigma of something déclassé" in music, a simplicity of instrumentation and rhythm, a repetitiveness;[51] or to trivial, irritating noise.[52] Sources have not commented on the etymology of

56

the term, but it likely resulted from onomatopoeia, which then begs the question, What aspect(s) of the music are the word sounds of "chanky-chank" supposed to suggest? The clanging of heavy chains comes to mind, not completely unlike the timbre of the triangle played in Cajun music or the rubboard used in zydeco, with the connotation of a sound that one might not consider as music. Repetitive rhythm is also suggested, such as what a triangle or rubboard might play with a two-step (chank-a-CHANK, chank-a-CHANK) or a waltz (CHANK, chank-a chank-a CHANK . . .). Others associate the accordion with the term; for example, Marc Savoy explains "chanky-chank style" as the practice of playing with frequent changes in bellows direction.[53] The Cajun accordionist Ray Abshire teaches a technique in workshops that he calls "the chanky-chank button," involving the use of button number 7 and a change of bellows direction when rendering a melody, which he regards as a key to the Cajun style of playing. Ancelet concurs with the onomatopoeia theory and with Marc Savoy's contention that it is the sound of the accordion in Cajun music, specifically the rapid alternation in bellows direction, to which "chanky-chank" refers.[54]

In the 1980s, when cultural tourism in southwestern Louisiana burgeoned and family restaurants featuring Cajun food and Cajun dancing to live music began to appear, the connotation of chanky-chank began to shift from one of derision to one of affection. Mulate's, one such restaurant in Breaux Bridge, Louisiana, created a bumper sticker to promote their business with the motto "I Love Chanky-Chank Music." Some still take umbrage at the term, but for others it has become a badge of pride. Likewise, Cajun accordion music has become a source of pride for Cajuns and the subject of delighted curiosity among some outside the ethnic group. Some outsiders go so far as to learn how to play the Cajun accordion themselves at summer music camps in Louisiana and other parts of the country. Cajuns now frequently refer to these accordion hobbyists as "Yankee chanks,"[55] playfully turning the tables on an insult formerly applied to them, recalling the Civil War and defending their culture from northern aggression.

The range of musical uses to which Cajuns and others have put the Cajun accordion is a testament to the instrument's power as a cultural symbol. Some Cajun accordionists like Marc Savoy or Walter Mouton prefer to spend most of their time playing in the traditional style described above and a traditional repertoire of standard Cajun songs, usually sung in French or occasionally instrumental. Rarely does a new composition become a hit and find its way into the rotation; more often, existing material is simply reworked or adapted to an individual player's preferences and abilities.

Other Cajun accordionists master the traditional style and repertoire and then expand their musical horizons. Horace Trahan won kudos and recognition from the Cajun French Music Association for his first recording *Ossun Blues*, performed in the traditional Cajun style.[56] He then scandalized some of the same people who praised him by picking up a wet-tuned accordion and recording a zydeco album, *Get On Board*, with a racially mixed band.[57] Steve Riley is a versatile musician who has recorded a wide variety of music over the past two decades with his band the Mamou Playboys, as well as with other lineups. It is not unusual at a Steve Riley show to hear a mixture of traditional songs and original compositions on the Cajun accordion, then for him to switch to fiddle to play some older double-fiddle tunes. In the second set, he might switch again to the triple-row button accordion to play some zydeco and Louisiana R&B selections sometimes known as "swamp pop," then return to the Cajun instrument and repertoire for the remainder of the evening.[58]

Other Cajun accordionists have ventured further into other American popular-music genres where it is unusual to hear an accordion. As noted above, the popularity of American country music temporarily pushed the accordion off the Cajun bandstand altogether in the 1930s and 1940s. When the accordion came back in style, some accordionists chose to continue covering the popular records out of Nashville, for which the singer would translate the lyrics into Cajun French. Belton Richard sang Hank Thompson's "Wild Side of Life," for example, as *le bord de la vie farouche* for a local audience.[59] By contrast, Jo-El Sonnier made some recordings of the traditional Cajun repertoire as a young prodigy. Then he went to Nashville and California to try to break through into the wider world of country music, trading mostly on his outstanding singing voice but also sprinkling French lyrics and accordion parts on some tracks to set himself apart at a time (the 1970s) when awareness of Cajun culture among the general public was much lower.[60] Sonnier also recorded an album of Cajun music for Rounder[61] and then three major-label country albums with modest success, the last in 1991. He eventually went back to recording and performing Cajun music, receiving three Grammy nominations for Best Traditional Folk Album.[62]

It is of course possible instead to rearrange traditional Cajun songs in the manner of another genre and to retain the accordion in the arrangement. The Cajun band Mamou (not to be confused with Steve Riley and the Mamou Playboys) recorded a self-titled album in the late 1980s that featured heavy rock versions of several Cajun standards such as "Jolie Blonde" and "La Danse de Mardi Gras." The texture they employed throughout included rock-tinged drumming, the bandleader Steve LaFleur's rock guitar and vocal stylings, fiddle, Cajun triangle, and (on four songs) accordion.[63]

The Cajun accordionist Wayne Toups has been one of the most prominent proponents of mixing rock (as well as other genres) with Cajun music. Toups made enough of a splash with his band Zydecajun in the 1980s that he was featured in the 1989 documentary film *J'Ai Été au Bal* (*I Went to the Dance*). Despite its name,

Zydecajun did not combine zydeco and Cajun music so much as it fused Cajun music with other popular music. In the film, Toups explains:

> You add a little bit of herbs and spices, of rhythm and blues, and a *little bit* of rock and roll. Not out of line, there's a border that you can just go by. And you can't cross the border, because then if you cross the border then you get away from the roots. So if you can just add little bits and pieces to it, you keep the fresh feeling and the energy to give to the younger generation, but still keep that roots, starcher strong Cajun feeling in your heart, you can go a long ways.[64]

The film cuts from this interview clip to its closing sequence: footage of Toups and his band playing at an outdoor dance in the small town of Rayne, Louisiana. They are midway through a rendition of "Allons à Lafayette," the first Cajun song ever recorded, with instrumentation that includes accordion, electric guitar, electric piano, bass guitar, and drums. The rock elements are clear: Toups's bluesy vocals, the barrelhouse electric piano and single-string electric-guitar solos, and the stop-time power chords during the singing of the second verse, shortly after the clip starts.[65] In the absence of the fiddle, the main reminders of "the roots" are the song's French lyrics (retained more or less from the 1928 recording) and Toups's accordion playing in the florid chanky-chank style that clearly borrows from the way previous accordion masters such as Aldus Roger[66] have played the song. At the same time, he puts his own high-energy twists into the accordion part, increasing the number of bellows changes during the main melody and playing repeating groups of three notes to create a momentary polyrhythm against the duple-meter background of the two-step. Underneath the guitar solo, he plays three- or four-note chords on the eighth-note offbeats, creating a strong syncopated feeling reminiscent of Jamaican ska. Here he is using the accordion not as an accordion, although its timbre is always there to remind you of its identity, but rather as a substitute for another instrument that would normally play a given figure, in this case a rhythm guitar.

In the film, Toups projects a macho image in his sleeveless muscle shirt, wearing a sweatband around his forehead with matching wristbands pulled up around his biceps. A few years later, I saw him in performance at the Great American Music Hall in San Francisco when he had developed this male-rock-star persona even further. He brought with him a more technologically advanced Falcon accordion, sporting six knobs on top (indicating six banks of reeds) instead of the usual four, playing with a band whose volume and arrangements ventured further into the genre of heavy metal. Several of the California dancers in attendance, whose tastes in Cajun music tend to be more conservative, were appalled. His recorded output, however, has been more varied. His 2004 album *Whoever Said It Was Easy* has some tracks that are clearly in the R&B vein, some more country, some Cajun. Like Sonnier, he does not feel obliged to play the accordion on every song. On a couple of tracks, "Leap of Faith" and "Cheap Imitation of You," the accordion plays simple lines that might have otherwise been assigned to a horn section.[67]

When another Cajun band, the Bluerunners, made its first record in 1991, it sounded like a rock band that happened to have an accordion and rubboard in it.[68] Except for the instrumentation, references to traditional culture were few, and the accordion was used mostly in place of a keyboard instrument in the arrangements, not played in the usual dance style. The band had a certain punk sensibility about it, and on tour in San Francisco that year, the accordion's bellows gave out, which caused the accordionist to smash it onstage. The band leader Mark Meaux told the journalist Michael Tisserand, "I was so proud of him, and proud of being in the band at that point." He also said, "We're not trying to destroy Cajun culture, we're trying to destroy the stereotypes."[69] This attitude has led the Bluerunners, through several stylistic and personnel transformations, to play with several ways of using the accordion, including traditional ones.[70] In addition to using the accordion to stand in for another instrument, they have had the accordion play along with a saxophone in a horn arrangement of sorts;[71] buried the busy chanky-chank sound in the mix instead of its customary foregrounding as a solo instrument;[72] composed a new two-step in the traditional style with accordion but in a significantly slower tempo;[73] kept the chanky-chank accordion in the background *and* slowed it down;[74] used a wet-tuned triple-row accordion to evoke a zydeco soundscape[75] or a Tex-Mex sound on a slow country ballad;[76] and featured the (dry-tuned) diatonic accordion as a lead melody instrument alongside a lead electric guitar in an original zydeco twelve-bar blues composition with horn-section accompaniment.[77]

The scholars Ryan Brasseaux and Kevin Fontenot attempt to come to terms with the heterogeneity of the twenty-first-century Louisiana audience for Cajun music by identifying three groups: the Cajun Renaissance/French movement, consisting of academics, state-agency officials at CODOFIL, other cultural elites, and the bands that follow their ideas; the Cajun French Music Association, the "Counter-Reformation" backlash to CODOFIL that gives out its Grammy-like "Le Cajun" awards to musicians who fit its notions of authenticity; and the working-class rank and file, whose eclectic tastes are reflected by the diverse playlists at radio stations like KBON-FM in Eunice.[78] Cajun music can hardly be said to be progressing in any one direction. Younger Cajun musicians—the bands Feufollet, the Pine Leaf Boys, the Lost Bayou Ramblers, and Kevin Naquin and the Ossun Playboys, just to name a few—are not simply picking up what Wayne Toups or Steve Riley or the Bluerunners started; all are finding their own ways among the many musical options available to them. If we then also take into account the legions of Cajun music fans and "Yankee chanks" in other parts of the country and abroad, then the field of possibilities for the Cajun accordion, for both reception and production of its music, becomes wide indeed.

Notes

1. Carl A. Brasseaux, *The Founding of New Acadia: The Beginnings of Acadian Life in Louisiana, 1765–1803* (Baton Rouge: Louisiana State University Press, 1987), 2–14, 20–89; Carl A. Brasseaux, *Acadian to Cajun: Transformation of a People, 1803–1877* (Jackson: University Press of Mississippi, 1992), 4.

2. Barry Jean Ancelet, *Cajun Music: Its Origins and Development* (Lafayette: Center for Louisiana Studies, University of Southwestern Louisiana, 1989), 2–17; Gérard Dôle, *Histoire musicale des Acadiens: De la Nouvelle-France à La Louisiane, 1604–1804* (Paris: Editions L'Harmattan, 1995); Claudie Marcel-Dubois, "Réflexions sur l'héritage musical français en Louisiane," *Selected Reports in Ethnomusicology* 3.1 (1978): 24–75.

3. Brasseaux, *Acadian to Cajun*, 46–47.

4. Ibid., 92–96.

5. Carl A. Brasseaux, *In Search of Evangeline: Birth and Evolution of the Evangeline Myth* (Thibodaux, La.: Blue Heron Press, 1988).

6. Brasseaux, *Acadian to Cajun*, 106–11; Rocky Sexton, "Cajuns, Germans, and Les Americains: A Historical Anthropology of Cultural and Demographic Transformations in Southwest Louisiana, 1880 to Present" (Ph.D. dissertation, University of Iowa, 1996), 147–55.

7. James H. Dormon, *The People Called Cajuns: Introduction to an Ethnohistory* (Lafayette: Center for Louisiana Studies, University of Southwestern Louisiana, 1983), 63–66.

8. Malcolm L. Comeaux, "Introduction and Use of Accordions in Cajun Dance Music," *Louisiana Folklore Miscellany* 14 (1999): 32.

9. Dormon, *People Called Cajuns*, 61.

10. Barry Jean Ancelet, Jay Edwards, and Glen Pitre, *Cajun Country* (Jackson: University Press of Mississippi, 1991), xvi.

11. Shane K. Bernard, *The Cajuns: Americanization of a People* (Jackson: University Press of Mississippi, 2003), xx, 18–19, 33–34; Mark F. DeWitt, *Cajun and Zydeco Dance Music in Northern California: Modern Pleasures in a Postmodern World* (Jackson: University Press of Mississippi, 2008), 72.

12. Dormon, *People Called Cajuns*, 69–76.

13. Barry Jean Ancelet, "Cultural Tourism in Cajun Country: Shotgun Wedding or Marriage Made in Heaven?" *Southern Folklore* 49.3 (1992): 256–66; Bernard, *Cajuns*, 58–145.

14. Barry Jean Ancelet and Elemore Morgan Jr., *The Makers of Cajun Music (Musiciens Cadiens et Creoles)* (Austin: University of Texas Press, 1984), 101; DeWitt, *Cajun and Zydeco*, 104. Lindahl has a different theory about motivations for punishment, having to do with the marriageability of musicians in Cajun culture. Carl Lindahl, "Grand Texas: Accordion Music and Lifestyle on the Cajun Frontière," *French American Review* 62 (1991): 26–36.

15. Columbia 15275-D; available on *J'Ai Été Au Bal: I Went to the Dance*, vol. 1, CD 331 (El Cerrito, Calif.: Arhoolie Records, 1990).

16. Comeaux, "Introduction and Use," 31–32.

17. "Fred Brown," in *The American Slave: A Composite Autobiography* (Supplement, Series 2), vol. 2: *Texas Narratives*, part 1, ed. George P. Rawick (Westport, Conn.: Greenwood Press, 1979), 464–70; "Virginia Newman," in *The American Slave: A Composite Autobiography* (Supplement, Series 2), vol. 7: *Texas Narratives*, part 1, ed. George P. Rawick (Westport, Conn.: Greenwood Press, 1979), 2902–8.

18. Ann Allen Savoy, *Cajun Music: A Reflection of a People* (Eunice, La.: Bluebird Press, 1984), 92.

19. Ibid., 80–81.

20. For more on how the musical technology of the Cajun accordion informs possibilities in Cajun music, see Mark F. DeWitt, "The Diatonic Button Accordion in Ethnic Context: Idiom and Style in Cajun Dance Music," *Popular Music and Society* 26.3 (2003): 305–30.

21. Hohner homepage, http://www.hohnerusa.com/index.php?209 (accessed January 11, 2009).

22. Savoy, *Cajun Music*, 92.

23. Qtd. in Michael Tisserand, *The Kingdom of Zydeco* (New York: Arcade Publishing, 1998), 44.

24. Savoy, *Cajun Music*, 13; Ancelet and Morgan, *Makers of Cajun Music*, 34–41.

25. Ancelet and Morgan, *Makers of Cajun Music*, 22.

26. Comeaux, "Introduction and Use," 34–35.

27. On Western swing, see Jean A. Boyd, *The Jazz of the Southwest: An Oral History of Western Swing* (Austin: University of Texas Press, 1998); Charles R. Townsend, *San Antonio Rose: The Life and Music of Bob Wills* (Urbana: University of Illinois Press, 1976).

28. Ben Sandmel, liner notes to Luderin Darbone's Hackberry Ramblers, *The Early Recordings: 1935–1950*, CD 7050 (El Cerrito, Calif.: Arhoolie Records, 2002).

29. Gold Star 1313; available on *J'Ai Été Au Bal*.

30. This narrative of the accordionless period in Cajun music, ending with the appearance of Iry Lejeune, is recounted in numerous sources, including Ancelet and Morgan, *Makers of Cajun Music*, 24–28; Ancelet, *Cajun Music*, 27–32; Savoy, *Cajun Music*, 14; and Les Blank, Chris Strachwitz, and Maureen Gosling, *J'Ai Été au Bal (I Went to the Dance)*, BF-103 DVD (El Cerrito, Calif.: Brazos Films, 1989). Broven goes further in chronicling the popularity of country music among Cajuns into the 1960s, even as the accordion had clearly reestablished an audience for itself. John Broven, *South to Louisiana: The Music of the Cajun Bayous* (Gretna, La.: Pelican Publishing, 1983), 19–75.

31. See www.savoymusiccenter.com (accessed January 16, 2009). His surname is pronounced "sah-VWAH."

32. Ancelet and Morgan, *Makers of Cajun Music*, 128–39.

33. Savoy, *Cajun Music*.

34. Malcolm L. Comeaux, "The Cajun Accordion," *Revue de Louisiane* 7.2 (1978): 125.

35. Ancelet, Edwards, and Pitre, *Cajun Country*, 169.

36. Ibid., 37–65. Comeaux reinforces this theme of Cajun versatility but maintains that subsistence skills were more specialized according to the environment in which people lived: bayou, swamp, prairie, or coastal marsh. Malcolm Comeaux, "Louisiana's Acadians: The Environmental Impact," in *The Cajuns: Essays on Their History and Culture*, ed. Glenn R. Conrad (Lafayette: Center for Louisiana Studies, University of Southwestern Louisiana, 1983), 109–26.

37. Ancelet, Edwards, and Pitre, *Cajun Country*, 163–70.

38. See www.savoymusiccenter.com.

39. Comeaux, "Cajun Accordion," 125.

40. Savoy Music Center, "Accordions in Louisiana," www.savoymusiccenter.com/accordions_in_louisiana.html (accessed January 22, 2012).

41. Ibid.

42. Clarence "Junior" Martin, personal communication, Scott, La., March 27, 1996; Comeaux, "Cajun Accordion," 121.

43. Tisserand, *Kingdom of Zydeco*, 263–64.

44. *How to Play the Cajun Accordion with Marc Savoy and Tracy Schwarz*, VHS (Eunice, La.: Bluebird Films, 1990).

45. For Québecois examples, listen to Philippe Bruneau, *Accordéon Diatonique/Diatonic Accordion*, Archives TCDA 19083–2 (Canadian Museum of Civilization, 2003). Irish players of the melodeon, as they call the diatonic accordion, include Bobby Gardiner and Johnny Connolly.

46. This is consistent with research on the practice of swing rhythms in jazz. Anders Friberg and Andreas Sundström, "Swing Ratios and Ensemble Timing in Jazz Performance: Evidence for a Common Rhythmic Pattern," *Music Perception* 19.3 (2002): 333–49.

47. All of the referenced Lejeune recordings can be found on Iry LeJeune, *Cajun's Greatest*, CDCHD 428 (London: Ace, 1992).

48. Consequently there is nothing about the instrument itself that prevents it from playing reels, jigs, polkas, mazurkas, contredanses, and other dance genres. This is evidenced by contemporary Irish and Québecois players and by historical accounts of slaves playing such dances in French Louisiana in the mid-nineteenth century, contrary to Comeaux's assertion that the introduction of the accordion contributed to the loss of such genres that were formerly part of Cajun tradition (Comeaux, "Cajun Accordion," 117).

49. Ancelet, *Cajun Music*, 37.

50. Nicholas R. Spitzer, accompanying booklet to *Zodico: Louisiana Créole Music*, LP 6009 (Somerville, Mass.: Rounder Records, 1979), 4.

51. Dormon, *People Called Cajuns*, 77.

52. Lindahl, "Grand Texas."

53. Tracy Schwarz, accompanying booklet to *How to Play the Cajun Accordion*, 20.

54. Barry Ancelet, personal communication, January 30, 2009; Ron A., Bravenet Cajun Accordion discussion list, January 19, 2009 (accessed February 9, 2012), http://pub21.bravenet.com/forum/static/show.php?usernum=1722942123&frmid=16&msgid=888392&cmd=show.

55. Barry Ancelet and Rocky L. Sexton, personal communications, February 3–4, 2009.

56. Horace Trahan, *Ossun Blues*, Swallow 6134 (Ville Platt, La.: Swallow Records, 1996).

57. Horace Trahan and the New Ossun Express, *Get On Board*, ZHR-1008 (Eunice, La.: Zydeco Hound Records, 2000).

58. Shane K. Bernard, *Swamp Pop: Cajun and Creole Rhythm and Blues* (Jackson: University Press of Mississippi, 1996); Ryan A. Brasseaux and Erik Charpentier, "Fabricating Authenticity: The Cajun Renaissance and Steve Riley and the Mamou Playboys," in *Accordions, Fiddles, Two-Step, and Swing: A Cajun Music Reader*, ed. Ryan A. Brasseaux and Kevin S. Fontenot (Lafayette: Center for Louisiana Studies, University of Louisiana at Lafayette, 2006), 487–94.

59. "Wild Side of Life," *The Essential Belton Richard Cajun Music Collection*, Swallow 6117 (Ville Platt, La.: Swallow Records, 1994).

60. Jo-el Sonnier, *The Complete Mercury Sessions*, Mercury 314–512645–2 (New York: Mercury, 1992).

61. Jo-el Sonnier, *Cajun Life*, LP 3049 (Cambridge, Mass.: Rounder Records, 1980). His three nominations came in 1997, 2000, and 2005, prior to the inauguration of the Cajun/zydeco category (Louise Spear, Grammy Archive, personal communication, February 24, 2009).

62. Other Cajuns have had more success in Nashville, most notably Jimmy C. Newman, but they were not accordionists.

63. Mamou, *Mamou*, MCAD-10124 (Austin, Tex.: MCA Records, 1988).

64. Blank, Strachwitz, and Gosling, *J'Ai Été au Bal.*

65. The full performance of the song can be heard on the soundtrack *J'Ai Été au Bal (I Went to the Dance)*, vol. 2, CD-332 (El Cerrito, Calif.: Arhoolie Records, 1990).

66. Listen to "Lafayette Two-Step" on *Aldus Roger: A Cajun Legend*, LLCD-1007 (Lafayette, La.: La Louisianne Records, 1993).

67. Wayne Toups, *Whoever Said It Was Easy*, SH 9037 (Shanachie, 2004).

68. The Bluerunners, *The Bluerunners*, Island 422–848 277–2 (New York: Island Records, 1991).

69. Michael Tisserand, "Never Mind the Bowties—Here's the Bluerunners," in *Accordions, Fiddles, Two-Step, and Swing*, 477–85.

70. For example, "Au Bord du Bayou" (a new composition) and "Ossun 2-Step" (a traditional standard) on *The Bluerunners, to the Country*, CD 6073 (Cambridge, Mass.: Rounder Records, 1998). The recordings cited here are all examples of particular uses of the accordion and not meant as an exhaustive catalogue of this band's accordion tracks.

71. "String Bean," on *To the Country.*

72. "Burn Up The Night," on *The Bluerunners, the Chateau Chuck*, MON 6118–2 (New Orleans: Monkey Hill Records, 1994); and "On and On," on *The Bluerunners, Le Grand Bleu*, LRHR 1137 (New Orleans: Louisiana Red Hot Records, 2001).

73. "Rhode Island" and "Au Festival" on *To the Country*; "Attention" on *Le Grand Bleu*. In addition, all three of these compositions feature innovative departures in song form from the traditional Cajun repeating AABB structure.

74. "Landslide" and "Doorway" on *To the Country*.

75. "Sound of Love" on *To the Country*.

76. "Go on Get Out," on *The Chateau Chuck*.

77. "Blueco" on *To the Country*.

78. Ryan A. Brasseaux and Kevin S. Fontenot, "Saving the Culture with a Song: Cajun Music and the Twenty-First Century," in *Accordions, Fiddles, Two-Step, and Swing: A Cajun Music Reader*, ed. Ryan A. Brasseaux and Kevin S. Fontenot (Lafayette: Center for Louisiana Studies, University of Louisiana at Lafayette, 2006), 501–5. See also Rocky L. Sexton, "The Cajun French Music Association: The Development of a Music-Centered Ethnic Organization," in ibid., 179–89.

4

'Garde ici et 'garde lá-bas

Creole Accordion in Louisiana

JARED SNYDER

Any effort to trace the history and development of Louisiana Creole accordion must first take on the task of defining the term "Creole" in the context of Louisiana. It may seem a simple task: take Mark DeWitt's definition for Cajun accordion in the previous chapter, and what does not fall under Cajun is Creole. However, Creole is too layered and nuanced a term for such a simple definition. Derived from the Portuguese *crioulo*, it once simply meant "native-born," as in a crop such as Creole garlic or Creole tomatoes, or in delineating between immigrants and those born in Louisiana. After becoming part of the United States in 1803, those of Spanish and French heritage self-identified as Creoles to distinguish themselves from the influx of English-speaking and, to their eyes, crude Americans. Seeing a commonality of religion and language, American observers expanded the grouping to include merchants, tradesmen, laborers, servants, and slaves among Creoles. Creoles' collective syncretic culture recombined elements from French, Native American, and African cultures, especially Bambara, resulting in a unique Creole culture distinguished by its language, foodways, and music. Faced with the choice of either inclusion in a multiracial group or forced identification with the crass Americans, most white Creoles distanced themselves from Creole identity, leaving the term to solely represent those of a nonwhite background.

While differences exist between the Creole communities of New Orleans, River Parishes, the Cane River region around Natchitoches, and those within the so-called Acadian Triangle in the Southwest (between Port Arthur, Texas, to the west, Mamou to the north, and Lafayette to the east), all fall within an inclusive definition that encompasses those who have some African lineage, historically spoken a

Figure 4.1 Sketch of a dance witnessed at Belair Plantation in 1887 (by Edward Windsor Kemble). This illustration is included in an article titled "Sugar-Making in Louisiana" by Eugene V. Smalley. The artist replaced the triangle described by the writer with a cello. *Century Illustrated Monthly Magazine* 35.1 (November 1887).

language with Gallic and African antecedents, and mainly practiced Catholicism. In terms of accordion styles, this eliminates Gallic-based traditions that synthesized African elements, such as Cajun, and also purely African American styles like that played in northwestern Louisiana by Lead Belly (a.k.a. Huddie Ledbetter).[1] It is within the Creole communities in the southern part of the state, including New Orleans, that we find the source of the Creole accordion tradition.

Music and dancing has always been an integral component of the social life of southern Louisiana. Writers visiting colonial New Orleans and its environs commented on the nightly social dances, where Creole musicians provided accompaniment while freemen watched from designated areas, joined clandestinely by slaves. Later, these same musicians performed for dances in their own community. By the early nineteenth century, the dominant dance, not only in Louisiana but across the French colonies and former colonies, was the quadrille.[2] This "set dance" has five distinct figures, originally based on popular French *contradanses*, with music made up of eight- or sixteen-bar themes, repeated as many times as was necessary until the four to eight couples completed the steps.[3] A *konmandé*, or caller, announces the steps using calls that punctuate and accent the rhythm. The Guadeloupean musicologist Marcel S. Mavounzy sees the quadrille as representing true Creole culture. Slaves deprived of their own dances adapted the quadrille, transforming it into a much more rhythmic dance than its European roots, but a more formal dance than its African antecedents.[4] On the Creole-speaking islands of Haiti, Martinique, Dominica, and Guadeloupe, the popular melody instrument for accompanying quadrilles was the button accordion.[5] The volume of the instrument allowed it to carry across a room full of dancers and over the accompanying rhythmic instruments.

In South Louisiana, both freeman and slave danced the quadrille. Virginia Newman, who was freeborn but apprenticed at the home of Governor Foster in Franklin, danced the quadrilles to the sounds of the accordion.[6] Adeline White, a slave in Opelousas, danced set dances complete with a caller, likely quadrilles, to the accompaniment of accordion and violin.[7] Fred Brown, a slave born in Baton Rouge, also heard dances accompanied by accordion and banjo.[8] Jonathan Cade at Southern University collected similar reminisces of accordions used for musical accompaniment at slave dances.[9] Quadrilles continued to be popular dances in the post–Civil War years, and often the accompaniment included an accordion.[10]

The earliest image extant of an accordionist is a daguerreotype dated from the early 1850s, taken in a photo studio in New Orleans. A seated, well-dressed black man plays a French-style accordion, probably a Busson and known in the local vernacular as a *flutina*. Although accordions were used as props in some photo studios, this man looks comfortable and ready to play. The first accordionist identified by name was Justin Follis, a black Civil War recruit from the New Orleans suburb of Carrolton who drowned in the Red River in 1865, leaving his ten-button two-stop German diatonic accordion behind.[11] By 1867, there was enough accordion business in New Orleans for the accordion builder Fredrick Christen to set up shop at 11 South Rampart.[12] The Prussian immigrant's shop served a city under dramatic change as thousands of newly freed slaves arrived in the city, needing accordions for quadrilles, gospel, and even voodoo ceremonies.[13]

This swelling population created a demand for string instruments as well, and some of that demand was met by a Creole accordionist and bandleader named William Henry Peyton (1856–1905). He also ran a small music shop where he built and repaired string instruments, and he was perhaps the only African American luthier working in his own shop in the nineteenth century.[14] He first advertised himself as a musician in the 1884 city directory and continued to do so until his death in 1905.[15] He started playing clubs on the corner of Customhouse and Franklin—an

Figure 4.2 "Accordion Player, daguerreotype," ca. 1855.
Photographer unknown. Courtesy of the Collections of the
Louisiana State Museum, New Orleans.

area known as the Tenderloin—at about the same time that he started advertising. An 1887 image of a club in the Tenderloin has black figures dancing in what
appears to be a quadrille formation, complete with a caller and four multiracial
musicians.[16] These clubs had names like The Big 25, The Pig Ankle, The Shoto-
Tonk, and The 28, and they bustled with well-paid roustabouts drinking whiskey
and claret mixed with cocaine. Another depiction from 1891 shows four musicians
playing for dancers in quadrille formation with the caller also playing bones.[17] The
pose of the caller and the formation of the dancers bear a strong resemblance to
a contemporary depiction of a roustabout dance on the New Orleans docks, accompanied by banjo and accordion.[18] An 1894 description of a dance called it
"incessant . . . a row of women and a row of men facing each other, but instead of
dancing in turns . . ., all those persons danced continually. Each man and woman

who faced one another danced at each other—the men jigging and shuffling, and the women were doing the *danse du ventre* (belly dance per 1893 World's Fair)."[19] A quadrille required the band to play until all couples finished, giving the musicians space to musically stretch out and embellish themes or try new variations. Musicians "often repeated the same selection, but never played it the same way twice," wrote O. G. Samuels, the New Orleans correspondent for *Variety*, about a band he heard in 1895 at Customhouse and Franklin.[20]

Peyton was not the only Creole accordion player in New Orleans. The Creole musician Albert Glenny learned on the French-style *flutina* with double keys (two rows), which allowed him to "get as much position on that accordion as you make on the violin," that is, to play a chromatic scale, but Glenny also played the German diatonic accordion.[21] The cornetist Freddie Keppard of the Original Creole Jazz Band received formal music lessons on the accordion before switching to the violin.[22] His fellow Creole musician Louis "Big Eye" (Delisle) Nelson, whose family had migrated to New Orleans, learned on his father's German-style accordion. The clarinetist Clem Raymond grew up listening to his father playing quadrilles on accordion at house dances near their home at St. Bernard and Dorgenois Street.[23] The bandleaders John Robichaux and Charlie Galloway both played some accordion in their groups.[24] The Creole bandleader and accordionist Numa Dauphin led a group that included several horn players.[25] Perhaps most intriguing are reports that Charles "Buddy" Bolden, considered the first jazz musician, played accordion at the start of his career and worked in Peyton's band.[26]

Witnesses recall Peyton playing a large two-row accordion.[27] These instruments were common enough that a short story published in the *New York Times* in 1874 made their abundance in New York City the object of a joke.[28] The German two-row diatonic accordion built upon the basic design of the single-row instrument. The external row (the one closer to the outside edge) contains the diatonic scale, with one note sounding in each bellows direction:[29]

| mi | sol | do | mi | sol | do | mi | sol | do | mi | sol | [push] |
| la | si | re | fa | la | si | re | fa | la | si | re | [pull] |

The second row is added inside of the first and mimics the pattern of the first, but sets the pitch a fourth higher. The desire to provide a richer tonal palette resulted in a number of alternative patterns for the second row. One solution, created by the French builder Maugein and then produced to perfection by the Italian master Paolo Soprani, called for a second row based on "si" (for a B/C accordion). This pattern allowed the performer almost a full chromatic scale to work with:

| fa♯ | si | re♯ | fa♯ | si | re♯ | fa♯ | si | re♯ | fa♯ | [push] |
| la♯ | do♯ | mi | sol♯ | la♯ | do♯ | mi | do♯ | la♯ | do♯ | [pull] |

Monichon, in *L'accordéon,* lists multiple arrangements besides these two that became popular in differing regions of Europe in the late 1800s.[30] Apparently, Nelson was unable to play Peyton's accordion when he was invited to sit in, suggesting that maybe Peyton played an instrument with the Maugein arrangement.[31]

The original design for the left-hand accompaniment on multi-row diatonic accordions was based on a design used for the single row: two buttons, one that sounds the bass of the root on the push and the fifth on the pull; the chord button sounds the major triad associated with the bass note (the root on the push and the fifth on the pull). Monichon dates the advent of more sophisticated bass systems using sets of between four and twenty-four accompaniment buttons to circa 1880.[32] The New Orleans Creole musician John Joseph recalled that Peyton's accordion had "little buttons" on the left side that allowed him to "play a real dance with an accordion," driving the music with both sides of the accordion in a style of playing that Joseph called "melody lead and lead melody."[33] That expanded accompaniment supplied Peyton with bass and chord combinations for tonic, subdominant, and dominant major chords, as well as some additional minor or diminished chords.

The core of Peyton's sound was a trio with Hugh Rankins on bass and the guitarist Richard Pain. He augmented his band with young players such as the clarinetists Alphonse Picou and Nelson, the trombonist Jules "Bouboul" Fortune, and the cornetists Buddy Bolden and Manny Gabriel. Several musicians, including Nelson and the bassist Albert Glenny, got their first professional work playing "low down" quadrilles with Peyton.[34]

The fifth dance in the Creole quadrille, a couple dance, could have been early blues songs like "Careless Love" or "Alabama Bound," or new rag dances such as the "Pas Me Las," already danced in New Orleans prior to 1894.[35] The very popularity of these new couple dances combined with the harmonic complexity of blues and rags signaled the demise of the accordion in New Orleans. The younger musicians who started out on the accordion—Nelson, Glenny, Bolden, and Manny Gabriel—had all switched to other instruments, and by the time of Peyton's death in 1905, there were no other accordion-led bands active in the city.

Like many New Orleans musicians, Peyton toured the outlying area, playing at docks and rail stops in the countryside.[36] New Orleans bands ventured into the southwestern part of the state, and musicians from that region filtered into New Orleans, but nothing points to Peyton playing for the Creole dancers in that region.[37] Kate Chopin described an 1897 dance outside of Marksville where a Creole accordionist and two fiddlers provided the music.[38] They probably came from the area west of Opelousas, where, Comeaux suggests, small Creole farmers were the innovators behind the Creole single-row style.[39] It was a rural area, where it was rare to hear chordal instruments such as the guitar. Hence, the combination of volume and built-in accompaniment made the accordion an immediate favorite for dances despite the instrument's drawbacks, such as poor responding keys, cheap reeds, and limited key selection. The keys choices (F and B flat), combined with its other shortcomings, crippled the ability of the accordionist to reproduce the nuances of the melodies played by the fiddle.

Amédée Ardoin was born before the turn of the century, the seventh of seven sons, somewhere on Bayou Teche.[40] When he was a boy, his family moved to work on a farm in an area called L'Anse des Rougeaux, between Mamou and Eunice. The Cajuns used the term *anse* (cove) to designate the wooded grove that would appear as an inlet on the sea of flat prairie. It was here that Ardoin met Adam Fontenot, who was about the same age.[41] Adam's father was an accordionist, and Adam would steal off with the accordion, knowing that he would be punished if he were caught playing the expensive instrument. His father gave him the accordion after hearing him play because he conceded that Adam had mastered the instrument.[42]

A new generation of accordions began to arrive on the prairies in the early 1920s. These brands—Monarch, Sterling, and Eagle—were smaller and lighter than the early models. The spring-loaded keys gave them much greater sensitivity of touch, while four sets of steel reeds held their tune much longer and projected much better than the old brass reeds. The bellows were stronger and reinforced to handle the rigors of hours of dance accompaniment. The Monarch was preferred by Ardoin and Fontenot for its combination of volume, control, and durability.[43] The small black-painted model was called "Le Petit Noir." Control was important to musicians, who felt that any use of the air-button was a sign of poor musicianship, regardless of the difficulties a tune presented—the accordionist should never run out of bellows space, either on the push or the pull.

At the Cajun and Creole dances, waltzes now alternated with other couple dances such as the one-step, two-step, and stomp, instead of the five movements of the set dances. New accordions tuned in the fiddle-friendly keys of D and C allowed the sophisticated style of accompaniment from the rich Cajun fiddle tradition to be applied to duets with accordion.[44] Fontenot regularly played with the fiddler Alphonse LeFleur, while Ardoin worked with a variety of fiddlers, including the most famous: Cajun Dennis McGee and Creole Douglas Belair. Both accordionists favored the D accordion because its higher pitch carried better over the crowded dance floor. It was also the ideal key for Ardoin's high, powerful voice. The melodies for the new couple dances drew from the existing fiddle tunes, recycled themes from quadrilles and folk songs. They also included new compositions that emphasized the scale patterns of the button accordion. Ardoin's gift for improvising verses about his audience dramatically increased his popularity.[45] Fontenot relied on Lefleur to sing, so he could concentrate on playing elaborate instrumental passages while maintaining an even rhythm.[46]

Creole accordionists kept their right hand in a position in which their first finger rested on the dominant push on the fifth button instead of the tonic push of the third button. For tunes played in the tonic, their hands drifted down to lower notes but always climbed back to the fifth button at the resolution. This allowed a natural fingering of a dominant octave with the fifth and eighth button on the push or slide up to the root octave on the sixth and ninth button also on the push. Creoles also played "cross position," with the key based on the dominant (on a C accordion this would be the key of G). Their hand position meant that the resolution remained in a push, but now using the fifth and eight buttons instead of the third and sixth. The "cross position" produced a key with a flatted seventh (used in the blues) and an accompaniment that would produce the tonic on the pull and the subdominant on the push. The dominant was implied on the pull of the fifth and seventh button that sounded the root and fifth of the chord only.

A common arrangement for a two-step started with fiddle and accordion playing the melody in unison, with the fiddle usually an octave above the accordion's middle range. This was followed by the singing of a verse or verses with the same melody, followed by a single instrumental restatement of the theme before the "turn": a short B section that was often used to demonstrate the skills of the accordionist. Quick bellows movements and octave jumps created a propulsive tension that built excitement on the dance floor until released with the final resolving octave. The "cross position" lent itself well to the turn, but because the accordion was designed around pushes rather than pulls, it meant that the musician had to exercise greater bellows control, since the bellows rapidly expanded on the turns. A well-played turn expressed the melody without depleting the bellows or using the air button. To highlight musical skill on the turn, the fiddle dropped to the low strings to "saw" a rhythm, while the accordion alone repeated the turn twice before the fiddle rejoined and the original theme was restated in unison.

Dancers demanded a steady rhythm, and the built-in accompaniment of the accordion fulfilled this desire. Two-steps used a steadily alternating bass-chord pattern regardless of the bellows direction with a slight pickup in the one. The rhythm was reinforced by tapping the foot on the one or stomping a steady four beat. The volume of the feet could be enhanced by having the musicians situated on top of a table or stomping on an overturned crate. Waltzes used a bass-chord-chord accompaniment, again regardless of bellows direction, that was offset with the foot tapping the third beat of the measure and the first beat of the next measure. Tunes played in "cross position" often gave the audio effect of sounding the subdominant accompaniment while playing the melody over the root. However, it was the steadiness and drive rather than the harmonic shape of the tune that made a good accompaniment. The fiddle repertoire included some tunes that did not fit a diatonic scale. For these, the Creole accordionists developed an accompaniment style that set a counter-melodic pattern in the right hand with a steady standard accompaniment in the left. The most famous piece in this style is "Les Barres de La Prison," recorded in 1929 by Bellard.[47]

Ardoin and McGee made their first recordings in 1929. McGee remembered that Ardoin was invited to record after winning an accordion contest. Most of the music Ardoin recorded at this and the following session later that year was likely what he played at the Cajun house dances where he made his living and where he found his major sponsors.[48] "Eunice 2-Step," played in A on the D accordion, has a classic turn that derives its melody exclusively from the fifth, sixth, and seventh buttons, using rapid bellows changes and an implied resolution at the close of each repetition.[49]

Of more concern for this essay are the tunes that were played at Creole dances, often held after the Cajun dances finished. Adam's son, Canray Fontenot, described these performances by Ardoin and his father: "Then he would really get hot. . . . Amédée would get down with some blues. . . . They would both play old French songs, old African songs and hollers, and then make up something new, just their own."[50] Ardoin recorded at least one piece drawn from his Creole repertoire at each of his first three recording sessions. "Blues a Basile," set in A, made extensive use of the flatted seventh and the implied fifth to create a uniquely Creole blues form—one that worked within the limits of the instrument, but captured the inflections of African American blues. Blues, except for slow blues in 3/4 called the *baisse bas*, were not considered proper music at Creole dances and were not played until later at night. Ardoin's blues were in 2/4 and had a uniquely Creole structure. As the aversion to African American forms began to weaken among the elders, dancers changed the type of dancing and how close they were dancing. Ardoin performed New Orleans–style blues as accompaniment for people dancing the Charleston.[51]

Ardoin felt comfortable enough about his blues repertoire to record two more blues at his critical 1934 Bluebird session. "Blues a Voyage" uses the same form as "Blues a Basile," but "Crowley Blues" is something new. Played out of the "cross position," the fiddler McGee is relegated to pure driving rhythm exclusively in the root-chord drone, while Ardoin plays what would become a ubiquitous ornament, using a pull of the seventh and tenth buttons (re and si) and hammering a staccato suspended over the rhythm. He builds an almost free-form melody around the flatted seventh and ends phrases with repetitive tags. This is clearly not Cajun music, and it defines a distinctively Creole music that was probably influenced by the unrecorded Creole musicians around him.

According to the Creole musician Thomas Fields, the one-row diatonic accordions were widespread on the prairies west of Opelousas, but to the south on the old plantations around the towns of Lafayette, Rayne, and Crowley, the two- and

Figure 4.3 "Negro musicians playing accordion and washboard in front of store, near New Iberia." Photograph by Russell Lee, 1938. Courtesy of the Library of Congress, Prints & Photographs Division, Farm Security Administration, Office of War Information Photograph Collection [LC-DIG-fsa-8a24838].

three-row accordions were preferred.[52] Peyton and others in Louisiana played multi-row accordions prior to the turn of the century, but those models did not start to penetrate the rural Southwest until the late 1920s and early 1930s. The fiddle that commonly accompanied prairie one-row accordionists was replaced with metal rubboards and occasionally augmented with another accordion or an iron triangle called the *tit fer* to go with the multi-row accordions. The rubboard wooden frame was tied around the player's neck with twine to free both hands to scrape the corrugated metal with spoons, bottle openers, or keys.[53] On a two-row accordion, a talented player could create flourishes in "cross position" using more blue notes than just the flat seventh and, hence, play musical forms derived directly from the surrounding African American culture. This style was called *la la* (in urban areas like Houston, the "French *la la*"), and the term referred to the music and the dance event itself. There were a number of influential practitioners of this style: Claude and Ernest Faulk; Jesse, Zozo, and Nanel Reynolds; Ambrose Sam; and most importantly, Sidney Babineaux from Rayne and Willie Green in Houston.

Babineaux was born in 1896, a contemporary of Ardoin and Fontenot. His father Oscar was a sharecropper and fiddler who provided the pioneering Cajun accordionist Joe Falcon with the basis for his popular song "Hip et Taïaut." Falcon was also familiar with Sidney's music.[54] He played a three-row diatonic accordion, likely a Hohner in C-F-G or G-C-D configurations. His band included his brother on guitar, a rubboard, and a string bass. Guitar and bass probably functioned as rhythm instruments, like in Peyton's band. The rubboard may have scraped a 6/8 pattern against the 4/4 rhythm of the guitar and bass. Percussion instruments were occasionally used by Ardoin and Fontenot, but in Babineaux's style, the scraper moved to a primary role in Creole music, both in sound and status. Pairing the scraper with the free reed brought Creole music from Louisiana closer to that of the Creole-speaking islands than the jointly shared quadrille ever did.[55]

Babineaux sometimes added a fiddler to the band, but most of the melody he carried himself. His band could play whatever was currently popular, but some of his tunes drew from the ragtime era, like "Tight Like That" and "Sweet Genevieve," while his "Pine Grove Blues" eventually became the trademark hit for the Cajun accordionist Nathan Abshire. Canray Fontenot preserved several Babineaux compositions in his repertoire, including "The Dipsy Doodle."[56] With the exception of Ardoin's recording sessions in 1934, the Depression destroyed the market for rural recordings, including Creoles. The only recordings of Babineaux were made at his home in Rayne in 1961, when the Arhoolie Records founder Chris Strachwitz visited him.[57] The "Rayne One-Step" slides back and forth between the root and the dominant in the pull position, with a short chromatic riff stuck at the end of each phase running from the sixth back up to the root. Babineaux's left hand remains steady with an almost 2/4 pulse of the alternating bass/chord pattern, while the rubboard, played by an unidentified relative, scrapes in a 6/8 pattern against the 4/4 melody. The three-row diatonic accordion has a much lighter sound than the single-row accordion because there is no bassoon set of reeds. "Pine Grove Blues" as played by Abshire emulates this sound by closing the bassoon register on his one-row and playing out of the third position (this is the key of D on a C accordion). This approach gives the player the flatted third and seventh that would commonly have been employed by the multi-row accordionist, but no accompaniment and no standard third or seventh to utilize the way Babineaux used on the "Rayne One Step."[58]

After oil was discovered Texas in 1901, Creoles followed the boom to "Grand Texas," the region from the Sabine River border through the coastal cities of Port Arthur, Beaumont, and Orange and west to the city of Houston. As Jim Crow laws limited opportunities in New Orleans, Creoles went West seeking a better future across the Texas state line. The onset of the Great Depression further accelerated their migration, and the massive road-construction projects initiated by Governor

Huey Long expanded connections between southwestern Louisiana and the Texas oil towns. Willie Green moved to the Creole neighborhood of "Frenchtown" in Houston's Fifth Ward in the 1920s. He found success playing his two-row button accordion at house parties in "Frenchtown," accompanied by a second accordionist and a rubboard player. He began a long-standing engagement at Irene's Cafe in the Fifth Ward on Christmas Day 1949, after the owner heard him playing a local party.[59] Strachwitz recorded four songs by Green's band in 1961.[60] The second accordion in Green's band plays a rhythmic pattern similar to the accompaniments rural accordionists concocted for accompanying fiddle tunes. These patterns alternate with short unison passages or short bursts of countermelodies. The Creole musician Alvin Rubin pointed out that *la la* is "less French music with more blues and R&B elements," and this was clearly the case with the *la la* scene in Houston. For example, the first tunes Anderson Moss learned, "Stormy Monday" and "Driftin' Blues," were not Creole tunes or rural blues but polished, urban blues.[61] Green demonstrates this by playing the R&B tunes "Baby, Please Don't Go" and the Joe Turner classic "Tell Me, Pretty Baby." The Creole quality was imparted by the distinct instrumentation and a distinctly Creole approach to African American materials. Segregation and the bad economy kept Creole music off the airwaves and out of the recording studio until 1954. Although musicians were paid for their music and respected within their communities, it was not a full-time profession. To sustain musicians full-time, it would take having a fully employed community with enough density of population to support them. Postwar Houston was just such a place.

Clifton Chenier was born in 1925 in Opelousas. Although he had been exposed to Creole music—his father played a single-row accordion and his uncle the fiddle—it was not until he heard the piano accordion that he became interested in music.[62] The instrument had a number of advantages over the diatonic accordion: It has a piano keyboard that supports a full chromatic scale, with each pitch sounding the same regardless of the bellows direction. The left-hand accompaniment features a bass and chord combination, but with a full complement of major, minor, seventh, and diminished chords. There had been jazz-piano accordionists, the most famous being Bus Moten, the brother of Benny Moten and a member of the Benny Moten Orchestra, but there were no antecedents in Creole music.[63] Piano accordions were already common in the Western swing bands that dominated broadcasts from Texas. They fused jazz and swing with the "sock rhythms" of Texas fiddle tunes and the sensibility of hillbilly music.[64] Chenier took these raw elements and his love for R&B and blues and created a new music.

Chenier started honing his craft in 1947, playing outside the gates of the Gulf oil refinery in Port Arthur, accompanied by his brother Cleveland on rubboard. To afford better stability, Clifton designed a corrugated vest with over-the-shoulder tabs, called the *frottoir*, that has since become ubiquitous in Creole music. Cleveland developed his own *frottoir* style using multiple bottle openers in each hand.[65] On the piano accordion, Clifton used his left hand to play the full accompaniment for blues and R&B tunes. The tonic, subdominant, and dominant chords and bass were voiced similar to the pumping bass lines heard on the records of Ray Charles. Meanwhile, his right hand comped[66] behind his singing like a good jazz pianist. He also played Creole tunes in keys of F sharp and G using a steady bass and chord pattern. In Clifton's hands, the accordion was a complete one-man band—when work was steady enough to add a third musician, he chose a drum over another melody instrument.

The major difference between Chenier's music and the R&B assimilations of Green and other *la la* musicians is that Chenier returned to an earlier Creole music to find the rhythmic underpinnings. Ardoin's recording of "Two Step de Prairie Soileau" was an adaptation of a *juré*, a Lenten Creole music performed in the post-Lent period, during which instrumental music is considered inappropriate among Creoles. In the adaptation by Ardoin and McGee, the single two-line melody is repeated over and over, getting its power from the intensity of the beat and tension built by repetition that is only relieved by the alternating vocal and instrumental passages and the occasional octave jumps carried out by the instruments. In New Orleans, *jurés* were strictly a cappella, but in the Southwest, *jurés* included polyphonic hand clapping and foot tapping with dense call-and-response singing. Ardoin and McGee may have been the first to adapt the *juré* for nonsecular dancing, but they could not capture the full power of the rhythm with accordion and fiddle only.[67] By getting his trap drummer to emulate the polyrhythm of the *juré*, Chenier put a drive behind his music that distinguished it from *la la*.[68]

Musicians in Houston began describing Chenier's music using an old Creole expression, *les haricots sont pas sale* (the snap beans are not salted). In common parlance, this became *les haricots*, which phonetically is pronounced in Creole as *zarico* and eventually came to be spelled as *zydeco*. As with *la la*, the term *zydeco* could refer to either the music being played or the dance event where the music was heard. The actual roots of the expression are lost, but it is thought to have come from either a Creole dance step that was popular in Houston or simply from the old Creole song played by zydeco musicians. The term was used on records made in the late 1940s by the Houston bluesman Lightnin' Hopkins and the R&B singer Clarence Garlow, although neither song was a zydeco.[69]

In Houston Chenier found an audience that had adapted to an urban lifestyle and was ready for his Creole interpretation of urban blues. He built his sound around piano accordion and rubboard, adding a trap drum to the band and then electric bass and guitar. The electric guitar was a rhythm instrument and a lead instrument. To attract an audience accustomed to popular blues records on the regional jukeboxes that prominently featured guitar solos, Chenier astutely hired a string of talented guitarists to work in his band. His repertoire was broad enough that he could play traditional Creole dances at Freeman Fontenot's club in Basile or the latest R&B hits at a club in Houston. He also mixed Creole lyrics with R&B rhythms and added the occasional blues passage to a Creole tune. In 1954 Chenier made his first recordings. These recordings achieved regional success and helped to expand his popularity further.

Wilson Anthony "Boozoo" Chavis was born in 1930 in a rural area outside of Lake Charles. Neither of his parents played music, but his grandmother's brother was Sidney Babineaux. Chavis started on a single-row accordion before moving up to a two-row instrument for playing house dances around Lake Charles. Chavis's rising popularity caught the attention of an electronics repairman named Eddie Shuler, who stocked the local jukeboxes and also ran a tiny recording studio in the back room of his shop. He teamed Chavis, who had never played with a band, with an R&B band that had never played with an accordionist before to record a soulful old *la la* song called "Paper in My Shoe."[70] The unlikely record became a massive regional hit that sold up to four hundred thousand copies. Chavis was not able to repeat his success, became disillusioned with the recording industry, and retired to a successful career as a horse breeder.[71]

Chavis's early exit from the scene was of no help to Chenier's career either, even though he made several excellent recordings for the Imperial label that emphasized his voice and accordion playing.[72] It did not discourage him, and he continued to tour relentlessly up and down the I-10 corridor between Lafayette and Houston. Chenier's luck changed when he began his long recording partnership with Strachwitz in the early 1960s. Strachwitz's interest in documenting Creole music ensured that Chenier's Creole repertoire would be equally represented with his blues and R&B tunes on his Arhoolie recordings. His Creole repertoire is best represented by recording of "Zydeco Sont Pas Sale," which shows Chenier's approach to zydeco stripped to just *frottoir* and drums.[73] The underlying 4/4 *juré* beat is played on the bass drum and accented with the snare, while Cleveland scratches a 6/8 pattern on the *frottoir*. Clifton's left hand plays the familiar alternating bass/chord, while adding blues ornaments around the straightforward Creole melody. As the melody slides back and forth between the root and the dominant, Chenier sings the lyrics in bursts while playing the response to his call on the accordion. The turn starts with a drop to the fifth and employs the harmony heard on Ardoin's "Crowley Blues" around a series of propulsive staccato phrases and octave jumps to build the tension. Resolving to the melody, he plays a nuanced matching unison line underneath his singing. The slurs and bends he achieves on the accordion are similar to the sound blues harmonica players achieve by overblowing the free reeds. Since the same technique is not possible with the mechanics of the piano accordion, Chenier overcomes this by utilizing the piano keyboard with superb bellows control to produce the desired vocal-like quality.

Chenier tirelessly performed, crisscrossing the circuit with shows that were legendary for their four- to six-hour length and the caliber of the musicianship. Through his music, Chenier promoted a Creole identity that was comfortable in the outside world and proud of its own unique culture. Strachwitz's recordings helped Chenier gain success outside of Creole communities among blues enthusiasts and rock audiences. He became an advocate for not only zydeco music but Creole identity in general, encouraging Creole musicians and convincing Floyd's, the Ville Platte record label, to start recording zydeco bands. The high standard of musicianship he adhered to profoundly influenced all zydeco musicians, as did his insistence on retaining the core instrumentation of accordion and *frottoir.*

Chenier's success created opportunities for other Creole accordionists, but none ever surpassed him in popularity during his career. Perhaps the strongest competition came from Rockin' Dopsie (Alton Rubin), a left-handed three-row button accordionist who was often called the "Crown Prince." His three-row playing took full advantage of the power of the instrument, and his band combined many of the elements that Chenier had established for zydeco. Chenier himself expanded his band to include saxophone and organ and distributed solos across all the melody instruments. He integrated elements of popular soul music and rock-guitar effects like the fuzz-tone and wah-wah pedal.

The modern sounds that Chenier championed were trumped in 1980 by the surprising success of a recording of an old Creole tune, "Joe Pitre a Deux Femmes," by John Delafose.[74] He played a single-row accordion in a style that harkened back to Ardoin, with no blues inflections and a loud and steady left hand clearly audible over the band. Although the drums and *frottoir* played similar roles to Chenier's group, the guitar and bass performed a minimalist role, pushing the beat behind Delafose—with the guitar rhythm accenting the one in a consistent pattern, while the bass played a simple three- or four-note melody. "Joe Pitre a Deux Femmes" came out on new Maison de Soul label that Floyd's had started at Clifton's insistence.

Times had changed since he retired to breed horses, but Boozoo Chavis never stopped playing for friends and family events. Electric instruments were now standard in every zydeco band, from the very rural Duralde Playboys to Chenier's Red Hot Band. Tunes were standardized in structure to accommodate the expanded lineups and promote the sharing of solos. Boozoo's playing retained a decidedly rural flavor, occasionally moving across bar lines, repeating parts unequal times, and changing between parts as he felt inspired to. Rather than trying to change his accordion playing, his band loosely followed the template suggested by "Joe Pitre a Deux Femmes," concentrating on playing a strong beat and following Chavis wherever he took the music. At times, his band seemed almost telepathic in their ability to follow the leader through his irregular but highly danceable tunes. This music focused on the interaction of Chavis's voice and accordion. Rather than adapting from African American sources, Chavis took Creole and Cajun tunes and performed a reductive editing on them, stripping out turns, eliminating passages, simplifying melodies, and syncopating tunes into something new. Over these he sang lyrics, often in English, drawn from nursery rhymes, folk tales, and expressions, rather than following the thematic structures found in urban blues. His lyrics were evocative of rural life and sensibility. Chenier's "I'm a Hog for You" sounds like a literary tour de force in comparison to Chavis's "Dog Hill," with its single-line message repeated over and over.[75] On stage, Chavis rapidly moved from one number to the next, wearing a cowboy hat and an apron to keep sweat from destroying his accordion. He only took breaks to light a cigarette or to move between single-, double-, and triple-row accordions.[76] Besides the "cross position," he exploited the relative minor keys, that is, playing in D minor or E minor (for the cross) on a C accordion—something that was always implied in old-time Creole music because of its lack of ways of sounding minor chords. Unlike earlier players, his left hand did not necessarily play the alternating pattern, but he always retained a steady rhythmic pulse that was part of the overall sound even if it conflicted with the harmonic structure. Chavis used the power of repetition in accordion and lyrics to drive the dancers into a frenzy in a relentless compact surge of a two- or three-minute song. He kept the beat that Chenier popularized but fused it with the looser instrumental structure of *la la* and the informed instrumentation of a modern zydeco band. His minimalist approach gave his music the ability to sound old-fashioned and modern at the same time. Chavis was wildly popular on the circuit of Creole clubs in Louisiana and garnered a hip audience among the general public.

Chenier died in 1987, leaving Chavis to be the dominant figure until his death in 2001. The difference in Chenier and Chavis could be said to represent the two main directions in Creole music: a worldly urban form with rural roots, or a rural form that manipulated external influences to its own design—reflected in the piano accordion of Chenier versus the diatonic button accordion of Chavis. However, this simple dichotomy does not do justice to the Creole musicians who have followed these two. Chenier's legacy can be heard most clearly in the music of his son, C. J. Chenier; his former organist, Stanley Dural, a.k.a. Buckwheat Zydeco; and Dural's protégé, Nathan Williams. All play piano accordion exclusively in a style that owes greatly to Chenier. In some ways, Chavis's style has had the more profound impact. In zydeco music, Creole culture has always interacted with popular African American culture, whether through a thorough assimilation of different forms (Chenier) or by ignoring popular trends (Chavis).

If anything, the dichotomy in zydeco music now rests with the competing demands of an international market that sees it as symbolic of Creole culture while at the same time carrying an underlying set of stereotypical assumptions about it (such as gumbo, dancing, good times), and a now predominately English-speaking and increasingly urban local community that is saturated by commercial popular culture. Creole musicians try to appeal to the tastes of the latter while negotiating with the former for recording contracts. Although they integrate the musical world around them—from funk, R&B, rap, and rock—they do so from a Creole perspective. Rather than modifying the accordion style, the overall sound is changed by incorporating popping bass, searing guitar, keyboard washes, or Creole-inflected rap.

The standards of musicianship are still very high among the current generation of accordionists. Cedric Watson has mastered fiddle and accordion, and his work with the accordionist Corey Ledet showcases not only his talents but also Ledet's mastery of both piano and button accordion.[77] Chris Ardoin, a great nephew to Amédé, has developed a style informed by popular performers like Sean Combs and Kanye West, but without giving up his superb one-row accordion playing. In contrast, his cousin Dexter, who has worked with both Cajun and Creole musicians, is perhaps the most thoroughly traditional sounding young accordionist.[78] Yet, among all of these young musicians, the accordion paired with the *frottoir* remains the core component of Creole music—built upon the legacy of Peyton, Ardoin, Chenier, and Chavis.

Notes

1. Jared Snyder, "Leadbelly and His Windjammer: Examining the African American Button Accordion Tradition," *American Music* 12.2 (1994): 148–66.

2. Henry A. Kmen, *Music in New Orleans: The Formative Years, 1791–1841* (Baton Rouge: Louisiana State University Press, 1966), 21.

3. William Barclay Squire, "Quadrilles (Fr.)," in *The New Grove Dictionary of Music and Musicians*, vol. 20, ed. Stanley Sadie (London: Macmillan, 2001), 653–54.

4. Marcel S. Mavounzy, *Cinquante ans de musique et de culture en Guadeloupe 1928–1978* (Paris: Présence Africaine, 2002), 20.

5. Kenneth Bilby and Morton Marks, liner notes to *Caribbean Voyage: The 1962 Field Recordings of Alan Lomax. Dominica: Creole Crossroads*, CD 1724 (Cambridge, Mass.: Rounder Records, 1999).

6. George P. Rawick, ed., *The American Slave: A Composite Autobiography* (Westport, Conn.: Greenwood Press, 1972–79); interview with Virginia Newman in *Born in Slavery: Slave Narratives from the Federal Writers' Project, 1936–1938: Texas Narratives*, ed. George P. Rawick, vol. 16, part 3, 1–2. All interviews resulting from this project were published by Rawick, *The American Slave*, without naming the individual interviewers nor giving

the dates of the interviews cited. See also http://freepages.genealogy.rootsweb.ancestry
.com/~ewyatt/_borders/Texas%20Slave%20Narratives/Texas%20W/White,%20Adeline
.html (accessed January 28, 2012).

7. Interview with Adeline White in *Born in Slavery*, vol. 16, part 4, 1.

8. Interview with Fred Brown in *Born in Slavery*, vol. 16, part 1, 3.

9. Qtd. in Dena J. Epstein, *Sinful Tunes and Spirituals: Black Folk Music to the Civil War* (Urbana: University of Illinois Press, 1977), 158.

10. Willie Foster, interview at the Ransome Hogan Jazz Archives (hereafter RHA), January 21, 1959, Special Collections Department, Howard-Tilton Memorial Library, Tulane University, New Orleans.

11. Francis Lord, *Civil War Collector's Encyclopedia*, vol. 4 (Edison, N.J.: Blue and Grey Press, 1995), 140.

12. L. Soard, *Soard's City Directory of New Orleans* (New Orleans: Soard's Directory Co., 1867), 54; 1870 U.S. Federal Census, Louisiana, Orleans, New Orleans, Ward 3, Series M593, Roll 520, 658.

13. Robert Tallant, *Voodoo in New Orleans* (Gretna, La.: Pelican Press, 1983), 77–79; Grace King, "The Christmas Story in the Little Church," *Harpers New Magazine* (December 1888-May 1889), 94–114.

14. Michael Holmes, personal correspondence, September 10, 2003.

15. Lawrence Gushee, "Black Professional Musicians in New Orleans ca. 1880," *Inter-American Music Review* 11.2 (1991): 53–63.

16. Alecia P. Long, *The Great Southern Babylon: Sex, Race, and Respectability in New Orleans, 1865–1920* (Baton Rouge: Louisiana State University Press, 2005), 62 (this is a reprint of the cover of *The Mascot*, January 22, 1887).

17. Vincent J. Panetta, "For Godsakes Stop! Improvised Music in the Streets of New Orleans, ca. 1890," *Musical Quarterly* 84.1 (2000): 19–21.

18. This painting was published in *The LIFE History of the United States*, vol. 7, *1877–1890, Steel and Steam*, ed. Sam Welles (New York: Time-Life Books, 1964), 121–22. The painting was in the collection of the New Orleans painter and collector Alonzo Lansford. The collection was dispersed upon his death; the painting's current location is unknown. The painting was used as the basis for a popular lithograph. The earliest print I have been able to find is 1900. The most famous use was for a Bessie Smith advertisement in the *Chicago Defender* in 1923.

19. "Ventre Dance Down South," *Washington Post*, January 28, 1894, 15.

20. Qtd. in Lawrence Gushee, "From Nineteenth-Century Origins of Jazz," *Black Music Research Journal* 14.2 (1994): 1–2.

21. Albert Glenny interview, March 27, 1957, RHA, Reel 1.

22. Jack Burkle and Danny Barker, *Bourbon Street Black* (New York: Oxford University Press, 1973), 16.

23. Clem Raymond interview, August 25, 1958, RHA, Reel 1.

24. Al Rose and Edward Souchon, eds., *New Orleans Jazz: A Family Album* (Baton Rouge: Louisiana State University Press, 1984), 107–8; Robert Goffin, *La Nouvelle Orleans Capitale du Jazz* (New York: Maison Francaise, 1945), 52.

25. Willie Parker interview, November 7, 1958, RHA, Reel 1. Parker identified a Creole accordionist and bandleader named Dauphin; Walter Dauphin (b. March 5, 1891) and Eleona Dauphin (b. June 10, 1888) identify their father as a musician named Numa Dauphin.

26. Morroe Berger, "Letters from New Orleans," *Annual Review of Jazz Studies* 7 (1994–95): 47–73; Donald M. Marquis, "The Bolden-Peyton Legend: A Re-valuation," *Jazz Journal* 30 (February 1977): 24–25; Robert Goffin, "'Big Eye' Louis Nelson," *The Jazz Record* (June 1946): 7–8.

27. Willie Parker interview, November 7, 1958, RHA, Reel 1; John Joseph interview, November 26, 1958, RHA, Reel 1; Eddie Dawson interview, June 28, 1961, RHA, Reel 1.

28. "A Sea Story," *New York Times*, July 26, 1874, 3.

29. This would apply regardless of the key of the diatonic scale.

30. Pierre Monichon, *L'accordéon* (Lausanne: Paysat, 1985), 64–68.

31. Alan Lomax, *Mister Jelly Roll: The Fortunes of Jelly Roll Morton, New Orleans Creole and "Inventor of Jazz"* (Berkeley: University of California Press, 1973), 90.

32. Monichon, *L'accordéon*, 73–75.

33. John Joseph interview, November 26, 1958, RHA Reel 1.

34. Lomax, *Mister Jelly Roll*, 61, 88, 90.

35. Kevin Sanders, "Kansas City's Black Ragtime Composers: Part 2," *Revelry Rag*, Newsletter of the Kansas City Ragtime Revelry (Summer 1996): 1.

36. Bill Russell, *New Orleans Style* (New Orleans: Jazzology Press, 1994), 171.

37. Austin Sonnier Jr., *Second Linin': Jazzmen of Southwest Louisiana, 1900–1950* (Lafayette: Center for Lousiana Studies, University of Southwestern Louisiana, 1989). Sonnier's book covers the jazz musicians that regularly moved back and forth between the Southwest and New Orleans.

38. Kate Chopin, "A Night in Acadia," in *The Complete Works of Kate Chopin*, ed. Peter Seyersted (Baton Rouge: Louisiana State University Press, 1969), 490.

39. Malcolm L. Comeaux, "Introduction and Use of Accordions in Cajun Music," in *Fiddles, Accordion, Two-Step, and Swing: A Cajun Musical Reader*, ed. Ryan A. Brasseaux and Kevin S. Fontenot (Lafayette: Center for Louisiana Studies, University of Southwestern Louisiana, 2006), 108–12.

40. Pierre Daigle, *Tears, Love, and Laughter: The Story of the Acadians* (Cecilia, La.: Hebert Publications, 1977), 83; Ann Allen Savoy, *Cajun Music: A Reflection of a People* (Eunice, La.: Bluebird Press, 1984), 312.

41. Savoy, *Cajun Music*, 66.

42. Ibid., 326; Barry Jean Ancelet, *The Makers of Cajun Music* (Austin: University of Texas Press, 1984), 10, 82; Raymond E. François, *Yé Yaille Chère!* (Lafayette: Thunderstone Press, 1990), 30.

43. Barry Jean Ancelet, Jay D. Edwards, and Glen Pitre, *Cajun Country* (Jackson: University of Mississippi Press, 1991), 168.

44. Dennis McGee, *The Complete Early Recordings of Dennis McGee* (Newton, N.J.: Yazoo, 1994). One can hear the superb accompaniment of Sady Courville and Ernest Frugé behind McGee's lead fiddling.

45. Savoy, *Cajun Music*, 45.

46. Carolyn Russell, liner notes to *The Louisiana Cajun Trio: Homage*, CD LTP-1 (Garden Grove, Calif.: Living Tradition Productions, 1992); Gérard Dôle, *Louisiana Creole Music*, FW 02622 (Washington, D.C.: Smithsonian Center for Folklife and Cultural Heritage, 1978).

47. Bellard and the six-fingered Riley recorded four songs in New Orleans for Vocalion Records on October 2, 1929. A single copy of the 78 rpm record "La Valse de La Prison" and "Mon Camon La Case Que Je Sue Cordane" survived but has never been reissued. No copy of the remaining two songs has been found. A more contemporary example of this song and style is "Les Barres de La Prison" (The prison bars) by Canray Fontenot, Adam Fontenot's son, with accordion accompaniment by Alphonse "Bois Sec" Ardoin, Amédée's cousin, found on *La Musique Creole*, 445 (El Cerrito, Calif.: Arhoolie Records, 1992). "Blue Runner," found on *The Carrière Brothers: Musique Creole*, 512 (El Cerrito, Calif.: Arhoolie Records, 2004), is another example in this style.

48. Savoy, *Cajun Music*, 327.

49. The first six songs recorded by Ardoin are found on *Cajun Dance Party: Fais Do-Do Legacy*, OK 46784 (New York: Sony Records, 1994), including "Eunice Two-Step." The remaining records, except for two, are found on *Amédé Ardoin, "I'm Never Coming Back": Roots of Zydeco*, 7007 (El Cerrito, Calif.: Arhoolie Records, 1995). This includes "Blues a Basile," "Blues a Voyage," and "Crowley Blues." Although Adam Fontenot did not record, recordings of his nephews Freeman and Ray-bee Fontenot give some idea of what he sounded like. They both can be heard on *Legendary Masters of Cajun and Creole Music: Les Haricots Sont Pas Sales* (Paris: Cinq Planetes, 1997).

50. Qtd. in Michael Doucet, liner notes to *Amédé Ardoin, "I'm Never Coming Back."*

51. Michael Tisserand, *Kingdom of Zydeco* (New York: Arcade Publishing, 1998), 60.

52. Ibid., 47.

53. Most non-Creole rubboard players use thimbles on their fingers and hold the board away from their body so that one hand can scrape on each side.

54. The 1900 census shows the whole Babineaux family, including Oscar and Sidney. The 1930 census shows Babineaux, listed as a musician, living with his widowed mother. 1900 U.S. Federal Census, Police Ward 1, Acadia, Louisiana, Sheet 3; 1930 U.S. Federal Census, Rayne, Acadia, Louisiana, Roll 782, Page 35B; Enumeration District 1; Savoy, *Cajun Music*, 95–96.

55. Jared Snyder, "Pumping and Scraping: Accordion Music in the Caribbean," *Kalinda!* (Summer 1995): 6–8.

56. Savoy, *Cajun Music*, 330.

57. *Zydeco: The Early Years*, CD 307 (El Cerrito, Calif.: Arhoolie Records, 1993).

58. *Nathan Abshire: French Blues*, CD 373 (El Cerrito, Calif.: Arhoolie Records, 1993). Abshire first uses this approach on the "One-Step de Lacassine" (1934), which is found on *Le Gran Mamou: A Cajun Music Anthology*, 13 (Nashville: Country Music Foundation, 1990).

59. Roger Wood, "Southeast Texas: Hotbed of Zydeco," *Journal of Texas Music History* 1.2 (2001): 11.

60. "Green's Zydeco," "Jolie Blon," "Tell Me, Pretty Baby," and "Baby Please Don't Go" are all issued on *Zydeco: The Early Years*, CD 307 (El Cerrito, Calif: Arhoolie Records, 1993).

61. Ibid., 8. Also see Tisserand, *Kingdom of Zydeco*, 76–78.

62. Savoy, *Cajun Music*, 370–81.

63. *Bennie Moten's Kansas City Orchestra: 1927–1929*, 558 (Paris: Chronological Classics Records, 1990); *Basie Beginnings: Bennie Moten's Kansas City Orchestra (1929–1932)* (New York: BMG, Bluebird, 1989).

64. *Adolph Hofner: South Texas Swing*, 7029 (El Cerrito, Calif.: Arhoolie Records, 1990); *OKeh Western Swing*, 37324 (New York: Epic, 1990).

65. Tisserand, *Kingdom of Zydeco*, 91–147.

66. "Comp" is a term used in jazz music to describe the chords, rhythms, and countermelodies that keyboard players (piano or organ) or guitar players use to support a jazz musician's improvised solo or melody lines.

67. *Cajun and Creole Music*, vol. 2: *1934–1937* (Cambridge, Mass.: Rounder Select, 1999) has examples of *jurés* recorded by John and Alan Lomax in southwestern Louisiana ("Je Veux Me Marier," "Feel Like Dying in His Army," "Rockaway").

68. Wood, "Southeast Texas," 5.

69. Tisserand, *Kingdom of Zydeco*, 11–20.

70. *Boozoo Chavis: The Lake Charles Atomic Bomb, Original Goldband Recordings by Boozoo Chavis*, 2097 (Cambridge, Mass.: Rounder Records, 1992).

71. Jared Snyder, "Boozoo Chavis, His Own Kind of Zydeco Man," *Sing Out!* 44.1 (1999): 34–41.

72. *Bayou Blues*, SPCD 2139–2 (Los Angeles: Specialty Records, 1970); this recording collects most of Chenier's early recordings and demonstrates how good they are.

73. *Clifton Chenier: Louisiana Blues And Zydeco*, 9053 (El Cerrito, Calif.: Arhoolie Records, 1993).

74. *John Delafose and the Eunice Playboys: Joe Pitre Got Two Women*, 335 (El Cerrito, Calif.: Arhoolie Records, 1993).

75. *Clifton Chenier: Sixty Minutes with the King of Zydeco*, 301 (El Cerrito, Calf.: Arhoolie Records, 1998); *Boozoo Chavis: Zydeco Trail Ride*, MDS1034 (Ville Platte, La.: Maison de Soul, 1995).

76. Tisserand, *Kingdom of Zydeco*, 235–54.

77. A fascinating project is *Cedric Watson and Corey Ledet: Goin' Down to Louisiana* (Lafayette, La.: Valcour Music, 2006), where Ledet plays piano accordion and Watson plays fiddle in a tribute to Clifton Chenier. *Cedric Watson* (Lafayette, La.: Valcour, 2008) has Watson playing both fiddle and accordion. *The Corey Ledet Instructional Triple-Row Accordion*, DVD (Lafayette, La.: Almena Films, 2008), gives examples of his three-row playing.

78. *Chris Ardoin and NuStep: MVP*, MDS 1086 (Ville Platte, La.: Maison de Soul, 2008); *Dexter Ardoin and the Creole Ramblers: What You Come to Do* (Lafayette, La.: Radio Records, 2008).

≥ 5 ≤

"Tejano and Proud"

Regional Accordion
Traditions of South Texas
and the Border Region

CATHY RAGLAND

At the 1993 Tejano Conjunto Festival en San Antonio, the pioneering accordionist Narciso Martínez did not perform as he had done almost every year since the first festival in 1982. His death in June 1992 marked for many conjunto musicians and enthusiasts the end of an era in the history of Mexican American music in Texas. And though the entire festival in 1993 was dedicated to the memory of Martínez, it continued on as it had in the past. The *raíces* (roots) night in which Martínez had been featured continued to celebrate the influence of conjunto's pioneers as it had in previous years. Each year since, the festival has been rejuvenated with a new roster of conjunto heroes replacing those who, like Martínez, had passed on. The term *conjunto*, it should be noted, simply means "group" or "ensemble," but in South Texas it refers to a musical style associated with the Mexican American or "Tejano"—the identifier many people in this region have come to prefer.

One notable aspect of 1993's *raíces* night was that not one of the accordionists performed without bass and drums. Up until his death, Martínez was one of a handful of accordionists who still performed accompanied only by the *bajo sexto* (a combination bass/rhythm guitar with twelve—six double-course—strings believed to have originated from the state of Durango in Mexico). In years past, the festival director Juan Tejeda introduced Martínez and his *bajo sexto* player (usually Fred Zimmerle or Toby Torres, each with his own story as a pioneering artist) as representing the "original conjunto style and where it all began, with just the

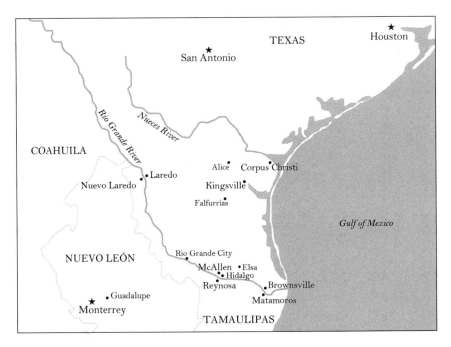

Figure 5.1 The South Texas-Mexico border region. Map by Helena Simonett.

acordeón y bajo sexto."[1] The double bass (known locally as the *tololoche*) was added in San Antonio during the late 1940s. Some sixteen years later, there are very few conjunto musicans at the festival who would have any memory of hearing the genre played live without the electric bass and drums. For them, the notion of "traditional conjunto style" means something different than what Tejeda described. Today, at the annual conjunto festival, there is no longer a "*raíces* night," where those who actually made some of the very first recordings of Tejano conjunto, in the 1930s, 1940s, and even the early 1950s, held forth as living proof of the music's staying power. Those influential artists and accordionists—Martínez, Valerio Longoria, Tony de La Rosa, Juan López—are all gone now, and the new "pioneers" are recognized for keeping the music alive as they travel the "taco circuit" of small towns and urban centers that takes them hundreds of miles throughout South Texas and, at times, to points further beyond. Some of these artists, like Flaco Jiménez, Santiago Jiménez Jr., Mingo Saldívar, and Joel Guzmán, have even played at the White House and to fans throughout Europe and Asia. These individuals have made the music their life's work, as the first "global" ambassadors of conjunto music and representatives of a people who had once struggled to be counted and recognized for their contributions to the unique culture and music of the region. But they also

Figure 5.2 San Antonio accordionist Santiago Jiménez Jr. continues the Jiménez family tradition of playing polkas and schottisches on the German-made Hohner accordion. Photograph by Jane Levine.

have much in common with the first pioneers. Many of these artists still play some of the same songs that the *raíces* artists made popular in their early recordings, and each is known for having crafted a distinct style of accordion playing.

Santiago Jiménez Jr., the son of the influential San Antonio accordionist Santiago Sr. (the original "El Flaco") and brother to Leonardo (Flaco), has said that, to him, "traditional conjunto style is the two-row Hohner accordion, *bajo sexto*, and *tololoche* (double bass) . . . with no drums. The drums came later, and that changed the style."[2] Tony de La Rosa, who was about a decade older than Santiago Jr. and is credited with having developed the "modern conjunto style" in the mid-1950s, when he added the electric bass and drums to the accordion and *bajo sexto* core, once said in an interview that "the *bajo* and I can sit there and play all day and all night long. But for me, if the drums aren't there I cannot get into the rhythm."[3] From this period on, conjunto accordionists (typically the ensemble leaders) could not imagine playing this music without the rhythm section. However, Martínez's early recordings in 1936 on Bluebird Records (a subsidiary of RCA), featuring only the accordion and *bajo sexto*, are considered by many to be the first recordings of conjunto music and, therefore, the beginning of a Tejano music tradition. By playing vibrant polkas, schottisches, mazurkas, waltzes, and Mexican *huapangos* (a folk dance with a rapidly alternating rhythmic pattern) on the treble buttons of the Hohner, two-row diatonic accordion and leaving the bass notes alone, Martínez allowed his *bajo sexto* player, Santiago Almeida, the opportunity to develop a distinctive style of playing by using a cross-picking technique with an alternating pattern and by playing the notes of the bass chord individually. This approach to playing the instrument produced a syncopated effect and increased the tempo of these rhythms (and the dancing), which set the Texas-Mexican sound apart from that of the local German and Czech population, who initially brought the accordion and early repertoire to the region. These early Martínez-Almeida recordings made the pairing of the accordion and *bajo sexto* central to what would become the modern conjunto style, as described by Manuel Peña in his important study of conjunto music, *The Texas-Mexican Conjunto: History of a Working-Class Music.*[4] It was a tradition that flourished in South Texas, specifically for members of the working-class community; and it served to bond the Mexican-American labor force together, linking families and friends from the Rio Grande Valley to San Antonio to Corpus Christi and even as far north as Lubbock. And while it is true that this instrumental core also represented the merging of Mexican and European influences, the accordion has emerged as the most visible symbol of the Texas-Mexican experience. On a larger scale, it still serves as the centerpiece of a distinctive regional American music phenomenon.

Like the Tejano people themselves, conjunto has weathered change and experimentation. In light of the elements that would seem to threaten the very notion of "tradition," conjunto maintains its popularity through perseverance of style, whether it is manifested in the accordion sound, vocal style, or the performance of European-derived rhythms such as the polka and schottische. Today, the accordion and conjunto music are more solidly ingrained in the definition of Tejano identity itself; and because the music is also a hybrid genre, it is a reflection of the local sense of self. The music's evolution, as argued by Peña, is connected to the social, political, and economic transformations within Texas-Mexican society that date back to the turn of the twentieth century. Conjunto music, with its two-row (and now three-row) button accordion, has become a powerful symbol of identity, initially among working-class Texas-Mexicans, and now within the local society as a whole. And while switching to the chromatic-button or keyboard-style accordion might offer greater range and more accommodating fingering options, the diatonic, three-row model persists because of its symbolic resonance. Conjunto is one of the most visible and celebrated folk (or roots) music traditions in Texas and the American Southwest. But as a locally produced popular music widely performed and recorded throughout Texas, it also finds itself in a rather ambiguous place, as it operates somewhere between the local music industry's definition of traditional (referred to as "regional") and popular music styles such as rock, pop, country, and *música tejana,* a modern incarnation of conjunto that sometimes pairs or replaces the accordion with keyboards and the *bajo sexto* with the electric guitar.[5]

With an Accordion in His Hands

"If you wanna play in Texas, you gotta have a squeeze-box," is the slogan one hears several times a day on KTXZ-FM, the Austin-based bilingual Tejano-music radio station located seventy miles north of San Antonio. Thanks in large part to the crossover success of Flaco Jiménez and the high-profile popularity of the Tejano Conjunto Festival en San Antonio, the accordion is the most visible and widely celebrated symbol of conjunto music and, in modern times, Tejano identity in Texas. The accordion is prominently displayed in the posters selected to represent the Tejano Conjunto Festival en San Antonio each year, and the accordion still dominates the airwaves of Spanish-language music in South Texas.

Each year the festival is celebrated with a new poster that is designed by a winning artist in a popular and highly competitive contest. Because the competition is open, the winning poster typically reflects the local community's relationship with the music and, most significantly, the accordion. The winning poster of 1985, for instance, featured Santiago Jiménez Sr. (1913–84) holding his accordion. Jiménez, a contemporary of Martínez, made early recordings of conjunto dating back to the late 1930s and into the 1960s. Jiménez's style of playing might be viewed as the prototype for a distinguishable "San Antonio sound." Though he always joined forces with the *bajo sexto* and took "liberties" with the melody, he remained more closely tied to the basic dancelike structure of the polka rhythm. Jiménez also altered the sound of his accordion by retuning it to suit his vocal register and, perhaps, to get a brighter sound, one that further emphasized the melodic line and diminished the *bajo sexto*'s role somewhat. In all, Jiménez's original polkas (*polkitas,* as they were affectionately called), his style of performance, and the "sound" of his accordion became well known among locals, many of whom still try to emulate it. He was also the father of two of conjunto's next generation of pioneers, Santiago Jr. and Leonardo (Flaco), each credited with maintaining the tradition as well as contributing to the modernizing process.

On the 1988 poster, the accordion appeared in the hands of an unidentified Tejano man with the clawed feet of a rooster and wearing a *guayabera* (traditional Mexican wedding) shirt. In only a few years, the accordion and conjunto music had evolved into folkoric artifacts and symbolic representations of the Tejano in search of his or her Mexican roots. The rooster often appears in Mexican storytelling and is associated with the devil. This man/creature's presence at conjunto dances is also represented in much of the valley's conjunto dance-hall folklore as a warning to young women who might accept a dance from the "wrong man."[6] In 1989 the accordion was featured in the hands of another unidentified Tejano musician wearing a suit, which may indicate a reference to the influential Kingsville-based El Conjunto Bernal, who broke from the tradition of cowboy hats and boots by wearing a suit as a means of attracting upwardly mobile Texas-Mexicans during their heyday in the 1960s. On the 1990 poster, the accordion was the chosen instrument of a coyote, symbol of the viral male, wearing a black cowboy hat (as opposed to the white cowboy hat typically worn by Anglo-Texas country musicians).

Also wearing a black cowboy hat in 1992 is a panther playing an accordion with the flag of the Lone Star State emblazoned on the accordion's bellows, as a means of asserting the Texas-Mexican's place in Texas history. In 1993 there was a simple drawing of a young man behind stylish sunglasses with long hair and a mustache, wearing a muscle-revealing undershirt. He is proudly standing behind a window, surveying the world with his accordion in his hand and with a somewhat smug, though proud look on his face. The indication here might be that Tejano conjunto and the accordion can also be seen as power symbols for Mexican American and Chicano youth throughout the Southwest. In 2000 a lone elderly man wearing a *guayabera* shirt sits in a cantina, and with a faraway look he appears to sing to himself while playing his button accordion. It is as if the old gentleman is yearning for the time when the music represented nothing more than a way to unwind from the day's work, just like a cold beer and a good game of cards. This nostalgic theme carried on to the next year, as the recently deceased *raíces* pioneer, Valerio Longoria (1924–2000), was featured with his accordion. In 2002, the image of a woman finally made it on a winning poster—and I don't mean the Virgin of Guadalupe, an image that has appeared in the background of some posters through the years. It is the image of a young woman with an accordion, representing the young students who take classes in Tejano conjunto accordion at the Guadalupe Cultural Arts Center—one of the few opportunities to learn the accordion available to young girls, since it is typically handed down from father to son within the family. The following year, a woman appeared on the poster wearing a *bajo sexto* on her shoulder as she cheers on her male companions, an accordionist and a drummer. In years past, there had been no images of women accordionists on the poster, as they rarely take it up seriously as do the men.

Figure 5.3 Accordionist and composer Eva Ybarra is the only female with a lifetime of experience in the male-dominated Texas-Mexican conjunto accordion tradition. Photograph by Jane Levine.

Traditionally, women in conjunto are featured singers, but mostly they are fans—the biggest fans, in fact. At the festival, they can be seen hocking CDs, posters, and t-shirts for their fathers, husbands, or brothers. There have been only two significant female accordionists who have appeared at the festival: Lupita Rodela and Eva Ybarra. Rodela, who is also blind, has had a sporadic career as a performer and made only a handful of local recordings, while Ybarra has released recordings of original music on the American independent roots-music label Rounder and has been performing and recording for over forty years, traveling widely to play at festivals throughout the United States.[7] She also spent a year as artist-in-residence at the University of Washington in Seattle. She has often complained that because she is a woman who plays the accordion and leads her own group, she has not been given the recognition she deserves in her hometown of San Antonio and among what she calls the "conjunto accordion boys club."[8] Though she has been regularly featured at the festival, she is typically scheduled on "Mother's Day," which is always on a Sunday. Mother's Day at the festival is also "family day," and she must play early in the afternoon, which, during the festival, is typically when lesser-known and younger up-and-coming artists perform, while the evening slots are reserved for more established male artists, the exception being female singers backed by all-male groups. Likewise, Ybarra must perform after a presentation of young children who are learning to play the accordion in the Guadalupe's Chicano Music Program, which, though she supports the program and has even been an instructor in the past, she feels diminishes her credibility as an established Texas-Mexican accordionist and songwriter. While many of the top accordionists praise her innovative and highly skilled accordion playing, they cannot seem to accept her as their peer. The fact that she has gained recognition as a top player outside of Texas has proven to be such a threat that many have perpetuated a rumor that she is a lesbian, which was reported to me in an interview by one of the most popular accordionists in the region.[9] While Ybarra vehemently denies this rumor, such a claim is evidence that a woman who makes her career playing the accordion in this male-dominated tradition is an outsider and somehow in their view not "feminine."

In 2008, the accordion that adorned that year's winning poster didn't feature a player at all; it had sprouted wings, fashioned from the Texas flag. The accordion appeared to have grown larger than life, perhaps in celebration of the community's resilience, growing economic wealth, and more pronounced presence in local politics. Through the years, the accordion had been the one constant in these posters as the ever-present instrument of the Tejano musician as well as a powerful symbol of the Texas-Mexican presence in the region. It is similar to the pistol in the hand of many border *corrido* (narrative ballad) heroes documented by the Mexican American folklorist and novelist Américo Paredes.[10] "Con su pistola en la mano" (with his pistol in his hand) is a line that appears in many traditional border *corridos* and represents the community's resilience and solidarity.

In these visual examples, the accordion remains constant in an ever-changing and increasingly evolving Tejano society. Several highly symbolic images of Mexican folklore appear with the accordion to validate its meaning, such as the panther, which represents the power and virility of the Mexican male, and the devil, which symbolizes the historic conflict between Anglos and Tejanos in Texas, particularly of men.[11] The coyote (*lobo*) was originally used by Spaniards to describe Mexicans, indicating a person of mixed-blood who was viewed as a lower species, close to an animal. In Chicano literature, the coyote has come to represent "an anomalous and effusive symbol" of Mexican American identity and culture.[12] It is a virile and proud image, but one that remains on the margins of Anglo-American society.[13] This image becomes further localized with the accordion in the hands of the coyote as well as every other figure, man or beast, on these posters. Like the ubiquitous "pistol en la mano" of the border hero and provider of justice in border ballad *corridos* dating back to the turn of the twentieth century, the accordion has become a fascinating symbol of Mexican American and Tejano working-class experience and the struggle to move from the margins to the center of local society.[14] And as billboards around San Antonio boldly proclaim, it is good to be "Tejano and Proud."

The accordion shown in each of these posters is the three-row, diatonic button accordion. For the Tejano migrant worker who originally was able to obtain this instrument in the early 1920s because it was cheaper and smaller than the larger chromatic, piano-style accordions used by other immigrant musicians, the diatonic model represents an act of defiance as well as of dedication to a tradition that evolved in spite of poverty and oppression. While other once-impoverished ethnic communities in Texas that feature accordions in their music, such as the Creoles who migrated from Louisiana to Texas in the early part of the twentieth century (see Jared Snyder's essay in chapter 4 of this volume), have since abandoned the small-button model for the more popular keyboard model, the Tejano has remained dedicated to the small-button accordion played by the first conjunto pioneers, making it central to the music's sound in spite of the contemporary stylistic and instrumental changes in the ensemble. For the Tejano, the three-row button accordion embodies the community's economic struggle while also distinguishing it as the core of an "authentic" Tejano conjunto sound. Rather than change to a more versatile, larger accordion, conjunto accordionists prefer to tinker with the instrument by re-voicing the reeds, adding more buttons and keys to the board as needed, and maintaining a sound that is in their mind uniquely "Tejano." In fact, one of conjunto's early pioneers, Valerio Longoria, is not only known for popularizing *boleros* and other romantic ballad songs but also for tuning his accordion to create, as Peña describes in his book, the *sonido ronco* (horse sound) that is the result of tuning one of the double reeds so that when a note is played it vibrates at the rate of a lower octave.[15] This technique would be taken up by other accordionists and is part of the retuning process a new accordion undergoes after it is purchased. The complexities of the music and community life, with its long history in the state, are boldly projected in the makeshift construction (and reconstruction) of this instrument. Though the button accordion was long ago rejected by musicians from other ethnic communities in Texas, it remains almost exclusively associated with conjunto music and with the Tejano musician.

As the folk music of Tejanos in Texas, conjunto is a product of diversity within the local culture. Responding to questions about San Antonio conjunto accordionists' devotion to the Hohner button accordion, Santiago Jiménez Jr. replied, "We stay with the Hohner because it is strong and durable. You can do anything to it, drop it, knock it around, and it survives."[16]

Conjunto music is just as durable. It was born in the fields among working-class Mexican Americans in the Rio Grande Valley, and it has survived decades of migrations across the country. Technology, the influence of popular-music styles such as country, pop, rock, and R&B, and the introduction of modern instruments such as the guitar, bass, drums, and keyboards have affected the evolution of the conjunto sound. However, the music's connection to its South Texas roots has kept the music well within the consciousness of Tejanos in Texas as well as for those who left to follow the migrant circuit and have settled in other states throughout the country. "When I perform at festivals and even in my hometown, I tell the people about the history of this music," says Jiménez Jr. "I tell them about the German influence and about the musicians like my father who helped make this music popular. This music may sound simple to some people, but it comes from my blood."[17]

Modern Conjunto Style and the Tejano Community

Conjunto today enjoys a prominent position within the Tejano community. It is the folk music of middle-class Tejanos, the popular music of working-class Tejanos, and the regional roots music of Texas and the Hispanic Southwest. For many it represents a history of struggles for identity and power, and for others it is a point of reference that validates an expanding contemporary Tejano music industry. At the annual Tejano Conjunto Festival en San Antonio, the music and the accordion are the voice of cultural expression and Tejano pride. However, within the local Tejano music industry, conjunto is also a popular music form that is recorded, promoted, and sold alongside contemporary *música tejana* and *música norteña* styles.[18] While both of these genres have a much wider distribution network and constant infusion of new ideas and new musicians, conjunto manages to comfortably survive in that hazy middle ground somewhere between pop and folk. This is, in part, due to its ability to absorb change and innovation, but more importantly, the genre maintains the traditional accordion and *bajo sexto* combination and serves a functional role as the music of weddings, anniversaries, birthdays, and other events within the local culture.

Hernando Abilez, a former director of promotions at the Capital/EMI-Latin branch office in San Antonio in the early 1990s, had been involved with the promotion and development of some of the top contemporary Tejano artists such as Selena, Emilio Navairra, and many others. Even though his label didn't necessarily record and promote conjunto, Abilez is aware of the importance of the accordion and conjunto music in the history of Tejano music:

The popularity of the accordion has to do with the culture, going back to our roots and family tradition. Here in San Antonio you have to speak Spanish because people here are so proud. It is reflected in their music and the popularity of the accordion, which is so symbolic of the roots of Hispanic people in Texas. One thing that makes Tejano musicians special is that our musicians grew up listening to Motown, country, rock, etc. but they also listened to the older Tejano music, which was conjunto in the early years and then *orquesta tejana.* The music takes from all those styles and has become a mixture which is what we now call Tejano music. It is regionalized, or from Texas, but it is being distributed all over the world. The Tejano label is opposed to salsa or cumbia so that people know it is from this region of the U.S. . . . from Texas.[19]

As Tejano identity has become more celebrated by the population as a whole in Texas, people within the community have come to celebrate conjunto as a highly visible and widely accepted link to their long-neglected history in the state. Renewed interest in the music among younger, middle-class Tejanos, particularly at festivals and community events, has increased the profile of the music over the years. However, the music has also undergone significant change and fragmentation as a result. Veteran musicians such as Mingo Saldívar, Flaco Jiménez, Eva Ybarra, and others who had been recognized by local scholars and music enthusiasts as pioneers and contemporary participants in the annual Tejano Conjunto Festival—which has been the one of the most important means for publicly honoring pioneering musicians and the conjunto tradition since 1981—and who perform more frequently at city- and state-sponsored Mexican American and Texas folk festivals are also promoted as "regional folk musicians." In addition to performing in South Texas, they also appear at folk and world-music festivals outside of the state as representatives of what is often described as "regional American music" or "American roots music." What allows them to survive and compete with contemporary *música tejana* and *música norteña* is their role as representatives of regional Texas-Mexican music, making it popular outside of the regional Tejano and Mexican markets. More commonly, local promoters and the tourist industry have begun to include traditional conjunto groups at events alongside highly produced and younger *música tejana* artists.

During the spring and summer in San Antonio, an outdoor Tejano music festival of some sort occurs nearly every weekend. Many of these events are cosponsored by major corporations, such as the Miller Brewing Company, R. J. Reynolds (the national tobacco company), Budweiser, and AT&T, who have actively courted the large Tejano market. As a major tourist center, an aspect of the city that has been magnified over the last two decades by the addition of Seaworld and Fiesta Texas, San Antonio is learning to capitalize on conjunto as a viable commodity and a major distinguishing cultural activity the city has to offer. Before the mid-1980s, conjunto music was heard predominantly in San Antonio's largely Hispanic West Side, most of South Texas, and in towns and cities in California and Colorado, where many Tejanos migrated as farm workers from the 1930s to the 1960s. In San Antonio, it was largely relegated to the A.M. dial of radio stations like KEDA (Radio Jalepeño) or to small clubs, dance halls, and flea markets. Heightened "external" interest in the music compounded with a newfound awareness of conjunto and its cultural significance within the history of Texas has broadened its audience. As the local Tejano music industry has become more sophisticated and complex, conjunto music must also respond to current changes to survive. But unlike *música tejana*, it must do so without shedding its "folk" status.

Today, conjunto music is also identified regionally (within Texas), thanks in part to a still thriving local music industry infrastructure. Focusing my research on San Antonio, Corpus Christi (Gulf Coastal Bend region), and the Rio Grande Valley allowed me to examine three distinctly regional styles of conjunto. Additionally, and relative to the Tejano industry in which conjunto has begun to reassert itself, conjunto is further defined in opposition to the two more commercially prominent popular music styles, *música tejana* and *música norteña*.

By comparison, conjunto is generally marginalized by its status as folk or "roots" music. It is still identified with, and primarily heard at, community-based events like weddings, *quinceañeras* (a coming-of-age ceremony for a fifteen-year-old girl), anniversaries, graduations, and festivals. Early recordings of conjunto artists like Narciso Martínez, Valerio Longoria, and Tony de La Rosa on independent Tejano labels such as IDEAL (now accessible through the California-based Arhoolie Records), Corona, Falcón, and others helped spawn the popular Tejano music industry in the state beginning in the mid-1940s. But while contemporary *música tejana* typically enjoys national and international distribution today, conjunto's popularity remains at a grassroots level, selling primarily in outdoor flea markets, independent Tejano record shops, in some regional Wal-Mart stores, and at local dance halls direct from the hands of the musicians themselves.

Conjunto Regional: The Fragmentation of Tejano Conjunto in South Texas

"Conjunto regional" is the Tejano industry's term for groups that still perform within the traditional conjunto style. In recent years at the Tejano Conjunto Festival, the term *puro conjunto pesado* (loosely translated as "pure, hardcore conjunto") has been used. This category is somewhat broad; it includes *raíces* musicians such as Tony de La Rosa, Valerio Longoria, and Rubén Vela, and more contemporary conjunto artists such as Los Dos Gilbertos, Mingo Saldívar, and Los Chamacos.

However, what all of these performers have in common is the accordion and *bajo sexto* forming the core of the sound. And since those two instruments historically created the foundation of conjunto, the tradition is still strongly upheld and recognized within the scope of *conjunto regional*. In fact, whenever the term "conjunto" is used to describe a group's sound, it is assumed that the accordion and *bajo sexto* are present. The repertoire of most *conjunto regional* groups is largely made up of popular *canciónes rancheras* (Mexican "country" songs in polka rhythm), polkas, *huapangos*, and some *corridos*. Of course, veteran conjunto musicians tend to stick primarily to the more traditional songs they are expected to play at community functions, and younger players include many in their repertoire.

The modern Tejano groups, however, are also motivated to perform original songs if they want to compete in the Tejano market. In most cases, their original songs are based on traditional conjunto song forms and instrumental rhythms. Moreover, post-*raíces* conjunto groups such as Jimmy Gonzalez y Mazz, David Lee Garza y Los Musicales, La Tropa F, and others are on the extreme edge of the *conjunto regional* groups, often referred to as *conjunto progressive*, which is the term now being used at the Tejano Conjunto Festival. These groups perform almost exclusively original tunes, and those traditional tunes that they do perform are often done in an untraditional manner, especially in the way that the accordion plays the melody. Rhythmically, these groups might incorporate contemporary influences from country, R&B, soul, rock, and rap. In the case of artists such as Albert Zamora y Talento, Bobby Pulido, and Mazz, who have further expanded conjunto's reach to include popular innovations that have had some influence on the contemporary *música norteña*, the genre associated with recent migrants from Mexico and those who remain undocumented. This would include a combination of a strong reliance on the *cumbia* (contemporary Mexican dance rhythm rooted in the northern Colombian folk tradition) and the popular romantic-ballad singing style, while still dipping into traditional conjunto and border-song repertoire (such as *corridos*, *rancheras*, and *boleros*). As a result of new interest in the music, conjunto is also evolving as a popular-music style. Younger musicians who once rejected conjunto and the accordion in the 1970s and 1980s, or those musicians who stopped performing due to lack of interest in conjunto, have since returned to the genre and have been playing before larger, multigenerational audiences.

Within *conjunto regional* or *puro conjunto*, substyles have evolved out of a move to maintain the music's connection with local audiences, something Tejano music is not able to do. Because conjunto is so closely identified with Tejano community life and individual interpretation of the tradition, focus on regional style has contributed to the popularity and the survival of conjunto in the highly competitive Tejano industry. The three major areas of South Texas where conjunto music is regularly performed live, heard on the radio, and supported by strong historical roots in the community are San Antonio; Corpus Christi and the Coastal Bend; and the Rio Grande Valley and Northeastern Mexico.

San Antonio

The San Antonio style represents the most fascinating amalgamation of American popular-music influences on traditional conjunto style, and it is the best known on national and international stages. Contemporary conjunto music in San Antonio reflects the urban, multiethnic setting in which the genre evolved. San Antonio was also one of the early recording centers for modern country, blues, and R&B, and over the years San Antonio conjuntos have absorbed strong stylistic and aesthetic influences from these genres. Because of the strong German presence, San Antonio accordionists have traditionally been the most loyal to the German Hohner three-row Corona II diatonic button accordion, while many of their Rio Grande Valley and Corpus Christi counterparts have gravitated toward the flashier Houston-based and Italian-made Gabbanelli brand and, more recently, other popular models made by the Italian companies Beltrami and Baffetti. San Antonio players are devoted to simple, memorable melody lines based on polka, waltz, and schottische dance rhythms. They are also distinguished by a stronger focus on the accordion as the primary lead (and often solo) instrument within the ensemble. This latter distinction has become a highly developed aspect of the sound, particularly by local accordionists in the San Antonio area. This is probably due, in part, to the international popularity of Flaco Jiménez not only as a modern pioneer of Tejano music and culture but of American roots music as well.

Flaco's own interpretations of his father's compositions, particularly "Viva Seguin" and "La piedrera," are almost as well known as the original songs. By the early 1970s, Flaco's accordion style was becoming more and more influenced by rock, country, and R&B, allowing him to treat it like a guitar with a highly syncopated and expressive playing style. For example, one distinguishing feature of modern conjunto accordion style introduced by Flaco Jimenez is the fermata (hold or pause), where he will sustain or hold a note for longer than its value would indicate—and often longer than is usual in music performance—to create tension and excitement in his performances, particularly when these are followed with rapid-fire chromatic runs on the scale. This is illustrated in my transcription of the primary melody of two recordings of "Viva Sequin" (see figure 5.5). One is an excerpt of Santiago Sr.'s accordion performance from a vintage recording made for the Los Angeles–based Imperial Records in 1947 and reissued by Arhoolie Records in 2001. The other is an excerpt of Flaco's version of the same song originally recorded in the late 1970s for the San Antonio–based DLB Record label and later issued in 1989 by Rounder Records.[20] I have arranged

Figure 5.4 Flaco Jiménez, on stage at the annual Tejano Conjunto Festival in San Antonio, is one of the first to incorporate elements of blues and rock in his accordion style, which has earned him fans worldwide. Photograph by Jane Levine.

the transcription so that both performances can be viewed simultaneously, one above the other, for easy comparison of Flaco's more "modern" interpretation of the accordion-playing style forged by his pioneering father. While Flaco remains focused on keeping the song's melody intact, his subtle elaborations and addition of notes show a modern approach to playing the accordion by ornamenting and extending simple folk melodies and using fermatas, thus allowing for a highly syncopated and lively new sound. Also note that in measures 2, 4, 5, and 16, Flaco adds grace notes to affect a slurred or "bent" note, an influence from blues and rock. In measures 10 and 13 he adds extra notes, moving by half-steps up and down the scale. Likewise, the lower approximate beats per minute better accommodate the slower two-step *tacuachito* dance associated with the music and influenced by the Texas "shuffle rhythm" played by local country bands. While Flaco's approach is more daring and creative than his father's, it is a reflection of his increasingly Americanized musical tastes, though he is careful not to make the melody unrecognizable to his audience.

Figure 5.5 Excerpt of "Viva Sequin" as played by Santiago Jiménez Sr. (S) and by Flaco Jiménez (F). Transcription by Cathy Ragland.

Today, San Antonio–based accordionists like Mingo Saldívar, Eva Ybarra, Santiago Jiménez Jr., Flaco Jiménez, Steve Jordan (originally from the Rio Grande Valley, but he spent much of his accordion-playing career in San Antonio), and others have each developed their own recognizable and highly expressive accordion styles, complete with technical nuances that make them unique among other players in the tradition. Mingo Saldívar, for example, is known for producing train whistles from his accordion and his call-and-response dialogues with his blues harmonica player; the late Steve Jordan was celebrated for adding phase-shifters and other effects that give his accordion an "otherworldly" sound. Establishing an individualized accordion-playing style and sound has become expected of conjunto players, particularly those in San Antonio. However, it is the San Antonio players who remain more dedicated to the traditional European rhythms such as the polka, waltz, *redova* (redowa, a Mexican folk dance with a rapidly alternating rhythmic pattern), and schottische, while players further south and along the border favor Latin and Mexican rhythms such as the *cumbia* and the *huapango*. The San Antonio–based accordionists often publicly credit German and Czech immigrants for their contributions to the conjunto tradition, even though they are also the most expressive and most innovative accordionists. The hybrid nature of the tradition is celebrated and maintained; however, it is open to individual interpretation, and that is what makes it distinctively "Tejano."

Corpus Christi–Coastal Bend

Tony de La Rosa's influence may have resonated throughout the valley and even into San Antonio, but his much-celebrated accordion style can still best be heard in the music of the Corpus Christi–Coastal Bend groups, as well as in groups located in surrounding areas such as Kingsville, Robstown, Riviera, Beeville, and stretching to Alice. As a result, the conjunto typically associated with this region of South Texas demonstrates La Rosa's fondness for articulating scales throughout the melody but without the elaborate solos and extended chromatic runs popular among San Antonio players. Several conjuntos in this region are also known for a preference toward three-part vocal harmonies rather than the more traditional *dueto* (duo) harmonies that predominate in the Rio Grande Valley and San Antonio. Some of the popular groups from this area include Rubén Naranjo y su Conjunto, Grupo Badd, and Angel Flores. This phenomenon is most likely attributable to the influence of the Kingsville-based El Conjunto Bernal, who were widely celebrated in the 1960s and early 1970s for their rich, three-part harmonies. This group was credited for having "modernized" the otherwise folksy singing style by taking in influences from local mariachis and popular Mexican singing trios of the 1940s, 1950s, and 1960s, such as Los Panchos and Los Dandys from the nearby northern Mexican state of Tamaulipas.

Rio Grande Valley and Northeastern Mexico

In the Rio Grande Valley, the focus is less on the accordionist and more on the songs themselves and the performance of the group as a whole. Due to this region's close proximity to the border, local conjuntos are subject to influences from Mexico and the still vibrant and more transnational *música norteña* (or simply *norteña*) tradition. Tejano conjunto owes its origins to the *norteña* tradition, which was born in the northeastern region of Mexico, bordering the United States, particularly in the states of Nuevo León and Tamaulipas, during the nineteenth century. German and Czech immigrants brought their popular dance styles to cities like Monterrey and Matamoros. Instrumental folk ensembles that existed in the region, called *tamborileros* (*picotas* in Tamaulipas), typically featured one or two clarinets and a hand-held *tambora* drum (likely introduced by Spanish Jesuits) and played at secular and religious celebrations in rural towns and villages.[21] Though there is evidence of the accordion's existence in Monterrey in the late nineteenth century, migrant workers who crossed the border to work as farm laborers, primarily in Texas, brought back to Mexico cheap diatonic button models in the early twentieth century, which quickly replaced the clarinet.[22] Continued migration spurred the popularity of accordion and *tambora* ensembles on both sides of the border. The *bajo sexto* was added, eventually replacing the *tambora*, and the ensemble was solidified with the dissemination of recordings in the 1930s by the Rio Grande Valley–based accordionist Narciso Martínez.

By the late 1950s, many South Texas groups, particularly those making their way further north into San Antonio and Corpus Christi, took on elements of country, R&B, and rock, as Texas-Mexicans in such urban areas were participating more and more in American popular culture and society. This would lead to the further development of a Tejano identity that had already begun in earnest after World War II. This population would also begin to separate itself from newer, often undocumented Mexican immigrants crossing the border. Paralleling this process was the fruition of a distinct Tejano conjunto style, with the accordion as the melodic and symbolic focus of the sound. Tejanos used the term "conjunto" to refer to these ensembles, and songs were increasingly bilingual or utilized less-complicated Spanish. This meant that the *corrido*, with its detailed story lines requiring an intimate knowledge of the language, all but disappeared from the Tejano conjunto repertoire by the early 1960s. The 1964 termination of the Bracero Program (allowing the temporary legal importation of contract workers from Mexico into the United States) coincided with a surge in undocumented Mexican migration that continues today. Groups primarily based on the other side of the border in Mexico as well as some on the Texas side maintained the *música norteña* identifier for their brand of accordion-based music and the *corrido* tradition. These songs shifted in topic and focus from stories of revolutionary heroes, the exploits of border bandits, and roustabouts to the border-crossing experience as well as other issues facing recent migrants, affecting a larger Mexican laborer population now traveling from regions further south in Mexico and spanning across the United States, such as immigration policy, racism, discrimination, drug trafficking, and, more recently, corruption in Mexican politics. By the early 1970s, *norteña* recordings were being produced and sold on both sides of the border by companies located in Monterrey, Corpus Christi, San Antonio, and San Jose, California.

Today, *norteña* music is part of a multimillion-dollar, transnational music industry that has since dwarfed the reach and popularity of Tejano conjunto, which is concentrated in central and southern Texas. In fact, at a recent convening of Tejano conjunto and *norteña* scholars from both sides of the border in October 2010 in the border town of Weslaco, Tejano music producers, musicians, and label executives lamented the fact that *norteña* and other Mexican regional genres that have emerged in the diaspora, such as *música duranguense, banda,* and *tropical,*[23] have begun to dominate the local airwaves, once the domain of *música tejana.* This phenomenon is also being felt as far north in San Antonio and has taken hold in other cities and towns across the Southwest. This is likely due to the fact that young Tejanos and Chicanos are listening to a wider range of American and Mexican-American popular-music genres, and their allegiances no longer lie solely with these regional genres. At the same time, local radio stations recognize that their potential for growth is tied to the musical taste of the increasing numbers of Mexican immigrants who tend to maintain stronger ties to Mexico and remain dedicated to regional Mexican popular-music genres.

Though *norteña* features the same instrumentation as the Texas-Mexican conjunto—accordion (sometimes paired with saxophone), *bajo sexto,* bass, and drums—the accordion's primary role in the ensemble is to introduce the song's melody and each verse of the *corrido* or *canción-corrido* (romantic verse-chorus song in *corrido* form). It provides a musical framework for the telling of the story. In Tejano conjunto, the accordion takes on a more central role, to guide dancers and as a means for the accordionist (generally the bandleader) to show off his (or her) virtuosic playing style.

Rogelio García, a Mexico-based border D.J. who has been on the air since the 1960s, said in a personal interview that "the accordion is fundamental in *norteña* music, just like it was in the early development of Texas conjunto. But for Mexicans, and for the immigrant on the other side who wants to remember his history and his family, the *corrido* is very important. In Texas it is gone and has been so for many years. But every Mexican knows that the *norteña* has to have the *corrido,* and not just those songs from the past, but from today."[24] Local radio stations, broadcasting from Mexican border towns such as Reynosa and Matamoros, feature programs that play traditional *corridos* as well as *corridos perrones* or *corridos pesados* (loosely translated as "badass" or "hardcore"), which tend to either glorify drug trafficking or to criticize the corruption and hypocrisy of the Mexican government and the criminalization of the border zone by the American government. The popular protagonists of these newer songs are either *narcotraficantes* (drug traffickers) or *mojados* (undocumented immigrants). Throughout the United States, these songs are popular among recent immigrants and those who have not assimilated (usually due to their undocumented and low economic status) and who maintain strong connections to Mexico and their Mexican identity. Historically, through their exploits, the *mojado* and the *narcotraficante* merge real life and fantasy amid the struggle for economic survival, against border patrol and authority figures, and the negation of social space, however marginal, all of which bonds the immigrant community—initially in the Texas-Mexican border region, and later (with the advent of cassettes, CDs, and now the Internet) in rural towns and urban centers throughout the United States.

In the border region, where speaking both Spanish and English is a must and travel across the border in both directions is more frequent, *norteña* style and the maintenance of the *corrido* song form have come to dominate the local sound-scape. However, *norteña* and Tejano conjunto artists, particularly in the border region, are often critical of each other's playing style. While conjunto artists tend to criticize *norteña* groups for their approach to rhythm—which is often unsteadied by irregular drum rolls and offbeat improvisations on the electric bass—*norteña* artists criticize the conjunto musicians' virtuosic instrumental display on the accordion and its dominance of the song's melody, which they claim takes away from the song's text and meaning. The Mexican-born accordionist Ramón Ayala, a longtime resident of Hidalgo, Texas (just three miles from the U.S.–Mexico border), and a Grammy-award-winning pioneer of the *norteña* style, made the following criticism regarding the role of the accordion in Tejano conjunto and, in so doing, addressed an important distinction between the two styles:

> The Tejano puts a lot more accordion in his songs, and for those of us who play *norteña* music, we only use it where it is necessary, like [for] connecting the verses of the song. Tejano accordionists also like to make a show with the accordion, you know, show off their playing. They even dance while they are playing. We don't do that because then, you lose the song, you know, the corrido, and that's what Mexicans want to hear.[25]

Another telling distinction is that Tejanos know conjunto groups by the names of their accordionists (e.g., Flaco Jiménez, Santiago Jiménez, Mingo Saldívar) or, in the more contemporary *música tejana* genre, by the vocalists' names (e.g., Selena Quintanilla, Emilio Navaira, Roberto Pulido, Michael Salgado), while *norteña* groups favor names with superhuman qualities and that locate them in a specific town or state in the *norteño* region (e.g., Los Cadetes de Linares, Los Invasores de Nuevo León, Los Alegres de Terán) or simply "del norte," indicating solidarity with the northernmost (or bordering) region of Mexico (e.g., Los Tigres del Norte, Los

Humildes del Norte, Los Terribles del Norte) and the Mexican migrant worker. Likewise, the majority of *norteña* groups are recognized for how successfully they interpret the songs that are overwhelmingly written by amateur songwriters, many of whom come from the border region (an exception is Los Tigres del Norte, with its exclusive stable of songwriters). A popular *corrido* might be recorded over and over by several different groups; however, it is the group's collective interpretation of that song that brings them notoriety, not necessarily the song itself. In *norteña* music, no one group "owns" a *corrido*.

The popularity of vocal music, particularly within the *corrido* tradition, has historically given more focus to the unfolding of the story. This influence can be heard in the rich but still "folksy" *dueto* (duo) harmonies of Tejano conjunto and *norteña* from both sides of the border. Historically, some of the most memorable vocal duets in the music's tradition can be traced to classic *norteña* groups such as Los Alegres de Terán and Los Donneños, who began their careers in Mexico and also became influential in the Rio Grande Valley of Texas. More recent locally based groups who have followed in this tradition include Los Dos Gilbertos, Los Fantasmas del Valle, and the late Rubén Vela y su Conjunto. The *dueto* style features close harmonies, typically in minor thirds, with the second, much higher voice sounding a nasalized whine. Popular *norteña* groups today—even those based in California, like Los Tigres del Norte—have adopted this *dueto* singing style as well, now a distinctive feature that sets conjunto and *norteña* groups apart.

Unlike the tendency of San Antonio accordionists—who focus more on dancing and instrumental virtuosity featuring elaborate solos and accordion acrobatics, as evidenced by San Antonio players like Saldívar, Jiménez, and Jordan—Rio Grande Valley and northeastern Mexican accordionists outline the melody developed by the singer(s) and play something similar to a coda at the end of each vocal phrase or stanza of the *corrido* or *canción-corrido*. While Valley and northeastern Mexican groups are quick to distinguish themselves based on style, which side of the border they live on, whether their audience is more "Mexican" or more "American," in performance they recognize that their audiences are largely Spanish-speaking and may identify with being Mexican, American, and/or Texan, and their sets reflect this with a healthy balance of *corridos*, instrumental polkas and *huapangos*, and popular *cumbia* hits. Ramón Ayala is perhaps the best representative of this cross-border, cross-cultural sound. The Tejano Conjunto Festival in San Antonio has taken notice by inviting Ayala to the festival in 1999 as a representative of the *norteña* style, but otherwise such groups are not featured. While *norteña* groups have been playing in local clubs, dance halls, and festivals throughout Texas for years and now throughout the United States, they are marginalized when it comes to high-profile, city- and state-supported festivals such as the Tejano Conjunto Festival.

In both cases, however, the accordion maintains its symbolic significance. For the Tejano it is a symbol of cultural memory of a working-class past that allows them to celebrate their role in making a prosperous Texan and American society. For the *norteño*, the accordion is a symbol of regional identity and a past that is built on cross-border and cross-cultural exchange and travel. *Norteña* music is the only accordion-based tradition in Mexico, and the *corrido*, though found in other parts of Mexico, is unique in form, structure, and content in this region. It is a source of pride for a region of the country that has a history of conflict and neglect in dealing with the Mexican government and cultural center.

Music of the People

Listening to the San Antonio radio station KEDA (1540AM), one of the few strongholds of traditional conjunto, one might hear the local accordion hero Mingo Saldívar perform his popular version of Johnny Cash's "Ring of Fire" ("Ruedo del fuego"). Saldívar takes up with his accordion where Cash's guitar left off by squeezing off a series of staccatos and wheezing sounds that erupt in the high-pitched whistle that so perfectly imitates that of a steam train. It is a fascinating Tejano interpretation of not only a country classic but of a truly American soundbite. It connects Tejanos today to a shared American experience that their parents and grandparents fought hard to be a part of. KEDA's mix of popular early rock 'n' roll and R&B classics alongside *conjunto regional* or *puro conjunto* from around South Texas, and even some lively fusions of *conjunto progressive* with country or Latin jazz, is representative of the genre's resilience and sustainability. Each day on the station there are also personal dedications and shout-outs, birthday, wedding, and anniversary congratulations interspersed between songs, just as they are at local dances in dance halls and nightclubs. Along the Texas-Mexican border, stations from the Mexican side, such as Reynosa's XHRR (known as "La Ley" or "The Law"), mix popular Mexican *cumbias* with *corridos perrones* played by Mexican and U.S.-based *norteña* groups. Similar to the San Antonio stations, there are personal dedications and shout-outs to listeners on both sides of the border. While in both cases, it is clear that the music has never lost its deep connection to its community-based roots and the accordion as a symbol of working-class identity, it is a constant in this local Texas-Mexican soundscape. In the border region, the popularity of this music—particularly *norteña*—transcends, or better yet, erases the political and economic borderline between these two countries.

The development of a distinctive Texas-Mexican music tradition in a region where poverty, oppressed laborers, and racial conflict dominated the Mexican-American experience helped to bond a community of people together amid the pressure to assimilate. It has continued in spite of its marginalization by American and Mexican popular-music industries. However, in light of ideological inroads made in the Chicano movement, conjunto has remained a strong symbol of a self-sustained Tejano society: acculturated, but never completely assimilated. Conjunto music was born and bred on South Texas soil with a history that is distinctly marked by regionalized innovators, from Narciso Martínez to Tony de La Rosa to Flaco Jiménez, and passed along through generations by way of a shared identity and love for a music all their own. The accordion traveled with workers on both sides of the border, where it came to symbolize accomplishment and modernity for those who returned to Mexico and pride in one's working-class identity and roots among migrants in Texas.

The emergence of Texas-Mexican conjunto and its modern incarnations presents a fascinating opportunity to study the construction of a separate regional society and identity based on selective local acculturation and assimilation. Likewise, *norteña*'s ability to embody a new sense of personal, regional, and transnational history and identity allows for a dynamic exploration by scholars and music enthusiasts of a newly mobilized population in response to the undocumented status of a large portion of its members. Despite limited socioeconomic advancement, many immigrants draw strength from extensive networks that span the diaspora, together creating an "imagined community" based on strong attachments to Mexican heritage and culture and to a uniquely "American" way of life.

Notes

1. This is part of Juan Tejeda's introduction heard at many of the annual Tejano Conjunto festivals over the years.

2. Santiago Jiménez Jr., personal communication, San Antonio, April 17, 1991.

3. Tony de La Rosa, personal communication, Riviera, Tex., July 20, 1991.

4. Manuel Peña, *The Texas-Mexican Conjunto: History of a Working-Class Music* (Austin: University of Texas Press, 1985), 38.

5. The term *música tejana* (Tejano music) came into common usage in the 1980s and gained international attention in the early 1990s as one of the fastest-growing types of Latin music in the United States. See also Manuel Peña, *Música Tejana: The Cultural Economy of Artistic Transformation* (College Station: Texas A&M University Press, 1999).

6. José E. Limón, "El Baile: Culture and Contradiction in Mexican-American Dancing," *Tonantzin* 5.2 (1988): 22–25.

7. *A Mi San Antonio*, CD 6056 (Cambridge, Mass.: Rounder Records, 1994), and *Romance Inolvidable*, CD 6062 (Cambridge, Mass.: Rounder Records, 1996).

8. Eva Ybarra, personal communication, San Antonio, November 10, 2003.

9. Mingo Saldívar, personal communication, San Antonio, May 28, 2003.

10. See Américo Paredes, *"With His Pistol in His Hand": A Border Ballad and Its Hero* (Austin: University of Texas Press, 1958); Américo Paredes, *Folklore and Culture on the Texas-Mexican Border* (Austin: University of Texas Press, 1993).

11. See José Limón, *Dancing with the Devil: Society and Cultural Poetics in Mexican-American South Texas* (Madison: University of Wisconsin Press, 1994); and José Limón, "Texas-Mexican Popular Music and Dancing: Some Notes on History and Symbolic Process," *Latin American Music Review* 4.2 (1983): 229–46.

12. Teresa Meléndez, "Coyote: Towards a Definition of a Concept," *Aztlán* 13.1–2 (1982): 298–99.

13. Ibid., 295–307.

14. Following Paredes's famous book title, *"With His Pistol in His Hand."*

15. Peña, *Texas-Mexican Conjunto*, 83.

16. Santiago Jiménez Jr., personal communication, San Antonio, April 17, 1991.

17. Ibid.

18. *Música norteña* refers to "music from northern Mexico," a very popular genre in Mexico and the United States, especially among the Mexican communities. See Cathy Ragland, *Música Norteña: Mexican Migrants Creating a Nation between Nations* (Philadelphia: Temple University Press, 2009).

19. Hernando Abilez, personal communication, San Antonio, August 5, 1993.

20. *Don Santiago Jiménez Sr. y sus Valedores: Viva Seguin*, CD 7023 (El Cerrito, Calif.: Arhoolie Records, 2001); and *Flaco Jiménez: Arriba el Norte*, CD 6032 (Burlington, Mass.: Rounder Records, 1989).

21. Carlos Jesús Gómez Flores, *A tambora batiente* (Monterrey: Dirección General de Culturas Populares/Unidad Regional Norte, 1997), 24.

22. Filiberto Molina Montelongo and Guadalupe Quezada Molina, "Nuevo León y su música de acordeón 1941–1961," in *Tradiciones y costumbres de Nuevo León*, ed. Rogelio Velázquez de León and Francisco Javier Alvarado Segovia (Monterrey: Departamento de Investigaciones Históricas, Secretaria de Desarrollo Social del Gobierno del Estado de Nuevo León, 1995), 97–104.

23. *Bandas* became popular among the immigrant population in Los Angeles in the early 1990s. They were modern interpretations of the brass ensembles found throughout rural Mexico, particularly in the states of Sinaloa, Oaxaca, and Guerrero. The music spread to other U.S. cities, particularly in the West and the Midwest, giving rise to a popular dance called *quebradita*. See Helena Simonett, *Banda: Mexican Musical Life across Borders* (Middletown, Conn.: Wesleyan University Press, 2001). *Música duranguense* is a popular-music genre that grew out of blending elements of *banda* and *norteña* among Chicago's immigrant population beginning in the mid-1990s. See Sydney Hutchinson, *From Quebradita to Duranguense: Dance in Mexican American Youth Culture* (Tucson: University of Arizona Press, 2007). There were many references to the northwestern Mexican state of Durango in early songs, and a close variant, known as *tamborazo*, is associated with nearby Zacatecas. Like *banda*, this style has gained momentum among immigrant youth throughout the United States and, more recently, in Mexico. *Tropical* is a popular Latin American dance form featuring romantic songs sung to a Mexican variant of the Colombian *cumbia* rhythm. It is also quite popular among immigrant youth and is sampled and mixed by D.J.s, known as *sonideros*, on both sides of the border. See

Cathy Ragland, "Mexican Deejays and the Transnational Space of Youth Dances in New York and New Jersey," *Ethnomusicology* 47.3 (2003): 338–54.

24. Rogelio García, personal communication, Monterrey, Nuevo León, Mexico, August 7, 2003.

25. Ramón Ayala, personal communication, McAllen, Tex., October 7, 1998.

≫ 6 ≪

Preserving Territory

The Changing Language of the Accordion in Tohono O'odham Waila Music

JANET L. STURMAN

"Waila Music"

It is 1:30 A.M.
Sleep won't come.
She listens to music.
O'odham waila music,
San Antonio Rose,
a wild saxophone and accordion.
In her mind she dances.
She dances with a handsome cowboy.
His hat is white, his boots are dusty.
They turn in rhythm together.
They don't miss a beat.
Their hearts beat in sync.
Their sweat is mixed as one.
The earthen dance floor beneath them,
the stars and the moon above them.
That rhythm, that rhythm,
it makes them one.

Waila music, like the poetry of the Tohono O'odham poet, linguist, and distinguished professor Ofelia Zepeda, is plain and direct, yet evocative and invigorating. The accordion and saxophone entwine like the dancers and celestial bodies that Zepeda calls to mind. Such simplicity belies its power. Connection—between people and music, language and instrumental performance, and music and memory—lies at the heart of the story of the accordion in waila music.

For the Tohono O'odham, the indigenous people of southern Arizona formerly known as Papagos,[1] the accordion is not a native instrument. It arrived by way of Texas and northern Mexico in the 1890s, along with German immigrants who farmed, raised cattle, and helped construct the factories, railroads, and mines in the region.[2] As prospectors and entrepreneurs traveled west, spurred by the growth of the mining industry, music traveled with them, and the accordion came along, aided by a nascent recording industry.[3] The O'odham adopted the Texas and northern Mexican music styles (see the previous chapter by Cathy Ragland), enriching them with influences from the West Coast and Los Angeles–based Chicano styles to create their own popular borderland music, calling it *waila.*

Essentially dance music, waila derives its name from the Spanish word for dance (*baile*), and most players prefer this term over "chicken scratch," another widely used label for the style, with its good-natured but faintly derisive reference to the appearance of the dancers in the desert dust. The term *waila* also refers to the polka beat, the defining dance rhythm in the waila repertoire. The earliest ensembles were string bands commonly featuring two fiddles and a guitar with a snare and bass drum or a bass fiddle, but by the late 1950s the accordion had become a signature instrument of waila.[4]

One of the fundamental distinctions between waila and *norteño, Tejano,* and other comparable traditions is that performances of waila customarily exclude parts for vocalists; the singing lines are performed by the saxophone(s) and accordion, expanding the role previously undertaken by the fiddlers in earlier O'odham instrumental groups.[5] The relationship between language use and accordion technique lies at the heart of the distinctions between these kindred styles. While Tejano accordionists play flashy, often elaborate interludes between sung verses delivered by vocalists, waila accordionists supply or reinforce the melodic content of the song.[6] Many O'odham players identify the accordion as "the voice of waila."[7] Brandis Joaquin, the accordionist for the Mario Brothers and Thee Express, explains: "It seems like everything fits to the accordion."[8] Even when saxophones are assigned the role of singer, the accordion may be retained. Brandis adds: "You might say it replaces the double saxes, but we like to combine saxophone with the accordion. In Thee Express we use two saxophones with accordion—this is a popular instrumentation today."[9]

Not only does the accordion stand at the heart of the contemporary waila practice, but recent changes in how players view singing illuminate new techniques in accordion performance. A focus on approaches to a single instrument also reveals that the style and practice of waila is far from uniform; there has always been considerable variation among performers. Varied techniques signal nuanced views of what waila contributes to modern O'odham life. Recognition of this fact calls for equal recognition in academic contexts.

Ethnographic focus on identifying shared cultural practice often obscures the fact that many times such choices result from individual desire and taste. One of my aims in this study is to illustrate the importance of such personal choices and to explore a means for including individuality in an explanation of shared cultural practice, similar in some ways to what the anthropologist Lila Abu-Lughod has called "the ethnography of the particular."[10] Despite variations in performance practices, O'odham listeners uniformly value waila because it connects them to each other and "makes them happy."[11] The focus on how and why waila musicians play the accordion the way they do allows us to see how the music also links O'odham to non-O'odham and to much wider social, musical, and even economic circles. Yet even as waila musicians engage with the non-O'odham world, they simultaneously hold it at bay.[12]

Methodology

While a study of the waila accordion implies a focus on the instrument as an object, the accordion itself matters much less than who plays it, what is played, and where, when, and why it is played. My service on the Tucson Waila Festival committee since 1995 has provided me with the opportunity to hear a wide range of waila bands, meet many waila musicians, and observe how O'odham and non-O'odham respond to the music.

The annual Waila Festival, held in Tucson, Arizona, since 1988, is one of the best ways to hear waila off-reservation.[13] The program for each festival typically features four different bands that alternate slots throughout a single Saturday night, performing from 5:00 until 11:00 P.M. O'odham and other American Indians comprise the majority of attendees; some drive several hundred miles to attend the event. Non-O'odham of many ages and backgrounds from the Tucson community also attend. My experience at this festival, as well as at other events, has taught me that the Tohono O'odham have a strong affiliation with place; waila players identify themselves by where they live and where they were raised. The interviews I conducted with accordionists for this article confirmed that this affiliation with place forms a backdrop for other observations regarding waila accordion performance.

My interviews with waila accordion players conducted in support of this essay spanned three generations of players. John Manuel, the accordionist for the American Indians, was sixty at the time of writing; Frank Valenzuela, of Valenzuela and Company, was fifty-nine. Damon Enriquez, the accordionist with the Cisco Band,

was forty years old when interviewed. The Cisco Band was established by his father, Francis Enriquez, in 1969; Damon joined full-time in 1990. Today the band
consists solely of Francis and his sons and grandsons. Steve Vavages, twenty-two,
plays with Thee Express, the Young Waila Musicians, and Passion, a Tucson Tejano band that has played regularly at the Yaqui-operated Casino of the Sun for
the past two or three years. Brandis Joaquin, twenty-four years old, is another
Thee Express member. In addition to these interviews, I drew on past experience,
conversations, and the testimonies of veteran performers who spoke at the Young
Waila Musicians' workshops in 1996 and 1998 about how they learned and what
waila meant to them. Daniel Joaquin and Al Pablo were two accordion players who
spoke at those events. Their observations regarding the accent of the accordion
prompted me to investigate language models for musical performance among the
O'odham and to compare the accent of waila accordionists to Tejano and *norteño*
counterparts. This investigation included comparing recorded examples of waila
accordion performance with examples of related styles.

Performance Places and Context

Music from cities and towns beyond Indian territory inspired the development of
waila, but the customs of performance and the circuit of engagements for O'odham
players center around reservation life. Waila bands play for rodeos, religious holidays and feast days, birthdays, and other special celebrations on the reservation—
everything from christenings to funerals. Musicians play in private homes and
community centers, and many events are held outdoors. Well-established bands
develop a following and a full calendar and may play as often as every weekend.
In addition to playing on the Tohono O'odham Reservation, bands also circulate among other reservations in the area. Valenzuela and Company, for example,
regularly performs on other American Indian reservations in the area, including
the Gila Indian Reservation, the reservations for the Salt River Apache, the San
Carlos Apache, and the White Mountain Apache.[14]

For a non-Indian like myself, the Tohono O'odham Reservation can seem stark,
isolated, and impoverished, but to those who call it home, it is a comforting place—
as one player told me, it is "where people look like me and where people know
each other."[15] Tohono O'odham means "desert people," and the land that belongs
to them is marked by vast stretches of dusty desert soil framed by breathtaking
mountain ranges and peppered with a mix of prickly plants: scrawny mesquite,
feathery palo verde trees, and a vast variety of cacti, including the majestic, treelike
sahuaro, whose giant trunks sprout arms and where, according to native belief,
the ancestral spirits of the O'odham reside. Those who live on this land learn to
appreciate the beauty of the harsh landscape, but this appreciation does not reduce

the hardship imposed by the conditions of nature, including the vast distances separating villages and communities and the limited economic opportunity endemic to reservation life.

There are currently twenty-four thousand registered Tohono O'odham tribal members. According to the 2000 census, approximately half of them live on one of four noncontiguous territories in the Tohono O'odham nation, all located in southern Arizona. The largest land reserve, often called the "main" reservation, comprises 2.7 million acres, with the northern boundary just south of Casa Grande extending south into Mexico.[16] The other reservations are the San Lucy District, south of Gila Bend, the twenty-acre village around Florence, and the oldest settlement, San Xavier, directly south of Tucson.

In the early twentieth century, most O'odham people resided on reservations and supported themselves primarily with subsistence farming on their territory. In the 1950s, the U.S. Bureau of Indian Affairs (BIA) began encouraging the O'odham to work on the large irrigated cotton fields in southern Arizona.[17] The accordionist John Manuel spoke of growing up in this farming environment in the memories documented later in this essay.

New ways of life resulted from the BIA Relocation and Employment programs of the 1950s and 1960s, spurred by the federal government's plans to terminate its legal obligations to Indian tribes. This act pushed American Indians, especially youth, to leave the reservation and relocate in major cities to find work. Life in Los Angeles and other big cities in the Southwest exposed O'odham to a wide array of music makers and styles and reinforced interest in popular Mexican and Chicano music. The waila bandleader Angelo Joaquin Sr. settled in Los Angeles during this period, and his music reflects his encounters with urban dance styles, especially those enjoyed by Latino audiences at the time.

After the state of Arizona authorized gambling on reservation lands in 1993, the Tohono O'odham tribe opened Desert Diamond Casino on S. Nogales Highway. Benefits from gaming include employment and distributions of profits made directly to O'odham tribal members. Every two years, all registered O'odham receive two thousand dollars from casino profits, which many use to purchase big-ticket items such as cars or even musical instruments. The windfall character of this support does not, however, provide steady income for insurance and maintenance. The growth of the casino industry has affected waila performance directly and indirectly. In addition to boosting individual spending, the Casino supports waila performance, hiring bands to perform on its premises and sponsoring offsite events, including the Tucson Waila Festival.

Other off-reservation venues where Tohono O'odham musicians perform waila include city parks, schools, museums, civic centers, and even prisons, where bands are hired to play for events ranging from summer entertainment programs to highway dedications. Some bands were even formed in response to off-reservation civic gatherings. The Tohono O'odham Veterans, for example, is a group of players who share experience in Vietnam. Regulars at the Waila Festival and also on the reservation, they formed in 1991 to play at Tucson's annual 'Nam Jam ceremonies.

Instrument Choice and Technique

Most waila musicians play the three-row diatonic button accordion. The Hohner Corona is the most widely used model. Apart from its reasonable cost and wide availability, the Hohner was also the instrument played by early Tejano and *norteño* artists, in particular Narciso Martinez, whose playing inspired the older generation of waila players.[18] However, in the past decade, younger waila players increasingly favor the more expensive and elaborate accordions made by Gabbanelli.[19] Their attraction to these instruments corresponds to their admiration for new and dynamic Tejano accordion players and for the status that accrues from association with such virtuosi and their signature instruments.

The Hohner Corona II has thirty-one treble buttons, each with two sets of treble- and middle-octave reeds. Pressing a button produces a tone with a distinctive warble that results from the simultaneous sounding of two reeds, each tuned four to five cents apart. Pushing the bellows while pressing a button produces one pitch, while pulling it produces another. The buttons are arranged so that the notes of diatonic triads lie in sequence along a row, and waila performance techniques exploit this layout.[20] There are also twelve bass-chord buttons on the left side of the instrument. Many waila players take out the bass reed boxes, making it "easier to move the bellows."[21] Even players who do not choose to alter their instruments rarely play the bass buttons while performing with the full band, since the guitar, bass, and drums handle rhythm and bass accompaniment. Hohner and Gabbanelli make accordions with five registers, three reed sets, and as many as five switches that can be used to produce different combination of reeds sets for a pitch.[22] These elaborate instruments, especially those with switches, are popular with contemporary Tejano accordionists but are rarely used by waila players who, no matter what instrument they play, favor a plain and even technique.

Damon Enriquez of the Cisco Band plays a Gabbanelli three-row button accordion that he bought in 1996; but he began on a Hohner. "The Gabbanelli has become the standard in the last five to ten years; before that everyone played a Hohner."[23] These new instruments have three registers and anywhere from three to six switches to allow a player to vary the combination of reeds used in producing any one tone. The Gabbanelli "Norteño" model has three switches. Gabbanelli accordions weigh more than the Hohner Corona and feature brilliantly colored designs and fancy metalwork on the boxes. "They have a great tone and are so visually attractive," says

Figure 6.1 Damon
Enriquez with his
Gabanelli accordion.
Photo courtesy of Damon
Enriquez, 2010.

Damon.[24] Like the younger players interviewed for this article, he mentioned his admiration for the Tejano accordionist Jaime de Anda of Los Chamacos, who often plays a Gabbanelli Model 2 Tone with six registers and four sets of reed blocks, although de Anda also sometimes plays a Hohner Corona II.

Not all players have abandoned the Hohner for the Gabbanelli. Frank Valenzuela has been playing a Hohner Corona for twenty years. He has also kept the bass reeds:

Some players keep the bass; it depends. Some of the players who play fancy and want to add lots of notes and play quickly take out the bass keys [reeds] so that the instrument will respond more quickly. Some people like the Gabbanelli; it's okay if you are only playing for an hour or two, but it is too heavy for a ten-hour gig.[25]

Versatility and Learning to Play

Most waila performers play more than one instrument, and all of the accordionists I interviewed began playing on a different instrument. Most began with rhythm instruments such as guitar or percussion.

Daniel Joaquin, who in addition to the accordion also plays saxophone, trumpet, and several other instruments, is typical in that he does not read or write music and plays by ear. He started in the 1930s when his father got him his first guitar for twelve dollars. "Music kept us all together and reminded us who we were," he recalled.[26] When he began playing accordion, he appreciated the range of the instrument. He liked being able to reach higher pitches on the accordion than was possible on the saxophone and felt that the "accordion offered a nice break from playing the saxophone."[27]

Damon Enriquez started playing waila on drums. Later, his father taught him how to play a song on the accordion, beginning with the first verse, and then later the second part; he learned "London Bridges"—based on the "London Bridge" song, of course, with the waila polka beat: "The first part of the song is similar, but part two is made up and more sped up."[28]

Many waila players perform with more than one band. While Damon's primary link is to the Cisco Band, when he was young he played with the Papago Warriors. That band took its name from the mascot for the school in Sells, where Damon grew up and still resides. He was in junior high school at the time, and the other players were either in junior high or high school. He distinguished this band from the contemporary band named Papago Warrior, a progressive group that obtained the right to use the name from Damon and his earlier bandmates, since "there was little chance that the earlier group would get together again."[29]

Frank Valenzuela was born in San Carmelo, a little town on the border of the reservation, and he now lives in Three Points. Frank taught himself to play on a Hohner accordion that he picked up. He never had formal lessons and, like most waila musicians, does not read music. He knows all his music by memory. For those players not born into musical families, the opportunity to play often results from serendipity more than by design. Frank was invited by the father of his son's girlfriend to perform with the Santa Rosa Band in 1987 after it lost its accordion player. In 1995 he started Valenzuela and Company, and he sometimes plays with the Alex Gomez Band.

Serendipity also played a role in how John Manuel, born in Tucson on the San Xavier Reservation, learned to play.

Dad used to work on a farm. We had a neighbor who was crippled. He played guitar, and I used to watch him play. One day this Mexican guy came by with an accordion. I bought it from him for thirty dollars. It was a Hohner. He was a drug dealer and had to get rid of it quickly. It was in bad shape; it did not even have a cover. I bought it right away and took it to my friend.

John remembers transferring O'odham fiddle band music as well as Mexican songs to the accordion:

I learned to play by ear. I would look and see [how my friend played]. First, I learned Mexican songs, but Chicken Scratch had its own songs. I used to listen to fiddle bands. People in town had a band with two violins, guitar, bass guitar, snare, fiddle bass, and drum.[30]

Like several other players I interviewed, John also played rock music, and he credits this with inspiring a more flexible approach to waila, even if the two styles remained distinct: "When I was a teenager I joined a rock band, and we played for five years. I played guitar and bass. I just kept the accordion on the side."[31] He joined the American Indians in 1970 and still plays with them. Over time, the group moved from a classic approach to more experimental practices.

We've been playing together for forty years. We do our own music. . . . On our new CD I also play harmonica, and the sax player sometimes switches off to play violin. We like to experiment with new combinations and see how people like it. We were in Gila River last week, and I received good comments from a lady who liked what we were playing.[32]

John made history in 1976 when he connected his accordion to a wah-wah pedal, producing an entirely new effect, which can be heard on his recording of "Cry Babe."[33]

Performance Practices and Influences

Waila accordionists typically play a single-voice melody, although the fluttering of the double-reed combination for each pitch enriches the sound. The warble of the accordion is typically matched by the wide vibrato preferred by waila saxophone players. Players tend to outline the melody using arpeggiated chords, occasionally adding harmonic chords at the ends of phrases or the close of a piece. If not supplying the melody alone, a popular early waila technique is to shadow or play in tandem with the saxophone. The song "Old-Timer Two Step," as performed by the American Indians with the accordionist John Manuel, offers a good example of a classic waila sound.[34]

John Manuel still plays a Hohner accordion, without the bass reeds: "There is no need for those reeds, and it makes the instrument lighter." John found most of his inspiration from other Chicken Scratch bands. He explained: "I liked practically all of them. There was one in particular, the Hickiwan Band, they had a different way of playing the accordion; Hickiwan played with more of a Mexican style."[35] It is easy to see the Mexican influence in the titles of songs recorded by this band, such as "La feria de las flores," "La palo millo," and "Jalisco, nunca."[36] While the leader of the Hickiwan Band, Alex Jose, inspired his technique, the two men also became friends. Alex told John that he was inspired by his songs and began to learn them. John also met Alex's brother Willie (Francisco), who taught him to play in the Texas style. Like other O'odham, Alex had learned the Texas style in California. John remembered how different that style seemed to him: "To me, the Texas style seemed almost backwards to Chicken Scratch. The chord changes work differently."[37]

While all the musicians interviewed cited Mexican and Tejano styles as influencing some aspect of how and what they learned to play on accordion, the styles they adopted differ in subtle ways. Daniel Joaquin pointed towards Narciso Martinez, the Tejano accordionist credited as the father of *conjunto* music in the 1930s and 1940s, as an important influence on his playing.[38] A recorded selection featuring Martinez that offers an example of the style and melody that transferred to waila is "Flor Marchita."[39] Daniel's debt to Narcisco Martinez includes a shared use of quick, staccato articulations, emphasis on the treble end of the instrument, and leaving the bass part to the other instruments. Martinez's technique for backing duo singers, an essential feature of Mexican *música norteña*, also found its way into waila, where the accordion backed duo saxophones.[40] Despite such similarities, waila accordionists tend to play with a more sustained, legato sound than *norteño* accordionists, even when playing similar patterns. Fingering technique accounts for some of this difference, but bellows technique is equally important, and interpretation is yet another factor. Daniel Joaquin explained that much as O'odham speak English with an accent, they play music with an accent.[41]

Like most waila accordionists, Damon Enriquez does not use the bass buttons, a decision that reflects the influence of his father, his first teacher: "He took out the buttons because of the weight and because it makes it easier to play loudly for a long time."[42] His father, Francisco "Cisco" Enriquez, influenced his playing, but he also cites as influences the twenty-five-year-old Albert Zamora, the accordionist for the Corpus Christi–based band Talento, and Jaime De Anda, who had been playing since the 1970s, when he, like Damon, began playing with his father's band. Both players prompted Damon's move to the Gabbinelli accordion. "Of course, I can't play even close to those guys,"[43] he modestly adds, but there is no question that his manner of playing reflects more recent Tejano practices. The Cisco Band adds decorative passages to the melodies performed by the saxophone in a manner akin to Tejano artists. Comparing Zamora's performance of the polka "Prieta Casada"[44] to Damon's playing of the waila selection "The Tailor"[45] reveals some essential differences. While Zamora introduces phrases with showy flourishes, playing harmonic triads in rapid succession and in different octaves, and inserting dramatic fills when the singers pause, Damon's accordion provides the lyric melody, adding flourishes generally at the end of a phrase. When the accordion plays the melody, the saxophones may add decorative elements, but none that would compete with Zamora's fills. In another example, when Damon plays the *cumbia* "Meeks,"[46] the saxophones carry the melody, and the accordion interjects decorative riffs built on repeated melodic motifs. These insistent phrases are not bursts of display in the style of Zamora, but they share a compelling effect. The aim to push listeners into a dancing frenzy is shared by both the Tejano and waila players. This more insistent approach sets the Cisco Band apart from older, more reserved bands. In addition, Damon and his fellow Cisco Band members also stand out for their choreography, performance demeanor,[47] and for including vocals in their performances.

Jaime de Anda was the player mentioned most frequently by the younger O'odham accordionists as an inspiration. However, Steve Vavages surprised me with the range of his influences. Clearly, he and his fellow band member Brandis Joaquin rely on the Internet to expand their access to other performers and, to a lesser extent, to promote their own work. Steve cited YouTube videos as a means of widening his experience. Among the models for these young players are Steve Jordan, Ramon Ayala, Renato Borghetti (the Italian *milonga* player), and Joel Guzman, all renowned for their virtuosity. "[They play] faster and more fancy. . . . To tell the truth, waila playing is often a little lower in standards and less clean,"[48] Steve notes, making clear the skills he hopes to emulate. An example of the stronger Latino influence in newer waila music can be heard on the track "Rinconcito" on Vavages's *Express Yourself* album, which positions the accordion at center stage. Played here by Steve's father Rupert Vavages, the performance opens with the repeated-note flourishes more customary of Tejano than mainstream waila.[49]

Knowing When to Throw Words in the Air

While it is useful to understand what kind of accordions waila musicians play and what techniques they use while performing, more significant is the role that the accordion plays in a waila band. Along with the saxophones, it provides the singing voice of waila. While modern *conjunto* (Tejano) and *norteño* music customarily includes singers, waila has not followed suit. This may result from how the Tohono O'odham traditionally view singing. According to Ofelia Zepeda, the O'odham conceptualize the oral arts, including singing, as "throwing words into the air."[50] Because of the power words carry, this is an act not to be taken lightly. The accordion sings but does not throw words in the air.

"I don't know how someone can write about Native American expressive culture and not refer to religion," one O'odham friend said to me on a long drive. He added: "Of course, some people may not appreciate the difference between spirituality and religion." We were talking about a recently published study of the popular music of another tribe and the author's opening statement that the book would not directly address religious practice.[51] Like that author, I did not anticipate discussing religion for this essay, since waila is popular social-dance music, and the O'odham do not typically consider it to be sacred music. Yet respect for spiritual boundaries may help explain why the O'odham conventionally prefer purely instrumental waila and why the accordion, along with the saxophone, stands in for the vocalist.

Despite the popular character of waila, spiritual matters often surface in discussions surrounding it. When I asked why O'odham don't sing while performing waila music, an O'odham friend told me that "there are maybe only two traditional songs in O'odham that would fit with the rhythm of waila." Colleen Fitzgerald's studies of language stress and metric accentuation in Tohono O'odham songs seem to support this claim; although the dominance of duple-meter dance rhythms that accentuate beat one of the measure in this popular repertoire invites consideration, the trochaic metric stress that Fitzgerald identifies as essential might be accommodated if desired.[52] I also sensed that my friend was suggesting that the O'odham language should be reserved for traditional songs, or at least for songs that do not borrow foreign rhythms and melodies. As if confirming my speculation, he added: "Many of the songs come from outside and are Mexican favorites; of course, Spanish isn't our language." The last point was particularly telling. Plenty of O'odham know how to speak Spanish, but it is not the tribe's indigenous language. O'odham consider waila to be their music; they do not view themselves as performing borrowed music. Singing in Spanish might reduce their claim on the music even as it might compromise the space and aesthetic that O'odham traditionally reserve for singing in their own language.

In an essay on native poetry and O'odham oral aesthetic arts, the linguist Ofelia Zepeda explains that O'odham speakers equate poetic speech with song and that the traditional O'odham oral aesthetic arts include formal speaking, prayer, and oratory, as well as song:

> My observations on O'odham song texts has led me to believe that singers who dream the song text are gifted with the ability to transfer the most beautiful ideas into song language. The language then itself becomes a thing of beauty meant to please spiritual beings, worldly beings such as animals, and of course, humans.[53]

Zepeda's observations remind us that songs in the O'odham language reflect a trust and a power conferred upon humans from spiritual sources. It would follow that using the O'odham language for waila songs could be construed as compromising that relationship. This reverence for the power of words sung in O'odham may help explain the reluctance of O'odham to incorporate sung lyrics into waila performance, but exceptions do and always have existed. Those exceptions correspond in significant ways to how different generations of players have approached the accordion.

Knowing When to Sing

In recent years, waila musicians have begun to document their own histories. Angelo Joaquin Jr, the founder of the Tucson Waila Festival, has prepared several as-yet-unpublished documentaries, one of them a study of the links between the Mexican *orquesta* traditions of the 1940s, exemplified by Beto Villa, with developing Tohono O'odham practices, exemplified by the Ajo Orchestra under the leadership of Angelo Mattia, an O'odham musician based in Ajo, Arizona. Mattia's orchestra included guitar, saxophones, and trumpet, but not accordion. The class distinctions that Manuel Peña[54] noted as distinguishing the working-class audiences for *ranchera*-inspired ensembles, including accordion, from the aspiring middle and upper classes, who favored the dance-band orchestras, were less sharply defined in Tohono O'odham communities, but each of the two paths influenced the development of waila. Mattias played for and was first inspired by the *orquesta* tradition, but rather like Beto Villa, he quickly integrated *ranchera*-style dance music into his waila repertory.

The story of the Joaquin Brothers illustrates a similar exchange between orchestral and band influences. Ron Joaquin, the leader of Southern Scratch, one the best-known contemporary waila bands, has prepared an homage to his late father, Angelo Joaquin Sr., the leader of the renowned Joaquin Brothers band (1957–93). The Joaquin Brothers began in Los Angeles in 1957 as Angelo Joaquin and His Orchestra. At that time, the group featured Angelo on guitar, his brother Fernando and his cousins Frank Celestine on saxophone, and Joe Celestine on bass fiddle.[55] With his return to the Tucson area in 1958, Angelo re-created the band as the Joaquin Brothers, including his brother Daniel on saxophone and later, accordion, and his nephews Leonard Joaquin on bass guitar and Jerome Joaquin on drums. For thirty-five years, the band performed for O'odham and mixed audiences throughout Arizona and at folk festivals elsewhere in the United States as well as Canada. The band's last major out-of-state performance was at Carnegie Hall in 1980. My sense, from talking with Angelo Joaquin's son and others, is that over the years the band served as a kind of conservatory for waila. From the beginning, its members helped train and initiate young up-and-coming players, and the network of living players who have some connection to this seminal group is extensive and links many different bands. Jerome and Leonard Joaquin play today with the band Valenzuela and Company, alongside Frank Valenzuela, who used to sit in with the Joaquin Brothers band and who is one of the accordionists interviewed for this project.

Ron Joaquin recalls a Yaqui singer named Nacho Armenta who would perform with the Joaquin Brothers.[56] His father enjoyed these songs—among them, "Amazing Grace," and "Cielito Lindo," both sung in Spanish—and Ron decided to include them on his tribute recording. There will be no attempt to present them in O'odham, nor will any O'odham performer sing them for the public; Ron hired two Chicana singers to record the songs that Nacho used to sing. Ron's older brother, Angelo Joaquin Jr., remarked that one of the keys to his father's success was "understanding his audience."[57] In the 1950s, there were enough O'odham in Los Angeles (following the BIA migration campaigns) that there was a ready audience for waila,[58] but when the Joaquin Brothers performed for mixed or non-O'odham audiences, especially for their Chicano audiences in Los Angeles, the band would include songs, but not ones performed in the O'odham language.[59] Waila for others might include songs, but songs in the O'odham language were not part of the repertoire of waila bands during this formative period.

O'odham elders still recall boarding-school proscriptions against speaking native languages. O'odham school children were punished for speaking their language. Such incidents are rarely discussed with non-O'odham, but this legacy may have also played a role in establishing the practice of not singing O'odham lyrics in mixed settings. Many waila performers learned instruments and started to play music in groups while in boarding school. Daniel Joaquin remembers his days at St. John's Indian School, where he started playing in the school band, which used a violin, guitar, bass violin, and two saxophones. He remarked that the fiddler was a San Carlos Apache who could play perfectly all the songs the old O'odham musicians played.[60] The chance to meet youth from other tribes was one aspect of boarding-school life that students seemed to appreciate, but instructors used the variety of tribal languages spoken by students as yet another reason to force Indian students to speak English.[61] While many began playing at school, others did not, and learning on one's own was an equally important route. Frank Valenzuela, for example, also attended St. John's as a youth, but he did not play with a band then.[62]

The growing popularity of waila may have even contributed to the weakening of O'odham language proficiency. At a Tucson performance of traditional dancers from Baboquivari School, the teacher and language advocate Danny Lopez told the audience: "The social round dance took place in the round house; today it has been replaced by waila. . . . Our traditional dances died out for a while as we got more into the Mexican music."[63] Despite his observations, Lopez supported waila, especially when it reinforced the bonds that linked O'odham to their community, their ancestors, and their traditions. He attended the first waila musicians' workshop in 1995 and spoke about the values that players could reinforce.

The practice of reserving O'odham songs for contexts that did not include outsiders or waila was not always strictly observed. The accordionist John Manuel recalled an early Chicken Scratch band led by Virgil Molina's band, the Molinas.[64] "They had a song they used to sing in Papago. . . . They sang a song called 'Oik Oik'—about a dance on the reservation and how one girl had no one who wanted to dance with her. . . . When I first heard it, I thought it would be pretty good to sing in O'odham instead of singing in English or Mexican, but it did not catch on."[65]

Damon Enriquez, the accordionist with the Cisco Band, one of a few bands that sing today, offered yet another explanation for the resistance to singing, noting how experience with rock music influenced attitudes toward singing in waila performance:

> Most people I meet don't mind letting the instruments do the singing for them. Honestly, I think it is because many O'odham are kind of shy in public; that's our way. Lots of them sing, but not on stage. The Cisco Band began singing in the 1990s. I remember my dad coming to me and saying, "What do you think about singing this song?" He wanted to sing some Texas Tornado covers. I was all for it. During my teen years I played rock with a separate band. I did that for ten years. I played drums with those garage bands. My father also had that experience; he played rock 'n' roll in the 1960s. So we added some songs with lyrics [to our waila performances]. We went through phases. We began with Tejano oldies and included some old country hits. In the 1990s we played "Neverending Love" [sung in English]. Now we are doing originals. Of course, once in a while we like trying something new; we'll listen and try anything we like . . . and [laughing] that we can do.

Unsung Stories and Female Players

Even without words, the sense of a good story remains an important aesthetic for waila musicians, especially for older players. Frederick Mattias told Angelo Joaquin Jr. that a good waila song needs to tell a story, and Daniel Joaquin echoed that sentiment.[66] Mattias explained, "The story in the music needs to be connected to some roots." For many, familiar melodies and rhythms are rooted in their memories of gatherings that defined their childhood and meaningful events for their families.

While women were part of these events, they rarely performed. As Danny Lopez once explained, "In O'odham culture women weren't seen; they stayed in the back of the house."[67] Women played supporting roles and often still do. Preparing food for the communal feasts that often accompany waila performances is a traditional female role, and the moment when the cook takes off her apron and comes out to dance is a special one—immortalized in the elegant stipple artwork of the late Tohono O'odham artist Leonard Chana.[68] Some bands set aside special songs for that moment.

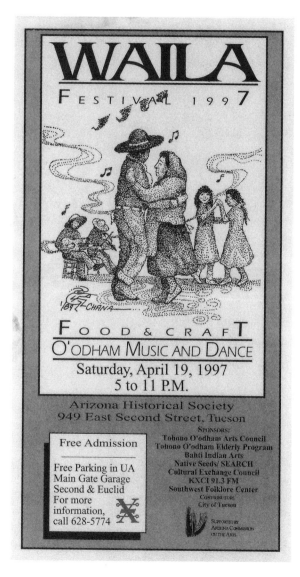

Figure 6.2 2008 Waila Festival poster with a print by the Tohono O'odham artist Leonard Chana (1950–2004). Courtesy of the Waila Festival.

In recent years, Tohono O'odham girls and young women have learned to play instruments. Most female waila musicians who play as children begin performing with family members, the same way that most male waila players learn. Ron Joaquin, the leader of Southern Scratch, included his daughter Sara in his band as a percussionist, a typical first assignment for young players. Sara and the rest of the band are joined by Melanie Farnsworth on saxophone on the Southern Scratch Christmas album.[69]

Al Pablo, the leader of the Pablo Waila Band, a family band from the Wa:k Village in the Xavier District, coached his daughters on saxophone and accordion and integrated them into the band first formed by his father Dave. At the 2005 Waila Festival, Al's daughter Amanda Pablo played saxophone, accordion, and bass. Al also plays accordion and sax in the band, and his brother Mike plays bass. Both girls have played with their peers in young waila musicians' groups.

Gertie Lopez is an independent female accordionist and leader of her own band. She lives in Tucson and works as a teacher on the San Xavier Reservation. A musician since childhood, she played in a mariachi led by her father Augustine and later performed with her brothers in waila bands.[70] Adopting an independent path, Gertie and her band the T. O. Boyz play each weekend at Antonio's, a south Tucson bar, but have never performed at the Waila Festival. Her waila band performs for the Borderland Theater's annual Tucson Pastorela[71] production every year, an engagement where waila joins a mélange of Spanish Christmas songs, as well as selected folk, classical, and popular music, in the service of the script. The job suits a group like Gertie's that already challenges stylistic and gender boundaries. Gertie not only leads her own waila band; she incorporates reggae beats into her waila performances and sometimes sings, as in "Sheila's Rasta."[72] Like the other players interviewed, Gertie doesn't limit herself to accordion; she plays guitar as well.

Old Fashion, New Fashion

While some might argue that the accordion is an old-fashioned instrument, most Tohono O'odham accordion players do not think of the accordion as modern or old. For Frank Valenzuela, "it's somewhere in between."[73] The questions that seem to count to players are: How is the accordion played, and is that playing making people happy? Daniel Joaquin stopped playing accordion in the 1960s, reporting that he found "it wasn't popular in the 1960s with O'odham audiences and dancers."[74] Damon Enriquez noted that some of his non-O'odham coworkers once questioned him about playing accordion: "It was obvious they were thinking Lawrence Welk or something. I told them it wasn't like that."[75] It appears that as long as waila players are able to adjust their technique to the changing tastes of their listeners, the instrument remains vital.

Some of the younger waila accordionists play in a style described as "aggressive" by their elders.[76] What constitutes aggression differs from band to band, but for some, the showier style of young accordionists counts as aggressive. Supplanting the accordion's time-honored role with vocals counts as another "aggressive" move, as does body language and dress. The most aggressive groups, like the new Papago Warrior (a.k.a. P-Dub), adopt a stage presence that mixes elements of hip-hop and *pachuco*. They wear dark clothing, pork-pie hats, and dark sunglasses known as "locs," and they play in large arenas. Younger players are taking waila in new directions, incorporating songs and playing techniques that connect them and their audiences to new pop music practices. Their video posts on YouTube and other websites reveal a desire to connect to the wider world of popular music, but equally evident is their aim to define waila on Tohono O'odham terms and retain its vitality for O'odham fans.

Conclusions

This focus on accordion players—their roles, concerns, and playing techniques—has confirmed that waila is changing. Those changes parallel fashions in American and international popular music as shaped by the realities of Tohono O'odham life along the southwestern U.S.–Mexican border. The influence of Mexican music persists, reflecting increasingly new Tejano and pan-Latino sounds as well as popular trends in rock and pop. Those influences may be rooted in place, but like Tejano and other popular commercial forms, they circulate without allegiance to geographic location. John Manuel described the changing role of the accordion in this larger context: "To me, waila is following a path like Rock. In the 1960s there was Woodstock and the British Invasion. Since then Rock has undergone many changes. Chicken Scratch is the same way; it is changing in different directions."[77] His remark alludes to a lack of uniformity resulting from individual choices.

A shared thread in the interviews was the importance of connection. Waila accordionists adopt techniques and instruments that connect them to players they admire and to the styles that please their audiences. The ways that accordionists treat melody, incorporate principles of Tohono O'odham speech accent, and tell stories without words help transform borrowed music into O'odham music. Waila music unites the Tohono O'odham within their own communities, but it has also always linked them to wider realms of popular and international music. In this way, waila performers contribute to shaping a modern sensibility that retains O'odham values.

The history of this relatively new musical practice supports this claim. Adopting the accordion helped transform the fiddle bands into contemporary popular ensembles. When the O'odham bandleaders merged *conjunto* with *orquesta*, they joined other borderland musicians in blending European, Mexican, and American styles to produce music that embraced their southwestern experiences. By placing the accordion in the service of retaining linguistic boundaries, by refusing to adopt outside language models, and by applying speechlike articulation principles in performance technique, Tohono O'odham musicians crafted a mode of performance that was distinctly theirs. Even individual experimenters acknowledged existing repertories of meaning. The older generation may lament some of the choices of young players, but there is plenty of evidence that young players continue to respect and even seek to reinforce the boundaries between Tohono O'odham and outside practice. Innovators who strive to incorporate showier accordion technique, more singing, and new gender responsibilities still insist that their music must first and foremost serve O'odham audiences. Like Angelo Joaquin Sr., the young musicians of Thee Express experiment with ways to include non-O'odham listeners and enhance the recognition of their music while maintaining cultural if not geographic boundaries. Native sovereignty has its counterpart in popular native music and the ongoing dance between resistance and accommodation. Left unchecked, individual innovations or borrowed practices might transform waila into a style no longer representing the people, but waila accordionists play their role in balancing the maintenance of traditional values with the competing forces of deterritorialization.

Notes

"Waila Music" from *Ocean Power, Poems of the Desert* by Ofelia Zepeda. © 1995 Ofelia Zepeda. Reprinted by permission of the University of Arizona Press.

1. In 1986, the Papago tribe adopted a new constitution and declared that it would be known by its own name, the Tohono O'odham. See the official website of the Tohono O'odham Nation, http://www.tonation-nsn.gov/ (accessed January 24, 2012); Charles F. Wilkinson, *Blood Struggle: The Rise of Modern Indian Nations* (New York: W. W. Norton and Co., 2005), 299.

2. Chris Strachwitz, liner notes to *Norteño and Tejano Accordion Pioneers*, CD 7016 (El Cerrito, Calif.: Arhoolie Records, 1995), 8.

3. For a stimulating history of industrial development, particularly the role played by copper mining along the U.S.-Mexican border, see Samuel Truett, *Fugitive Landscapes: The Forgotten History of the U.S.-Mexico Borderlands* (New Haven, Conn.: Yale University Press, 2006).

4. The earliest documentation of the fiddle bands appears in an 1860 journal, according to Jim Griffith, liner notes to *Old Time Music of the Tohono O'odham, vols. 1 and 2*, 8082 (Phoenix: Canyon Records, 1997). This is a CD rerelease combining two earlier recordings, *The Gu-achi Fiddlers*, CR 8082 and 8092 (Phoenix: Canyon Records, 1988,

1991). Examples also appear on *Borderlands: From Conjunto to Chicken Scratch*, SF40418 (Washington, D.C.: Smithsonian Folkways, 1994).

5. While scholars studying waila have made much of this distinction, few acknowledge that the early Tejano and *norteño* music was also predominantly instrumental. Chris Strachwitz notes that the early Tejano accordionists in the 1930s played only with bass and guitar and that it was not until the following decade that vocalists joined the ensemble and came to be viewed as essential to the style. Chris Strachwitz, liner notes to *Norteño and Tejano Accordion Pioneers*, 2.

6. Damon Enriquez, personal interview, Tucson, December 29, 2008.

7. Brandis Joaquin, personal interview, Tucson, December 28, 2008.

8. Ibid.

9. Ibid. The band can be heard on Thee Express, *Express Yourself*, CR8119 (Phoenix: Canyon Records, 2007).

10. Lila Abu-Lughod, "Writing against Culture," In *Recapturing Anthropology*, ed. Richard G. Fox (Santa Fe: School of American Research Press, 1991), 137–62.

11. *Waila! Making the People Happy*, DVD, dir. Daniel Golding (Native American Public Telecommunications/PBS, 2005). This sixty-minute documentary profiles the Joaquin Brothers over four generations, illustrating their signature contributions to waila music.

12. David W. Samuels speaks of the ironic and contradictory views the Apache express toward their reservation, viewing it as incorporated into the American mainstream yet simultaneously apart and distinct. David W. Samuels, *Putting a Song on Top of It: Expression and Identity on the San Carlos Apache Reservation* (Tucson: University of Arizona Press, 2004), 83.

13. Although out of print, *Dancing in the Dust: The Waila Festival—Live!* (Tucson: Blue Bhikku Records, 1998) remains the best audio documentary of the festival.

14. Frank Valenzuela, personal interview, Tucson, December 30, 2008.

15. Angelo Joaquin Jr., personal communication, Tucson, January 4, 2009.

16. The Gadsden Purchase in 1853 (ratified in 1854) bisected Tohono O'odham territory when it defined the current border between the United States and Mexico, leaving residents in the southern portion in Mexico and placing those in the north in the United States. Even today, O'odham view the border as an arbitrary divide separating kin and shared traditions.

17. Wilkinson, *Blood Struggle*, 301. The promotion of agribusiness led to the widespread abandonment of small-scale subsistence farming on the reservation. The crippling growth of diabetes among the O'odham appears directly linked to the abandonment of a diet based on traditional crops and foods such as tepary beans, mesquite flour, squash, corn, peppers, and various cacti, crops the O'odham now seek to recover—an effort supported by Angelo Joaquin Jr. and other waila leaders. See Jim Kent, "Traditional Native American Crops Face Extinction: Native Seeds / SEARCH Group Works to Preserve Culture and History through Seed Gathering and Preservation," *Native Voice*, July 5, 2002, 3; Gary Paul Nabhan, *The Desert Smells Like Rain* (Tucson: University of Arizona Press, 2002).

18. Martinez played a two-row button Hohner prior to 1940, when one- and two-row models were the norm. Strachwitz, liner notes to *Norteño and Tejano Accordion Pioneers*, 5.

19. There are several accordions that bear this name. A popular *norteño* model in the Gabbanelli line is actually manufactured in China and costs considerably less (around six hundred dollars) than the two thousand dollars or more that the models produced in Houston or Italy cost.

20. For example, on the F row (row 3) in a G/C/F accordion, buttons 2, 3, 4 are C, F, A, respectively; 5, 6, 7 are C,' F,' A,' and 8, 9, 10 are F," A," C" while pushing. While pulling these same buttons outlines an E diminished chord in 6/4 position, E, G, B flat, or a root-position G-minor triad, depending upon whether you start on 2 or 3: G, B flat, D, E,' G,' B flat,' D," E," G." The top buttons on each row supply chromatic pitches, so button one in this row is either D sharp pushing, or C sharp pulling.

21. Frank Valenzuela, personal interview.

22. An illustrated explanation of accordion switches can be found at http://www.reyesaccordions.com/Paco4512/FAQ/AccordionSwitches.htm (accessed December 2008).

23. Damon Enriquez, personal interview.

24. Ibid.

25. Frank Valenzuela, personal interview.

26. Daniel Joaquin, Veteran's Panel, Young Waila Musicians' Workshop, University of Arizona, Tucson, August 1998.

27. Daniel Joaquin, interview, in Angelo Joaquin Jr., "The Influence of Orquesta Tejano on Tohono O'odham Waila Bands" (unpublished report, Tucson, December 2006).

28. Damon Enriquez, personal interview. "London Bridge" can be heard on Larry S. Albright, *Carl and Buddies: For Our O'odham Elders* (Casa Grande, Ariz.: Rock-a-Bye Records, 2002). In this performance, the structure that Damon describes is reversed: the first section of the song is an original tune, followed by a variant of the familiar nursery tune (if sung, it would be "London Bridge is falling, falling, falling" [the tones for "down" are omitted]). An earlier version of this song appears on the Santa Rosa Band's recording *Papago Chicken Scratch, Vol. 3*, CR 8071 (Phoenix: Canyon Records, 1984).

29. Damon Enriquez, personal interview. Papago is a band known for its singing as well for gang and rap stylings.

30. John Manuel, personal interview, Tucson, January 9, 2009.

31. Ibid.

32. Ibid.

33. *The American Indians Play Waila Music*, CR6120 (Phoenix: Canyon Records, 2006). This CD combines two earlier Canyon releases, *The American Indians Play Chicken Scratch*, C6120 (1974), and *Waila Social Dance Music: The American Indians, Vol. 2*, 6155 (1976). I am grateful to Kristen Butler of Canyon Records for drawing my attention to this technique. Her podcast, the *History of Waila Music/Chicken Scratch* (2009), appears on the Canyon Records website, http://store.canyonrecords.com/index.php?app=cms&ns=display&ref=HistoryOfWaila (accessed December 22, 2011).

34. *The American Indians Play Waila Music*.

35. John Manuel, personal interview.

36. *Alex Jose and His Hickiwan Band*, LP-SWF008–87 (Phoenix: Canyon Records, 1975).

37. John Manuel, personal interview.

38. Chris Strachwitz, liner notes to *Narciso Martínez*, *"Father of the Texas-Mexican Conjunto,"* CD 361 (El Cerrito, Calif.: Ideal/Arhoolie, 1993).

39. *Norteño and Tejano Accordion Pioneers.*

40. Chris Strachwitz, liner notes to *Narciso Martínez*, *"El Huracan del Valle,"* LP 9017 (El Cerrito, Calif.: Arhoolie/Folklyric, 1977).

41. Daniel Joaquin, Veteran's Panel, Young Waila Musicians' Workshop, University of Arizona, Tucson, August 2003. See also Joaquin, "Influence of Orquesta Tejano."

42. Damon Enriquez, personal interview.

43. Ibid.

44. Albert Zamora, *Qué Viva la Música de Acordeón*, FRCD1938 (Corpus Christi, Tex.: Freddie Records, 2006).

45. "The Tailor" is a track on the Cisco Band's 2007 CD *The More Things Change*. The band posts occasionally to YouTube; see the group singing "Dance with Me" in English at http://www.youtube.com/user/ciscoband#p/u/1/9WW2Ljed8yI (accessed February 15, 2012). Their MySpace page is at http://www.myspace.com/theciscoband (accessed January 24, 2012).

46. "Meeks" is a track on *The Cisco Band* (1998).

47. I discuss the Cisco Band's choreography in Janet Sturman, "Movement Analysis as a Tool for Understanding Identity: Retentions, Borrowings, and Transformations in Native American Waila," *the world of music* 39.3 (1997): 51–69. Some of these changes can be seen in the videos on the band's YouTube site, and the video loop there illustrates the choreographed movements that the band practices (http://www.youtube.com/user/ciscoband; accessed January 26, 2012).

48. Steve Vavages, personal interview, Tucson, December 28, 2008.

49. Thee Express, *Express Yourself.*

50. Ofelia Zepeda, "Indigenous Language Education and Literacy: Introduction to the Theme Issue," *Bilingual Research Journal* 19.1 (1995): 5–6.

51. Angelo Joaquin Jr., personal communication.

52. Colleen M. Fitzgerald, "The Meter of Tohono O'odham Songs," *International Journal of American Linguistics* 64.1 (1998): 1–36. Tohono O'odham song texts set to borrowed or contemporary popular melodies and the relationship of language stress to musical rhythm, phrasing and articulation in that context, are topics that have not, to my knowledge, been studied. Such investigation, though promising, would require a command of the Tohono O'odham language and more training in linguistics than I currently possess.

53. Ofelia Zepeda, "Written Statement: O'odham Language," in *Stabilizing Indigenous Languages*, ed. Gina Cantoni-Harvey (Flagstaff: Northern Arizona University, Bilingual/Multicultural Education Program, Center for Excellence in Education, 1996), http://www.ncela.gwu.edu/files/rcd/BE020488/Stabilizing_Indigenous_Languages.pdf (accessed January 24, 2012).

54. Manuel Peña, *The Texas-Mexican Conjunto: History of a Working-Class Music* (Austin: University of Texas Press, 1985); and Manuel Peña, *Música Tejana: The Cultural Economy*

of Artistic Transformation (College Station: Texas A&M University Press, 1999). Class associations separating orchestra from the bands hold in many other contexts in the Americas. In chapter 12 of this volume, Sydney Hutchinson observes similar divisions along lines of social class in her analysis of *merengue típico* in the Dominican Republic.

55. Pinal County Historical Society, *Florence* (Mount Pleasant, S.C.: Arcadia Publishing, 2007), 58.

56. Ron Joaquin, personal communication, Tucson, December 12, 2008.

57. Angelo Joaquin Jr., personal communication.

58. There still is a sizeable Tohono O'odham community in Los Angeles, and waila bands from Arizona sometimes travel to the Los Angeles metropolitan area to perform.

59. Anjelo Joaquin Jr., personal communication.

60. Daniel Joaquin qtd. in Joaquin, "Influence of Orquesta Tejano."

61. Recorded spoken reflections and documents attest to these experience. "Remembering Our Indian School Days: The Boarding School Experience," Permanent Exhibit at the Heard Museum, North Scottsdale, Ariz.; see also Margaret L. Archuleta, *Away from Home: American Indian Boarding School Experiences* (Scottsdale, Ariz.: Heard Museum, 2000).

62. Frank Valenzuela, personal interview.

63. Danny Lopez, "Desert Voices," public lecture, Arizona Historical Society, Tucson, February 28, 1996.

64. *The Molinas: Super Scratch Kings*, CR 6128 (Phoenix: Canyon Records, 1979).

65. John Manuel, personal interview.

66. Joaquin, "Influence of Orquesta Tejano."

67. Lopez, "Desert Voices."

68. Chana died in 2003. For additional reproductions of his artwork and a transcript of the artist's observations on the art of Tohono O'odham life, see Leonard F. Chana, Susan Lobo, and Barbara Chana, *The Sweet Smell of Home* (Tucson: University of Arizona Press, 2009).

69. Southern Scratch, *Chicken Scratch Christmas*, CR 8101 (Phoenix: Canyon Records, 1994).

70. The anthropologist Stephen Nugent of Goldsmiths College, University of London, made a film documenting Gertie Lopez's life: *Waila: The Music of the Tohono O'odham Featuring Gertie Lopez and the TO Boyz*, dir. Stephen Nugent and Ricardo Leiazaola (2009), available at http://anthrofilm.onlinefilm.org/en_EN/film/47403 (accessed February 15, 2012).

71. Tucson's Borderlands Theater has offered its annual *pastorela* since 1995 in a multilingual production that brings together diverse segments of the community. The *pastorela* is an advent tradition popular in Mexico and Hispanic America dating back to the sixteenth century. The pageant players customarily mix the silly with the sublime and include classic and contemporary music, while enacting the story of shepherds, pilgrims, sheep, and a dog as they follow the star to Bethlehem to celebrate Jesus's birth. On the way, they encounter devils trying to deter them with wiley ruses. Fortunately, archangels

step in to vanquish the devils, with tactics that might include such unlikely tools as Elvis Presley songs and Star Wars light sabers to get the travelers back on track.

72. Gertie's Band has several YouTube postings, and while these links are rarely stable, "Sheila's Rasta" as performed by Gertie and the T.O. Boyz can be found at http://www .youtube.com/watch?v=eZxK4BDMI0A (accessed February 15, 2012).

73. Frank Valenzuela, personal interview.

74. Joaquin, "The Influence of Orquesta Tejano."

75. Damon Enriquez, personal interview.

76. Frederick Mattias qtd. in Joaquin, "Influence of Orquesta Tejano."

77. John Manuel, personal interview.

⤃ 7 ⤄

Accordions and Working-Class Culture along Lake Superior's South Shore

JAMES P. LEARY

"Robust and Rowdy"

In the winter of 1981, Bruno Synkula of Ashland, Wisconsin—a house-party musician and maintenance worker born in 1919 to Polish immigrant parents—told me that he learned to play button accordion as a kid from an Italian neighbor, a disabled "ore puncher" who had toiled atop a dock jutting into Lake Superior to push iron ore from bottom-opening rail cars into the holds of Great Lakes vessels. One of Synkula's favorite tunes, "Livet i Finnskogarna" (Life in the Finnish Woods), is a Swedish waltz associated with Finns that he first heard in the aftermath of a turkey shoot at a rural tavern frequented by French Canadians, Germans, Irish, Scandinavians, and Slavs. Its performer, Ole Lear, a former Great Lakes deck hand of Norwegian descent, had acquired the tune from Germans.[1]

Such occurrences were common in Synkula's home region. From the 1880s through the early decades of the twentieth century, European immigrants of mostly peasant origins and their descendants, settling alongside and sometimes intermarrying with Ojibwes, labored along Lake Superior's South Shore. Extending east to west from the Upper Peninsula of Michigan through northern Wisconsin to the port cities of Superior and Duluth, the South Shore's citizens worked in mines, lumber camps, and mills; on shipping vessels and loading docks; in boarding houses, shops, and taverns; and on fishing boats and small hardscrabble farms. Mixing their respective languages with "broken English" on the job, they relied heavily on accordionists to create a musical *lingua franca* amid the house parties and hall dances that highlighted their scant hours of leisure.

As workers who "play," whose labor is occasional, and whose workplace shifts, social-dance musicians, accordionists especially, have toiled mostly at the structural margins of everyday social orders, typically bundling varied repertoires and banding together with fellow border-crossing performers to unify often diverse audiences in festive settings that are dark, crowded, noisy, and rambunctious. In his pathbreaking book *The Making of the English Working Class*, E. P. Thompson chronicles ruling-class alarm about "Satan's Strongholds," evident in the "tendency of authority to regard taverns, fairs, any large congregation of people, as a nuisance—sources of idleness, brawls, sedition, or contagion." Perhaps worse, such condemnations of unruly behavior had been long endorsed, albeit tacitly, whenever "those who have wished to emphasize the sober constitutional ancestry of the working-class movement have sometimes minimized its more robust and rowdy features."[2]

Although Thompson's study is confined to England from roughly 1750 to 1830, a pre-accordion era when ballad-singers and fiddlers stirred crowds, the self-serving, moralizing, top-down rhetoric he documents was later echoed throughout Europe by accordion opponents disturbed about the instrument's proliferation. Mass-produced, portable, inexpensive, loud, pretuned, and enabling both novice and skilled musicians to play melody, harmony, and rhythm simultaneously, the accordion emerged alongside and was associated with such threats to social order as scandalous new couple dances like the polka and the waltz, emigrants' abandonment of hierarchically stratified homelands, and gatherings of industrial workers inclined toward organizing. In 1907 the Swedish composer Hugo Alfvén advocated genocidal measures: "Chop up all the accordions that come in your way, stamp them to a jelly, cut them to pieces, and throw them into the pigsty, because that is where they belong."[3] In Finland, an equally brutal coalition of churchmen, educators, composers, and romantic nationalists, including folklorists, argued that, like heretics, accordions should be burned as "the arch enemy of folk music."[4]

The essays in this volume testify to the accordion's defiant, persistent global vitality, especially as wielded by and for the people who have made their living through physical labor in an industrializing world. In America's Upper Midwest, the accordion, broadly considered, has been the most ubiquitous and emblematic folk-musical instrument from the late nineteenth century through the present. In its varied yet kindred manifestations (diatonic and chromatic button accordions, piano accordions, "Chemnitzer" or "German" concertinas, and Bandonions), the free-reed, push-pull squeezebox has been not only an integral part of numerous ethnically distinct "polka" traditions but also essential to the Upper Midwest's pervasive, creolized "polkabilly" sound.[5] The immigrant and ethnic populations of the region's major urban centers—Chicago, Milwaukee, the "twin cities" of Minneapolis and St. Paul, and the "twin ports" of Duluth and Superior—have likewise fostered a profusion of accordion importers and manufacturers, accordion schools, accordion-instructional publications and sheet music, accordion clubs, and, most recently, an accordion-repair curriculum in a state-supported technical school, several musical halls of fame dominated by accordionists, and an accordion museum.

Thanks to the sustained efforts of musicians, entrepreneurs, cultural activists, and, in recent decades, scholars, we know a good deal about the Upper Midwest's array of accordion-based genres, its virtuoso performers and influential proponents, and its primarily urban accordion infrastructures. We know less, however, about the historical emergence, human particulars, and cultural significance of the accordion as an instrument of choice among local performers in the region's rural and industrialized hinterlands. Heeding E. P. Thompson's admonition that considerations of working-class culture must focus on "real people" living "in a real context,"[6] this essay draws from interviews and field-recording sessions conducted from February 1979 through June 1981 with dozens of rural and working-class musicians and their audiences in the accordion-infused subregion of the Upper Midwest that is the South Shore of Lake Superior. Although they included indigenous peoples, European Americans whose ancestors had arrived several generations earlier, and a few born in the old country, most were the children of immigrants. Ranging from their sixties through their eighties, they collectively recalled the accordion's regional emergence. Complementing their firsthand testimony with newspaper accounts, the work of other folklorists, and subsequent interviews with musicians, my focus here concerns: 1) how South Shore musicians acquired and learned to play assorted accordions; 2) the audiences for whom and contexts within which they performed; and 3) the sources and nature of their repertoires. The resulting cumulative historical and ethnographic portrait illuminates the accordion's significant role in establishing a common, creolized, regional, and enduring working-class culture that was substantially formed between the 1890s and the 1930s.

"Accordion in a Gunny Sack"

In 1899, four-year-old Lucille Milanowski arrived in Wisconsin with her Polish-immigrant parents, settling in a small frame house beneath Ashland's massive ore dock, where so many newcomers toiled through sweltering summers and freezing winters. As she told me more than eighty years later, button accordions were simply around. Compelled by their sound, Lucille began "fooling" with one while in her teens. "Nobody taught me."[7] Her experience as a self-motivated young musician who learned to play "by ear" in a working-class milieu with access to accordions mirrors that of many along the South Shore.

John Wroblewski, for example, was born in Washburn, Wisconsin, in 1907, the eldest of Adolph and Elizabeth Wroblewski's eleven children. Adolph, a Polish immigrant, worked on the city's coal dock and as a seasonal hired man on sur-rounding farms. Of German and Polish descent and raised downstate in Stevens Point, his wife took in boarders, a common practice in that era. Either single men or sojourners who had left wives and children to earn money, the Wroblew-skis' boarders included musicians who entertained and doted upon the family's many children. When John Wroblewski was seven, as his widow Frances told me, a boarder "bought John a little button accordion. . . . That started it. John wore out five accordions. . . . He wouldn't put that thing down. He ate and slept with it. His mother said they couldn't control him." Born likewise in 1907 to Polish im-migrant parents, but just across Chequamegon Bay in the port and sawmill city of Ashland, Frances Milenski Wroblewski was the eldest of eight children. Her father also worked on the docks, while her mother, like Elizabeth Wroblewski, ran one of many boarding houses on Ashland's east side. Here too were musicians aplenty. "In those days you either played a harmonica, or a fiddle, or an accordion."[8]

More than a few played several instruments. Fritz Swanson, born in 1897 to im-migrants from Småland, encountered a fellow Swede, John Nyquist, while working as a cook in his father's Ashland County lumber camp around 1913. An itinerant logger and woodworker, Nyquist toted a gunny sack that held a bucksaw and his precious fiddle. As an old man in the 1930s, he often "played for drinks" by pair-ing his fiddle with Swanson's accordion in the latter's Indian Lake tavern. Once Nyquist fell after having a few too many, smashed his fiddle, and had to rely on the harmonica.[9] Other immigrants—like the Finns Kalle Piirainen, who worked as a miner in Iron Mountain, Michigan, and Matti Maki, who toiled successively in Minnesota lumber camps and in mines on the Gogebic Range before home-steading north of Washburn—were adept at both fiddle and accordion.[10]

Harmonica and accordion, however, and especially button accordion, were the most common combination for the region's multi-instrumentalists in the late nineteenth and early twentieth centuries. Stan Stangle's Czech-born mother, Ludmila, learned to play harmonica and button accordion on the family farm. When she emigrated as teenager around 1905, she slipped the harmonica in her pocket, while her parents made room for her accordion in a big steamship trunk.[11] Since each harmonica's reeds are tuned in a particular key, with each reed yield-ing a different note depending on whether the player is exhaling or inhaling, the instrument's design is fundamentally the same as the button accordion, sub-stituting breath for bellows. Youngsters raised around both instruments often progressed from harmonica to button accordion. Art Moilanen, born in 1917 in the Finnish logging hamlet of Mass City, Michigan, took up harmonica but was soon squeezing out tunes on a button accordion.[12] Matti Maki's son Hugo did the same. Matt Radosevich (b. 1914) began playing harmonica as an eight-year-old farm boy in Benoit, Wisconsin. After "goofing around" secretly with his older brother's three-row button accordion, he entertained for house parties hosted by his Croatian-immigrant parents.[13] Similarly, Tom Johanik, the son of Slovak immigrants who farmed near Moquah, Wisconsin, began playing "harmonica before grade school," then "started out goofing around with an accordion, an old leaky one that my dad had."[14] Bill Hendrickson (b. 1901) was raised to the west of Johanik in the Finnish settlement of Herbster, where he worked in the woods and fished commercially before running a grocery store. His immigrant father "played mouth organ and could sing real good." When Bill showed promise, his dad offered to buy him "a two-row 'cordeen."[15]

Some were content with the harmonica, which was far more portable and inexpensive than a button accordion. Bill Hendrickson's neighbor, Helmer Olavie Wintturi, stuck with harmonica like his father, Matti, who had learned in Finland.[16] In the nearby Finnish settlement of Oulu, Einard Maki recalled that "all the kids used to play harmonica." He purchased his first at age fifteen for fifty cents from an Iron River candy store in 1922.[17] Les Ross Sr. was born in Eben Junction, Michigan, a year later into what he called a "harmonica family." His grandfather, Franz Rosendahl (b. 1864), who immigrated from Finland in 1898, played harmonica, as did both of Les's parents, Frank Ross and Helmi Herrala. "Grandpa played a longer harmonica, maybe eight inches. His moustache was draped over the plates. . . . He mostly played church hymns." When Les was very young, his grandpa bought him a harmonica, and he and his sisters all played.[18] Significantly, however, Les Ross, Einard Maki, Olavie Wintturi, and many other harmonica players in the South Shore region used their tongues deftly to open and close certain reeds, producing both melody and bass rhythm. The resulting sound simulated the right- and left-hand button/reed workings of an accordion and was aptly dubbed "accordion style"—a testimony to the primacy of the button accordion.

Despite their greater weight and bulk relative to fiddles and harmonicas, accordions were among the prized possessions brought to the South Shore region by more than a few immigrants. Reino Maki remarked that his father left Finland with "a button accordion in a gunny sack, that's about all he had." Similarly, Matti Pelto's father Emil and his Uncle Anton, immigrants from Finland to Michigan's Copper Country, as well as Eskel Hokenson's mother, who came from Sweden to settle on Wisconsin's Bayfield Peninsula, Clara Sveda's Czech immigrant father Joe Belofsky, who toiled as a seasonal harvest and mill hand before finding steady work on Ashland's coal dock, and Phil Johanik, who left Slovakia for a cutover farm near Moquah, all packed and played their accordions across oceans and continents.[19] When I visited Tom Johanik in 1981, he had preserved two of his father's old button boxes, both made in Czechoslovakia, as family heirlooms: a small one-row model and a fancy inlaid two-row instrument with leather bellows, still in its original case along with the bill of sale, a tune book, and a catalog of instruments from the Antonín Hlaváek Company.

"German" or "Chemnitzer" concertinas, as well as Bandonions, although not as abundant as button accordions, were also brought by immigrants to the South Shore region. In the Upper Peninsula of Michigan, Julius Chopp (b. 1912) recalled that his father arrived from Croatia in Copper City with "a beat-up concertina."[20] Born the same year as Chopp, his fellow Croatian John Kezele remembered:

> One of our neighbors had a concertina. That was my first love. I didn't think there was sweeter music than listening to a concertina half a mile away, especially on a quiet summer evening when he'd be out on his porch and we'd be out on our porch—listening to the music. Nobody wanted to breathe deep for fear we were going to miss something.[21]

Earl Otchingwanigan, of Ojibwe and Swedish heritage, learned to play Bandonion from Poles in the Crystal Falls area.[22] And Alan Lomax recorded a Lithuanian immigrant concertinist, Charles Ketvirtis (1893–1968), in Newberry, Michigan, for the Library of Congress in 1938.[23] In Wisconsin, Bob Mathiowetz (1918–2008) was raised in a Czech-German musical family in Ashland, where his father led the Mathiowetz Concertina Orchestra in the 1920s.[24] Mathiowetz's Polish friend Louie Kolonko was another Ashland concertinist, while Anton Wolfe in Moquah was such a devoted concertina player that he eventually learned to make them.[25] There were also players in the port cities of Duluth/Superior, where Polish immigrants like Ignatz Czerniak formed trios with fiddle, clarinet, and concertina.[26]

Sometimes conserved within families for decades, the button accordions and related squeezeboxes brought by immigrants more often fell apart from frequent use, or were sold and traded to eager youngsters from the second generation. Such transactions generally originated in local dance halls and lumber camps. Founders of the Finn Settlement north of Washburn built a hall where Matti Maki played the button accordion he'd brought from Finland. His sons Reino, Hugo, and Walter admired their dad's playing but were forbidden to touch his precious instrument. Reino learned nonetheless when his father was out and "Mother turned her back," while Hugo acquired a castoff instrument from a neighbor who also played at the Finn Hall. Young Eskel Hokenson worked in a lumber camp with Ojibwes and French Indians from the nearby Red Cliff Reservation. There the DePerry family and others hosted house parties with square and step dancing to fiddle, pump organ, and accordion.[27] Hokenson bought "a one-row button accordion from an Indian" about 1913. When it burned in a fire a few years later, he purchased a two-row from a neighbor that eventually fell apart. Fritz Swanson acquired his button accordion as a teenager in a lumber camp in 1913, while Matt Saari, born

Figure 7.1 Bob Mathiowetz brandishes his concertina in a trio of photos on display in his basement "music room." Ashland, Wisconsin, 1980. Photograph by James P. Leary.

in 1902 to Finnish immigrants on a farm near Maple, Wisconsin, was inspired by the playing of lumberjacks like Jack Kauti. A kid with little money, he brought a team of horses to help a neighbor make hay and received a button accordion in payment.[28] Saari's neighbor, Ed Pearson, born in 1911 to Swedish immigrants, saved money from trapping weasels to buy a neighbor's button accordion, then practiced in the "back forty" (rural area) until he mastered several tunes.[29]

Rudy Kemppa, raised in the Finnish settlement of Toivola, Michigan, likewise ran a trap line but coveted a new accordion he had seen advertised in a Sears catalog for $4.50. He caught a large weasel, then sent its pelt to a fur company with a note asking them to either send him $4.50 or return the pelt. He received a check for the exact amount and soon possessed a new Hohner two-row.[30] While mail-order suppliers like Sears were often the best new-accordion option for dwellers in such hamlets as Toivola, the port and sawmill town of Ashland, the "Garland City of the North," had stores like Garland City Music by the early twentieth century.[31] Felix Milanowski was only three in 1915 when his Aunt Lucille and her husband bought him the two-row Hohner he still played sixty-five years later.[32] In 1939 Tom Marincel, raised in the Croatian farming community of Sanborn, south of

Ashland, allied with his brother to purchase a three-row button accordion, crafted by the Cleveland-based Slovenian immigrant Anton Mervar, from Garland City Music. Lacking the necessary nineteen dollars, the Marincel boys put down a few dollars each, then conspired with the salesman to conceal the full price from their father, who, amazed by an apparent bargain, paid the balance.[33]

By the late 1930s, however, the button accordion had been losing popularity for more than a decade to the piano accordion, referred to by some, like Eskel Hokenson, as "the big accordion." It is impossible to determine exactly when the modern piano accordion entered the South Shore region. The Ironwood (Michigan) Museum's collection includes a photograph of John Shawbitz, posing with an Italian piano accordion manufactured by the Olverini Company sometime prior to World War I. Although developed earlier, the piano accordion was not well known in the United States before Guido Deiro, who arrived in Seattle from Italy in 1908, began performing on the vaudeville circuit in 1910 and made influential recordings a year later.[34] Perhaps the critical mass of Italians and Slovenians like Shawbitz on the Gogebic Range, centered around Ironwood and Hurley, fostered an early awareness of Deiro and his instrumental innovations.

Many of the musicians I interviewed along the South Shore had listened to 78 rpm recordings made before World War I, like "Sharpshooter's March," by Guido Deiro and his younger brother Pietro, but their recollections of the piano accordion's emergence were roughly a decade later. John Kezele recalled a few piano accordions in Michigan's Copper Country in the early 1920s, but they were not common until later that decade. Clara Sveda remarked similarly about Ashland, where the former button accordionist Fritz Swanson bought his first piano accordion in 1926, with Lucille Milanowski and John Wroblewski following suit about that time. Stan Stangle mentioned a piano accordion "boom" in the late 1920s, when George Vivian sold them "like crazy" out of his Ashland music store. Swanson, Milanowski, Wroblewski, Bill Koskela,[35] and many more were former button accordionists. Even left-handed Elizabeth Bowers Lind, who had learned to play button accordion upside down and backwards, soon did the same with the piano accordion.[36] By the early 1930s, used piano accordions were also common outside of cities like Ashland. John Kezele bought one for forty dollars, while the button accordionist Art Moilanen acquired one through his older brother, whose piano accordionist coworker was killed in a mining accident.

Like any innovation, the piano accordion was embraced by some and shunned by others. Heavier, more expensive, and arguably more complicated to play than the button accordion, the piano accordion was valued for, in the words of the quickly converted Hugo Maki, "its tone, range, versatility." Most crucially, since button accordions were limited to one or two keys, musicians wishing to play

Figure 7.2 Bill Koskela with his piano accordion. Ironwood, Michigan, 1981. Photograph by James P. Leary.

semiprofessionally in ensembles quickly saw the piano accordion's advantages, since it could be played in any key. As Frances Wroblewski put it, the piano accordion was "in style."

Local musicians were also clearly inspired to make instrumental changes by stellar piano accordionists who barnstormed through the region in the 1920s, some of whom doubled as sales agents. Lacking the money to buy piano accordions on their own, Eino Okkonen (b. 1903) and Bill Hendrickson of Herbster pooled their resources to purchase a single piano accordion from a touring performer. The Norwegian-born Thorstein Skarning and His Entertainers from Rice Lake, Wisconsin, featuring the twin piano accordions of Otto and Iva Rindlisbacher, made appearances in the Ashland area.[37] Meanwhile, Viola Turpeinen, who had learned to play button accordion from her Finnish immigrant mother in Crystal Falls, switched to piano accordion in the early 1920s, then teamed with the fiddler John Rosendahl and the piano accordionist Sylvia Polso from Ironwood to form the most influential Finnish American band of her generation. Turpeinen and company made scores of 78 rpm recordings in New York City, toured Finnish American communities from coast to coast, and were even renowned in Finland, but they were especially beloved in their home region, where her distinctive playing is still emulated.[38]

The rise of the piano accordion in the 1920s did not, however, result in the disappearance of button-accordion and concertina players. While some performers welcomed the new, others held fast to the old, often within the same extended family. Lucille Milanowski made the switch, while her nephew Felix did not. Hugo Maki, Gus Mattson, and Eddie Pelto abandoned the button box, but their brothers Reino, Charles, and Matti remained steadfast. Some working musicians—Tom Johanik, Tom Marincel, Bob Mathiowetz, and Matt Radosevich among them—even continued well into the 1980s to lug several button accordions or concertinas to dances so they could switch instruments to play in a range of keys. For the most part, however, those who "played out" for public dances favored the piano accordion, while button-accordion devotees performed at home and "helped out" with music at neighborhood house parties.

"They Made Their Own Music"

For South Shore dwellers in the late nineteenth and early twentieth centuries, home and neighborhood were where most first heard and played accordions. In the case of Stan Stangle,

> We had a little band of our own in the family. My dad played clarinet, mother would play 'cordion, I'd play trumpet, my brother would play baritone horn. My sisters both played baritone. And it was that way almost through the whole neighborhood. . . . They made their own music.

Stangle's parents were Czech or, as they sometimes called themselves, Bohemian, as were most of their neighbors on Ashland's east side. Well-organized, they built a spacious Bohemian Hall with a stage, ample bar and kitchen, and a wooden dance floor. Polish immigrants had their own enclave on Ashland's east side, where Alex Siedlecki was born in 1908. His maternal uncle Leo Chmieleski and brother Ed were fine accordionists, and neighborhood social gatherings were frequent: "Someone would bring an accordion or a violin, we'd roll up the rugs and have a little party." Although there was no formal Polish hall, several family-run taverns served the purpose. Moskau's "Sailor's Retreat," for example, had a hall for extended Polish weddings.[39] Tom Johanik was raised similarly to the strains of his father's button accordion, while the family enjoyed house parties with fellow Slovaks and eventually built a hall in Moquah. Reino and Hugo Maki in Washburn's

Finn Settlement likewise heard their dad squeeze out tunes and enjoyed parties in neighbors' homes and in the community's Finn Hall.

Widespread though it was, this pattern of an accordionist raised in an accordion-playing family, surrounded by house-partying kindred immigrants and enjoying dances at an ethnic hall, was not universal. Communities with mixed ethnicity, whether clustered around a workplace or made up of small farms, were as common as ethnic enclaves. Just as the accordion helped sustain a group's sense of being Czech or Polish or Finnish, so also did the instrument unite musicians and dancers who, despite various cultural backgrounds, were nonetheless conjoined as farmers or laborers in a common locale. Within such settings, where large families prevailed, musically inclined second-generation Americans commingled easily with youthful peers of diverse heritage.

Vivian Eckholm Brevak (b. 1919) was one of eleven children. Her father, Carl, emigrated from Sweden at age fifteen, while her second-generation Norwegian American mother hailed from Clear Lake, Wisconsin. The family lived on a small farm near Barksdale, a railroad stop between Ashland and Washburn, where DuPont ran a munitions factory. Carl Eckholm worked there, while the family kept a few cows and took in boarders. He was a fiddler, his wife played guitar, and Frank Holmes, a Finnish lumberjack boarder with an Anglicized surname, played accordion. Carl Eckholm also made "moonshine" during Prohibition, supplying neighbors and hosting house parties. Vivian played some "second fiddle" but mostly accordion. "All the neighbors got together," she told me, including Anglo-Canadians, Swedes, Norwegians, Finns, Germans, and Hungarians, one of whom she married.[40]

One of thirteen children on a farm in southern Ashland County near Mason and Grandview, Fritz Swanson had similar experiences. His Swedish-immigrant father and a fellow countryman, Bill Lind, played accordion. The elder Swanson also ran lumber camps, employing Norwegians and French Canadians, where music flourished in the evenings. The Swansons' rural neighborhood likewise included many musical families—including the Vervilles and their six boys and six girls—who enjoyed house parties and a few drinks. Rose Verville Swanson, who married one of Fritz's brothers, told me that her father, a French Canadian timber cruiser and butcher born on Isle Royale, and her mother, from St. Paul's Irish community, often played fiddle and harmonica for house parties, joined by local accordionists like the Swansons. In the 1920s Fritz roamed to Detroit for training as an auto mechanic, then worked in Milwaukee and Chicago, where he enjoyed performances by the stellar New York City–based Swedish piano accordionists John Lager and Eric Olzen. When hard times hit in 1929, he returned home to purchase "ten acres with a log cabin" and a dance hall. With the end of Prohibition, Swanson's Indian Lake Tavern quickly became a hangout for musicians and dancers, including Charlie Guski, an accordionist from "Polack Hill" in Washburn, and his sister Angie, whom Fritz soon married. Attracting all sorts of people—including the renowned Norwegian accordionist Ole Lear, who would "chew two boxes of snuff and drink a quart of booze in an evening of playing"—Fritz hosted midsummer picnics for members of the Swedish American Vasa Order and sometimes played for "Swede-Finn" dances at the Runeberg Society Hall on Ashland's west side. Although none of the Swedish Baptists settled just across Indian Lake set foot in Swanson's tavern, they enjoyed his music too as it wafted to their farms on summer evenings.

Unifying though it often was, the accordion also contributed to social divisions. Prior to Father Frank Perkovich's invention of polka masses on Minnesota's Iron Range in the 1970s, the accordion in the Lake Superior region was regarded as an almost exclusively secular instrument associated with dancing and drinking. Like Vivian Eckholm's father, Matt Radosevich's parents made "moonshine and homebrew" to share at house parties, while teenage Felix Milanowski played button accordion for house parties "with dancing and lunch, homebrew and whisky, just about every weekend." Those of an especially pietistic religious orientation, including Swedish Baptists and Finnish Apostolic Lutherans, might appreciate dance melodies from afar but regarded dancing as devilry. Meanwhile, mainstream Finnish and Scandinavian Lutherans, many secular left-wing Finns, and some traditionalist and Christian Ojibwes enjoyed dancing but were strong temperance advocates. Their inclination aligned with federal law during the Prohibition era (1919–32), but even before and after its duration certain public accordion-driven dances accommodated temperance-minded clientele by officially banning alcohol. Einard Maki recalled, however, that while there was no drinking inside at Oulu's Finnish Hall, plenty had a drink outside "on the sly." Eskel Hokenson remembered similarly that the mostly Swedish and Red Cliff Ojibwe musicians and dancers thronging the Men's Club on Little Sand Bay were not permitted to drink openly, yet "there were a hundred cars parked there and, by every steering wheel, a pint of whiskey."

Accordion-smitten teens from anti-dance families paralleled these surreptitious drinkers as, anticipating the guitar-driven teenage rock rebellion of the 1950s, they fell in with bad companions to have fun unbeknownst to strait-laced elders. Les Ross Sr.'s childhood home in Eben Junction was a short walk from the Blue Moon Tavern, frequented by Finnish and a few Irish lumberjacks: "I'd ask them to sing a song, and I'd play along. . . . Many a time I was told, 'You're underage.' I'd go outside, and then they'd accommodate me. There's many, many songs I learned from them boys . . . a rowdy bunch." Later, while they were piling wood, Les's pietistic grandfather, who played only church hymns, asked: "'Did you learn to play yet?' I said, 'Yes.' He said, 'What did you learn?' I said, 'The Five Card.' He said, 'My boy, that's a sin.' After that we mixed our signals." The Finnish Lutheran parents of Matt Saari similarly opposed dancing in Maple, yet he too learned tunes from old lumberjacks. As a teenager, Matt and likeminded pals climbed through the window of the local one-room school to dance in secret. In Oulu, where many Finns regarded dancing as sinful, young Einard Maki, Eino Sarkinen, and their friends sneaked into houses abandoned during the Depression: "We'd walk five, six miles and be up all night dancing."

Teens in Slavic Catholic communities also gathered mostly on their own for dances to an accordionist. Although their festivities occurred with drinking, they were generally undertaken with their parents' knowledge and sometimes culminated in religious worship. Joe Johanik reminisced with his cousins, Tom and Elmer, about teenage parties with fellow Slovaks near Moquah.

> We built that shack on Zurian's land somewhere in the Depression years—'33, '34? And we used to get George Letko to play over there. . . . He was an easier man to wake up than Tom's dad [Philip Johanik]. . . . We could get organized there at ten o'clock and go and get Mr. Letko. And he'd gladly come down and play until any hour of the night [on a one-row button accordion]. We'd be sure that he had something to drink, pass the hat. Maybe he'd get a dollar, dollar and a quarter.

Letko's bellows came apart, unfortunately, on a particularly rowdy occasion: "That's the last time Letko played. The last time I saw his accordion it was sitting on the lilac bush."[41] When Felix Milanowski was fifteen or sixteen, he began playing at house parties for a group of mostly Polish-American peers. In winter, they went on "sleigh-ride parties" to barn dances in the country. "We'd leave the party at three or four in the morning, then make it to church in Ashland, 5:30 mass."

Although accordion playing regularly countered ethnic and religious constraints along the South Shore, it seldom transcended class divisions. It was a thoroughly rural and working-class instrument fostering egalitarian social relations. In contrast to the American South, for example, where African American musicians entertained upper-class whites regularly, I encountered only one instance wherein an accordionist performed for so-called betters. Felix Milanowski's dad was working on Ashland's ore dock in the mid-1920s when his boss, knowing that Milanowski's youngster played button accordion, asked if Felix might entertain his guests at a little party. As Felix told me, his father reckoned, "I don't know if he's good enough for this type of thing, but I'll ask him." The boss replied that it didn't matter, as long as they had a little live music. When Felix agreed to play, his father took him to a big house on Ellis Avenue just after midnight, where he push-pulled "polkas and waltzes until 6:00 in the morning." It was Prohibition, but instead of the usual "home brew" and "moonshine" colored with brown sugar or charcoal, these "big shots," as Felix regarded them, drank and even shared "good stuff" smuggled in from Canada. "I was about fourteen, fifteen, or sixteen at the time.

Then the food came out, and I never seen a table so saturated with food." Nor did he ever again play for such an event.

"Everyone Knew These Tunes"

Perhaps Felix Milanowski's upper-class audience was slumming; perhaps they were rags-to-riches sorts reconnecting with their cultural roots. We'll never know, but we do know that live music for social occasions, eventually dominated by the accordion, was pervasive along the South Shore in the late nineteenth and early twentieth centuries. At the era's outset, in the words of Stan Stangle, "There was no radio, TV, no piano, no Victrola." Tunes were learned by ear, by watching, by trying to play. The region's overall repertoire was comprised chiefly of non-Anglo-European Old World songs and "couple" or "round" dances (polkas, waltzes, schottisches), as well as Anglo-Celtic-French-Indian jigs and reels for step and square dancing. These distinctive yet complementary repertoires were linked historically with fiddling.

The most pervasive European folk-musical instrument from the eighteenth century through much of the nineteenth century, the fiddle—established along the South Shore in the late 1700s, sustained through the fur trade and lumber camps—persisted well into the twentieth century. In 1938, for example, Alan Lomax recorded fiddle tunes like "Devil's Dream" and "Red River Jig" on the Bad River Ojibwe Reservation from Joe Cloud. Born in 1885, Cloud learned to play in 1900 from his father, Menogwaniosh Anakwad (1849–1911), a fiddling lumberjack also known as George Cloud.[42] Likely the first late nineteenth-century immigrant musicians to juxtapose their recently imported old-country melodies with established New World sounds were lumber-camp fiddlers like the aforementioned Swede, John Nyquist. According to Fritz Swanson, Nyquist "could play anything," from Swedish dance tunes to Irish reels.

Just such a mixture of round dances and square dances, ranging from Swedish waltzes to "Turkey in the Straw," characterized Eskel Hokenson's early twentieth-century experience in the Little Sand Bay and Red Cliff area, where Swedes, Ojibwes, and French Indians mingled in lumber camps and community halls. By this time, however, button accordionists like Hokenson shared instrumental prominence with fiddlers. Edith Hukkala told me that around 1914, in southern Ashland County, her mother joined a throng of Finnish immigrants and old-stock Americans to enjoy round and square dances in High Bridge to the strains of a solo button accordion.[43] By the 1920s, active fiddlers were scarce, as accordionists held sway.

In that decade, the old lumber-camp stock of jigs and reels was also fading, in part because of the emergence of "modern" couple dances like the fox trot, in part because older fiddle tunes were superseded by a new crop of "hillbilly" tunes spread by radio and records, but also because a good many new immigrants never learned them in the first place. At Washburn's Finn Hall, according to Reino Maki, accordionists like his father squeezed out "waltzes, polkas, and schottisches" almost exclusively. There was "not much square dancing, like the Swedes and Norwegians [do]." Partially confirming Maki's sweeping assertion, Fritz Swanson, who enjoyed John Nyquist's square-dance fiddling, nonetheless paralleled Reino in favoring his father's mostly Swedish repertoire of "polkas, waltzes, schottisches, and hambos."

Such ethnically specific dance-hall repertoires were often first encountered as the music of home and heart. Eskel Hokenson and Stan Stangle learned Swedish tunes like "Nikolina" and Czech tunes like "Baruška," respectively, from the singing and playing of their button-accordionist mothers. Tom Johanik's father played button accordion at home, while his mother sang Slovak songs, with the kids joining in. "Some people like to fight, but we would sing." Les Ross Sr. likewise long remembered Finnish polkas his father sang and played around the house. Bruno Synkula's parents were married in Poland, but his father emigrated first to work in Pennsylvania mines, Chicago slaughterhouses, Dakota wheat fields, northern Wisconsin lumber camps, and on the Ashland ore docks before earning enough to send for his wife. Neither parent was a musician, but "Mother liked to sing and hum tunes . . . some of them old pieces she heard in the old country." Those tunes stayed with Bruno, and he worked them out on button accordion. "I used to play 'em for her, and she really enjoyed that." Mary Stelmach was born in Ashland in 1904, but her button-accordionist older brother Stanley spent his early childhood in Poland. "He was a shy mama's boy" who never married. Steeped in melodies learned at home from his parents, "he could hear a song once and then he could do it," and so he was in demand for Polish weddings. "They'd ask him to play, but he would not do it unless my mother was there. She had to sit there. Then he would do it."[44] Immigrant households along the South Shore frequently reverberated with songs and hummed melodies, whether accompanied or not, and these were in demand amid public events. As Frances Wroblewski said of her accordion-playing husband's experience: "Everyone knew these tunes, people sang 'em, fellows would hum tunes to John at dances, and then he'd play the tunes."

Many of the tunes that "everyone knew" were, of course, learned through oral/aural tradition and had well-known names in, for example, Croatian ("Samo Nemoj Ti," "Sinoč Si Meni Rekla"), Czech ("Modré Oči," "Svestkova Alej"), Finnish ("Iitin Tiltu," "Isontalon Antti ja Rannanjärvi"), Swedish ("Kväsar Vals," "Johann På Snippen"), and more. Limited at first to a family, neighborhood, or ethnic group, such tunes became widely known by the 1920s, and dedicated accordionists might be expected to play them. More obscure yet compelling melodies sometimes lacked names altogether, or their names were long forgotten and thus reinvented, or they had names that varied. Charles Mattson learned a tune from a fellow worker's hum-

Figure 7.3 Tom Johanik with his father's leather-bellowed button accordion in the community hall, Moquah, Wisconsin, 1980. Photograph by James P. Leary.

ming as they cut hay in 1925. When I recorded him fifty-six years later, he simply called it a "hayfield tune." Vivian Eckholm Brevak knew no proper titles for many tunes she learned from her father and the family's Finnish boarder. Instead, she kept a list of personalized titles in her accordion case—"Dad's Waltz," "Leonard's Schottische," "Sweetie Pie's Polka"—that she jokingly called "sheet music." Many polkas that Les Ross's father performed lacked names, while others had recognized names but combined musical phrases from several sources, thus departing from the standard tune. And although Fritz Swanson knew the real name for "Spikkroks Valsen" (Stove Poker Waltz), he and his pals called it "Pluggen's Roost" in reference to a local hangout of hard-drinking French Canadian lumberjacks.

The titles and musical structures of many pieces played by accordionists stabilized in the 1920s, as what American labels called "foreign series" records became widely available in the region. Some records featured old standards; others offered new compositions. As might be expected, what Alex Siedlecki called "tough ones that can't be sung in church" remained exclusively in oral tradition. Siedlecki, Tom and Elmer Johanik, Matt Saari, Rudy Kemppa, Jingo Viitala Vachon, Les Ross Sr., Matti and Eddie Pelto, and many more performed a few earthy peasant or bawdy lumberjack tunes with colorful titles like one Matti Pelto translated from Finnish as "GetYour Hands Off My Tits before I SockYou in the Mouth."[45] Likewise, Vivian Eckholm Brevak's parents and their large family could not afford to buy records, perhaps because, as she put it, they were already "instrument poor" and preferred homemade music. Nonetheless, most of the region's accordionists learned some of their repertoire from records, including records made by touring performers who frequented the region.

In the early 1920s, Rudy Kemppa bought his first records at Dover Music in Hancock, Michigan. "Somehow that grew into me." Eventually he became a disc jockey for a Finnish-American radio program. Finns in northwestern Wisconsin sometimes bought records while visiting Duluth or Superior, where the Finnish socialist newspaper, *Tyomies*, advertised the latest by such regionally based performers as Arthur Kylander, Elmer Lamppa, the Maki Trio, Hiski Salomaa, and Viola Turpeinen. Stores in Ashland sold records aplenty too. Ed Siedlecki bought Polish 78s from Garland City Music, then played them over and over until he could replicate what he heard on button accordion. Julia Gaik, who worked in an Ashland dime store, invited pals like Felix Malinowski to hear new Polish records she'd purchased on labels like Columbia, Okeh, and White Eagle: "We used to go there and listen to 'em, and then we'd go home and see if we could play 'em on the accordion." Dazzled by Viola Turpeinen's accordion wizardry at Minersville Hall near Marengo, Fritz Swanson bought several of her records. Turpeinen's driving style and minor-key melodies departed from his usual Swedish repertoire, but he persisted: "After three weeks I could play a Finn polka." As was the case in house-party or dance-hall contexts, many of the region's accordionists not only crossed ethnic lines in their record-buying, repertoire-building pursuits, but also acquired popular tunes like "Red Wing" and "It Ain't Gonna Rain No More" from the American musical mainstream.

Established from the 1890s through the 1930s as the South Shore's central house-party and dance-hall instrument, the accordion flourished in immediately ensuing decades, especially as its regional prominence was reinforced by larger, mass-mediated musical trends in American culture. To cite the most significant examples, in the mid-1930s Frank Kuczynski, a Polish American piano accordionist from Milwaukee, joined the guitar-picking Texas-born crooner Gene Autry to create an accordion/string band "singing cowboy" fusion that swept the nation.[46] In the late 1940s, Cleveland's Frankie Yankovic popularized a modern polka sound, combining twin piano accordions with stringed instruments and harmonized English vocals, which resulted in million-selling records, incessant touring, and numerous network-television appearances.[47] And in the early 1950s, having settled in Los Angeles, the North Dakota accordionist and bandleader Lawrence Welk launched his eponymous musical variety show that would become the longest-running program of its kind on national television.[48] Accordionists followed suit along the South Shore, forming ethnic-country polkabilly bands, emulating Yankovic's Americanized Slovenian polka sound, and producing their own regional variety shows, like the still-syndicated *Chmielewski Funtime.*

Successive honky-tonk, rock, and folk-music explosions in the 1950s and 1960s, however, moved many third- and fourth-generation South Shore residents to abandon accordions for guitars. Captivated by Hank Williams, Elvis Presley, and the Duluth-born Bob Dylan, the sons of Vivian Eckholm Brevak, Tom Marincel, and Les Ross Jr., for example, formed country and rock bands. Yet none forgot their regional squeezebox roots. They all continued to make music with their parents. And in the 1990s, the younger Les Ross formed a Finnish-American reggae/rock band, Conga Se Menne, that paid periodic homage to the regional accordion sound by featuring his dad and other old-timers in live and recorded performances. More recently, in late 2008, the second *Wisconsin* CD by the roots rock guitarist Bucky Halker was dedicated to the memory of fellow musician and Ashland resident Bob Mathiowetz (1918–2008): "I'm glad I was able to communicate with and see him again while I worked on these recordings. Bob was elected to the World Concertina Congress in 1999 and kept performing right until the end."[49]

The album's final track, "Concertina Galop," combines a field recording I made of Mathiowetz in 1981 with guitar backup laid down twenty-seven years later by Bucky Halker and Steve Yates. In a similarly retro-contemporary tribute to the South Shore's squeezebox spirit, and at just about the same time that Halker and Yates laid down their rhythm and bass tracks, J. Karjalainen, often dubbed "the Finnish Bruce Springsteen," teamed with the two-row button-box player Veli-Matti Järvenpää on an album, *Paratiisin Pojat* (Paradise Boys), that likewise concludes with a revitalized field recording paying tribute to the accordion.[50] Originally performed for the folklorist Alan Lomax in Newberry, Michigan, 1938, to the tune of "The Battle Hymn of the Republic," Emil Mäki's fanciful lyrics imagine a house party in heaven where St. Peter and the prophets laugh and swing their beards as strings and free reeds resound eternally:

> *Sun kloorin kloorin halleluuja!*
> *Siellä harput ja hanurit ne soi.*
> [Glory, glory hallelujah!
> The lyres and accordions ring out.]

Notes

Interviews with individuals are only cited the first time. Unless otherwise indicated, all interviews were conducted by the author and are part of the Ethnic Music in Northern Wisconsin and Michigan Collection, Mills Music Library, University of Wisconsin. Place names are in Wisconsin, unless otherwise indicated.

1. Bruno Synkula, personal interview, Ashland, 1981.

2. E. P. Thompson, *The Making of the English Working Class* (New York: Vintage Books, 1963), 57, 59.

3. Qtd. in Birgit Kjellström, "Dragspel," *Sohlman's Musiklexikon* 2 (1975): 329–35.

4. Ilkka Kolehmainen, "'Do Not Dance to the Screeching, Insidious Accordions: Burn Them': The Accordion in Finnish Folk Music," *Finnish Musical Quarterly* 2 (1989): 29–31.

5. See Victor Greene, *A Passion for Polkas: Ethnic Old-Time Music in America, 1880–1960* (Berkeley: University of California Press, 1992); James P. Leary, "The German Concertina in the Upper Midwest," in *Land without Nightingales: Music in the Making of German-America*, ed. Philip V. Bohlman and Otto Holzapfel (Madison, Wisc.: Max Kade Institute for German American Studies, 2002), 191–232; and James P. Leary, *Polkabilly: How the Goose Island Ramblers Redefined American Folk Music* (New York: Oxford University Press, 2006).

6. Thompson, *Making of the English Working Class*, 9.

7. Lucille Milanowski, personal interview, Ashland, 1980.

8. Frances Milenski Wroblewski, personal interview, Washburn, 1981.

9. Fritz Swanson, personal interview, Ashland, 1980.

10. Charles Mattson, Covington, Mich.; Hugo Maki, Washburn; Reino Maki, Washburn; interviews by the author and Matthew Gallman, 1981.

11. Stanley Stangle, personal interview, Ashland, 1980.

12. Art Moilanen, interview by the author and Matthew Gallmann, Mass City, Mich., 1981.

13. Matt Radosevich, interview by the author and Matthew Gallmann, Benoit, 1981.

14. Tom Johanik, interview by the author and Matthew Gallmann, Moquah, 1981.

15. Bill Hendrickson, interview by the author and Matthew Gallmann, Herbster, 1981.

16. Helmer Olavie Wintturi, interview by the author and Joel Glickman, Herbster, 1979.

17. Einard Maki, interview by the author and Matthew Gallmann, Oulu, 1981.

18. Les Ross Sr., interview for the Michigan Traditional Arts Program, Negaunee, Mich., 2002.

19. Matti Pelto, interview by Matthew Gallmann, Boston Location, Mich., 1979; Eskel Hokenson, interview by the author and Matthew Gallmann, Little Sand Bay, Bayfield County, 1981; Clara Belsky Sveda, personal interview, Ashland, 1980.

20. Julius Chopp, personal interview, Copper City, Mich., 1984.

21. John Kezele, interview by Joel Glickman and Marina Herman, Copper Country, Mich., 1979.

22. Earl Otchingwanigan, personal interview, Crystal Falls, Mich., 1996.

23. *Traditional Music and Spoken Word Catalog* (American Folklife Center, Library of Congress, Washington, D.C.). Ketvirtis is misspelled as "Ketvertis" in the catalog (Patti Ketvirtis to Hilary Virtanen, email communication, January 14, 2009).

24. Robert Mathiowetz, personal interview, Ashland, 1980.

25. Anton Wolfe, interview for the John Michael Kohler Arts Center, Stevens Point, 1986.

26. Joe Czerniak, interview by Richard March for the Wisconsin Arts Board, Duluth, Minn., 1988.

27. Dolores "Dee" Bainbridge, interview for the Wisconsin Arts Board, Ashland, 1996.

28. Matt Saari, interview by the author and Matthew Gallmann, Maple, 1981.

29. Edwin Pearson, interview by the author and Matthew Gallmann, Maple, 1981.

30. Rudy Kemppa, interview by Matthew Gallmann and Sarah Poynter, Hancock, Mich., 1979.

31. Anonymous, "Garland City Music," *Edison Phonograph Monthly* 6.6 (1908): 14.

32. Felix Milanowski, interviews by the author and Matthew Gallmann, Ashland, 1979–81.

33. Tom Marincel, interview by Richard March and Joel Glickman, Sanborn, 1979.

34. Henry Doktorski and Count Guido Deiro, liner notes to *Guido Deiro, Complete Recorded Works, Vol. 1*, CD 5012 (Champaign, Ill.: Archeophone Records, 2007).

35. Bill Koskela, personal interview, Ironwood, Mich., 1981.

36. Rose Verville Swanson, personal interview, Mason, 1980.

37. James P. Leary, "Ethnic Country Music along Superior's South Shore," *JEMF Quarterly* 19.72 (1983): 219–30; and James P. Leary, "Old-Time Music in Northern Wisconsin," *American Music* 2.1 (1984): 71–87.

38. James P. Leary, "The Legacy of Viola Turpeinen," *Finnish Americana* 8 (1990): 6–11.

39. Alexei Siedlecki, personal interview, Ashland, 1981.

40. Vivian Eckholm Brevak, personal interview, Barksdale, 1981.

41. Joe Johanik, interview by the author and Matthew Gallmann, Moquah, 1981.

42. James P. Leary, "Sawdust and Devils: Indian Fiddling in the Western Great Lakes Region," in *Medicine Fiddle*, ed. James P. Leary (Bismarck: North Dakota Humanities Council, 1992), 30–35.

43. Edith Hukkala, interview by the author and Matthew Gallmann, Washburn, 1981.

44. Mary Stelmach, personal interview, Ashland, 1981.

45. James P. Leary, "Woodsmen, Shanty Boys, Bawdy Songs, and Folklorists in America's Upper Midwest," *Folklore Historian* 24 (2007): 41–63.

46. Wade Hall, *Hell Bent for Music: The Life of Pee Wee King* (Lexington: University Press of Kentucky, 1996), 30–31.

47. Robert Dolgan and Frank Yankovic, *The Polka King: The Life of Frankie Yankovic* (Cleveland: Dillon and Liederbach, 1977).

48. Lawrence Welk, *Wunnerful, Wunnerful! The Autobiography of Lawrence Welk* (New York: Bantam, 1971).

49. Bucky Halker, *Wisconsin 2, 13, 63, vol. 2*, CD 08 (Chicago: Revolting Records, 2008).

50. J. Karjalainen and Veli-Matti Järvenpää, *Paratiisin Pojat: Finnish-American Folksongs*, CD 367 (Tampere, Finland: Poko Rekords, 2008).

⤸ 8 ⤹

Play Me a Tarantella,
a Polka, or Jazz

Italian Americans and the
Currency of Piano-Accordion Music

CHRISTINE F. ZINNI

In 1971, Roxy and Nellie Caccamise traveled from the small town of Batavia, New York, to Bruge, Belgium. Pioneers of the piano accordion in upstate New York, they had been selected to represent the American Accordion Association at the World Championship competition. Among the competitors was one of their students, John Torcello. Like other first- and second-generation Italian American accordionists, the group from western New York first heard the strains of accordion music at neighborhood gatherings of friends and relatives. Unlike earlier generations, Torcello was able to develop a wide-ranging repertoire of Italian folk and classical music, American popular music, and jazz by studying at Roxy and Nellie's accordion school. He became a member of a forty-piece accordion band and shared the local stage with celebrities like the famed concert performer, composer, and radio star Charles Magnante, the jazz artist Art Van Damme, and the orchestra leader Lionel Hampton. Early exposure to accordion music on the streets, as well as the concert stage, inspired Torcello to further his studies. Years later, he went on to play with Luciano Pavarotti and the Los Angeles Philharmonic.

I come to this accordion story from growing up on Batavia's south side. Music was the glue in our neighborhood—a place where, like in other Little Italies across western New York State, Italians and Poles lived side by side. While the *ethos* of our neighborhood has changed, the echo of Italian operas, tarantellas, mazurkas, waltzes, and polkas continues to haunt the streets. Roxy and Nellie's music store still stands, now run by their daughter Rose. Rows of accordions line the walls of the store. The names of the models—Stradella, Soprani, Excelsior, Giulietti, Guerrini, Bell, Pan American, and Italo-American—suggest the breadth and scope of the story and some of its Italian roots. While my love of accordion music evolved out of childhood experiences, it was only years later, when I was conducting oral history research for a video documentary on Italian Americans in the region, that I began to realize the larger significance of our neighborhood story. Following the echo that bellowed back and forth between local, national, and transnational venues, I discovered how Roxy and Nellie's accordion school reflected the Italian American influence on American popular music.

As the anthropologist Dennis Tedlock has stressed, culture is an emergent phenomenon made in the interstices between people.[1] In this essay, I look at the emergence of accordion schools and accordion bands in the United States established by Italian Americans. Approaching the subject from the perspective of grassroots oral history and performance theory, I map the ways in which Roxy and Nellie's efforts were connected to a longer history and larger matrix of Italian American musicians, composers, publishing houses, and manufacturers in New York City, Chicago, and San Francisco. This essay also suggests how the interactions and interplay of peoples within, and through, these community-based networks functioned to create a parallel economy and a cultural space that was not only imbricated in the politics of identity but helped span gaps between folk and fame. Taking an actor/action-centered approach to life-history narratives, I submit that the accordion schools created by Italian Americans operated through the interstices of two cultures and proved to be a strategic intervention in American cultural life with polysemous meanings.

The Beginnings

As the noted Italian American authors Jerre Mangione and Ben Morreale suggested more than fifty years ago, music was the art most closely associated with Italians in the first waves of immigration to the Americas.[2] This is evidenced by the number of Italian stage performers, opera singers, and band musicians that gained prominence between the mid-nineteenth and the early twentieth century. As Victor Greene and Harry W. Swartz assert, by the turn of the century, band music was ubiquitous in the Americas, and Italian musicians were everywhere.[3] Performing selections from grand opera, the flamboyant Alessandro Liberati directed his band from horseback. Known as "The Toscanini of Band Music" and "Svengali of the Baton," Giuseppe Creatore played off the cultural capital of his Neapolitan roots and enthralled audiences with the warmth of his smile, his emotional displays, and demonstrative feelings for his operatic repertoire. The success of Creatore's Italian Band prompted the influx of other musicians from Italy to America—and a host of bandleaders sporting mustachios and wild, long hair. Compared to the strict regimentation of the military ensembles led by Germans and Czechs, Creatore's intense, athletic performances were controversial. Commenting on the hypnotic effect the conductor reportedly had on his audiences, a journalist from the *Chicago Tribune* remarked: "Tone is the wireless medium he uses to reach you, but the current he sends to you is his own intense individuality, and you feel it and obey it just unresistingly as do his men."[4]

Crisscrossing the country to perform at diverse venues, from the mid to the late nineteenth century Italian touring bands led by Italian conductors like Cappa, Grafulla, Scala, Minoliti, Liberati, Franciulli, Creatore, Corrado, Gallo, Vesella, Don Phillipini, Tommasino, Ferulla, Satriano, Cassassa, Donatelli, Ruzzi, and Sorrentini competed with band luminaries like Victor Herbert and John Philip Sousa by featuring Italian *bel canto* pieces, operatic overtures by Verdi, Bellini, and Rossini, as well as popular American marches and ragtime. Towns and cities across the country took up the standard by proudly supporting local municipal bands and incorporating similar repertoires. As Victor Greene opines, "[T]he proliferation of Italian bands reflected the appeal of Italian classical music across class lines"; moreover, "the Italian bands helped define in ethnic terms the music regarded in general as popular music."[5] In the port city of New Orleans, which by 1920 harbored a population of approximately three hundred thousand Italian immigrants, bandleaders like Nick La Rocca, the founder of the Original Dixieland Band, joined African Americans in taking band music in another direction: jazz.

While some Italian band musicians were trained in conservatories abroad, the majority honed their art by playing brass and wind instruments in local bands in their *paese*, or village of origin. Whether leading processions that celebrated the feasts of patron saints or performing for civic holidays and weddings, the "musicking"[6] of Italian bands not only expressed the fervor of *campanilismo* (or "the sense of intense loyalty to one's village or province") but the widely known Italian aesthetic of *fare bella figura* or *fare figura*. Literally meaning "to make a beautiful figure" and/or "to sound good," *fare bella figura* is a cultural code that refers to one's social currency and "style, appearance, flair . . . [and] to succeeding well; to obtaining appreciation and respect—in short, self-presentation and identity, performance, and display."[7] As such, it is intricately related to the idea of *grazia*, or civility and grace. As Christopher Small has noted, "[T]he fundamental nature, and thus the meaning, of music lies not in objects but in the act of musicking. It lies in what people do. Musical objects have meaning only in so far as they contribute to the human activity which is musicking."[8]

Involving *paesani* or villagers in dancing and singing, Italian band music encouraged anything but passivity. Interaction, interplay, and participation were prized features of Italian bands' spectacular aural and visual performances. Little distinction was made between high and low genres, as the repertoire of the bands included Italian operas and overtures as well as local folk songs.

Portable and easy to play, *mandolino* (the mandolin), *chittara battente* (an antique form of the guitar), and the *lira* (lyre) were popular string instruments for backyard gatherings and serenades. Like band music, solo performances allowed musicians to *fare figura* by mixing genres and expressing classical Appolonian elements of civility and grace as well as the ecstatic Dionysian elements of revelry, song, and dance.[9]

During the 1860s, the *organetta* (diatonic button accordion) and *fisarmonica* (chromatic piano accordion) manufactured in Italy arrived on the scene. As the story goes, a pilgrim passing though the territory of Castelfidardo stopped by chance at Antonio Soprani's farmhouse. He gave the rudimentary *accordeon* he was carrying to the farmer's son Paulo, who was so fascinated with the workings of the instrument that he opened a small studio and started to make improvements to the music box. Within a decade, Mariano Dallapè from the town of Stradella had also started crafting accordions. The accordion industry expanded quickly, and accordion music became woven into Italian lifestyles.[10]

By 1900, almost half a million Italians had emigrated to the United States from diverse regions in Italy. Within ten years this number grew to 1.34 million.[11] The music of the immigrants had particular currency inside and outside of their diasporic communities. Contributing to the process of ethnogenesis, it encouraged immigrants who identified primarily with their region to shape a common Italian American identity. From religious and public affairs to weddings, funerals, and carnivals, performances of, and participation in, live musical events served to enact an Italian presence on the American streets as well as to forge ethnic bonds. In this way, musicking became part of a fabric of life that not only expressed the Italian aesthetic of *fare bella figura* but also promoted good intergroup relations. Drawing on folk traditions as well as opera, music was standard fare at social and community centers that featured vaudeville performances. In New York City's Little Italy alone, this musical atmosphere lent itself to a concomitant trade in instrument making and commercial music markets, as community booksellers, music retailers, and publishers promoting *italianità* (representations of Italian culture) sprang up around Mulberry Street on Manhattan's Lower East Side. There, Italian immigrant entrepreneurs fueled the musical pump and filled the need for folk and popular music by publishing sheet music, selling musical instruments, and developing a network of national ties with other dealers in other large cities across the United States and Canada.[12]

Outside of ethnic communities, the currency of Italian music was perhaps most evident at some of the largest attractions of the last century: world's fairs, such as the Pan-American Exposition in Buffalo, New York, in 1901. Drawn to the Queen City on the Lakes through chain migrations and the desire for *pane e lavoro* (bread and work), Italians and Poles were relative newcomers to the ethnic mix of Germans and Irish that had settled western New York. At the turn of the century, Buffalo's burgeoning Little Italy boasted one of the largest Italian populations outside of New York City, San Francisco, Chicago, and New Orleans. Segregated for the most part in a ghetto, incongruities abounded between the material circumstance of immigrants who earned their livelihood as artisans, longshoremen, skilled and unskilled laborers, and shopkeepers, and the widespread appeal of Italian music and opera.

Eclipsing the harsher realities of the city streets and the contingencies of immigrants' everyday lives, the Pan-American's utopian "City of Light" promulgated the idea of human progress from "savagery to civilization" and a new world order based on the Industrial Revolution and education of the masses. Seen as a civilizing influence, band music and opera were considered an integral part of this education. Nina Morgana, a beloved Italian American coloratura soprano who sang opera locally in Buffalo churches and schools, was a featured performer at one of the exposition's main attractions, the Venice in America exhibit. Other great drawing cards at the exposition were the bands of Francesco Fancuilli, the leader of a regiment band based in New York City, a local band directed by Serafina Scinta, and a mandolin band.[13] Along with his activities as director of his concert band, Scinta was also the conductor of a mandolin band at the University of Buffalo. As Jean Dickson points out in her study of the mandolin craze that developed during the later part of the nineteenth century, mandolin music was well incorporated into Buffalo's educational system. It "carried an air of European culture and sophistication." Italian mandolin "orchestras" performed at private parties and mainstream theaters as well as church services, hotels, restaurants, benefits, and Italian clubs like the Aurora, the Filodrammatico, the Cicolo Musicale Bellini, and the Circolo Savoia within the Italian *colonia* (colony).[14]

The currency of Italian bands was also evident in smaller towns with large Italian populations less than sixty miles from the Queen City. During the early part of the century, a string band called the Italian Mascarade or Clown Band was a regular part of celebrations by Batavia's South-Siders. Local newspapers note how the appearance of the newly formed Italian Imperial Concert Band "put a good face" on the Italian communities in Batavia and LeRoy. Significantly, the band staged its performances on the same streets where some of the cities' elites were taking part in Ku Klux Klan demonstrations against the influx of the olive-skinned newcomers and their "immigrant Catholicism."[15]

Roxy and His Accordions

These were some of the local sights and sounds that Roxy's father, Giuseppe Caccamise, witnessed during the early twentieth century after he emigrated to the upstate region together with other *paesani* from Valledormo, Sicily. Giuseppe opened a grocery store on LeRoy's Pleasant Street and contributed to this musical landscape by playing his twelve-bass button accordion from Castelfidardo at backyard gatherings and social events like weddings and *feste* (festivals). He taught his son Roxy how to play a number of traditional folk and popular songs. One's range was limited with the button accordion, however, and Roxy yearned to play the versatile new piano accordion, which had chord buttons for all major and minor keys on the left and three or more chromatic octaves on the right. Roxy recalled years later that his own father thought that asking for accordion lessons was such a luxury, "it was a joke." "I dug ditches and worked on farms to get money for lessons. Then, when I was in my late teens, I was finally able to purchase an accordion and used to spend seven or eight hours a day practicing."[16] After studying classical piano-accordion technique with a local graduate of the Eastman School of Music, Roxy began traveling thirty miles east to the flourishing metropolis of Rochester to meet with James (Jiggs) Carrol, also a graduate of Eastman and the leader of a jazz group called the Harmonicats. Jiggs, who later became the celebrated arranger for the Mitch Miller Orchestra, convinced Roxy to play popular as well as classical and folk music on the accordion.

By 1910, the piano had become the main accompanying instrument for dance orchestras across New York. By the 1930s, "everything seemed faster, microphones had arrived . . . violins were still around, as were pianos (though not so reliably maintained). Important new instruments to western New York dance bands included piano accordion, guitar, and tenor banjo."[17] The pianist and guitarist Roger Kelly, whose extended family entertained regional audiences for more than a century, recalled that his brother Woody played the button accordion since he was ten years old. Eager to learn the piano accordion, Woody purchased one from Roxy.

> Roxy's the guy [who] started accordions around here. He gave Woody lessons. He started everybody. Roxy had an old Chevy coupe with a rumble seat, and he put accordions in there. . . . He'd bring 'em over, and he'd get you started, and he'd sell 'em an "according" and give 'em a lesson. He'd get 'em started; then he'd send another guy around. Roxy had the candle burning on both ends. He was always goin' here in the early thirties—'33, '34 . . . he had everybody playin' accordion.[18]

For Roger, the accordions were "magical things" with their inlaid mother-of-pearl and ivory and their deep crimson, cobalt blue, and jet black casings glistening in the sunlight. Roxy indeed was selling more than material objects—he was also

Figure 8.1 Roxy Caccamise with accordion in peasant dress, ca. 1930. Used by permission of Rose Caccamise.

selling dreams. Roxy successfully convinced the parents of the young Joe Gambino and their neighbor, Sandy Consiglio, that the piano accordion was the thing of the future—an instrument that could launch their sons' fame and fortune. Yet, "they had to look for me under the bridge . . . on Saturday, that was lesson day, see?" said Joe, recalling his aversion to the discipline of practicing.[19] In nearby Mt. Morris, the musical Passamonte brothers remembered how the sound and *look* of the piano accordion captured peoples' imagination during the 1930s. Nick Passamonte recollected a musician named Dutch Longini being the first in the area to buy a piano accordion. "Then," said Nick, "everyone had one. My brother Jim . . . we would get together at [their brother] Gus's barber shop—Gus cutting hair and others playing and challenging one other."[20] Gambino and Consiglio would come over to play at family gatherings. Joe La Barbera, who lived up the road on Stanley Street, also worked for Roxy selling accordions. He started up a successful dance band with his wife and boys.

Roxy's efforts to promote the piano accordion were inspired by the success of Italian accordionists and composers that pioneered the new technology. Building on the legacy of opera stars and band conductors from the last part of nineteenth century and the early twentieth century, these accordionists found that American audiences were not only receptive to Italian music but to an expressive "Italian" style of performance as well. Promoting the new piano accordion's versatility and portability, their wide-ranging repertoires and compositions advanced the new technology's association with modernity.

The Deiro Brothers and Their Magical "Music Boxes"

Coming to America as a "business agent" for Ronco Vercelli, one of numerous accordion manufacturers established by craftsmen in Castelfidardo, Italy, Guido Deiro used the venue of the 1909 Seattle's Alaska-Yukon-Pacific Exposition as a platform for introducing the piano accordion to international audiences. In 1916, Guido joined his brother Pietro, the Pezzolo brothers, and Pietro Frosini to found an accordion club in San Francisco. Originally consisting of thirty-nine accordionists, all of whom were of Italian descent, within a decade membership had grown to 250 musicians. The activities of the club laid the groundwork for a string of accordion schools and bands that began emerging in large cities like San Francisco, Chicago, and New York. In 1927, preceding the performance of his original accordion band at Il Grande Pic-Nic Dell'Accordeon Club, the spectacular picnic in Marin County's Fairfax Park, Guido led a parade and motorcade of several hundred vehicles through the streets of San Francisco. Hailed as a hero of sorts by the local Italian press and termed "the most popular Italian in the city" by English-language newspapers, Guido and his musical protégés helped usher in the accordion craze that would last until the 1970s.[21]

Between his performance at the Alaska-Yukon-Pacific Exposition in Seattle in 1909 and the accordion club's triumphant ride through the streets of San Francisco in 1927, Guido had served as an agent for the Guerrini Accordion Company at the Panama Pacific Exposition in San Diego of 1916, where he won the gold medal for music. Founded by Italian American craftsmen from Castelfidardo who had set up shop in San Francisco, Guerrini became the first American company to fashion

Figure 8.2 Studio photograph of Guido Deiro to publicize his appearance as a headliner at the Palace Theatre, Alpeda Studios, New York,
1909. Used by permission of Count Guido Roberto Deiro.

accordions with piano keyboards, by utilizing some of the designs of Pietro Deiro.[22]
Following the musician Pietro Frosini, who had perfected the "bellows shake" on
his button accordion in vaudeville shows, the Deiro Brothers succeeded in building up a receptive national audience for piano-accordion music. Testifying to the
newfound popularity of the instrument they had helped promote across the nation, Guido proudly declared, that the accordion was being used "everywhere—at
dance halls and in orchestras."[23]

Newspaper clippings from 1910 to 1930 reveal how Guido and Pietro's magical
"music boxes" were important features of the brothers' legendary whistle-stop
tours across several continents. A one San Antonio journalist wrote, "Once the
accordion was the instrument of the proletariat, and to confess a liking for accor-

dion music was to betray exceedingly bad taste. . . . What a change [Guido] Deiro
has wrought! He has made the accordion one of the most musical of instruments,
one who can play it well is accepted as an artist, and there is no better evidence of
discriminating taste than appreciation of such music as Deiro's."[24] Arguably, this
epiphany had much to do with Guido's performance style: his onstage histrionics,
bravado, and "dazzling techniques"—trills, runs, cadenzas, diminuendos, glis-
sando effects, and coloration. Reminiscent of articles praising the band conductor Giuseppe Creatore, critics of the time seemed hypnotized by the physicality
of Guido's act—his "warmth," "physical magnetism," "fire, feeling, and tempo,"
and the way he "threw himself into the rippling, lilting, dancing syncopations of
his music—with his hands, feet, and eyes." *Fare figura*—cutting a beautiful figure,
dressed all in white—the Deiro Brothers projected an air of respectability and
sophistication. The sense of magic, wonderment, and awe surrounding their acts
on the curious "meloaccordeon" was evident in the terms used to describe them:
"maestro," "master," "svengali," "magician," and "wizard."[25]

Performing a wide-ranging repertoire in multiple keys and modes, these
early pioneers of the piano accordion consciously chose to demonstrate to audiences that an instrument associated with the Dionysian elements of Italian folk
music—dance, song, romance, and happiness—was also capable of evoking the
cool Apollonian heights of Italian classical music. Boldly moving from Italian
operatic overtures and light classics to ethnic folk tunes and waltzes to fast-paced
polkas, mazurkas, marches, and rags, their performances had a visceral effect on
crowds. Proud of his fluency in diverse musical idioms, Guido proclaimed that
his instrument "knows every language!"[26]

The Matrix

The development of the recording industry and mass-media technologies in the
early twentieth century decisively advanced the image of the Italian maestros'
cosmopolitanism and fluency in diverse musical idioms.[27] As Peter Muir notes,
during the early 1910s, record companies like Victor and Columbia started tar-
geting domestic as well as mainstream markets: "Though Italian Americans constituted the second-largest ethnic community in the United States after German
Americans, Italians bought more records than their German counterparts. Indeed, according to the ethnic discographer Pekka Gronow, far more records were
distributed to Italian Americans than to any other single ethnic group."[28] From
1894 to 1943, almost five hundred Italian American individuals and groups made
ethnic recordings in America.

Over the course of a few decades, Guido released a stunning "103 sides with
Columbia—four with the independent Harmony label and two Edison cylinders.

His brother Pietro released 152 sides over [a] quarter of a century."[29] Building on the vaudeville routines that brought them to national prominence, the Deiro Brothers, Pietro Frosini, and Antonio Galla-Rini recorded across a wide range of styles, from light classical and operatic to Neapolitans songs, marches, waltzes, mazurka, polkas, and rags. Cutting his first record in 1911 through Columbia, Deiro recorded two compositions that were destined to become favorites of the accordion public: "Sharpshooters March" and "Ciribiribin." Reissued nine different times, "Ciribiribin" reportedly "outsold almost everything else in the catalogue."[30]

Print technologies came into play, as an intricate network of community-based Italian American publishing houses, like those run by Biaggio Quattrociocche and Octavi Pagani, not only set the standard but also created a parallel capitalist economy by publishing the sheet music of the accordion stars. Pietro Deiro entered the lucrative business by founding his own publishing company.

Like the entrepreneuring Italian Americans involved in the production and distribution of accordion music, accordion manufacturers created an alternative economy revolving around production of the instrument. A number of Italian Americans also set up dealerships for instruments crafted in the United States and Italy. This matrix of manufacturers and dealers worked together with the accordion stars to develop the technology of the instrument and to create signature brands and custom-made models for recording artists from diverse ethnic groups. The piano accordions they designed effectively bore the signature mark of their Italian and Italian American makers, thus further inscribing associations of the instrument with Italian style and artistry. Personalizing the accordions according to ethnicity, color, shape, and size, models not only were made to the specifications of particular recording artists but often stamped with their names.

In this way, on a personal as well as professional basis, the first- and second-generation Italian American founders of accordion schools became wedded to the development of the material objects that brought them fame and fortune. Underscoring how the look and sound of the "dry-tuned" Excelsior achieved iconic stature among Italian American musicians, the composer and accordionist William Schimmel writes: "The Excelsior was Sinatra, it was the 21 Club. It was the Stork Club! It was a musical culmination of the Italian American mentality and its relations to the cultural mainstream of art and entertainment. No shades of gray. [It said,] 'I can afford it!'"[31]

Après Vaudeville: Emergence of Accordion Schools

Gaining a foothold in the public spotlight through records, radio, movies, and the publication of sheet music, and bolstered by the appeal of well-crafted instruments

Figure 8.3 Italo-American Accordion Manufacturing Company
advertisement for the "Guido Deiro Italotone," *Accordion News*, July
1935. Used by permission of The Deiro Archive, The Center for the
Study of Free-Reed Instruments, Mina Rees Library Collection, the
Graduate Center of the City University of New York. I am especially
grateful to Allan Atlas, the director of the Center for the Study of
Free-Reed Instruments, and Michael Handis, the associate librarian
for Collection Management, The Mina Rees Library, for their help in
locating information.

made by compatriots, Italian American accordionists used their celebrity status to form accordion clubs, schools, and bands. The success of accordion schools like those set up by the Deiro Brothers, Frosini, and Galla-Rini served as a template for Italian American musicians across the country to follow suit.

The acclaim surrounding the original accordion club in San Francisco, started in 1916, encouraged Guido Deiro and Antonio Galla-Rini, who had spent twenty years in vaudeville, to open their own accordion studios along the Pacific Coast. Galla-Rini later established a chain of accordion schools on the East Coast. Like Pietro Deiro, Galla-Rini wrote his own accordion-method books and produced his own radio shows. Frosini, the master of the bellows shakes, also opened an accordion studio in New York City, mentoring talented students for local venues and the concert stage.

Across the country, a community-based alternative economy emerged as accordion schools and studios, run predominately by Italian Americans, competed with Wurlitzer for young male and female students. As Greene notes, by the end of 1939, "[O]ne estimate anticipated there would be 35,000 students in accordion schools . . . one observer counted thirty-six accordion schools in sixteen states."[32] The idea of becoming fluent in diverse musical languages, and thus being able to negotiate cultural divides and distinctions of race, class, and gender, was an explicit part of the instruction in the schools and was particularly appealing to ethnic peoples. In *The Golden Age of the Accordions,* Manny Quartucci notes how Leo Piersanti, the exclusive Excelsior dealer in Chicago, founded an accordion school that offered instruction books in English and Italian. According to Quartucci, one of the largest schools in Chicago was run by Dave Biasco, who, during the heyday of the accordion craze in the 1930s and 1940s, employed over twenty teachers and trained up to one thousand students per week at its peak.[33]

Interactions between accordion teachers, students, accordion makers, and producers and distributors of sheet music led to elaborately staged spectacles of accordion bands, which in turn helped promote the Italian American accordion schools that fostered them. Since the founding of the San Francisco Accordion Club in 1916, two of the original members, Caesar and John Pezzolo, had organized yearly accordion picnics in the Bay Area. Participatory communal events publicized in English- and Italian-language newspapers, the picnics reportedly reached their apotheosis of Dionysian splendor in 1933, when Caesar Pezzolo staged a thousand-piece accordion-band concert in Marin County's California Park, featuring headliners like Pietro Deiro. The concert was attended by approximately ten thousand people. As Guido Canevari, the owner of one of the largest accordion centers and schools in the area, recalls: "I never saw so much Italian salami, bread, cheese, and red wine in my life! People danced to their heart's content."[34] Not to be outdone by their neighbors to the north, Guido Deiro organized and directed the world's largest accordion band of 1,500 players for the First Annual Southern California Music Festival at the Los Angeles Coliseum in 1940. Apparently, "[T]he only group larger than Guido's accordion band was the [brass] band of 2,500 players."[35]

Things coalesced in a somewhat different manner on the East Coast during the later part of the 1930s, with the combined efforts of Pietro Deiro, Pietro Frosini, and the talented accordionists Charles Magnante and Joe Biviano, who aimed at "classizing" the instrument and bringing its players to the concert stage. Together with his protégés, Magnante founded the American Accordion Association in 1939. Intent on altering perceptions about the instrument's "limitations" and highlighting its capacity for Apollonian perfection, Magnante's groundbreaking performance at Carnegie Hall in 1939 was clearly a strategic intervention in the historical record of the instrument's—and by association, Italian American musicians'—capabilities.[36]

Local Legacies

This climate of excitement was the backdrop against which Roxy and Nellie ventured into the accordion world. Nellie Barsocchi (b. 1918) was only fifteen years old when she met Roxy, but she had already established a reputation in Niagara Country as a *wunderkind* of sorts on the accordion. Participating in numerous amateur contests, like the one at Amedola Theater, where she and her father received five dollars as first prize, in her early teens Nellie exhibited all the makings of a successful stage career. Her father took her to hear Pietro Deiro at Toronto's Eaton Hall when she was twelve years old. Thus, when Nellie met Roxy three years later, she was not only able to play some of Deiro's most difficult compositions, she had also mastered the bellows shake of Pietro Frosini. Regularly commissioned to play before bigwigs like the Rands, the owners of Marine Trust Bank, and other members of Buffalo's high-society circuit, with her ability to perform on her accordion Italian operas such as "Il Trovatore," Nellie's repertoire included well-known American marches, overtures, and folk and popular music.[37]

Nellie recalled how she and Roxy started out with two accordions in the 1930s: the Superior that her father had traded in for her well-worn Ranco Antonio, and Roxy's Italo-American. Renting studio rooms in the nearby towns of Mt. Morris and Geneseo, where they gave lessons on weekends, the couple put most of their energy into staking a musical claim in Batavia. Eventually handing over the responsibility of teaching students in the outlying districts to one of their star students, Jimmy Cassiano, Roxy and Nellie focused on growing their Batavia "studio" cum music store, which quickly became a social center and gathering place for regional musicians, music lovers, and musicking.

Figure 8.4 Nellie Barsocchi with accordion at age twelve, early 1930s. Used by permission of Rose Caccamise.

Characterizing their early beginnings as "barter days," with customers trading coal, vinegar, tomatoes, and other useful items in exchange for lessons, the couple turned into dealers of prestigious lines of accordions like Excelsior, Hohner, Soprani, Giulietti, Superior, and Italo-American. Presenting themselves as teachers, concert accordionists, and specialists of classical and folk music, Roxy and Nellie started their own accordion school in 1939, which quickly attracted local and national acclaim.[38] Ambassadors of the piano accordion and Italian style, the couple taught their students a variety of Italian folk tunes, tarantellas, mazurkas, and polkas, as well as Italian classical songs, waltzes, sonatas, overtures, and Tin Pan Alley hits. By doing so, they afforded the sons and daughters of Italian immigrants the opportunity to perform at venues ranging from Italian and Polish weddings, to country-and-western gigs, to concert halls. The students' mastery of different musical languages on the accordion catapulted them into a larger public sphere, where they could demonstrate the modernity and versatility of instrument and artist alike.

Coinciding with the heyday of the national accordion craze, Roxy and Nellie's rise to musical stardom and the success of their accordion school marked the transition of Italian music from the back yard to the concert stage. By the late 1940s, radio and television, along with the outreach of the record and movie industries, made fame seem within the reach of numerous musicians living in the rural countryside. Building on the legacy of Italian opera singers, popular vocalists, and stage performers from earlier decades, the modern media served to solidify the associations between music and identity—often bringing the ethnic musicians and their music from the margins to the center stage.

The currency of accordion music was evident in the kinds of high-profile venues where Roxy and Nellie were invited to perform. Booked into gigs at local political events and rallies in and around Batavia, the couple loomed large in the cultural landscape of the region, playing duets and solos for Eleanor Roosevelt as well as the governor of New York, Herbert Lehman. Stimulated by a sense of place, in his "spare time" Roxy composed songs like the "Jackson Street Polka," "LeRoy March," and "Friendship Polka"—tunes that were performed in local nightspots, at regional civic events, and on the national stage by close friends, students, and compatriots. Quoted in *Accordion World* magazine, the jazz great Lionel Hampton heralded Roxy's "Jackson Street Polka" as "the best polka I ever heard."[39]

In the mid-1940s, the Caccamises broadcast a weekly program from Batavia's WBTA radio station. Following the example of popular Italian radio programs airing from Rochester, Niagara Falls, and New York City, their show highlighted requests and dedications, but it went one step further: opening with original compositions by Roxy like "My Friendship Polka" and/or duets with Nellie and female accordionists and protégées like Dolores Penepento, the program showcased the proficiency of the young accordion students performing a range of musical styles, from Italian folk and classical to American Tin Pan Alley hits, marches, and country and western. As the strains of "Speranze Perdute" flowed into the "Blue Danube Waltz," the audiences became versed in numerous musical styles.

The agency of the Caccamises in utilizing communication technologies mirrored that of Pietro Deiro and Frosini, as well as second-generation accordion stars like Magnante and Biviano, with whom they became fast friends. At meetings on Mulberry Street in New York City's Little Italy, Roxy and Nellie gained firsthand knowledge about Frosini's broadcasts of a radio show six mornings a week, as well as Magnante's and Biviano's commercial recordings for NBC.

From these experiences, Roxy and Nellie learned much about production and promotion. Their work organizing regional seminars on accordion music and their involvement in the school and stage not only provided a service to students and the community, it also illustrated a fact underscored in trade publications like *Accordion World*: accordions were "a Big Business."[40] Regularly traveling to Chicago to attend trade shows at the Palmer House with her parents, Rose Caccamise remembers how "it was the place where they all assembled, and it was a wonderful time! To *see* and *hear* the latest new models that would come out: new features like the electronic ones . . . and the wonderful experience of meeting the artists and hearing them perform. They were all there!"[41]

Developing a personal relationship with celebrities like Magnante as well as manufacturers, who would mention them by name in articles and/or on radio programs when the couple started organizing local media events, celebrity accordion artists agreed to come to their community and perform.

Scheduled at the local entrepreneur (and their friend) Charles Mancuso's theater in Batavia, national celebrities shared the stage with the Caccamises' forty-member accordion band. Playing to packed houses and people traveling long distances to see them perform, the retinue of accordion "stars" shifted boundary lines between town and country, ostensibly putting the township of Batavia in a league with larger cities like Buffalo and Rochester.

By the 1960s, the couple had achieved local and national acclaim and passed on their knowledge to a host of musical prodigies. Giving their students a way of entertaining others while making the Italian standard visible, accordion music not only provided entrée into the worlds "across the tracks" and recognition for musicians of ethnic descent but also regular travel and a wealth of experiences.

Rooted in civic ties and local connections, the Caccamises' accordion story continued to bellow back and forth between global, national, and local venues. On the local level, the couples' reputation as ambassadors of accordion music and Italian style influenced local politics and supported their school, while their work with students impacted their national prestige. Encouraged to enter regional and national competitions, a number of Roxy and Nellie's students, like Joe Robusto, Marilyn Strogen, and John Torcello, went on to win national and international championships. Torcello toured with Luciano Pavarotti, worked in Hollywood, and became a famous recording artist and entrepreneur.

Roxy and Nellie's school and advocacy of accordion music had an impact not only on the future and fate of individual students but also on the character and ambience of their community at large. Local musicians and residents attest to how the Caccamises and their students put Batavia on the map as "an accordion town."

By the 1950s and 1960s, the most popular bars and restaurants sported dance halls and clubs, and, according to Joe and Virginia Gambino, Roxy and Nellie's "progenies" were "playing 'em all." Alluding to the impact of the beloved Chordovox accordion and other instruments purchased from Roxy, Joe claimed, "Without the accordion I wouldn't have existed. . . . There was not one place I didn't play in . . . hotels, clubs, you name it. I played in 'em all."[42]

The relevance of accordion music in the lives of second-generation Italian Americans in the Genesee Valley is illustrated in the testimony of yet another student of Roxy's, Sandy Consiglio. A butcher by trade, Consiglio spent his days "cutting meat," but his nights were devoted to practicing the accordion. Modeling his playing after the Italian American star Charles Magnante, Consiglio claimed that he possessed all of Magnante's records, and in developing his own style, he took inspiration from studying the celebrity's style of playing riffs and arpeggios on an Excelsior. Consiglio recalls that the greatest thrill of his life came one day in 1957, when Roxy asked him "to do him a favor" and pick up Magnante at the airport.[43]

By the mid-1960s, rock 'n' roll and cool jazz were "in," and Roxy found himself selling more guitars than accordions. Although Roxy is no longer around, the strains of young people studying accordion music still resound through the store, now run by his daughter Rose. Across a wide swath of counties, local accordion stars continue to draw on their folk traditions to create a "useable present," inspire younger protégés, and move audiences of all ages to dance—thus demonstrating, in so many ways, the dynamic links between music and culture, actively produced and renegotiated in the interstices between people(s) and place(s).

Conclusion

From the early part of the twentieth century to the present day, accordion music has variously served as a counterhegemonic force and means of assimilation among Italian Americans. The accordion schools and bands that emerged out of a matrix of Italian American musicians and entrepreneurs during the 1920s through the 1960s had a dynamic impact on American popular culture—contributing, like the Italian concert and mandolin bands that preceded them, to the appreciation of an Italian style.

Creating an alternative economy during a crucial period in American culture, when Italian immigrants were vying for economic and political power, the production and distribution of accordion music was, literally and figuratively, instrumental in transforming individuals' material circumstances. Perhaps its greatest currency, however, lay in the way musicking on the piano accordion helped create a sense of *communitas* in Little Italies, shape Italian American identities, and enact their presence in America. Learning to perform diverse musical idioms by studying at an accordion school held out the promise of a measure of respect and advancement across lines of race and class—and something more: the demonstration that, in the musical sphere, Italian Americans were a veritable force that could not be confined to the margins.

Notes

1. Dennis Tedlock and Bruce Mannheim, Introduction to *The Dialogic Emergence of Culture*, ed. Dennis Tedlock and Bruce Mannheim (Urbana: University of Illinois Press, 1995), 1–33. On how Italian American identity is "situational and labile," see Robert A. Orsi, "Introduction: Crossing the City Line," in *Gods of the City: Religion and the American Urban Landscape*, ed. Robert A. Orsi (Bloomington: Indiana University Press, 1999), 1–78; and Harris M. Berger and Giovanna P. Del Negro, *Identity and Everyday Life: Essays in the Study of Folklore, Music, and Popular Culture* (Middletown, Conn.: Wesleyan University Press, 2004). On performance style(s) and the ways in which class relations and power differentials inform the emergent qualities of music, see Charles Keil and Steve Feld, eds., *Music Grooves: Essays and Dialogues* (Chicago: University of Chicago Press, 1994); and Helena Simonett, *Banda: Mexican Musical Life across Borders* (Middletown, Conn.: Wesleyan University Press, 2001).

2. Jerre Mangione and Ben Morreale, *La Storia: Five Centuries of the Italian American Experience* (New York: Harper-Collins, 1992).

3. Victor Greene, "Ethnic Music and American Band Music" and "Italian Bands and American Popular Music," in *A Passion for Polka: Old-Time Ethnic Music in America* (Berkeley: University of California Press, 1992), 31–46; Harry W. Swartz, "Creatore Starts Italian Band Vogue," in *Bands of America* (New York: DeCapo Press, 1975), 212–23.

4. Qtd. in Swartz, *Bands of America*, 212–23.

5. Greene, *Passion for Polka*, 35–39. Greene notes that there were more than five thousand wind bands representing every community in Italy during the nineteenth century.

6. The term "musicking," the present participle of the verb "to music," was originally coined by the ethnomusicologist Christopher Small to emphasize the active, "emergent," dynamic elements occurring between and among musicians, audiences, dancers, and composers in any musical event. See Christopher Small, "Whose Music Do We Teach Anyway?" address to the Music Educators National Conference in Washington, D.C., 1990, featured on the website of MUSE (Musicians United for a Superior Education). Small uses the term to underscore "that remarkable form of human encounter in which people come together to make meanings, to explore and affirm and, yes, celebrate for a while their common humanity and their sense of who they are and of where they belong." See http://www.musekids.org/whose.html (accessed December 27, 2011). Charles Keil also takes up the term to highlight the interactive elements of sounding, singing, dancing, and celebrating. See Charles Keil, Angeliki Vellou Keil, and Dick Blau, *Polka Happiness* (Philadelphia: Temple Press, 1992); Keil and Feld, *Music Grooves*. For a comparative study of how brass-band music became part of the lifestyle and identity among Sinaloan rural and urban working classes, see Simonett, *Banda*.

7. Gloria Nardini, *Che Bella Figura! The Power of Performance in an Italian Ladies' Club in Chicago* (New York: State University of New York Press, 1997), 5–33; Giovanna P. Del Negro, *The Passeggiata and Popular Culture in an Italian Town: Folklore and the Performance of Modernity* (Montreal: McGill-Queen's University Press, 2004). Both authors note how form and substance come together in the concept of *fare bella figura,* a central metaphor of Italian life and arbiter of Italian social mores. For performance traditions in Italian music, see the work of Alan Lomax and Anna Lomax Wood, http://research.culturalequity.org/get-radio-detailed-show.do?showId=28 (accessed January 23, 2012); Luisa Del Giudice and Nancy Van Deusen, eds., *Performing Ecstasies: Music, Dance, and Ritual in the Mediterranean* (Ottawa: Institute of Mediaeval Music, 2005).

8. Christopher Small, "Musicking: A Ritual in Social Space," lecture at the University of Melbourne, June 6, 1995, http://www.musekids.org/musicking.html (accessed January 30, 2009).

9. Keil posits a dialectic in which the Apollonian style as expressive of a concern with perfection, and individuation is contrasted with the Dionysian or Bacchic loss of self, primal urge-to-merge, ecstasy, and revelry. He notes that "both styles have required a balancing of both forces to grow . . . [and] are confused and confusing due to the pervasive influence of mass mediation on music in this century" (Keil and Feld, "People's Music Comparatively," in *Music Grooves,* 211–17). Ann Hetzel-Gunkel takes up this issue in "Polka as a Counter-Hegemonic Practice," *Popular Music and Society* 27.4 (2004): 407–27.

10. Ivo Baldoni and Beniamino Bugiolacchi, "The Fascinating History of the Accordion," in *Who's Who in the World of Accordions,* ed. Norman N. Seaton (Dallas: Texas Accordion Association Production, 1994), 72–73.

11. U.S. Census Bureau, Population Division.

12. Greene, *Passion for Polka,* 31–46. See also Michael Schlesinger, "Italian Music in New York," *New York Journal of Folklore* 14.3 (1988): 129–38. Orsi, Introduction, 1–78, notes that Italian immigrants have enacted their presence on city streets through religious processions, backyard serenades, sidewalk conversations, and games. See also Joseph Sciorra, "We Go Where the Italians Live: Religious Processions as Ethnic and Territorial Markers in a Multi-ethnic Brooklyn Neighborhood," in *Gods of the City: Religion and the American Urban Landscape,* ed. Robert Orsi (Bloomington: Indiana University Press, 1999), 314–40; Anna Lomax Chairetakis and Alan Lomax, liner notes and recordings of musicians in Niagara frontier and South Ontario, *Chesta a la Voci ca Canuscite (This Is the Voice You Know)* LP GVM675 (New York: Global Village, 1986).

13. Virginia Yans-McLaughlin, *Family and Community: Italian Immigrants in Buffalo, 1880–1930* (Urbana: University of Illinois Press, 1982); see also Frank Cipolla, "Schedule of the Scinta Band—August 21, 1901," http://library.buffalo.edu/libraries/exhibits/panam/music/bands/scintaaug21.html, and "The Italian Community of Buffalo and the Pan-American Exposition," http://library.buffalo.edu/libraries/exhibits/panam/immigrants/italians.html (accessed December 28, 2011).

14. Jean Dickson, "Mandolin Mania in Buffalo's Italian Community 1895–1918," *Journal of World Anthropology: Occasional Papers* 2.2 (2006): 1–15; Ferdinando Magnani, *La*

città di Buffalo, N.Y.: E paesi circonvicini e le colonie Italiane (Buffalo: Tipografia Editrice Italiana, 1908).

15. Irene Gates and Katherine Gill, eds., *The Legacy of Italian Americans in Genesee County* (Interlacken, N.Y.: Heart of Lakes Pubishing, 1992).

16. Christine F. Zinni, "An Accordion Story: Following the Trail of Roxy and Nellie Caccamise," *Voices: The New York Journal of Folklore* 31 (2005): 3–4, 28–34. "Meet Roxie Caccamise," *Accordion World Magazine: Convention Issue* 60.8 (June, 1950): 45; "The Roxy Caccamise Family," *Accordion and Guitar World* 31.8 (December 1967-January 1968): 15; Roxy qtd. in Lynn Bellusicio, "The LeRoy March," *LeRoy Daily Pennysaver*, March 1986.

17. Jim Kimball elaborates on this issue in "Roger Kelly: Reminiscing On Old Time Music," in *Praisin', Pickin', and Prancin'*, ed. Daniel Ward (Batavia, N.Y.: Genesee Arts Council, 1992), 16. See also Karen Park Canning and Jim Kimball, "The Italian Troubadours and Italian Music of the Genesee Valley," in *Order and Creativity: Dynamic Expression of a Shared Way of Life*, ed. Dan Ward (Batavia, N.Y.: Genesee-Orleans Regional Arts Council, 1994), 6–9; Jim Kimball, "Accordions and Concertina: A Historical Perspective," in *Folk Arts: Our Living Traditions* (Batavia, N.Y.: Genesee-Orleans Regional Arts Council, 1978), 6–16.

18. Nellie and Rose Caccamise, personal interviews, Batavia, N.Y.; and Roger Kelly, personal interviews, Perry, N.Y., December 1997 through March 1998.

19. Joe and Virginia Gambino, personal interview, Geneso, N.Y., December 1998.

20. Nick and Frank Passamonte, personal interview (with Karen Park Canning), Mt. Morris, N.Y., November 1997.

21. "Il Grande Pic-Nic Dell'Accordeon Club" (August 21, 1927), in *Guido Deiro Scrapbook*, no. 2, pp. 27 and 30, Guido Deiro Archives, City College of New York (hereafter *Guido Deiro Scrapbook*); see also Ronald Flynn, Edwin Davidson, and Edward Chavez, eds., *The Golden Age of the Accordion* (Shertz, Tex.: Flynn Publishing, 1992), Peter C. Muir, "Looks Like a Cash Register and Sounds Worse," *Free Reed Journal* 3 (2001): 55–79; "Guido and Accordion Clubs," Guido Deiro Homepage, http://guidodeiro.com/accordionclubs .html (accessed November 22, 2008).

22. "Deiro Wins Gold Medal," *San Diego Union*, July 12, 1916, in *Guido Deiro Scrapbook* no. 1, p. 43.

23. "Famous Musician to Play at Expo," *San Diego Union*, ca. 1916, in *Guido Deiro Scrapbook* no. 1, p. 41.

24. "Deiro Tops Majestic Bill," *San Antonio Times*, ca. 1916–1917, in *Guido Deiro Scrapbook* no. 1, p. 46.

25. The terms attributed to the Deiro Brothers are taken from newspaper articles in *Guido Deiro Scrapbook* nos. 1 and 2.

26. "Deiro Most Famed Accordionist," *Long Beach Times*, ca. 1923, in *Guido Deiro Scrapbook* no. 1, p. 63.

27. Keil claims that "style is a reflection of class forces" and that "style has its basis in community recreation through ritual . . . in class society the media of the dominant class must be utilized for the style to be legitimized" (Keil, "People's Music Comparatively," 202). See also Hetzel-Gunkel, "Polka as a Counter-Hegemonic Practice," 407–27; Mark

Kohan, "The Polka and the Accordion," *Voices: The New York Journal of Folklore* 27.1 (2001): 22–23.

28. Peter Muir, "The Deiro Recordings," *Free Reed Journal* 4 (2002): 9. His assessment is based on Pekka Gronow, "Ethnic Recording: An Introduction," in *Ethnic Recordings in America* (Washington DC: American Folklife Center/Library of Congress, 1982), 23.

29. Muir, "Looks Like a Cash Register," 63.

30. Ibid.

31. William Schimmel, "Excelsior! The Best and Nothing but the Best," *Free Reed Journal* 4 (2002): 61–62.

32. Greene, *Passion for Polka*, 125.

33. Manny Quartucci, "Some Thoughts about the Accordion in Chicago and the Midwest," in *The Golden Age of the Accordion*, ed. Ronald Flynn, Edwin Davidson, and Edward Chavez (Shertz, Tex.: Flynn Publishing, 1992), 93.

34. Guido Canevari, "San Francisco—The Early Beginnings," in *The Golden Age of the Accordion*, ed. Ronald Flynn, Edwin Davidson, and Edward Chavez (Shertz, Tex.: Flynn Publishing, 1992), 9–10.

35. Ibid., 9; and "Saturday Fixed as Fiesta Day," *Los Angeles Times*, May 28, 1940, in *Guido Deiro Notebooks*, no. 2, p. 72.

36. Joe Biviano, "History is Made at the Carnegie!" in *The Golden Age of the Accordion*, ed. Ronald Flynn, Edwin Davidson, and Edward Chavez (Shertz, Tex.: Flynn Publishing, 1992), 184–86.

37. Nellie Caccamise, personal interviews, Roxy's Music Store, Batavia, N.Y., December 28, 1997 and January 4, 1998

38. Lela Hart Dunn, "Roxy Caccamise, Famed Accordionist," *Accordion and Guitar World* 28.4 (August-September 1963): 19; "Meet Roxy Caccamise," *Accordion World: Convention Issue* 60.8 (June 1950): 45.

39. Qtd. in ibid.

40. "The Accordion Is a Big Business," *Accordion World* 60.8 (June 1950): 28–29, 56–57.

41. Rose Caccamise, personal interview, Batavia, N.Y., December 2008.

42. Joe Gambino, personal interview, Geneseo, N.Y., 1997.

43. Sandy Consiglio and Al Mastrolio, personal interview, Perry, N.Y., July 29, 1998.

⚘ **9** ⚘

The Klezmer Accordion

An Outsider among Outsiders

JOSHUA HOROWITZ

There are many Jewish musical cultures spread across the world today, yet klezmer, the instrumental music of the Eastern European Jews, enjoys almost universal popularity.[1] It is generally accepted that clarinet and violin are traditional klezmer instruments, as defined by the instrumental parameters of recorded documentation from the earliest years. The "klezmer revival" has encouraged modern-day klezmer musicians to learn the style of their Old World predecessors by studying the vast corpus of 78 rpm discs still available. Because most of the recordings made in the United States between 1915 and 1942 feature clarinet as the lead instrument, it is considered the most "traditional" instrument in klezmer music today. Whereas only three tunes by two of the early solo accordionists (Yankowitz and Tsiganoff) recorded between 1906 and 1930 are featured on reissues of klezmer recordings that have become available in the past twenty years, there were at least sixty-nine sides of relevant solo-accordion tunes and twenty-eight harmonium solos released during that earlier period. In comparison, the legendary klezmer clarinetist Naftule Brandwein, whose recordings have practically defined the older style of contemporary klezmer music, released only about fifty-three recordings during the same period; the less prolific but nonetheless refined clarinetist Shloimke Beckerman recorded only fourteen. The clarinetist Dave Tarras subsequently recorded many more, imprinting the tastes of American klezmer musicians today more than any other figure in its history and thereby achieving cult status for himself and the instrument.

As valuable as early recordings are for documenting musical history in the twentieth century, it should be kept in mind that U.S. recordings and their catalogs are an incomplete certificate of musical history—an often misleading source upon which to make conclusions. For instance, in tracing the use of the accordion in the klezmer ensemble through early recordings and catalogs, single instruments are often not listed in the ensembles. This is especially true when the ensemble features more than fourteen instruments; but since as early as 1912, klezmer ensembles have also simply been listed as "orchestras" of seven-, nine-, twelve-, or thirteen-men groupings. The accordion appears in the ensemble listings only when the ensemble was small enough to allow mention in the label catalogs, or when the label decided to be diligent enough to list all the instruments. In the larger orchestras, only the names of conductor and soloist appear.

In short, it is only possible to trace the accordion's first entry into the klezmer ensemble via recordings when the ensemble was blessed with a detailed discographic catalog. As a result of drawing on only this partial evidence of recordings, scholars have sometimes misunderstood the accordion's role and have concluded that the instrument is a more recent accessory. As Ottens and Rubin have written:

> The "neo-traditionalists" among the revivalists propagate a newly fabricated standardized style, which is put together out of only a few "traditional" elements. . . . The inclusion of the accordion as an historical instrument of the East European Klezmer tradition belongs to this "newly fabricated tradition"; in fact, it was first used by klezmer ensembles in the 1930s. The resulting traditions that have come out of these standardizations and mythifications have transformed music into a symbol, and with it a romantic replacement for Judaism, the reality and history of which the revival generation willingly closes its eyes to.[2]

Even a cursory survey of the recordings and performance documents from the era of early 78 rpm through the modern revival show that the accordion, far from being a peripheral outsider to the klezmer genre, as it is sometimes portrayed in the literature, has been an integral member. The important role that the accordion plays and its power in transmitting, defining, and changing tradition in the genre is evident from its earliest incursions into klezmer music in the late nineteenth century. Thus one might conceive the honorary title of "klezmer accordion" for the instrument that has been a favored member of the ensemble even among the earliest-dated recordings of klezmer music.

The Solo and Duo Recording Era (ca. 1899–1929)

The earliest known klezmer accordion recordings cataloged in the United States are those by A. Greenberg in New York, made for the United Hebrew Disc and Cylinder Record Company. Greenberg recorded the Jewish "Breiges Tanz"[3] in 1906, along with a Russian "Walse," Natalka Poltavka "Kamarinskaja," and a "Troika."

In 1907 he again recorded the "Kamarinskaja" and "Breigas Tanz," this time on organ. Although nothing is known about Greenberg's personal history, his style was typically accordionistic, with simply ornamented melody lines, occasional thirds or chord melodies in the right hand supported by offbeat left-hand chords, and a straightforward rhythmic delivery.[4]

Pioneering Virtuoso: Grigori Matusewitch

One of the first outstanding Jewish accordionists to make recordings was Grigori Matusewitch. Grigori was one of the nine sons of Hyman Matusevicz, who owned a large house-furnishing shop in Belorussia; he studied violin as a child with a private teacher in Minsk.[5] As a teenager, he happened upon Mulka, an inebriated Tartar who appeared in Minsk playing the English concertina. Matusewitch was so fascinated by the instrument that he bought Mulka a bottle of vodka, to which the drunk replied by handing over his concertina in gratitude. Matusewitch taught himself to play the instrument and developed a rich career, which included playing for the czar's family. In 1920, Matusewitch moved with his family to the free city of Danzig, Germany, where he gave frequent concerts and was able to obtain a League of Nations passport, which enabled him to play concerts on both sides of the Atlantic until 1923.

Although only three recordings of Matusewitch's Yiddish-style concertina playing exist,[6] he deserves to be considered as one of the finest of the early Yiddish-music "accordionists." He was primarily a classical concertinist, but he enjoyed playing folk music and delighted his audience by including some in almost every program.[7] Matusewitch later enjoyed an illustrious, though brief, career in the United States from 1923 to 1939.

Matusewitch's style represents a well-balanced amalgamation of the classical and the folk klezmer style. In the nineteenth century, there were klezmer performers who actually composed longer works in a folk style, showing complete familiarity with the klezmer genre but combining it with a classical sensibility. Well-known composers in this vein were Joseph Michael Guzikov, xylophone (Sklov, Russia-Poland, 1806 or 1809–37), Aron Moyshe Kholodenko, violin (Berdichev, 1828–1902, also known as Pedotser),[8] and Alter Goizman, violin (also known as Alter Tshudnover, 1846–1912).[9]

Matusewitch can be considered as belonging to this tradition—a crossover musician at home in both worlds. Often accompanied by a classically trained pianist, he made use of a plethora of techniques, which are usually considered part and parcel of the classical world—extensive use of broad rubato (the folk style also uses rubato, but usually in much shorter time spans), a clear tone, and a wide, carefully mapped-out and controlled dynamic range. His bellows technique was immaculate, and his long notes often featured a "Saratov tremolo."[10]

On January 27, 1928, a review in the *Houston Post-Dispatch* described his style thus:

> Under his fingers the small instrument resounded with bell-like tones resembling a flute, trills of a violin expertly fingered, the baritone of a cello, the mellow richness of a clarinet, and then dropped to a softer key, giving the illusion of the murmurings of the woodwinds of a large orchestra.

Indeed, a characteristic of Matusewitch's "folk" style was his frequent use of a warbling fast trill using the upper third. When playing klezmer tunes, he made ample use of vocalistic escape tones (or Nachschläge, sometimes known in Yid-

Figure 9.1 Grigori Matusewitch, Russia 1909, with a two-row bayan and surrounded by what seem to be Vyatskaya accordions. Photo courtesy Eric Matusewitch.

Figure 9.2 Virtuoso
Grigori Matusewitch,
1920s. Photo courtesy
Eric Matusewitch.

dish as "Krekhtsn"), appoggiaturas, trills, and occasional syncopation. Favorites of
Matusewitch's repertoire were the Jewish liturgical prayer "Kol Nidre," a potpourri
of Yiddish melodies called "Yiddishe Melodien," his original klezmerish tunes
entitled "Oriental" and "Wolach," Russian and Ukrainan folk songs, a "London
Polka," a "Serenade," and in a more crowd-pleasing vein, Monti's "Czardas" and
Sarasate's "Zigeunerweisen," popular tunes composed in a quasi-Gypsy salon
style. His main concert fare concentrated upon classical violin repertoire.

Grigori was survived by his sons, Boris Gregory (English concertina) and Sergei
(piano accordion). Concerning the continuity of klezmer music in the family's repertoire, Eric (Boris's son)—who still occasionally plays the concertina in concert—
wrote that Boris was "'a very serious' classical musician, sticking to pieces found
in a typical violin recital. . . . Boris did, however, arrange many Jewish pieces for
his students, immigrants from Eastern Europe who enjoyed that musical style."[11]

The Klezmer Accordion

Intercultural Influences:
Andónios "Papadzís" Amirális and Rembetika

One accordionist who seemed to embody the typical klezmer sound more than any other, though he never actually recorded any klezmer tunes, was Andónios "Papadzís" Amirális (birthplace and dates unknown). He recorded frequently with the great singer of early Smyrniac rembetika music, Antonis Diamantidis (otherwise known as Dalgas), in the 1920s and 1930s. His style was as close to a synthesis of vocal and instrumental Yiddish style as could be found. It is generally recognized that Greek music and klezmer music share many stylistic characteristics. One reason is that under the rule of the Ottoman Empire, Greek Phanariots were set up as rulers in many of the regions where Jews played klezmer music. The *klezmorim* (klezmer players) of Bessarabia and Vallachia, especially, commuted regularly to Constantinople, where contact with Greeks and Turks was assured. Amirális's playing exemplifies those elements common to—though not exclusively—klezmer musicians at the end of the nineteenth century.

The first such overlapping feature was the use of the *krekhts* mentioned above— the sobbing sound produced upon the release of a note that is typical to Yiddish music, but also found throughout Balkan and Turko-Arabic musical systems. The second element was the use of a klezmer Nokhshpil (postlude), found at the end of the rembetika *hasapiko* "Hasapaki Dhen Se Thélo Pia," featuring Dalgas, Papadzís, and an unknown *mandóla* or guitar player. This Nokhshpil features a simple, slow, descending line often typically used as a transitional phrase in klezmer—but also in non-Jewish Romanian music—between the slow *doina* and the medium Hora dance that follows. It was first observed by Martin Schwartz, who interpreted it as possible evidence of the activity of Ashkenazi Jewish musicians in the early rembetika scene. Previously, the only hard evidence of that interaction had been the few scattered descriptions and documents of klezmer musicians frequenting Constantinople in the late nineteenth and early twentieth centuries. Subsequent to Schwartz's observation, the collector and Turkologist Hugo Strötbaum unearthed some fascinating "missing link" 78 rpm recordings of the Blumenthal Brothers.[12]

The third element was Amirális's flowing, constant ornamentation of the melody, which was as pervasive as it was inconspicuous. Here was a way of dealing with the melody that seemed so typically klezmerish: nuances on every note of the phrase, yet the impression of a crystal clear melody line. Perhaps what made this melodic transparency possible was the fourth element: a jagged way of phrasing that brought out every curve and resting point of the line, which emphasized the asymmetry of the melody and clarified its contours. Underscoring it was a notable absence of unrelenting chords, which not only would have obscured the subtle ornamentation but also softened the modal dissonances. The early recordings

183

thus highlight the extent to which "recognizable" klezmer styles are inextricably connected to a range of intercultural influences.

The Klezmer Accordion as Voice: Max Yankowitz

The essence of the earliest klezmer style derives from the characteristics of the voice as used in liturgical, paraliturgical, and Yiddish song. In other words, the accordion comes nearest to being a representative mouthpiece for klezmer music when it is not being used an accordion at all, but rather a voice disguised as an accordion. As Alan Bern explains:

> From the beginning . . . I approached the accordion as a wind instrument that accidentally happens to have buttons and keys. In Yiddish and all other musics I play on the accordion, I listen to what wind instruments and the voice do and model my playing on them.[13]

This is particularly true of the music of Max Yankowitz (birthplace and dates unknown). Listening to it, one becomes aware of a combination of qualities coming together to form his sound. The "inefficiency" of the bellows, with only nine to fourteen folds—typical for the three-row instruments of the time—made it possible to ornament a main melody note with trills or escape tones by touching other notes on the instrument, without having them come out too clearly. In other words, the limited air volume of the bellows made the ornamental notes softer. The tuning of only one pair of reeds for each tone also provided a more plaintive sound and forced the player to imply timbral variation through phrasing, since there are no register buttons to hit that would magically change the timbre. The reeds were tuned almost at the unison, lending the instrument a dry, slightly melancholy sound that didn't drip with sentimentality.

Virtually nothing is known of the life of Max Yankowitz. The only recordings we have of his music are in a duo formation, either with *tsimbl* (dulcimer)—for instance, those with Goldberg from 1913—or with piano, as in the 1929 recordings with Abe Schwartz. Yankowitz remained active as an accordionist at least until 1937, after which no further recordings appear.

The 1913 recordings create an understated pastoral atmosphere, with sparse, tasteful ornamentation and a subtly "vocal" sound. Yankowitz often accents notes in a phrase through the use of the crushed grace note—whereby the melody is played simultaneously with the note a semitone above it, creating a dissonant effect. What first struck me about these recordings was the way in which Yankowitz uses the left hand. In the slow pieces, it often doubles the melody in antiphonal passages, or for short spurts *colla parta*, or in parts of the melody that move stepwise. Otherwise he leaves the bass part to the accompanist, but doubles it occasionally to accentuate parts of the melody. Because the *tsimbl* often doubles his own melody in the bass register, at first the listener may not notice this.[14] The technique of weaving in and out of the melody is indigenous to early klezmer arranging style. In larger ensembles, one often hears an instrument that appears for a snippet of the melody and then leaves again. Listening to Yankowitz, one gets the impression that this technique adds definition to the melody.

The fact that Yankowitz used the bass so sparsely was the first indication that his instrument may have been a three-row chromatic right-hand with a push-pull left-hand system, as it would have been difficult, though not impossible, to have continuously doubled some of the fast-moving bass lines of the *tsimbl* with the gracious right-hand phrasing Yankowitz displays.[15] Among Yankowitz's repertoire we find the solemn and stoic "Kol Nidre," which is anything but disgraced by the backwoods accordion and *tsimbl* instrumentation. Indeed, it is disarmingly straightforward, delicately ornamented, and exquisitely phrased with no extra filigree.

The "Gypsy Accordionist": Misha Tsiganoff

Misha Demitro Tsiganoff (1889–1967; his surname means "Gypsy," but he was commonly called by his nickname, Mishka)[16] was born in Odessa, lived in Brooklyn and Manhattan, was Christian, and spoke fluent Yiddish. Any speculation as to his having been Jewish on the basis of his familiarity with the klezmer style should be seen in relation to the fact that he identified himself, on his U.S. Social Security application, as Gypsy when he was forty-seven years old. It is possible, as some have claimed, that he later converted to Judaism, though this has never been substantiated.

Tsiganoff began his recording career in New York in 1919 and made his last solo record ten years later. In the 1930s he was billed as "The Gypsy Accordionist" on the Philadelphia radio station WPEN.[17]

In contrast to Matusewitch and Yankowitz, Tsiganoff's style is more distinctly accordionistic. He does use the vocal-imitation ornaments typical to Jewish and Gypsy style, but above and beyond that, his approach features audible bass lines that enter at asymmetric points of the melody and a more hard-driving attack in the right hand. In contrast to Yankowitz, Tsiganoff accents the melodic rhythm of a phrase by sporadically adding an octave to certain melody notes, using a harder bellows press, and sometimes adding a dissonant bass note in the left hand. His fast lines are aggressive and clearly articulated, with syncopated accents that give his music a danceable quality. One significant aesthetic difference exists between Tsiganoff and the others: when varying the melody, Tsiganoff strays further away from it than either Matusewitch or Yankowitz, who stay very close to the melody.

He tends to fill out the lines with more notes than the other accordionists. On two of the 1919 recordings there is a second voice, which is probably a simple register-organ melody line, or clarinet, played by Nathaniel Shilkret.[18] The second melody is ornamented somewhat differently from the main line and is a good example of early klezmer heterophony, as is frequently heard on the European ensemble recordings of early klezmer music. Tsiganoff's instrument may have been a *bayan*, which was commonly played in Odessa, his birthplace, as his name is listed in 1937 under "accordion," as opposed to "piano accordion," in the same section as Yankowitz,[19] which seems to have indicated the button accordion.

Standard repertoires are always bound to arise out of the collection of pieces each era brings forth. Certainly in the case of the above three accordionists, a miniature selection of "signature tunes"[20] has emerged. Rather than merely having become fair game for the ensembles of the recent klezmer revival, they have curiously become musical banners of the instrument itself. The first of these was a signature medley commonly played by Matusewitch as a choice example of his popular concertina repertoire (*Yidisher Melodien*), and the other two have been played as envoys of the klezmer accordion in recent years. They include "Shulems Bulgarish Part 1 and Part 2" (Yankowitz) and "Koilen Dance" (Tsiganoff). No klezmer accordion case should be without them, and rarely is.

Orchestral Cross-influences (1930–36)

Although we know that most of the klezmer accordionists who recorded in the early years presented solos and duos, many of them also played with various groups of artists and were active in the many orchestras that existed, most noticeably in the studios of the recording companies and the Yiddish theater. By the end of the 1930s, there were around forty accordionists with Jewish family names listed in the New York City Musicians Directory—which tells us nothing about the kind of music they performed, however, as some of the best players of klezmer music were not Jewish (such as Mishka Tsiganoff).[21]

We encounter a delicious enigma at this point: it would seem as if in the 1930s, the accordion was used by leading klezmer orchestras specifically to give an "ethnic" sound to their ensembles when playing the music of any culture other than klezmer. The 1935 Russian, Polish, and Lithuanian recordings of the Abe Schwartz Orchestra (one of the leading klezmer groups of all time) use the accordion on most of the sessions, whereas it is not present on Schwartz's klezmer recordings of the same period. Perhaps this tendency was merely the result of engaging available players who knew the repertoire. Though Matusewitch used the concertina for Russian and Hungarian music in the 1922 ensemble recordings, it does not seem to have been a gesture intended to project the image of the instrument onto another ethnic group, as his solo klezmer recordings clearly would disprove such a claim.

We do know that great Yiddish singers, such as the prolific David Medoff (1888–1972), used the accordion throughout their recording careers. Medoff recorded mostly Ukrainian and Russian, but also Yiddish music from 1917–38. His orchestras and duo recordings were graced with the accordion playing of Mario Perry, Basil Fomeen, and Tsiganoff (1926). It is not officially accepted historical practice, however, to consider vocal music as belonging to the realm of "klezmer music," even when the instrumentalists backing up Yiddish vocal music often play in a klezmer style. This explains why, when the klezmer accordion accompanies the Yiddish voice, it has still not been considered a "klezmer accordion" by historians intent on excluding it (see Ottens, and Rubin's quote above).

The Ensemble Enlightenment Era (1937–42)

Two years after the Abe Schwartz Orchestra's Russian, Polish, and Lithuanian discs came out, non-Jewish musicians began increasingly to record klezmer tunes in their ensembles with the accordion. In June 1937, the Greek clarinetist Kostas Gadinis formed his Jewish Orchestra and recorded the klezmer tune "Lechayim," with himself on clarinet, a guitar or *lauto*, and an unknown accordionist. Alongside Greek, Turkish, and Romanian tunes, Gadinis went on to record the klezmer titles "In Vain Keller" (In the Wine Cellar) and "Zol Zein Freilach" (May It Be Joyful) in 1939. In 1940, his Greek accordionist was listed as John K. Gianaros.

The accordion on these recordings is used for chordal accompaniment. The playing is as brash as the clarinet, driving and unadorned yet showing little evidence of an integration of the instrument with the melody. Since this seems to be the first appearance of the accordion in listings of klezmer ensemble recordings, are we to conclude that innovations in klezmer instrumentation were initiated by non-Jews? After all, Gadinis was Greek. Perhaps it would be more accurate to consider the question in the light of differences in cataloging practices as regards precision; some were satisfied to use the term "orchestra," with no indication as to instrumentation or personnel, while others detailed both.

The misleading information about the treatment of the accordion in ensembles has more to do with the development of arranging techniques than it does with the acceptance or rejection of the instrument as such. Prior to its transplantation to the New World, arrangements for klezmer ensemble reflected the given hierarchic positions of the ensemble members. The roles of soloist and director were usually performed by the same person. In the nineteenth century, this was usually the violinist; later on, more often the clarinetist. It was a position that meant being heard and seen at all times and being able to play and direct at the same time. Even in the early recordings of Brandwein, Beckerman, Schwartz, Kandel, and others, one almost always hears the soloist/ensemble constellation, with only momentary breaks given to other instruments. And, of course, even the concertina players and accordionists were earlier presented as soloists when the recording featured them. Yet their position in the later ensemble recordings was not as soloists, probably for the simple reason that none of them led their own ensembles.

The Abe Ellstein (1907–63) Orchestra was the first klezmer ensemble to catalog an unnamed klezmer accordionist as early as October 1939 on the six sides that the orchestra recorded with Dave Tarras on clarinet. The anonymous accordion that backs up Dave Tarras's clarinet playing in the Abe Ellstein Orchestra is featured as an equal, moving freely between rhythmic playing in the right hand and extensive melody doublings and thirds as clearly audible as the clarinet itself, swiftly departing at times to execute a fill in the spaces where the clarinet breathes and at the end of phrases. Here we hear the accordion in a variety of functions, as a true orchestral and also sometimes a solo instrument. In the ten Ellstein recordings made at the 1940s session, however, the accordion and its player managed, in a typical moment of cataloging oversight, to escape entry in the label listings, a singular omission the likes of which have contributed to obscuring the true history of the accordion and its heroes.[22]

The beginning of the 1940s witnessed a new wave of recording activity in the Jewish scene, centering on the most popular clarinetist of the period, Dave Tarras (1897–1989). Although not listed in the recordings of Al Glaser's Bucovina Kapelle with Dave Tarras in June 1939, the accordion was later included in his band, as can be seen in photos of the period. Later, the Dave Tarras Instrumental Trio, with Sammy Beckerman on accordion and Irving Gratz on drums, recorded over forty-three tracks between October 1940 (as the Kwartet D. Tarasiego, playing Polish music) and March 1942. Besides the accordionist E. Schlein, who played many of the Polish gigs with Tarras, his other klezmer (piano) accordionist was Jack Fiedel.[23] But Tarras was to continue playing with Sammy Beckerman beyond their memorable reunion concert in 1978 at the Balkan Arts Centre. Beckerman's style gave the earlier Tarras smoothness a tinny edge, which the snare drum of Gratz underlined. He rarely comes to the foreground, except for a few generously granted solos to add timbral relief, and therefore remains the classic background accordionist kept in his place by the frontman. He used the right hand to play rhythmic chords with an occasional doubling of a line to accent a phrase of the clarinet. His accompaniment patterns are light (probably so as not to overshadow the clarinet) and asymmetric, harking back to the *secunda* violin style,[24] whose challenge it was to play rhythm solidly, flexibly, but never mechanically. Beckerman's occasional doublings with the clarinet also show a familiarity with the earlier klezmer ensemble style, which used the high instruments to weave in and out of the melody, playing fragments of it and then dropping out.

The Hasidic and Israeli Years (1943–75)

In New York in the late 1940s, klezmer musicians mostly found work playing for various Hasidic communities in Brooklyn, owing to the large wave of immigrants who crossed the ocean after the destruction of their hometowns in Eastern Europe. The klezmer jobs changed almost overnight into marathon sessions, which required immense physical stamina. Describing Dave Tarras's feelings about the new wave of Hasidic music, Henry Sapoznik wrote that "Despite having been approached by the Hasidic community in the 1940s to play jobs for them, he had a great disdain for the music and the ecstatic responses of the community to it."[25]

Summing up the role of the accordion in the period that saw the transition from a somewhat traditional style of klezmer music to the new Israeli trend in the late 1940s, the American klezmer clarinetist Sid Beckerman explained that "all the good piano players, you know, who couldn't convert . . . played lousy accordion because none of them actually played. . . . So the bands did suffer. All of a sudden [it] became a style."[26]

In Philadelphia—the next-largest klezmer scene in the United States outside of New York—the situation was different. The standard repertoire, while showing overlap with the New York strains, was distinct and traceable to the areas of Iasi, Kiev, and West Ukraine. It remained somewhat conservative up to the mid-1920s, changing more slowly than its New York counterpart. The 1940s brought to Philadelphia an influx of "exotic" repertoire (Latin American tunes and mummers' reels), and while Palestinian[27] and Israeli tunes were also brought in, the older klezmer style remained intact for a longer period of time than it did in New York for Jewish music.[28]

However, a new ensemble sound was emerging at that time. In New York, Sam Musiker (clarinet, saxophone, 1916–64), the son-in-law and student of Dave Tarras, emerged as one of the main catalysts for integrating the accordion organically into that new sound world. Musiker was a classically trained musician who had gained notoriety, mainly as the saxophone—and occasionally clarinet—player in Gene Krupa's Swing Orchestra. He brought his extensive arranging experience, as well as the virtuoso accordionist Harry Harden, into his orchestra in the 1950s. Musiker's arrangements show an ingenious use of the accordion as an "orchestral" instrument, voiced downward from the violins' melody note, or peppering the arrangements with broad, full chords like the brass-section-padding of a classical symphony. Harden's hard-driving, clearly phrased accordion style was ideal for the brassy sound of the Musiker orchestra. One fine example of his playing can be found on the Abe Ellstein tune "A Heimisher Bulgar," recorded in 1952 and rereleased in 1993.[29] The tune provides a break[30] for his brilliant solo playing, which in the ensemble featured plenty of connecting phrases, endings, and supporting harmonies. Sam and his younger brother Ray (clarinet, saxophone) also played throughout the 1950s with the accordionist Seymour Megenheimer.[31]

In the 1950s, the pianist and accordionist Joe King was the bandleader who supplied most of the jobs to the working *klezmorim* (plural of *klezmer*), while at the same time responding to the new Israeli style, a new departure from the earlier klezmer repertoire and style. Howie Leess, who played saxophone for the King band, described his playing as "very poor, but [he was] a gentleman, and a very nice man, very nice to work for. But I didn't want to spend the rest of my musical life working for him."[32]

One of King's musicians, Rudy Tepel (clarinet), split off to make his own orchestra, using the talents of Peter Begelman and eventually "Sleepy" Walter Weinberg on accordion, whose style became the source of various and sundry stories regarding his questionable choice of chords. Although the Rudy Tepel Orchestra repertoire in the 1950s and 1960s still retained many of the older strains of Jewish dances, his music underwent the same process as King's style, embracing the Israeli music of its time as well as earlier "Palestinian" music. Tepel's style, like King's, met with occasional harsh comments from some of his sidemen as being too far removed from the "klezmer style." Sy Kushner, the founder and accordionist of Mark 3, which later would become one of the most popular Hasidic bands of the 1960s, developed a more inclusive perspective of the period. Regarding the style they were trying to create, Kushner remarked:

> We were not at all involved in backbeats or rock in the 1960s, but rather in an ensemble sound that *included* the clarinet . . . but did not *feature* the clarinet. We sought an ensemble blend of clarinet, alto, trombone, tenor, accordion, bass, and drums. The driving drumbeat was a bulgar beat[33] as used in klezmer. We were rather unique in that respect. Other bands that followed used a 2/4 beat [emphasis mine].[34]

Kushner has remained a permanent fixture of the Hasidic scene since the inception of Mark 3. He later went on to found the Sy Kushner Jewish Music Ensemble, which looks back to the older style of klezmer music but integrates the accordion as a lead instrument while still using it for "harmonic and rhythmic accompaniment."[35]

In Israel, the new style evolved from the popular-music movements that arose following the establishment of the state in 1948, a national music that expressed the aspirations of the varied immigrant culture. Like the Yiddish language, with its accompanying associations of the *shtetls* of Eastern Europe, klezmer music as it

existed in Eastern Europe before the Holocaust took on a role as just one more element within the rich tapestry of influences. Yet, significantly, it was the accordion
that, transplanted from its klezmer role, emerged as the pan-national, generic,
symbolic folk instrument representative of the Kibbutz and Zionist movements.
After 1948, there was hardly a Kibbutz that didn't feature an accordion playing
"Hatikvah"[36] or the Israeli Hora, as well as any number of officially conglomerated
dances for use in the schools and clubs abounding in Israel. One wonders how the
boatloads of forgotten Russian, Polish, and Romanian *klezmorim* with accordion
laments at their fingertips adapted to Israel's new musical culture, some of their
music perhaps never to be heard again.[37]

The Accordion in the "Klezmer Revival" (1975–2001)

In spite of the quixotic efforts of some of the best musicians of the klezmer scene,
the Hasidic pop and disco style that eventually developed in the early 1970s in the
United States seemingly edged the once self-evident Eastern European klezmer
style onto the periphery.[38] But at a time when it seemed that the entire klezmer culture—its repertoire, styles, instrumental functions, and even musical language—
had disappeared altogether, three groups emerged that were to define the stylistic
parameters of what was to be termed the "klezmer revival." On the East Coast,
Andy Statman and Walter Zev Feldman formed an "Old World" duo with clarinet
and *tsimbl*; Henry Sapoznik founded and led the ensemble Kapelye; and on the
West Coast, Lev Liberman and David Skuse began the group the Klezmorim. Only
the Statman and Feldman duo remained stoically loyal to their version of a recon-
structed classical klezmer style without the resources of the accordion.

It has always struck me as symbolic that the Klezmorim's first LP,[39] so consciously traditional in its first attempts, would include the accordion (played by
David Skuse) as one of its representatives. Yet even Kapelye placed the accordion
(played by Lauren Brody) in its center. Speaking about this decision, Sapoznik
commented:

> The first Kapelye record was "Future and Past" (1981). . . . Lauren was the first
> accordionist, and I hired her despite the fact I hated the accordion. (I wanted a
> cello.) Shortly after, however, I found out how wrong I was, as she singlehandedly
> (okay, she used both hands to play) made me change my mind about the instru-
> ment, and I was glad she was in the band . . . as she is a marvelous and nimble
> player full of musical integrity and taste. After she left, we had other part-time
> accordionists, including Hankus Netsky, Lorin Sklamberg, Sy Kushner, Alan
> Bern. We ran out of accordionists after that and went to piano, including Zalmen
> Mlotek and Pete Sokolow.[40]

The next group to come along, the Klezmer Conservatory Band, also accepted the accordion without reservation. Had the klezmer accordion silently reconstituted itself within one century from an unclassifiable solo or duo experiment into an inseparable icon of the klezmer revival?

While the accordion is now more present than ever in klezmer ensembles worldwide, having established its place within modern (see Lorin Sklamberg of the Klezmatics) and traditionally oriented klezmer groups, this is not the area in which its profile is highest. Notable exceptions, however, are to be found in the work of Alan Bern in Brave Old World (United States), the Sy Kushner Ensemble (United States), Emuk Kungl in Fialke (Germany), Kathrin Pfeifer in Ahava Raba (Germany), and perhaps my own attempts in Rubin and Horowitz and Budowitz.

The large number of duos that have emerged in the past thirty years alone shows not only the continuance of a constellation that existed at the beginning of the accordion's klezmer history, but also an appreciation of the developments yet to follow.[41]

One significant new development in the new era of klezmer music is the increasingly important role of women accordionists. In the 1930s, the Pincus Sisters sang as one of the several harmonizing sister acts that popped up around the time of the Andrews and Barry Sisters (eventually called the Bagelman Sisters). Two of the Pincus Sisters played accordion. An unpublished photo features a nameless young woman standing in an angelic white dress next to Dave Tarras on a 1940s bandstand, and one or two female names appear among the accordion listings of the New York City Musicians Directory, but otherwise there is woefully little evidence of a female presence among the early players. However, might Eddie Cantor's lyrics to an Original Dixieland Jazz Band rendition of Jewish tunes from 1920 be read as a reflection of a new trend in changing gender roles?

> Leena is the queen of Palesteena
> Just because she plays her concertina.
> She plays it day and night,
> She plays with all her might,
> But how they love her, want more of her.

The growing presence of female accordionists could appear to further entrench the instrument's image as a minority within a minority, were it not for their substantial musical contribution. It is significant that the first accordionist of the early years of the "klezmer revival" was Lauren Brody, leading a discipleless crusade at that time, armed only with a Bell piano model and an impressive background of experience in Bulgarian music. Since then, many other women have enriched the klezmer-accordion scene with exceptional musicality, among them Christina Crowder, Franka Lampe, Kathrin Pfeifer, Sanne Möricke, and Wendy Morrison, to mention but a few. Yet despite the virtuosity and omnipresence of the accordion in contemporary klezmer ensembles, female and male, it seems that the accordion has yet to establish itself as a solo klezmer instrument in its own right.

Conclusion

The pattern whereby new instruments "replace" older instruments in the world of classical music often results from composers working closely with instrument makers to solve technical problems. Ironically, the term *clarino* (Italian for "little trumpet") denoted those high trumpet passages of Baroque church music that would later become the preserve of the new reed instrument, the clarinet. But in the case of the klezmer accordion, the process is somewhat more complex. This is well illustrated by the case of the Jewish *secunda* (chord violin or viola) player, a member of practically every Jewish trio, quartet, or quintet whose function was to play the "um-cha, um-cha, um-chata cha-chas." It is a well-known fact that the *secunda* players all but disappeared during the widespread immigration of klezmer musicians from Eastern Europe and Russia to the United States already beginning in the 1880s.[42] Ben Bayzler, when talking about the Polish *secunda* violins (which he called *fturkes*), spoke with respect and awe about their art:

> They were regular violins, but held down low, at the shoulder. They provided such rhythm that even if my uncle sent me off somewhere and there was no drum, people would keep dancing.[43]

Bayzler later played with accordionists, but there is no mention of these accordionists putting the *secunda* players out of business.

Perhaps the most solid *secunda* fiddle tradition still intact in Eastern Europe is in Transylvania, where Gypsy musicians played with Jews before the war. I asked Béla, the amputee accordionist of Méra, Transylvania, why Mezöség and Kalotaszeg[44] music uses so many chords. He answered:

> It didn't always. Before the war the *contra*[45] played like this, "Jewish style" [one chord, maybe two]. Then after the war the accordion came. You could play any chord just by pushing a button. So because the new accordion players could play as many chords as they wanted to, they played as many as they could. It changed the *contra* style. Some *contra* players changed over to accordion. Now all *contra* players play like that. But it was the accordion that made them do it.[46]

So in the end, at least near Cluj, Romania, the accordion didn't replace the *contra* or *secunda*; it simply challenged it and served as a catalyst in changing its style.

In spite of its prevalence prior to the First World War, the *secunda* fiddle in klezmer music has remained an oddity, while the accordion has persisted. And in the modern klezmer scene, in spite of the recent resurgence of fiddle playing, the accordion has, more often than not, assumed the role of the earlier *secunda*. Yet it would be presumptuous to say that the accordion "replaced" the *secunda* violin simply because both instruments have performed the same musical function. Other factors, such as the fashion of ever larger klezmer ensembles and the brass-instrument craze of Sousa and jazz at the turn of the twentieth century, were more decisive in forcing the obsolescence of the violin in klezmer music. Is it not possible that the *secunda* violin will return to its original place in the klezmer ensemble, thereby freeing the klezmer accordion to take center stage again as a solo instrument in its own right?

The accordion has been present at every stage of klezmer music in both the Old and New Worlds for at least the last hundred years. History shows that there has never been a decisive break in the tradition of klezmer music or in the use of the accordion since its appearance on the scene, and certainly nothing warranting the retroactive implication of death and resurrection that is implied in the term "revival." On the contrary, its role changed, evolved, and adapted to new styles and contexts, for which it often acted as catalyst. Thus any ideological attempts to exclude the accordion from the klezmer tradition cannot be sustained against the klezmer accordion's complex and varied history. The accordion never "entered" and "left" klezmer musical culture. It arrived there and, with the help of its greatest exponents, both male and female, Jewish and non-Jewish, seems determined to remain.

Notes

1. The term "klezmer" is derived from two Hebrew words: *kle* (vessel) and *zemer* (song). The term thus refers both to the music and its player as a "vessel of song."

2. Rita Ottens and Joel Rubin, *Klezmer-Musik* (Munich: Bärenreiter-Verlag, dtv, n.d.), 298.

3. Commonly spelled "Broyges" or "Broiges," this is a traditional Eastern European Jewish wedding dance that depicts quarrel and reconciliation.

4. My thanks go to Peter Nahon for providing the Greenberg recordings.

5. The spelling of the family name today is Matusewitch, but various spellings were used for the record catalogs.

6. "Waltz Tel-Aviv," Vi[ctor] rej (BVE 55821–2), "Yidisher Wulach" (Jewish Dance), 2 Vi[ctor] V-9018, V-9035, 25–5002 (BVE 55823–2), "Yidisher Melodien," 1 Vi[ctor] V-9018, V-9035, 25–5002 (BVE 55824–2), September 24, 1929, New York.

7. Although the popularity of the Wheatstone concertina—first produced in 1829, exactly one hundred years before Matusewitch recorded his *Yiddishe Melodien* for Victor—had already waned by the time Matusewitch hit the stage, demoted to the rank of a circus or seafarer's instrument, in 1870s Russia its appeal was rekindled by Professor

Marenitch of the St. Petersburg Conservatory. He suggested that it be taught to women in secondary schools on account of its portability and accessibility, which eventually led to the formation of a concertina orchestra in 1887 by the St. Petersburg Teacher's Academy.

8. Joachim Braun, referring to Pedotser's compositional variation techniques, interprets him as belonging to the eighteenth-century Russian classical violin tradition, having "absorbed both the traditions of the Khandoshkin type . . . and the art of the Moldavian violinists." Joachim Braun, "The Unpublished Volumes of Moshe Beregovski's Jewish Musical Folklore," *Israel Studies in Musicology* 4 (1987): 138.

9. Goizman composed violin solos using the theme-with-variations form, which he called Yidisher Kontsert (Yiddish Concerto). His works, as well as those of Pedotser, represent an organic synthesis of klezmer style and nineteenth-century art music.

10. The Saratov accordion factory created a large selection of accordions ranging from tiny to huge button accordions, which were used all over Russia in accordion orchestras. The small changing-tone Saratov accordions inspired a particular feature, which would become known as the Saratov style: the use of an extremely fast bellows tremolo played on each note. Probably this style was known to Matusewitch and may have inspired his use of the tremolo on his recordings, though they are not present everywhere, only on certain long notes. When asked about Grigori's connection to Saratov, Eric Matusewitch wrote: "Gregory's wife, Manya [who died in 1976], told me that she and Gregory had relatives in Saratov . . . they were unable to visit those relatives because that city [during the cold war] was off limits to westerners" (email correspondence with the author, 1999).

11. Eric Gregory, email correspondence with the author, 1999.

12. The Blumenthal Brothers made recordings of Ottoman, Sephardic, Armenian, Greek, and Egyptian music, as well as Ashkenazi klezmer music. See "Sirba," recorded by the Orchestra Orfeon in 1912, and "Kleftico Vlachiko," recorded by the Orchestra Goldberg in 1908 by Odeon. Both of these recordings and more information appear on Martin Schwartz's klezmer 78 rpm reissues, *Early Yiddish Instrumental Music, 1908–1927*, CD 7034 (El Cerrito, Calif.: Arhoolie/Folklyric, 1997).

13. Alan Bern, personal correspondence, May 28, 1999.

14. According to Rita Ottens and Joel Rubin, "Typical for the solo accordion playing in the East European music, Yankowitz used only the right hand." Both the basis and the generalized conclusion of Ottens and Rubin are wrong. Not only did Yankowitz in fact use the left hand of his instrument, there is virtually no evidence of anything typical about the lack of the left hand in the broad category of "Eastern European music." Furthermore, other klezmer accordionists used the left hand extensively in both the presence and absence of a bass instrument. The above quotation appears in the liner notes to the CD *Yikhes, Frühe Klezmer-Aufnahmen von 1907–1939*, US-0179 (Munich, Germany: Trikont, 1991), 20.

15. Yankowitz is listed in the 1937 AFM Local 802 New York City Musicians Directory. At that time, there were about two and a half pages of people listed under "accordion," and slightly fewer than four pages listed separately under "piano accordion." Among

the "accordion" listing there appear a lot of Irish names, which might indicate that the "accordion" in this context referred to a button construction, whereas the "piano accordion" was specified. Among the "piano accordion" listings there appear many Italian names. I thank Paul Gifford for this information.

16. The various alternative spellings of Tsiganoff's name include: Mikas Cigonu, Michal Cygan, Mishka Cyganoff, Miska Czigany, M. Tsinganidis, Mishka Tzyganoff, M. Zigan, and Mishka Ziganoff. Names on the early 78 rpm discs were typically "ethnicized" to match the type of music being recorded. So the name Cigonu, for instance, would be used when Tsiganoff played Lithuanian music.

17. He performed frequently with Molly Picon, the Pincus Sisters, David Medoff, and Moishe Oysher, among others.

18. The recordings are listed under Lieu. J. Frankel in Spottswood's discography as follows: 4819–2 *Der Chosid Tanzt*—Pt. 2 Em 13128; 4824–2 *Der Chosid Tanzt*—Pt. 1 Em 13128, cl solo, unk acn NY ca. January 1920. The unknown accordionist ("unk acn") is fairly certainly Tsiganoff. On most of the many recordings involving another instrument, Shilkret is playing organ, though apparently he also played clarinet on occasion. It is difficult to tell which instrument he is playing on this recording. The sound is thin and in the background.

19. See n.12.

20. "Signature tunes" can also be attached to performers from outside sources by virtue of their popularity, and thus may not be favored by the performer at all—such a case would be "Take the 'A' Train" by Duke Ellington. In the case of Yankowitz and Tsiganoff, the signature tunes came about as a result of their reappearance on recent CD reissues. Matusewitch, however, played his "Yidisher Melodien" often at concerts. The concept of signature tunes was common in the Middle East, and the practice can still be found today. A performer will play on the streets, improvising a text that advertises his merits as a wedding performer. The Ladino tune "Alevanta Gaco" is an example of this. Aron Saltiel and Joshua Horowitz, *The Judeo-Sephardic Songbook: Fifty-One Judeo-Spanish Songs* (Frankfurt: C.F. Peters Verlag, 2001).

21. Probably most of the accordionists playing klezmer music today are not Jewish. Certainly in Germany this is the case. Sam Barnett, for example, has been the main accordionist for the Jewish affairs in Detroit (clarinet and violin); Dominic Cortese in New York and Tony DiJulio in Philadelphia are well-known Italian accordionists and mainstays of their respective klezmer music scenes. I thank Paul Gifford and Hankus Netsky for this information.

22. One month before the October klezmer sessions with Tarras, the Abe Ellstein Orchestra (calling itself the Leon Steiner Orchestra) made a series of recordings of American dance music that also used the accordion. More sessions were made of the same following the klezmer recordings as well.

23. A photo also exists from the 1940s of Tarras standing on a bandstand with a very young, unidentified woman accordionist in a white dress. He seems to have played with many accordionists, as can be seen from various other unpublished photos of the period.

24. "Secunda" denotes a traditional accompanimental role, as explained below.

25. Henry Sapoznik, liner notes to *Dave Tarras: Yiddish-American Klezmer Music, 1925–1956*, Yazoo CD 7001 (Newton, N.J.: Shanachie, 1992), 22.

26. Ibid., 25; unpublished interview by with Sid Beckerman and Pete Sokolow, by Henry Sapoznik, in the author's possession.

27. The term "Palestine" in this essay refers to Israel prior to its independence in 1948.

28. Hankus Netsky, "Klezmer Music in an American Community: The Philadelphia Example" (unpublished manuscript in the author's possession, 1998).

29. Henry Sapoznik, *Klezmer Pioneers: European and American Recordings 1905–1952*, CD 1089 (Cambridge, Mass.: Rounder Records, 1993).

30. "Break" here denotes a solo in jazz terminology.

31. To list the entire roster of bands in the 1940s-60s containing accordionists would take pages. Two other bands, however, merit mention: the Murray Lehrer Orchestra and the Epstein Brothers, both of whom worked steadily with accordionists. The Epstein Brothers were seminal figures in the klezmer scene in its early years and exerted an influence on today's klezmer revival through the 1990s.

32. Qtd. in Henry Sapoznik, *Klezmer! Jewish Music from Old World to Our World* (New York: Schirmer Books, 1999), 161.

33. Kushner refers to the underlying rhythmic accompaniment pattern, which was actually an 8/8 meter divided 3+3+2, as opposed to the straight 2/4 "oom-pah" patterns.

34. Sy Kushner, personal correspondence, January 9, 2000.

35. Sy Kushner, personal correspondence, May 27, 1999.

36. The national anthem of Israel.

37. One accordionist I have interviewed, the Israeli accordionist and bassist Naftali Aharoni (born in Vilna, 1919), composed and arranged pieces strongly rooted in the klezmer style of Eastern Europe using sophisticated dancehall harmonies, basslines, and counterlines that are reminiscent of Dave Tarras's postwar ensemble arrangements. They are strongly rooted in the "tradition," with plenty of accordion fills and breaks—useful at any function where dancing occurred.

38. One often-overlooked musician who returned to the klezmer style before the so-called revival is the Israeli clarinetist Moussa Berlin, who was playing older repertoire and style and learning from 78 rpm records of the 1920s in the 1960s.

39. The Klezmorim, *East Side Wedding*, Arhoolie 3006 (El Cerrito, Calif.: Arhoolie Records, 1977).

40. Henry Sapoznik, personal correspondence, January 8, 2000.

41. A selection of accordion duos, 1913–29: Grigori Matusewitch/J. Samos (concertina/piano), United States; Max Yankowitz/Goldberg (accordion/tsimbl), United States; Max Yankowitz/Abe Schwartz (accordion/piano), United States; Mishka Tsiganoff/Nathaniel Shilkrets (accordion/organ or clarinet), United States; 1940s: Dave Tarras/Samuel Beckerman (clarinet/accordion), United States; Aslavinsky/Bilinson (violin/bayan), Ukraine/United States; Avram Bughici/Dumitru Bughici (violin/accordion), Romania; 1975–2001: Joel Rubin/Alan Bern (clarinet/accordion), United States; Rubin and Horowitz (clarinet/accordion), United States/Europe; Horowitz and Lässer (ac-

cordion/accordion; accordion/*tsimbl*), Austria; Andy Statman/Alan Bern (clarinet/ac-cordion), United States; Salomon/Van Tol of Salomon Klezmorim (clarinet/accordion), Holland; Sanne Möricke/Christian Dawid of Khupe (clarinet/accordion), Germany; Len Feldman/Rob Goldberg of Khazerayim (concertina/guitar; concertina/*tsimbl*), United States; Aslavinsky/Bilinson (violin/bayan), Ukraine/United States; Czernovitzer Duo (father/son duo, bayan/bayan), Ukraine.

42. Between 1880 and 1917, the population of New York Jews had grown from 80,000 to 1,250,000, mostly Russian immigrants.

43. Qtd. in Michael Alpert, "Brave Old World," liner notes to *Beyond the Pale*, CC 3135 (Rounder, 1994): 17–21.

44. The music played in the area around Cluj in Transylvania. Bartók had a special interest in the music of this area.

45. The term *contra* is used by most musicians of Hungarian descent who play through-out Hungary and Romania to denote the same function as the *secunda* violin (chord playing).

46. Béla Berki Árus (b. 1931), personal interview, September 28, 1995, Méra, Tran-sylvania.

Discography of Klezmer Accordionists

Bern, Alan. "Brave Old World," on *Beyond the Pale* (1994, Rounder CC 3135, Licensed from Pinorrekk Records).

Brody, Lauren. *Kapelye: Future and Past* (1981, Flying Fish/Rounder CD FF 249).

Horowitz, Joshua, and Joel Rubin. *Rubin and Horowitz Bessarabian Symphony* (1994, Wergo, Mainz, SM 1606-2).

Kushner, Sy (The Sy Kushner Jewish Music Ensemble). *KlezSqueeze!* (1996, Bon Air Recordings; see http://nulitemusic.com/site/index.php?act=viewProd&productId=5.

Möricke, Sanne. *Khupe Live: Mit der Kale Tantsn* (1999, Yellowjacket Music LC 01371).

Tsiganoff, Mishka. "Odessa Bulgar" (1920). Reissued on *Klezmer Pioneers 1905–1952* (Rounder CD 1089).

Van Tol, Theo. "Salomon Klezmorim," on *Klezt Best* (1993, Syncoop 5753 CD 158).

Yankowitz, Max, playing with Tsimbler Goldberg. "Shulems Bulgarish" (1913). Reissued on *Klezmer Music 1910–1942* (Global Village CD 104).

⩗ 10 ⩘

Beyond Vallenato

The Accordion Traditions in Colombia

EGBERTO BERMÚDEZ

In memory of Jacques Gilard (1943–2008)

The accordion[1] is considered to be at the core of vallenato style and sound, and vallenato itself is undoubtedly the most widely recognized Colombian popular music genre in and outside Colombia since Carlos Vives's stunning success with his 1994 pop-fusion album *Clásicos de la Provincia* (Classics of the Province).[2] The Costeño singer had made a name for himself nationally in 1991 starring in *Escalona*, a popular *telenovela* (soap opera) about the life of the vallenato composer Rafael Escalona (1927–2009). Viewed by millions, the *telenovela* further cemented the perception of vallenato as Colombia's foremost accordion music—a claim made by Escalona and other prominent members of the elite of the Valledupar region who, in the late 1940s, began to call their regional style of music "vallenato." Before that time, there existed a traditional style of accordion music in the northern Colombian coastal region that had already undergone some modifications after entering the emergent Colombian music industry in the early 1940s. Accordion players, composers, and singers who were part of this early commercialization, however, were fully aware of the co-option of Colombian accordion music by the Valledupar elite.[3] One of the music's main figures, the accordionist Francisco "Pacho" Rada (1907–2003), for example, refused to call the music he played "vallenato" because he did not hail from the Valledupar region.[4] Another accordionist complained that the Valledupar residents "believed themselves the owners of the accordion tradition."[5] The vallenato composer Adolfo Pacheco denounced the

Figure 10.1 Main states and cities of Colombia. Map by Helena Simonett.

appropriation of accordion music by the political and cultural elite of Valledupar in one of his songs, "El engaño" (The Hoax). In it, the former president Alfonso López Michelsen and the Nobel Prize–winning author Gabriel García Márquez are blamed for having further endorsed the idea of Valledupar as the sole home of accordion music in Colombia through their unrestricted access to the Colombian national media.[6]

The conflation of the accordion with vallenato indeed has widespread circulation, at home as well as abroad, and has led to peculiar interpretations of the history of the accordion in Colombia. Two recent films reiterate the legendary stories of the vallenato accordion set in the breathtaking background of the exotic Caribbean coast of Colombia, suspended in time and in naive bliss: *El ángel del acordeón* (The Angel of the Accordion),[7] a partly government-sponsored film that tells the magical journey of a boy who becomes the king of the Vallenato Legend Festival, and the documentary *El acordeón del diablo* (The Devil's Accordion),[8] about the accordionist Francisco "Pacho" Rada, who had previously been fictionalized as Francisco El Hombre in García Márquez's famous novel *One Hundred Years of Solitude.* Under the spell of García Márquez's "magic realism," the documentary starts with the story of the spectacular arrival of the accordion, washed ashore after a German ship loaded with accordions heading for Argentina ran aground at the Guajira coast.

This shipwreck tale is not unique, however; it had also been used in *El lápiz del carpintero* (The Carpenter's Pencil), a 2002 film by the Galician filmmaker Anton Reixa, based on the novel published in 1998 by his fellow countryman Manuel Rivas. In this version, a ship loaded with accordions sinks off the coast of Galicia. The use of this story in the Spanish-speaking context comes as no surprise, since Basque maritime lore related to the accordion—as part of the novel *Paradox Rey*, by Pio Baroja (1872–1956)—appears to have been the inspiration behind García Márquez's first article on the accordion (one of his first published pieces) that in the decades to come contributed greatly to locate accordion music, later called "vallenato," at the center of Colombian cultural expressions.[9]

Accordion music in Colombia has a much longer history than the music that is called "vallenato" and is not confined to the Valledupar region that allegedly gave it its name. In this essay, I examine the development of accordion music in Colombia (including Panama before its separation from Colombia in 1903) and its role in Colombian traditional and popular music. Drawing on archival research and oral history, I will begin with the accordion's arrival in Colombian territory in the second half of the nineteenth century and conclude with vallenato's incorporation into the national and international popular-music circuits.

Figure 10.2 Francisco "Pacho" Rada starred in the documentary *El acordeón del diablo* (The Devil's Accordion) by Stefan Schwietert, 2000. Used by permission of Zero One Film, Berlin.

Early History

The first known mention of the accordion in Colombia appears in the travel accounts of Dr. Charles Saffray, a French physician and botanist.[10] When disembarking in Santa Marta on Colombia's northern coast in 1869, Saffray recalled that he was greeted by the sound of the accordion. Unfortunately, he did not specify whether it was played by a local seaman, a travel companion, or a member of his vessel's foreign (possibly French) crew. From the busy Colombian Caribbean ports of Santa Marta, Cartagena, Sabanilla, and Riohacha—including Aspinwall and Chagres in Panama—new cultural influences (including European and American popular music, musical instruments, and dances) made their way into mainland Colombia in the following decades. The accordion seemed to have been popular among European seamen traveling to South America and the Caribbean. According to a report from the mid-1800s, sailors docking in Havana, Cuba, sang hymns accompanied by accordion.[11]

In 1869, several accordion prototypes were current in Europe, and it is likely that the instrument mentioned by Saffray would have been either a single-row

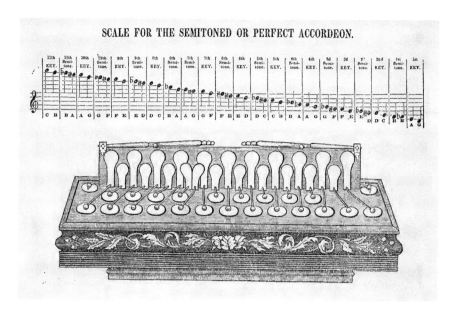

Figure 10.3 Drawing of the twenty-one-lever French model, 1843.

diatonic ten- to twelve-key accordion with two to four bass buttons, or a chromatic accordion with two rows of twenty-one to thirty melodic levers and one to four bass and chord levers. Both types were common in France between the 1840s and the 1870s, before the introduction of the mass-produced (double-row) models made by the Dedenis factory in Brive, Corrèze, in the late 1880s. The French instruments by Constant Busson or Georges Kannéguissert would have been the most likely candidates.[12] Those instruments had been known in the United States for some decades, particularly since the early 1840s, when the impact of European immigration was on the rise. In 1843 in Boston, Elias Howe Jr. (1820–95)—not to be confused with the sewing-machine inventor—published a tutorial and music anthology for both types of instruments, calling the diatonic "common or whole toned" and the chromatic the "semitoned or perfect accordeon," which, according to the drawings provided, refer to a ten-key instrument and to a French model with twenty-one levers, respectively.[13]

The same author (under the pseudonym Gumbo Chaff) published another accordion tutorial in 1850 aimed at all-white minstrel-show musicians and probably also at black musicians (see the photo of a Creole accordionist from the early 1850s in New Orleans in Snyder's essay in chapter 4 of this volume).[14] In the Latin American context, there are early mentions of accordions (*acordeones*) being sold in music shops in Havana, Cuba, in the mid- to late-1840s.[15] We can hence only assume that the instrument mentioned by Saffray in 1869 was French because by then, different models of Austrian, German, Italian, Swiss, and even Russian provenance were already available.[16] Most likely, accordions and harmonicas had been integrated much earlier into Panama's local musical culture (at that time, Panama was part of Colombian territory). As the Chagres-Aspinwall-Panama (waterway, dirt-road, and railroad) was the most secure and viable east-west transit route for the thousands of people drawn by the California Gold Rush, a large number of those easily portable and relatively cheap free-reed instruments must have passed through the isthmus and left an important musical imprint on local populations.

One of the characteristics of the trading societies developing in the Colombian (then New Granadian) coastal cities in the late eighteenth and early nineteenth centuries was cosmopolitanism. The port city of Cartagena and its foreign trade and contraband fostered innovation, liberalism, free-masonry, and democratic ideas. The so-called Jamaican connection, trade relations that started with contraband in the late eighteenth century and were later developed by Simón Bolívar and other Colombian pro-independence intellectuals and entrepreneurs in the earlier part of the nineteenth century, opened a window for modernity. By the 1870s, Barranquilla had developed into a vibrant port with a substantial foreign population. A Frenchman reported frequent dancing to the piano in expatriates' homes in which the resident English and American girls showed much vigor "in spite of the debilitating climate."[17] Already in 1855, a traveler had found German, American, English, and Dutch citizens living in Barranquilla and recalled that on arriving in Aspinwall (present-day Colón, Panama), he and a fellow traveler heard a crowd of Caribbean and local blacks, Americans, Irish, Chinese, and Indian "coolies" speaking in the purest English and French to "all kinds of Creole and pidgin."[18]

Cosmopolitanism and modernization were symbolized by imports fueled by the Colombian tobacco boom. In the mid-1860s, Costeño General Joaquín Posada Gutiérrez, a staunch traditionalist, noticed some sociocultural side effects of the economic development, such as changes in fashion and drinking habits.[19] Mompóx, the Magdalena River's main trading center, imported and marketed musical instruments and sheet music that comprised scores for wind bands, chamber ensembles, and piano between 1869 and 1876. Newspaper advertisements in 1876 showed band instruments such as clarinets, oboes, flutes and piccolos, valve trombones, cymbals, and snare and bass drums. Moreover, they included relatively new instruments such as the three-valve B-flat *cornet a piston*; alto, tenor, and baritone horns; the ophicleide (a keyed tuba); and saxhorns. Newly available musical instruments also included string double basses and *dulzainas* (harmonicas).[20] The newspaper mentioned above, *La Palestra*, was the property of a merchant trading house involved in tobacco exports to the Hanseatic ports of

Hamburg and Bremen. The owners belonged to the Sephardic Jewish merchant community from Curaçao, which had been involved in hide and Brazil-wood trade and contraband from the northern Colombian coast since the eighteenth century and kept an important profile in the region of Ciénaga, Riohacha, and Barranquilla throughout the nineteenth century.[21] Most likely, their merchant ships brought in the harmonicas that would ultimately be mass-produced and popularized by the Hohner factory in Trossingen, Germany, beginning in 1857.[22] The harmonica was perhaps the first free-reed instrument to be sold commercially in Colombian territory; as a novelty, it also reached inner Colombia (Bogotá), where it became available in shops in the early 1860s.[23] By the turn of the century, harmonicas were widespread. One of the members of the Lira Colombiana—the first Colombian musical ensemble to travel abroad—played the harmonica in concert in several Colombian cities in 1898.[24]

Other accordion-family instruments were also documented in the coastal region. In 1872, the previously mentioned Mompóx newspaper advertised lessons for the "bandonión," a variant of the German concertina.[25] In 1877, a French explorer in Valledupar reported a harmonium—probably French made—that was occasionally played in church services by its owner, Monsieur Pavageau, a Saint-Domingue physician, amateur musician, and politician.[26] The bandonión was still played in the 1890s by several amateur and semiprofessional middle-class musicians in Mompóx and used by a dance band.[27] Due to the strong trade connections with the Hanseatic ports, German accordion and concertina models dominated the region.

Colombian tobacco production and exports, after having declined in the interior provinces, concentrated in the northern coastal areas, where local production doubled in four years (1865–69), as did the population in major towns of the producing areas between 1850 and 1870.[28] The trading circuits of Sephardic Jewish merchants in the hide and tobacco business between the Colombian coast, Curaçao, and the Hanseatic ports included other important accordion territories such as Haiti and the Dominican Republic, where these merchants had also been prominent in the tobacco and sugar trades since the late 1850s.[29] Due to these intense economic interconnections, by the turn of the century, the accordion had been incorporated into several Caribbean musical styles, including *meringue, merengue, beguine,* and *plena.* In Santiago de Cuba, the accordion was documented in the late 1860s in combination with a scraper and later, in the 1890s, with *marugas* (metal shakers); it was used as an accompanying instrument in early *bolero* and, in central Cuba, of *danza* and early *danzón.*[30]

In 1893, a two-button (two bass/chord) instrument was described in an instruction book for wind-band musicians published by Eusebio C. Fernández in Cartagena. The author, a professional musician and wind-band director, was aware of at least three other accordion-family instruments: the Bandonion, the harmonium, and the concertina (here probably referring to the English variety).[31] The same year, a French traveler and explorer described an ensemble consisting of an accordion, a hand-played drum, and a scraped tube (*guacharaca*), which played for a *cumbiamba*, an open-air circle dance for men and women of the popular class.[32] Oral testimonies attest to the presence of both accordion and concertina in musical circles of neighboring Ciénaga in 1894, where drums, *tiple* (four-course metal-strung small guitar), guitar, and flute playing had also been reported.[33] One year later, an accordion was observed in a serenade in Puerto Colombia, Barranquilla.[34] The descriptions of these clearly Caribbean musical practices support Snyder's thesis about a preference to combine the accordion with scraped idiophones in the Caribbean and circum-Caribbean region.[35]

During the Civil War of 1895, *dulzainas* (harmonicas), accordions, and other instruments such as flute, *bandola* (plucked lute with flat back and metal double strings), and *tiple*, were part of the soldiers' entertainment when marching from Bogotá to the northern campaigns.[36] Most likely, these accordions were single-row German or Italian instruments.[37] German instruments available at that time included one-row (ten-button), two basses/chords models with two to four registers, branded "Universal" and "International-Accordion." From the late 1880s on, several manufacturers in Germany (mainly Saxony) produced them for export around the world (principally the United States, Australia, and New Zealand) under the names of Bruno, Globe, Sterling, Mezon, Lester, and Monarch.[38]

Accordions were sold in miscellaneous shops owned by Italians in Aracataca, a river town located fifty miles south of Santa Marta in the Colombian coastal banana-growing area under the control of the United Fruit Company.[39] Most likely, the accordions were one- or two-row instruments and had been manufactured by Paolo Soprani in Castelfidardo and Luigi Savoia in San Giovanni in Croce (Cremona, northern Italy).[40] The Trossingen factories of Matthias Hohner and Andreas Koch began production of accordions in 1903 (see Simonett's essay in chapter 1 of this volume); a few years later, Hohner produced its "Marca Registrada" (trademark), intended for export to the Spanish Caribbean and Latin America.[41] Hohner accordions continue to be the preferred instruments in Colombia.

Documentation of the import of accordions through the ports of Cartagena and Barranquilla begins to appear in 1900. In the midst of the bloody Thousand Days Civil War (1899–1902), a German merchant residing in Barranquilla imported from his native country one accordion weighing 1.5 kilograms—along with ties, scissors, padlocks, woolen cloth, and machetes. The following year, the quantity of imported instruments increased as a parcel of eighty kilograms arrived from Hamburg. Later that year, another 180 kilograms of shipments came from Germany and the United States. During 1902, several parcels containing accordions arrived in the port of Cartagena, again from Germany and the United States, in the total amount of 696 kilograms.[42] The weight of these shipments translates to approximately one hundred accordions and thirty harmonicas imported in 1901 and around 260 accordions in 1902. The dramatic increase of imported instruments in 1902 was due to the revival of foreign trade after the Civil War fighting, concentrated in Panama early that year, had come to an end with the peace treaties of Neerlandia (in the banana-growing zone near Ciénaga) in October and November 1902. The list of imported instruments also included three harmoniums (one from France and two from Germany), several pianos, guitar strings, brass-band instruments, and sizable quantities of phonographs and zonophones (a variety of the gramophone).[43]

A 1905 newspaper documents the presence of the accordion (along with triangle and side drum) among the English-speaking Caribbean workers of the United Fruit Company–owned plantations at the coast of Costa Rica.[44] By 1913, accordions, harmonicas, and harmoniums had reached San Andrés Island, a Colombian possession in the western Caribbean and home of a substantial English-speaking black and mainly Baptist (later also Adventist) population with strong ties to other black communities in the United States, Jamaica, the Cayman Islands, Nicaragua, Costa Rica, and Panama.[45] There, the accordion, along with the guitar and sometimes the harmonica, were the main instruments providing music for dance; where available, the harmonium was also used.[46] The Catholic religion encroached into Protestant territory through religious policies prone to cultural syncretism. American (and later English) Josephite missionaries, for example, allowed the use of banjo and harmonium in a Christmas service around 1911.[47] In the 1930s, ensembles of strings (violins and double bass) and harmonium were promoted by the Valencian Capuchins, who had replaced the Josephites in 1926.[48] Around that time, the first mentions of the presence of Romani people in Colombia appear.

Written and oral reports about the presence of the accordion proliferate in the 1910s. Accordions and local *gaitas* (paired duct flutes with two- and five-finger holes) were popular in El Molino and Urumita in southern Guajira.[49] In El Molino, three-register, one-row German accordions were mentioned in reference to Chico Bolaño, one of the first accordionists in the 1920s.[50] In Chiriquí, a province of southwestern Panama, ensembles of accordion and conical drum (*caja*) provided music for circular dances (*rueda de tambor, punto,* and *cumbia*) around 1920.[51] Some decades later, the accordion and drum accompanied the "bailes de pindín," a practice extended later to the "national" *punto* in various Panamanian provinces.[52] Thus, the new instrument became part of an established Panamanian "national music" that decades later would be called *música típica* (typical music). It was not until the mid-1960s, however, that through the successful participation of the vallenato accordionist Alfredo Gutiérrez in the Guararé National Music

Festival the cultural ties between Panama and Colombia, separated in 1903, would be renewed. This was an important step toward the internationalization of Costeño music and vallenato in particular.[53]

Colombia has not been seen as a country with a significant immigrant population. Yet the presence of foreigners, mainly artisans and merchants in the coastal cities, was obvious enough to provoke xenophobic screeds in local newspapers.[54] During the three first decades of the twentieth century, the banana-growing zones around Ciénaga and Santa Marta attracted a substantial flow of seasonal workers, peasant colonists, and middlemen, mainly from the neighboring coastal area—and to a lesser extent the interior provinces (Santander, Antioquia, Boyacá, Tolima). Others, attracted by the United Fruit Company, came from the English, French and Dutch Caribbean.[55] There were Venezuelan peasants and tradesman, Italian and Spanish socialists, anarchist artisans and entrepreneurs, Afro-Caribbean prostitutes and middlemen, and Syrian-Lebanese merchants—all part of a different type of cosmopolitanism, perhaps less refined than that of the urban centers, but still active agents of new ideas and cultural trends.[56] In 1925 in Ciénaga, the economic epicenter of the zone, Alvarez-Correa Díaz-Granados documented the presence of foreigners, including a Venezuelan violin player and Italian merchants and artisans who sold pianos and Victor phonographs.[57] However, a massacre of workers in 1928 and the international economic collapse of the Great Depression triggered tensions between locals and outsiders. In 1933, Aracatata newspapers reported outbursts of murderous rage by locals—aimed at Colombian non-Costeño workers and traders who had become scapegoats for the region's economic and social crisis. The following year, local authorities issued a decree to close the *academias*, or public salons, in which indoor dances, liquor consumption, and prostitution had flourished during the banana-boom years.[58]

The banana boom had a tremendous impact on society in the Colombian coastal region.[59] Its effect was felt beyond the commercial areas of Ciénaga and Aracataca, in regions as far as southern Bolívar, Magdalena, and Valledupar, as those areas became agricultural and cattle suppliers for the banana-growing region.[60] Accordions with register knobs on top of the sound boxes arrived from the banana-growing zone in cattle-driving trips and returned to the Plato and Chivolo areas (the eastern side of the lower Magdalena river).[61]

In spite of being historically less significant, the booming coffee-growing economy in the same areas (mostly around the northern slopes of the Sierra Nevada and the Valledupar corridor) attracted people from within and outside the region. Thus, the mobility and commercial and leisure activities described in the banana-growing zone were to a certain extent replicated in the areas around Valledupar and Villanueva, on the road to Riohacha. This export boom also reinforced the older economic ties with Germany as the main destination for Costeño

Colombian coffee.[62] In his memoirs, García Márquez quotes his mother, who re-calls that the *cumbiambas* in the red-light district of their hometown were being danced to the burning of handfuls of bills instead of candles.[63] In moralistic *coplas* written after the banana boom, the accordion is mentioned as part of the music of those *cumbiambas.*[64]

In the late 1920s in Bogotá, the jazz-band leader Anastasio Bolívar played a piano accordion in the performance of what he called "tango colombiano" (Colom-bian tango).[65] In the following years, the first recordings of Colombian accordion music were made in New York. Pablo Baquero and his Cuarteto Don Pablo and Ramón Carrasco with his Grupo Carrasco recorded several *pasillos, bambucos,* and songs for Victor between 1934 and 1936. Carrasco, a singer, may have also been the accordion player on the 1934 recordings.[66] The first Colombian recordings with the button accordion—along with voices, guitars, *caja,* and *guacharaca*—were made in Barranquilla in the mid to late 1940s. Abel Antonio Villa (1924–2006) and lesser-known accordionists such as Alejandro Barros and José Miguel Cuesta were recorded first, followed by Luis Enrique Martínez (1923–95), Francisco "Pacho" Rada, and Julio Torres (1929–51), the latter in Bogotá in 1950. The harmonica—with *guacharaca* to accompany the voice—was also present in those recordings.[67] At the time when the first accordion recordings began to circulate in the region, reports of accordions being sold in shops in Barranquilla appear too.[68]

In the mid-1930s, the folklorist Emirto de Lima described competitions of singers (*duelos de cantores*) accompanied by accordion, drums, and idiophones (*guacharaca* and triangle) in the old Provincia de Padilla, a region comprising present-day Cesar and southern Guajira, where they coexisted with *cantos de gui-tarra* (guitar songs), located in more urban marginal contexts.[69] In the early years of the decade, German harmonicas could also be bought—along with local *tiples*—in Pacho, a small town northwest of Bogotá. Harmonicas had been reported almost a decade earlier (1923) as being played by a crewmember of a steamer in the banana-growing zone near Santa Marta.[70] In the 1930s and 1940s, harmonicas seem to have had a more widespread national dissemination than accordions and were used by peasants in Boyacá and in Santander under the name of *sinfonía.*[71]

Information from the oral tradition is also useful to understand the confluence of the old traditions with the newly available instruments. The local composer and musician Cresencio Salcedo (1913–76) played the harmonica in his youth, accompanied by one or two guitars. He recalled that around 1930 harmonicas were "all over the place, and later came the little accordions with 'piston-like' registers"[72]—models traditionally used in Cajun and zydeco, mostly diatonic with two to four registers operated by knobs on top the sound box, which in coastal Colombia were referred to as "machine screws" (*tornillo e' máquina*). Born in the same region (Plato, Magdalena), Antonio Maria Peñalosa (1916–2005) recalled that his grandfather played the accordion and that he grew up in a hacienda (in Ariguaní, present-day El Difícil, Magdalena), which was frequently visited by accordion players from Fonseca and other near and distant places.[73] This was also the location of another, less-documented agricultural boom: that of the *balsameros*, or Tolu's balsam-resin extractors, an economic activity that many accordion players recalled as having led to the colonization of vast zones between the Magdalena and the Cesar Rivers, thus creating trading and cultural routes that disseminated accordions and their music. Pacheco recalled that accordions were also present on the other side of the Magdalena, having heard of players in Mahates, San Jacinto, and Sincelejo in the 1930s.[74]

Many accordionists seem to have started their careers playing harmonica, an instrument that in the 1930s was locally sometimes referred to as *violina*. In Valledupar, the harmonica was used in ensembles that included maracas as well as snare and bass drums.[75] By the late 1940s, accordions were part of the public dances of Christmas and New Year's street-music festivities in the lower Magdalena River region. These dances included the circular *cumbiamba* (including subgenres such as *merengue, son,* and *puya*), performed on either *flauta de millo* or accordion, *caja,* and *guacharaca*.[76] Two decades later, in the newly created Festival Vallenato in Valledupar (1968), the instrument (along with the harmonica, drums, and *guacharaca*) also appeared in the music of traditional dances in the same region (Mompóx, Magdalena), and in the 1980s in neighboring Chimichagua (Cesar province).[77] In 1959, researchers on one of the first recording expeditions organized in the country found in Quibdó (Chocó, Pacific coast) an ensemble that combined a one-row, four-bass Hohner accordion with guitar, *bongos, conga,* and *maracas*.[78] Similar ensembles (accordion, *caja,* and *guacharaca*) were also documented one year later in Atánquez (Cesar) by an Anglo-Colombian recording expedition.[79] In the late 1980s, the accordion had largely replaced the *gaita* in the traditional music of Atánquez, although the traditional instruments (*gaita, carrizos* [flutes], drums) were still used for the Corpus Christi dances.[80] In the 1990s, the accordion (along with metal spurs as sounding objects) was used for the traditional "Diablos" Corpus Christi dance in Valledupar and for the Carnival *pilón* (wooden mortar) dances, both in Valledupar and Riohacha.[81]

Vallenato

From the mid-1950s on, we find photographic evidence of Hohner "Corona" accordions in the Valledupar area, where the instrument was combined with guitar, *caja,* and *guacharaca*.[82] "New" musical instruments were also reported from Atánquez, including harmonicas, guitars, and accordions—the latter used for some communal public dances such as the *cumbia*. Recorded music was not yet present in a significant way, and the traditional local instruments (*gaitas, carrizos, maracas,* drums) still held their important place in dances such as the *gaita*.[83]

By that time, economic decline and stagnation characterized the northern coast.[84] After a series of economic booms had ended in the 1940s, cattle remained the only reliable source of income in the Colombian coastal region until cotton production renewed agricultural interest in the Valledupar region. One of the initial steps in a process that would eventually lead to the creation of the new department of Cesar was the naming of the prominent Valledupar politician and landowner Pedro Castro Monsalvo as minister of agriculture in 1948. Castro implemented radical changes in the central government's agricultural policies by stimulating cotton production through the creation of a special agency. The regulation of internal trade and prices brought about an immediate expansion of cotton cultivation in the southern Magdalena region around Valledupar—Castro's homeland.[85] Many small landholders, like the vallenato composer Rafael Escalona, ventured into cotton. By the 1960s, the region had established itself as the main supplier for the prosperous national textile industries. When the Cesar province became a department in 1967, the new government promoted vallenato as an important musical genre and the accordion as its emblematic instrument. Minister of Communications Alfredo Riascos Labarcés, who was originally from the Magdalena region, orchestrated the first nationally televised appearance of an accordion player, Nicolas "Colacho" Mendoza, accompanied by Rafael Escalona. Vallenato became firmly established as a cultural symbol of the nation with the election of Cesar's first governor, Alfonso López Michelsen, the son of the former two-time president López Pumarejo and later president himself (1974–78), aided by Gabriel García Márquez and the journalists Daniel Samper and Consuelo Araujo de Noguera, who worked for the national newspapers *El Tiempo* and *El Espectador*. Together they helped to create the Vallenato Legend Festival, one of Colombia's most important annual cultural events.

The elevation of vallenato to the status of national music brought about profound changes in the perceptions of the accordion and its players. Until then, accordion players had been treated "not even as people but as less than people," as the accordionist-composer Emiliano Zuleta (1912–2005) said. Leandro Díaz recalled that "in the old days," accordion players were poor and "despised by everyone."[86] In fact, during its earlier history (1870–1930), the accordion took root among the lower strata of the Costeño population, comprised mainly of landless agricultural laborers. A by-product of deeply rooted colonial institutions (*terraje, arrendamiento, concierto*), laborers worked a parcel of land that they rented from a landowner or his intermediaries. This population, as Pérez Arbeláez mentioned in the 1940s, enjoyed social mobility throughout the region. Village patron saints' feasts were poles of attraction that also helped migrating laborers renew family ties. Zuleta recalled his childhood as a "concertado" (a landless, poorly paid servant) in Valledupar.[87] Peasant laborers' mobility was particularly significant in regions where economic booms had developed during the nineteenth and early twentieth centuries.[88] Itinerant cowboys, immigrants, and internal migrants in search of work in towns and cities were, like the agricultural workers, active agents of the dissemination of accordions and accordion music throughout the region.

Deeply rooted in Colombia's colonial period, the exchange of contraband continues to be an important feature of the Atlantic coastal region's social and economic profile. As Posada Carbó observes, "its social acceptability, and the conditions under which it was established, exceeded the national government's powers."[89] Indeed, the scene in Schwietert's documentary, *El acordeón del diablo*, in which Pacho Rada's son takes a bus ride to Maicao (southern Guajira, near the Venezuelan border) to buy a new, tax-free Hohner Corona III, is more than familiar to Costeños and Colombians.[90] Many accordion players recall that in the 1960s and 1970s, instruments were difficult to come by, even in Maicao.[91] Contraband routes such as those from Aruba and Curaçao, two small islands just off the Venezuelan coast, though the northern Guajira ports had been active since the eighteenth century.[92] Because of their important position as trading centers, accordions became popular on those islands, and they are still an important feature of their traditional and popular music, especially in the *dande* style (accordion, rasp, and cylindrical traverse drum) in Aruba and in street-music ensembles (accordion, metal tubular scraper, cylindrical drum, guitar, and *marimbula*, a bass lamellophone) in Curaçao. In the Venezuelan Cumaná region, *aguinaldos* and *joropo oriental* have been performed since the 1950s by ensembles that include the button accordion.[93]

In the mid-1960s, marijuana cultivation began to displace cotton and other cash crops in the Colombian coastal region (Sierra Nevada and Valledupar zones), causing profound ecological, social, political, economic, and cultural changes.[94] In 1975, vallenato appeared only at the bottom of the radio top-ten lists, well below salsa and Costeño dance music.[95] After vallenato music became associated with the new local culture that had been brought along by the prosperity of the illicit trade, it began to expand beyond its local confines. The naming of *mafiosi* in vallenato songs became a standard practice.[96] In the course of only one decade, vallenato had entered the national and international music industries.

An important source of the vallenato accordion's early history is a series of photographs taken by Nereo López around 1953 in Valledupar and its neighboring area. There, in private and public music-making contexts, we observe the coexistence of several models of one-, two-, and early three-row Club III BS and Corona III button accordions made by Hohner. The simplest of them is the one-row/four-bass Vienna style with one set of reeds (without registers), similar to the model V still in production today.[97] By the 1980s, the preferred model among vallenato accordionists had become the Corona III, with three sets of treble reeds, three rows (10–11–10) of melodic buttons, and twelve bass buttons (six basses, six chords), without registers. The Corona III model comes in several key combinations; the most popular ones are tuned in the keys of ADG, GCF, FbbEb, and BbEbAb. In Spanish, the latter two are simply called "Cuatro letras" (FBEs) and "Cinco letras" (BEsAs), referring to the four and five letters, respectively, of the keys as they are named in the German language.

The design of the Hohner Corona II and III has changed since their inception in the 1930s. Their originally square cases feature a more rounded shape. Although the two- and three-reed blocks characteristic of Coronas II and III already existed in the 1930s and 1940s, the Corona models familiar to vallenato (as well as *merengue, norteño,* and *conjunto*) musicians began to be produced in the mid-1950s. The logo position, keyboard material, the system of attaching the leather straps, number of sound holes, type of buttons, and the placing of the tuning letterings changed during the period between the 1950s and 1980s. In the 1980s, a black plastic keyboard base replaced the wooden celluloid-lined keyboard base common in the 1960s. The golden color of the lettering of early models changed; grills were no longer chromed, and the metal cloth of the tightly knitted pattern that covered the sound holes was replaced by a lid with a light metal appearance. The melody buttons, at first small and rounded, became bigger and flatter and then again small and round in the 1970s. The round-shaped bass buttons turned into simple knobs; and the forty-seven sound holes were reduced to twenty.[98] When the smooth round design came on the market, it was locally referred to as "moruno"— a young steer without horns. Earlier Hohner models lined with brightly colored celluloid were called "guacamayos" (macaws).[99]

Besides the popular Corona III model, vallenato accordionists in the 1950s and 1960s also used Corona II and Hohner Club models with registers. The Club model is a hybrid diatonic/chromatic instrument: its third (inner) four- to ten-button "helping" row provides accidentals for the principal and secondary tonalities.[100] Photographs show Alejo Durán playing these instruments in the early 1950s (Model III M with five registers), and there is evidence of the use of later Club II B, Club III BS, and Victoria Club type models.[101] Corona III accordions are also produced with registers LMM, 16'-8'-8' (Corona III R and the Corona III MS), and there is evidence (mainly iconographic) of their use in Colombia from the mid-1960s on.[102] The Club Models III B and III BS were locally called "dos y medio" because of their two and a half treble rows.

Modification of accordions in Colombia (in the vallenato style) means transposition to other keys by altering the original factory-tuned instruments by either combining reeds from other accordions or retuning them.[103] Quiroz describes this procedure as *transporte* (transposition). The most common transpositions are to B, E, G, A, Bb, and Ab.[104] As part of its 150th anniversary celebration in 2007, Hohner issued three new models, one of them especially designed for vallenato—El Rey del Vallenato model—and additional register accordions suitable for vallenato (Corona III V Xtreme), *norteño* (Corona III N Xtreme), and *conjunto* (Corona II Xtreme).[105] The vallenato models (V Xtreme and Rey del Vallenato) come in five key combinations (EAD, ADG, GCF, FbbEb, and BbEbAb). The RV is basically the same as the Corona III, while the V Xtreme comes with five registers—MMM (8')—double tremolo, with Musette disposition, and with three additional treble buttons (thirty-four in all). Its basses follow the Hohner Corso model, which couples the bass reeds with two additional treble reeds.[106] Additional modifications, although rare, can substitute or add bass reeds to the treble keyboard to play bass sequences melodically—as done by the accordion player Calixto Ochoa. These modifications may also include widening the gaps of the "wet" tuning, as in Irish or French/Italian piano-accordion tunings.[107] Tunings in vallenato accordions are sometimes called "armonizado" (harmonized) and "brillante" (bright).[108]

Oñate reports that Italian and French accordion makers' attempts to make inroads into the *norteño* and *conjunto* markets were unsuccessful in Colombia. Vallenato musicians remain loyal to the Hohner Corona. Some have attempted to design new models, but these remain in very limited circles.[109]

Beyond Vallenato

ROMA

Since the early 1920s, the accordion has been present in the music and dances of the Colombian Romani (Rrom, Gom, Roma) communities. Stemming from Eastern European, Balkan, and Russian Romani people, including several lineages of Kalderash and some Ludar or Boyash, Roma immigrants began to arrive in Colombia in the 1910s, mainly via France and Spain. Nowadays, Roma number between five to eight thousand and are dispersed over the whole country. In spite of being recognized by the Colombian constitution as a separate ethnic group, Roma still face discrimination and prejudice in mainstream Colombian society. Lately, they have suffered greatly under the country's armed conflicts.

Accordions had been available to Russian Roma (Ruska Roma) since the mid-nineteenth century in numerous variants, such as the *saratovskaya garmonika*, similar to the Vienna style but with inverted push/pull action, or the *bayan*, a chromatic button accordion with a special keyboard layout and reed arrangement.[110] Russian Roma and other Eastern European Kalderash distinguished themselves as artists and entertainers, and their family "dynasties" played a major role in the development of the *Teatr Romen* (Romani Theater) in Moscow in the 1930s.

They were also prominent as choir singers in Moscow and St. Petersburg before the Russian Revolution.[111] Roma and Sinti musicians throughout Europe have traditionally used both button and piano accordions. Roma musicians in Romania, for instance, use it in the *muzika lautareasca* ensembles, and in Hungary, the accordion is an essential part of their professional musical activities. The accordion has become one of the key instruments in Sinti jazz and is prominent today in Roma and Sinti music groups who perform around the world.[112]

The Colombian Roma make use of the accordion, sometimes in combination with the violin, guitar, and tambourine, in their traditional song-and-dance repertoire that exhibits strong Eastern European (Russian, Balkan, and Turkish) connections. Residing in Bogotá, Lilio Cristo Gomanovich (b. 1938), a *phure Rom* (Rom elder) of the Ghusa (Gussó, Ruska) clan of Russian and Greek parentage, plays a *harmonika* (or *garmonika*), a two-row, twenty-button/eight-basses/chords accordion.[113] The younger generation of the Cristo-Gomanovich extended family plays this instrument (as well as other types of piano accordions) in modern ensembles that include guitar, drum set, and electronic keyboard. Vallenato also attracts attention among the young Colombian Roma, resulting in stylistic fusions (using *caja* and *guacharaca*) with the older Eastern European dance repertoire (polkas, etc.).[114]

The character of Melquiades the Gypsy in García Márquez's *One Hundred Years of Solitude* hints at the history of the Romani people in Colombia. Their strong presence in the Atlantic coastal region (Patillal, Cesar) is also acknowledged and described by the vallenato composer Rafael Escalona in a narrative that, disguised as literary "costumbrismo," reflects local racial and social prejudices against the Roma.[115] Although more research needs to be done before making any conclusions about the use of the accordion among the diverse Roma communities in Colombia and other Latin American countries, the button and piano accordions seem to be widespread in Romani musical traditions.[116]

I'KA

The accordion has a long tradition among the I'ka[117] indigenous people of the eastern slopes of the Sierra Nevada de Santa Marta, as reflected in the narrative of the late *cabildo gobernador* (council governor) Bunkwanavinguma, a.k.a Luis Napoleón Torres (1945–90; interviewed in Nabusimake, northwest of Valledupar, in 1983). Although fully aware of the instrument's recent arrival and place in popular entertainment, Bunkwanavinguma referred to the accordion when explaining the role of song and instrumental music in a mythical story about the origins of light. The anthropologist Donald Tayler had already reported in the early 1970s about the presence of the accordion in the I'ka sacred narrative of creation. In the "coming of the Sun" (a version of Torres's origin of light), mother (Earth) is deceived by men (priests) who play different musical instruments (including the accordion, pan-pipes, horns, and conch-shell trumpets) until she is captivated by the sound of two types of flutes, thus letting the Sun (and in another version the Moon) escape from her lap.[118]

Bunkwanavinguma performed on a Hohner Corona III of the type frequently used in contemporary vallenato music.[119] An earlier Hohner model, known as Vienna Style, that had been very popular in the region in the 1950s was still in use in the 1990s, as I found during a visit to the village of Simunurúa (Las Cuevas), located in the same region.[120] The music played on the accordion included voice and gourd rattles and accompanied the *chicote* couple dances. Similar instruments and musical style had been documented amongst the I'ka in the mid-1960s, when there was still a Capuchin mission on their territory (in San Sebastián de Rábago, now Nabusimake, a settlement returned to the control of the I'ka in 1982). Jim Billipp made recordings of the harmonica and the accordion music of *chicote* I'ka dancing in the 1970s, accompanied by the *guacharaca* common in neighboring peasant areas.[121]

Free-reed instruments introduced in the 1920s and 1930s seem to have become important in the cosmology and musical practices of other Colombian Indian groups. In the mid-1950s, shamans of the Kamemtxá of the Sibundoy area used the accordion, among other ritual paraphernalia comprising a crown and a cape of macaw and parrot feathers, necklaces of jaguar teeth and glass beads, collars of dry seed shells and handfuls of jungle leaves, along with songs as a curing tool. In the Putumayo region, harmonicas, along with cow-horn trumpets, bells, traverse flutes, and drums, were used in the early 1960s for parading carnival dances among the Inga (San Andrés) ethnic group.[122]

SAN ANDRÉS AND OLD PROVIDENCE

As mentioned above, in the 1910s, accordions (together with harmonicas and harmoniums) were part of the local music ensembles among the native population of the Archipelago of San Andrés, Old Providence, and Catalina, a Creole-English-speaking, black, and mainly Protestant community that voluntarily annexed to the Republic of Colombia in 1821. Located in the western Caribbean off the coast of Nicaragua, the archipelago has a long history, starting with a very early and brief colonization by English and Scottish settlers in the 1630s, who quickly abandoned the islands to move to New England. Largely unpopulated for several decades, the population of the islands grew again in the nineteenth century with the arrival of black people from Jamaica who had family ties to the timber-exporting centers on the coast of British Honduras, Nicaragua, Costa Rica, and Panama. Until the 1910s, coconut planters, Baptist and Adventist pastors, and Catholic missionaries from the United States gained a strong foothold on the islands and its community, an expansion confronted by Colombianization policies from Bogotá through Valencian Capuchin and Catalonian missionaries and the transfer of a growing number of Spanish-speaking administrators and bureaucrats to the islands. In 1953, the status of "free port" was awarded to San Andrés, converting it into a center of legal, as well as illegal, distribution of much-coveted goods, such as high-fidelity sound equipment, TV sets, expensive clothing, perfume, and liquor. The expansion of a local community of Jewish, Muslim Palestinian, Syrian, and Lebanese merchants, and the increase in numbers of mainland Colombian unskilled workers, created great pressure on the native inhabitants—who today are a minority in their own land.

Since the 1990s, music has been a key element in the revitalization of the local culture, largely affected, since the 1920s and 1930s, by trade, the phonograph industry, and media that brought to the islands musical styles from Trinidadian calypso and U.S. country music to reggae, *soca*, Colombian vallenato, and international *reggaeton*. In Old Providence, Trujillo Hawkins has maintained button-accordion playing—a tradition documented from the earlier part of the twentieth century with musicians such as Tristram Fox and Dario Manuel. Hawkins's ensemble includes guitars, maracas, jawbone, and washtub bass, as well as the accompanying instruments of the traditional local ensembles that feature mandolin or violin as the main melodic instruments. They play everything from European-Caribbean instrumental dances such as the polka, mazurka, schottish, and quadrille to mainland Colombian genres such as the *pasillo*. Sentimental songs as well as witty calypsos and *mentos,* some by local composers, portray a long-gone idyllic society that underscores harsh local realities such as political corruption, unemployment, and mainly the continuing and pervasive influence of drug trafficking spurred by the privileged strategic location of the archipelago.

Mexican Norteño Music Influence

The existence of *norteño* music in Colombia can be seen as the result of the early presence of the accordion in Colombian popular music such as vallenato and the consolidation of foreign cultural trends among Colombian rural and urban marginal populations.[123] Since the 1940s, Mexican songs, cinema, radio shows, and later soap operas have been central to the development of Colombian popular culture. Nowadays, small towns in rural Central Colombia constitute the epicenter of *norteño* music, especially in northern Cundinamarca, Boyacá, and southern Santander, where there is evidence of the popularity of one-row button accordions since the late 1950s.[124] Moreover, being a highly mediacized musical style, *norteño* music has rapidly acquired national coverage and gained a spectacular foothold in colonized frontier areas that are affected by drug trafficking and armed conflict.

German Hohner Coronas and Italian Gabbanelli accordions, some decorated in the colors of the Mexican flag, along with young artists like Giovanny Ayala, Jhonny Rivera, and Charrito Negro, are now a common sight at public venues in the region and at the Festival de Música Norteña, celebrated in Chivatá (Boyacá) since November 2005. Lyrics center on unrequited love, in particular those related to social differences; thus sentimental or romantic vallenato belongs to the so-called despecho (unrequited love) genre. *Narcocorridos* (*corridos* dealing with the illegal drug culture and also known as *corridos prohibidos* or *prohibited corridos*) are also part of this repertoire but are mainly performed locally and recorded informally.[125] The style is a *norteño* fusion of the Mexican "nueva ola" (new wave) and 1970s *baladas* (soft pop ballads) featuring a singer/accordion player. Video clips posted on YouTube come with violent images and the familiar icons of consumer culture: powerful motorcycles, flashy cars, sexy women, cellular phones, gold jewelry, horses, and alcohol. Live performances of vallenato and *norteño* today include electric bass and electronic keyboard, amplified acoustic guitar, congas (*tumbadoras*), and drum kit alongside the customary accordion, *caja*, and scraper. These ensembles also feature two or three background singers and female dancers. The "Mexican sound" of Colombian *norteño* ensembles is achieved through the use of electronic keyboards, acoustic guitar, *vihuela* (small mariachi guitar), electric bass, trumpets, and accordion, as well as the electronic drum set. Sometimes a mariachi ensemble or guitars are used for the "despecho" repertoire, particularly in the coffee-growing area in western-central Colombia.

Vallenato Today

In the last two decades, the Colombian northern coast has been deeply transformed by political and economic factors that have had a great impact on the local and national music market where vallenato reigns. Key to this process are the development of palm-oil and coal-mining industries and Colombian government policies encouraging foreign investment in local natural resources.[126] Colombia's principal open-air mines are located in the vallenato heartland (Guajira and Cesar), where production has expanded dramatically since 2005 to become Colombia's second largest source of foreign currency.[127] The local share from that income has surpassed fiscal income in this area and thus strengthened local and regional governments that invest in the culture sector, and especially in the music-entertainment business. Thus, an extensive cultural industry has linked vallenato, local politicians, the Colombian entertainment industry, and the mass media. As Hernandez-Mora describes it, prestigious local families have managed the festival as if it were a private enterprise, using state funds to advance their political and economic interests.[128] Recent reports in the Colombian media link money-laundering entertainment enterprises to megaconcerts promoting the government's political agenda.[129] Moreover, the northern coast in general, and particularly the Cesar department, the vallenato epicenter, has become infamous in the recent widely publicized indictments of politicians with ties to paramilitary groups. A former governor, two senators, and four representatives have been jailed, some accused and some already sentenced.[130] Gustavo Duncan stresses the regional elite's participation in the expansion of the paramilitary phenomenon in the Colombian northern coast and the central role played by national capital elites in tolerating it.[131]

Due to its increasing national popularity in the mid-1980s, vallenato became an efficient means of promoting clearly contrasting political, cultural, and religious agendas, ranging from those of Christian churches to those of guerrilla groups (particularly FARC).[132] The latter's vallenatos (*música fariana*) gained national visibility during the 1999–2002 FARC-Colombian government peace talks and have circulated in the informal music market and through the Internet. Lately, however, they have been severely censored by the Colombian government and media as part of its War on Drugs/War on Terror policy. In 2007, government officials removed the Colombian documentary film *Los rebeldes del sur* (Rebels of the South, 2002) by the Colombian artist Wilson Díaz from an exhibition on contemporary Colombian art in England, sparking debate about censorship and freedom of speech. One of the scenes documents the musical activities of FARC guerillas, including an accordionist playing a Hohner instrument featuring the colors of the Colombian flag (yellow, blue, and red) on its bellows—a fashion adopted by both Colombian vallenato and Mexican *norteño* musicians. Undoubtedly, national flags on accordions highlight the emblematic use of the instrument and its enormous symbolic power potential in both countries. The journalist Elijah Wald, in an article on the censorship of Mexican *narcocorridos*, states that the Mexican government has called for enforcement of broadcasting laws and the necessary political measures to regulate or prevent the diffusion of this music because drug trafficking has become a serious problem of national security and national health.[133] Commenting on the censorship of Díaz's work, the art critic and historian William López concludes that the case amounts to "a paranoid reading of the work, made possible in a climate of strong political polarization where the enemy is dehumanized and filled with the utmost possible amount of anti-values."[134] Vallenato has also become part of this polarization. When Los Hermanos Zuleta won a Grammy Award in the Latin Music category in 2006, a newspaper revealed that during a visit to Astrea (southwestern Cesar) a couple of years before, the duet apparently had engaged in a *piquería* (song duel) hailing the local paramilitaries. This song duel circulated in a live recording. Vallenato fans stood beyond the Zuleta brothers: if they had refused to sing for the death squads, as one cynic noted, "Grammy celebrations would have been made *in memoriam.*"[135] This seems to be a shallow excuse, however: in 2005 Los Hermanos Zuleta, along with their own sons, performed at the wedding of the prominent paramilitary leader Salvatore Mancuso, now imprisoned in the United States.[136] Unfortunately, accordions and vallenatos accompanied not only significant family events but massacres as well. In early 2000, the perpetrators of El Salado (Bolívar) massacre "celebrated" each brutal killing with accordions and drums.[137] Nonetheless, Alfonso "Poncho" Zuleta, the singer of the duet and owner of the group who broke with his brother (the accordion player Emiliano Zuleta) months before the Grammy award, is featured as a guest artist in the partly government-sponsored film *El ángel del acordeón.* At the Bogotá premiere, Zuleta's new accordion player, Gonzalo "Cocha" Molina, was presented with the Hohner Colombian-flag accordion he played in the film.[138]

Although nowadays vallenato seems to dominate the public discourse about popular accordion-driven music in Colombia, this essay has shown that the history of the accordion in Colombia is not only that of vallenato as claimed by prominent public figures. The pioneering work of the French musicologist Jacques Gilard has located vallenato's early history within a wider academic cultural and literary discourse and has inspired much of my own research.[139] A careful examination of historical sources reveals that vallenato is a media-propagated tradition whose authenticity has been fabricated effectively by powerful forces within Colombia's political and cultural realms, thus relegating all other accordion traditions to a marginal position within Colombia's music history.

Notes

1. The Spanish term *acordeón* is used for both the button and the piano accordion.

2. On Carlos Vives's early career, see Juan Vicente Contreras, "Carlos Vives and Colombian Vallenato Music," in *Musical Cultures in Latin America: Global Effects, Past and Present,* ed. Steve Loza (Los Angeles: University of California and Ethnomusicology Publications, 2003), 337–45.

3. Before the 1940s, accordion music "didn't have a name," according to an interview Carlos Bernal did with the accordionist Leandro Díaz (the link to the interview online is no longer active). Egberto Bermúdez, "¿Que es el vallenato? Una aproximación musicológica," *Ensayos: Teoría e historia del arte* 9.9 (2004): 11–62; Egberto Bermúdez, "Por dentro y por fuera: El vallenato, su música, y sus tradiciones escritas y canónicas," in *Música Popular na América Latina. Pontos de escuta,* ed. Martha Ulhôa and Ana Maria Ochoa (Porto Alegre: Universidade Federal do Rio Grande do Sul, 2005), 214–45; Egberto Bermúdez, "Detrás de la música: el vallenato y sus 'tradiciones canónicas' escritas y mediáticas," in *El Caribe en la nación colombiana: Memorias. X Cátedra Anual de Historia 'Ernesto Restrepo Tirado,'* ed. Alberto Abello (Bogotá: Museo Nacional de Colombia and Observatorio del Caribe Colombiano, 2006), 476–516. I employ the term "vallenato"

exclusively to refer to the musical genre. Adjectives such as "Antioqueño" (Antioquia), "Bogotano" (Bogotá), "Cachaco" (Bogotá and interior provinces), "Costeño" (Atlantic Coast), and "Vallenato" (Valledupar and surrounding areas) further distinguish the regional origins.

4. Francisco Rada (1907–2003), interview in "Testimonio 1," in Rito Llerena Villalobos, *Memoria cultural del vallenato: Un modelo de textualidad en la canción folklórica colombiana* (Medellín: Universidad de Antioquia, 1985), 167.

5. Juan Muñoz (1916–85), interview in "Testimonio 11," in Rito Llerena Villalobos, *Memoria cultural del vallenato: Un modelo de textualidad en la canción folklórica colombiana* (Medellín: Universidad de Antioquia, 1985), 272.

6. Adolfo Pacheco (b. 1939), interview in "Testimonio 6," in Rito Llerena Villalobos, *Memoria cultural del vallenato: Un modelo de textualidad en la canción folklórica colombiana* (Medellín: Universidad de Antioquia, 1985), 231. The song lyrics can be translated as follows (all translations are mine): "They brought in Alfonso Lopez, invented a festival / and used the national press proclaiming that local and regional music / noisy, legendary, and autochthonous, belonged only to Valledupar / and as in *One Hundred Years of Solitude* they glorified Rafael Escalona, / and today if you do not play that musical genre people think you do not play anything at all / . . . / and the national press proclaimed with its ferocious dragon's mouth / that the best music was that of the east side of the Magdalena River." In his memoirs, Gabriel García Márquez endorses the idea of Valledupar as being the sole home of accordion music in Colombia; see *Vivir para contarla* (Bogotá: Norma, 2002), 456.

7. *El ángel del acordeón*, dir. María Camila Lizarazo, prod. Clara María Ochoa Domínguez (Bogotá: Cine Colombia, Latido, CMO/Producciones, 2008). Based on the novel of the same title by Ketty María Cuello.

8. *El acordeón del diablo: Vallenato, Cumbia, und Son*, dir. Stefan Schwietert (Berlin: Zero Film, Absolut Medien, Arte Edition, DVE 743, 2000).

9. Gabriel García Márquez, "No sé que tiene el acordeón," *El Universal* (Cartagena), May 22, 1948. Baroja's fragment about the accordion has also been published separately. See Pio Baroja, *Fantasías vascas* (Buenos Aires: Espasa Calpe, 1941). See also Bermúdez, "Detrás de la música," 495–96.

10. Charles Saffray, "Voyage a la Nouvelle-Grenade," *Le Tour de Monde: Nouveau Journal des Voyages* 24.2 (1872): 82.

11. Luis Martínez-Fernández, *Fighting Slavery in the Caribbean: The Life and Times of a British Family in Nineteenth-Century Havana* (Armonk, N.Y.: M. E. Sharpe, 1998), 115.

12. Musée de la Musique, Paris, Instrument in E flat cat. no. E.995.29.22, Paris, ca. 1855, by Georges Kannéguissert, and Museum of Fine Arts, Boston, cat. no. 1998.100, Paris, ca. 1840–60, by Constant Busson. See Darcy Kuronen, *Musical Instruments: MFA Highlights* (Boston: MFA Publications, 2004), 74; and Haik Wenzel, "Alle Welt spielt Ziehharmonika," in *"In Aller Munde": Mundharmonika, Handharmonika, Harmonium*, ed. Conny Restle (Berlin: Musikinstrumenten-Museums, 2002), 31, 76.

13. Elias Howe Jr., *The Complete Preceptor for the Accordeon, Containing a Scale for the Common or Whole Toned, and a Scale for the Semitoned or Perfect Accordeon; Together with a*

Large Collection of Popular and Fashionable Music, Arranged Expressly for This Instrument (Boston: Elias Howe Jr., 1843).

14. Gumbo Chaff [Elias Howe Jr.], *The Complete Ethiopian Accordeon Instructor* (Boston: Oliver Ditson, 1850). See also Jared M. Snyder, "Squeezebox: The Legacy of the Afro-Mississippi Accordionists," *Black Music Research Journal* 17.1 (1997): 37–57.

15. Undated flyleaf advertisement in Zoila Lapique, *Música colonial cubana: En las publicaciones periódicas (1812–1902)*, vol. 1 (Havana: Letras Cubanas, 1979), 19.

16. *L'instrument de musique populaire. Usages et symboles* (Paris: Editions de la Réunion des Musées Nationaux, 1980), 174–76; Jean Jenkins, *Horniman Museum: Musical Instruments* (London: Horniman Museum and Inner London Education Authority, 1977), 60, plate 17, no. 99 (French, thirty levers); Pierre Monichon, *L'accordéon* (Lausanne: Van der Welde and Payot, 1985), 133–35; Cristina Bordas, *Instrumentos musicales en colecciones españolas*, vol. 1 (Madrid: Centro de Documentación de Música y Danza, Instituto Nacional de las Artes Escénicas y de la Música 1999), 98. Madrid, Museo Nacional de Artes Decorativas, No. 157 (French, twenty-three levers, two bass buttons); Paris, Musée de la Musique, Instruments Nos. E 995.20.30 (in D, twenty-seven levers); E 995.20.31 (in G, twenty-three levers); and E 995.20.32 (in C, twenty-three levers), all made anonymously in Paris around 1860.

17. Gustavo Bell Lemos, "La conexión Jamaiquina y la Nueva Granada, 1760–1840," *Cartagena de Indias: De la Colonia a la República* (Bogotá: Fundación Simón y Lola Guberek, 1991), 11–37; Miguel Samper qtd. in Eduardo Posada Carbo, *The Colombian Caribbean: A Regional History, 1870–1950* (Oxford: Oxford University Press, 1996), 188; and Edouard André, "L'Amerique Equinoxiale (Colombie-Equateur-Perou) 1875–1876," *Le Tour de Monde: Nouveau Journal des Voyages* 35.1 (1878): 11.

18. Elisée Reclus, *Voyage a la Sierra Nevada de Sainte-Marthe* (Paris: Lib. Hachette et Cie., 1881); first Spanish translation: *Viaje a la Sierra Nevada de Santa Marta* (1869; reprint, Bogotá: Instituto Colombiano de Cultura, 1992), 24–25, 74–75 (quotations are from the Spanish edition); Robert Tomes, *Panama in 1855: An Account of the Panama Rail-Road of the Cities of Panama and Aspinwall, with Sketches of Life and Character on the Isthmus* (New York: Harper and Brothers, 1855), 59.

19. Joaquín Posada Gutiérrez, *Memorias histórico-politicas*, vol. 1 (Bogotá: Foción Mantilla, 1865), 402–3.

20. Jesús Zapata Obregón, "Mompóx: Música, autores, y notas" (1992), unpublished ms., available at the Academia de Historia de Santa Cruz de Mompóx, 66. I thank Jesús Zapata Obregón for kindly supplying me with a copy of his work and allowing me to quote its information. Another term used for harmonica was "eolina." "Eolina" might be the origin of the current use of "violina" to refer to the harmonica. See Adolfo Sundheim, *Vocabulario Costeño o Lexicografía de la región septentrional de la República de Colombia* (Paris: Librería Cervantes, 1922), 7, 272; and Pedro Maria Revollo, *Costeñismos Colombianos o Apuntamientos sobre el Lenguaje Costeño de Colombia* (Barranquilla: n.p., 1942), 3, 71.

21. Celestino Andrés Arauz Monfante, *El contrabando holandés en el Caribe durante la primera mitad del siglo XVIII* (Caracas: Academia Nacional de la Historia, 1984), 111–15;

Ismael Alvarez-Correa Díaz-Granados, *Anotaciones para una historia de Ciénaga (Magdalena)* (Medellín: N.p., 1996), 384–87.

22. James Howarth, "Free Reed Instruments," in *Musical Instruments through the Ages* (Harmodsworth, U.K.: Penguin Books, 1974), 325–26; Zapata Obregón, "Mompóx," 70–72. Hohner's market expansion had been marked by its initial growth in the United States. By 1895, with the seizure of the U.S. market, Matthias Hohner's motto "My marketplace is the world" became a reality; see Haik Wenzel and Martin Häffner, *Legende Hohner Harmonika: Mundharmonika und Akkordeon in der Welt der Musik* (Bergkirchen: PPV Medien and Edition Bochinsky, 2006), 20.

23. Ricardo Silva, "Ponga usted tienda" (ca. 1862), in *Artículos de costumbres* (Bogotá: Biblioteca Banco Popular, 1973), 55.

24. As recalled by another of its members, Gregorio Silva, interviewed by Jorge Añez, *Canciones y recuerdos* (Bogotá: Ediciones Mundial, 1951), 62.

25. Although the title of this advertisement refers to the "Bandonión," in the main body the instrument is called a "concertina." On the Bandonion/*bandoneón*, see María Susana Azzi's essay in chapter 11 of this volume; see also Allan W. Atlas, "Concertina," *New Grove Dictionary of Music and Musicians*, vol. 6, 2d ed., ed. Stanley Sadie (London and New York: Macmillar Publisher, 2001): 236–40.

26. Zapata Obregón, "Mompóx," 297; Luis Striffler, *El río Cesar: Relación de un viaje a la Sierra Nevada de Santa Marta en 1876* (Cartagena: Tipografía de Antonio Araujo, a cargo de O'Byrne, 1881), 160. A French-made harmonium of this period belongs to the Perdomo Musical Instrument Collection of the Biblioteca Luis A. Arango, Banco de la República, Bogotá. See Egberto Bermúdez, *Colección de instrumentos musicales José I. Perdomo Escobar: Catálogo* (Bogotá: Banco de la República, 1986), 71. On harmoniums and their history, see Conny Restle, "'... als strahle von dort ein mytischer Zauber: Zur Geschichte des Harmoniums," in *"In Aller Munde": Mundharmonika, Handharmonika, Harmonium*, ed. Conny Restle (Berlin: Musikinstrumenten-Museums, 2002), 7–20.

27. Zapata Obregón, "Mompóx," 69, 407.

28. Posada Carbó, *Colombian Caribbean*, 42–43.

29. Michiel Baud, "The Origins of Capitalist Agriculture in the Dominican Republic," *Latin American Research Review* 22.2 (1987): 136–37.

30. Walter Goodman qtd. in Fernando Ortiz, *Los instrumentos de la música afro-cubana (1952–55)*, vol. 2 (Madrid: Editorial Musica Mundana Maqueda, 1996), 469; Laureano Fuentes Matons, *Las artes en Santiago de Cuba* (1893; reprint, Havana: Letras Cubanas, 1981), 255; Miguel Barnet, *Biografía de un cimarrón* (Barcelona: Ariel, 1968), 30, 46, and 71. See also Paul Austerlitz, *Merengue: Dominican Music and Dominican Identity* (Philadelphia: Temple University Press, 1997), 25–66; and particularly Sydney Hutchinson's essay in chapter 12 of this volume.

31. Eusebio Celio Fernández, *Tratado de música en general para el uso de las escuelas primarias y para consulta de músicos mayores* (Cartagena: Imprenta "El Esfuerzo," 1893), 188.

32. Henri Candelier, *Riohacha et les Indiens Goajiro* (Paris: Firmin Didot, 1893), 88–89.

33. Alvarez-Correa Díaz-Granados, *Anotaciones*, 278.

34. Charles Emerson qtd. in Guillermo Henríquez Torres, "La música del Magdalena grande en el siglo XIX. Eulalio Meléndez," in *Historia, identidades, cultura popular, y música tradicional en el Caribe colombiano*, eds. Hugues Sánchez and Leovedis Martínez (Valledupar: Ediciones Unicesar, 2004), 122.

35. Jared M. Snyder, "Pumping and Scraping: Accordion Music in the Caribbean," *Kalinda: The Newsletter of the Caribbean and U.S. Black Music Interconnections* (Summer 1995): 6–8.

36. Luís María Mora qtd. in Harry Davidson, *Diccionario folklórico de Colombia*, vol. 1 (Bogotá: Banco de la República, 1970), 195–96.

37. Gotthard Richter, *Akkordeon: Handbuch für Musiker und Instrumentenbauer* (Wilhelmshaven: Florian Noetzel, 1990), 52; Haik Wenzel, Martin Häffner, Petra Schramböhmer, and Anselm Rössler, *Ewig jung trotz vieler Falten: History Unfolds!* (Bergkirchen: PPVMedien, Edition Bochinsky, 2004), 79–94; François Billard and Didier Roussin, *Histoires de l'accordéon* (Paris: Climats-INA, 1991), 153–68.

38. Very little research has been done in this field. One of the most important factories seems to have been that of Eduard Dienst, established in Leipzig in 1871. See Maria Dunkel, "Innovation im Harmonikabau vor 1919 und ihre Ost-West-Zirkulation," in *Musikinstrumentenbau im interkulturellen Diskurs*, ed. Erik Fischer (Stuttgart: Franz Steiner Verlag, 2006), 96–97, 102–3; see also Spiers and Boden message board, http://melodeon.aimoo.com/category/MEZON-ACCORDIONS-1-780566.html (accessed December 29, 2011).

39. Luis F. Palencia Carat, "El gentilicio cataquero," in *Hijos ilustres de Aracataca*, ed. Rafael D. Jiménez (Santa Marta: Ediciones Aracataca, 1994), 157; Vittorio Cappelli, "Entre 'Macondo' y Barranquilla: Los italianos en la Colombia caribeña, De finales del siglo XIX hasta la Segunda Guerra Mundial," *Memoria y Sociedad* 10.20 (2006): 39–43.

40. By 1902, the Italians had designed a fully chromatic button accordion, popularized by the acclaimed soloist Giovanni Gagliardi (1882–1964) throughout Europe. See Monichon, *L'accordéon*, 134–35; see also "Giovanni Gagliardi," http://www.giovanni-gagliardi.net/Index.html (accessed December 29, 2011).

41. Claude Thermes Private Collection, Paris, single-row accordion with ten melodic buttons and four basses tuned AD and bearing the script: "M. HOHNER/Accordeon/Made in Germany/Best Made/Gold Medal St. Louis, 1904/Highest Award/Steel Bronze Reeds." Hohner's turn-of-the-century harmonicas came with printed brochures in four languages (English, French, Spanish, and Portuguese). Accordions Worldwide, "Hohner History," *150th Anniversary Weekend Celebration Saturday 8th, Sunday 9th September 2007*, http://www.accordions.com/hohner/2007anni/history.htm (accessed December 29, 2011). See also Walter Maurer, *Accordion: Handbuch eines Instruments, seiner historischen Entwicklung und seiner Literatur* (Vienna: Edition Harmonia, 1983), 108.

42. Archivo General de la Nación, Bogotá (henceforth AGNC), República, Ministerio de Hacienda, 440, ff. 337ss; 441, ff. 293 and 304; 445, ff. 479, 488, 507, 520, and 530. Calculations are based on one-row accordions weighing three to four pounds each and harmonicas calculated as weighing 125 grams.

43. AGNC, República, Hacienda, 441.

44. Ronald Soto-Quirós, "Y el olor . . . y el color de: Racismo en la Costa Rica de comienzos del siglo XX," *Aguaita: Revista del Observatorio del Caribe Colombiano* 17–18 (2007–8): 55.

45. See Egberto Bermúdez, "La tradición musical religiosa de las comunidades afro-americanas de habla inglesa: El caso de San Andrés y Providencia, sus iglesias y su música," in *Las iglesias de madera de San Andrés y Providencia: Arquitectura y Música* (Bogotá: Fundación de Música, 1998), 83, 86–88.

46. Emilio Eiton, *El archipiélago* (Cartagena; Mogollón Editor, 1913), 86–87.

47. Isabel Clemente, "Educación y cultura isleñas," in *San Andrés y Providencia: Tradiciones culturales y coyuntura política*, ed. Isabel Clemente (Bogotá: Ediciones Uniandes, 1989), 193. Clemente translated a letter by Father James Albert in the Lazy Hill Parrish church archive (Old Providence) that refers to an "órgano." What is meant here is most likely a harmonium, since there is no evidence of the use of pipe organs in those churches. In England and the United States harmoniums were often called "reed organs," "pump organs," or "parlor organs."

48. Bermúdez, "La tradición musical religiosa," 83.

49. Pedro Pablo Rojas Villero (1901) and Pureza del Rosario Vence Bolaño in Tomás Gutiérrez Hinojosa, *Cultura vallenata: Origen teoría y pruebas* (Bogotá: Plaza y Janes, 1992), 453, 578, 593.

50. Pureza del Rosario Vence Bolaño (1904) interviewed in ibid., 593. I thank Constanza Toquica (Bogotá) for information on Donato Annicchiarico and accordions in Fonseca around 1920–30.

51. Narciso Garay, *Tradiciones y cantares de Panamá* (Brussels: Presses de l'Expansion Belge, 1930), 120.

52. Manuel Zárate, "El Punto, Baile de la Mejorana Panameña (III)," *Boletín de Música: Casa de las Américas* 49 (1974): 11.

53. The Guararé (Los Santos province, Panama) Festival Nacional de la Mejorana was established in 1949.

54. Eduardo Posada Carbó, "Progreso y Estancamiento: 1850–1950," in *Historia económica y social del Caribe colombiano*, ed. Adolfo Meisel Roca (Barranquilla: Ediciones Uninorte, 1994), 236–37; Cappelli, "Entre 'Macondo' y Barranquilla," 28.

55. Catherine Le Grand, "Campesinos y asalariados en la zona bananera de Santa Marta, 1900–1935," *Anuario Colombiano de Historia Social y de la Cultura* 11 (1983): 235–50 ; Catherine Le Grand, "El conflicto de las bananeras," in *Nueva Historia de Colombia*, vol. 3 (Bogotá: Planeta, 1989), 183–217.

56. Rafael D. Jimenez, "Mario Criales. Un año después," "Cataqueros regionales," and "Cataqueros populares," in *Hijos ilustres de Aracataca* (Santa Marta: Ediciones Aracataca, 1994), 12, 117–18, 148; Roberto Herrera Soto and Rafael Romero Castañeda, *La zona bananera del Magdalena: Historia y léxico* (Bogotá: N.p., 1979), 33; Cappelli, "Entre 'Macondo' y Barranquilla," 25–48.

57. Alvarez-Correa Díaz-Granados, *Anotaciones*, 376, 380, 392.

58. Carlos Rincón, "Sobre Aracataca a principios de los años 1930," *Cuadernos de Literatura* 9.17 (2003): 19–20.

59. Posada Carbó, *Colombian Caribbean*, 198–207.

60. Posada Carbó, "Progreso y Estancamiento," 256.

61. Juan Muñoz (1916), interviewed in Llerena Villalobos, "Testimonio 11," *Memoria cultural*, 272.

62. Joaquín Viloria de la Hoz, "Café Caribe: la economía cafetera en la Sierra Nevada de Santa Marta," in *Experiencias exportadoras del Caribe Colombiano*, ed. Adolfo Meisel Roca (Cartagena: Banco de la República, 2002), 17–30.

63. García Márquez, *Vivir para contarla*, 30.

64. Anonymous *coplas* collected by Abimael Caballero, ca. 1935, in Herrera Soto and Castañeda, *La zona bananera*, 83.

65. Jaime Cortés, *La música nacional popular colombiana en la colección Mundo al Día (1924–38)*, Bogotá: Universidad Nacional de Colombia and Facultad de Artes, 2004), 101.

66. In the previous years, the accordion had been included in recordings of Puerto Rican *plena* and Mexican *corridos*; the Argentinean *bandoneón* also appeared on vinyl. See Richard K. Spottswood, *Ethnic Music on Records: A Discography of Ethnic Recordings Produced in the United States, 1893–1942*, vol. 4 (Urbana: University of Illinois Press, 1990), 1667, 1747.

67. Julio Oñate Martínez, *El ABC del Vallenato* (Bogotá: Taurus, 2003), 465–68; Ariel Castillo Mier, "Respirando el Caribe en un prolongado prólogo," in *Respirando el Caribe: Memorias de la Catedra del Caribe Colombiano*, vol. 1, ed. Ariel Castillo Mier (Cartagena/ Barranquilla: Observatorio del Caribe and Universidad del Atlántico, 2001), xix. Oñate Martinez is also the author of a sketchy description of contemporary use of the accordion in other Caribbean countries. Julio Oñate Martínez, "El acordeón en el Caribe," in *Respirando el Caribe: Memorias de la Catedra del Caribe Colombiano*, vol. 1, ed. Ariel Castillo Mier (Cartagena/Barranquilla: Observatorio del Caribe and Universidad del Atlántico, 2001), 181–90.

68. Enrique Pérez Arbeláez, *La cuna del porro: Insinuación folklórica del departamento del Magdalena* (Bogotá: Editorial Antares, 1953), 77.

69. Emirto de Lima, "Diverses manifestations folkloriques sur la cote des Antilles en Colombie," *Acta Musicologica* 6.4 (1935): 169; "Diversas manifestaciones folklóricas en la Costa Atlántica de Colombia," in *Folklore Colombiano* (Barranquilla: N.p., 1942), 14–17. In the Spanish version, Lima mentions the *pilón* (wooden mortar with pestle) as another of the instruments in the ensemble.

70. Virginia Paxton, *Penthouse in Bogotá* (New York: Reynal and Hitchcock, 1943), 206; Blair Niles, *Colombia, Land of Miracles* (New York: Century Co., 1924), 185.

71. Davidson, *Diccionario folklórico*, vol. 1, 195–96. *Symphonium* was the name given by Charles Wheatstone to the mouth organ with keys patented in 1829; this was the prototype for his later concertina. Howarth, "Free Reed Instruments," 322.

72. "Primero las dulzainas se regaron por todas partes, después ya vinieron esos acordioncitos de piston," in *Cresencio Salcedo: Mi Vida*, ed. Jorge Villegas and Hernando Grisales (Medellín: Ed. Hombre Nuevo, 1976), 21–22, 30, 36, and 112–13.

73. Interviewed by Peter Wade and Egberto Bermúdez, Barranquilla, February 5, 1995.

I thank Peter Wade and the Leverhulme Trust (Liverpool, U.K.) for sponsoring field-work in 1995.

74. Adolfo Pacheco, "Vallenato sabanero," in *Respirando el Caribe: Memorias de la Cat-edra del Caribe Colombiano*, vol. 1, ed. Ariel Castillo Mier (Cartagena/Barranquilla: Observatorio del Caribe and Universidad del Atlántico, 2001), 193.

75. Alberto Salcedo Ramos, "La tristeza de Leandro," in *Diez juglares en su patio* (Bogotá: Ecoe Editores, 1994), 94; Alejo Duran interviewed in Gutiérrez Hinojosa, *Cultura vallenata*, 569–72; Luis Zuleta Ramos (1922), interviewed in Gutiérrez Hinojosa, *Cultura vallenata*, 583.

76. Gnecco Rangel Pava, *Aires Guamalenses* (Bogotá: N.p., 1948), 46, 79–81, 99–101.

77. Ibid., 99, 93. See also Oscar Vahos Ramiro Álvarez et al., *Tres danzas de Mompós* (Medellín: Centro de Estudios y Promociones Folclóricas, 1970), 12–13; 17–18. The "Danza de Coyongos" involves accordion and drum. See Gloria Triana, "Reportaje a la Música: Encuentro de Barranquilla," (TV program, Instituto Colombiano de Cultura, 1983). On the carnival dance called "Pío-Pío" with "tambor, violina, y guacharaca," see Davidson, *Diccionario folklórico*, vol. 3, 84.

78. Photograph by Andrés Pardo Tovar of Centro de Estudios Folclóricos y Musicales, expedition to Chocó, 1959, in Instituto Colombiano de Antropología e Historia, Bogotá. I thank Jaime Cortés for referring me to this source.

79. Donald Tayler, *The Music of Some Indian Tribes of Colombia* (London: British Institute of Recorded Sound, 1972), 18.

80. Antonio Serje Cantillo et al., "Procesión de Corpus Christi en Atánquez: Kukambas, Diablos, y Negritos," *Nueva Revista Colombiana de Folclor* 2.9 (1990): 69.

81. Tomás Gutiérrez Hinojosa, personal communication, Valledupar, September 25, 2008; Gloria Castro Maya, "El Pilón Vallenato," *Nueva Revista Colombiana de Folclor* 2.10 (1991): 36; Victor Manuel Pacheco, "El por qué los Embarradores y el Pilón," *Nueva Revista Colombiana de Folclor* 3.12 (1992): 123.

82. Photograph by Jesús Martínez, Valledupar; Hermes Martínez, personal communication, Valledupar, September 25, 2008. I thank Hermes Martínez for providing me with a copy of this photograph.

83. Gerardo Reichel-Dolmatoff and Alicia Reichel-Dolmatoff, *The People of Aritama: The Cultural Personality of a Colombian Mestizo Village* (Chicago: University of Chicago Press, 1961), 198, 245.

84. Posada Carbó, *Progreso y estancamiento*, 279; Adolfo Meisel Roca, "Rezago relativo y creciente integración, 1950–1994," in *Historia económica y social del Caribe colombiano*, ed. Adolfo Meisel Roca (Barranquilla: Ediciones Uninorte, 1994), 322–23.

85. Jaime Bonet Morón, "Las exportaciones de algodón del Caribe colombiano," in *Experiencias exportadoras del Caribe Colombiano*, ed. Adolfo Meisel Roca (Cartagena: Banco de la República, 2002), 146–48; Astrid Martínez, *Planes de desarrollo y política agraria en Colombia: 1940–1976* (Bogotá: Universidad Nacional de Colombia, 1986), 89; Absalón Machado, Prologue to *Bonanza y crisis del oro blanco en Colombia: 1960–1980*, ed. Yezid Soler and Fabio Prieto (Bogotá: N.p., 1982).

86. "El acordeonero no era de la gente sino de la menos gente." Emiliano Zuleta qtd.

in Ciro Quiroz Otero, *Vallenato hombre y canto* (Bogotá: Icaro Editores, 1983), 19; Leandro Díaz qtd. in Jorge Nieves Oviedo, *De los sonidos del patio a la música mundo: semiosis nómadas en el Caribe* (Cartagena: Observatorio del Caribe Colombiano and Convenio Andrés Bello, 2008), 93.

87. Interviewed by Gutiérrez Hinojosa, *Cultura vallenata*, 585.

88. Pérez Arbeláez, *La cuna del porro*, 42, 78; Hermes Tovar, "Orígenes y características de los sistemas de terraje y arrendamiento en la sociedad colonial durante el siglo XVIII: El caso Neogranadino," in *Peones, conciertos, y arrendamientos en América Latina* (Bogotá: Universidad Nacional de Colombia, 1987), 124–29.

89. Posada Carbó, *Colombian Caribbean*, 228–29.

90. The film's episode is also quoted in the publication issued by Hohner on its 150th anniversary. See Wenzel and Häffner, *Legende Hohner Harmonika*, 93.

91. Liliana Martínez Polo, "Reyes vallenatos recuerdan cómo consiguieron su primer acordeón," *El Tiempo*, April 4, 2007.

92. Arauz Monfante, *El contrabando holandés*.

93. Isabel Aretz, *Los instrumentos musicales en Venezuela* (Cumaná: Universidad de Oriente, 1967), photo no. 2; Ocarina Castillo, *Los hacedores, rostros, manos, voces: Valle de Cumanacoa, Golfo de Cariaco*, CD no. 8 (Caracas: Consejo Nacional de la Cultura, 2002).

94. Eduardo Saenz Rovner, "La 'prehistoria' de la marihuana en Colombia: consumos y cultivos entre los años 30 y 60," *Cuadernos de Economía: Universidad Nacional de Colombia* 26.47 (2007): 205–22.

95. Fernando Gastelbondo, "Elementos para una caracterización de la industria fonográfica en Colombia" (Senior thesis in economics, Universidad de los Andes, Bogotá, 1977), 28.

96. Martín López González, "Cambios en los procesos académicos, políticos, y culturales de la sociedad riohachera producto de la bonanza marimbera (1975–1985)" (Senior thesis in sociology, Universidad Nacional Abierta y a Distancia, Riohacha, 2008), 5, 13, 43, 83. I thank Wilder Guerra (Riohacha) for kindly referring me to this source.

97. A selection of them are included in Antonio Cruz Cárdenas and Manuel Zapata Olivella, *Homenaje Nacional de Música Popular 1998: Rafael Escalona* (Bogotá: Ministerio de Cultura, 1998). One-row instrument (p. 40); two-row instruments (pp. 9, 24, 39, 44, 50–56); Club III BS (pp. 58–59); early three-row (pp. 20–23, 60–61, 67, 93–95); and Corona III (pp. 84, 86, 98).

98. Information on the Hohner Coronas can be found in Universidad de Reyes Accordions, "Open Forum," http://www.reyesaccordions.com/site.htm (accessed December 30, 2011).

99. Quiroz Otero, *Vallenato hombre y canto*, 205; Oñate Martínez, *El ABC del Vallenato*, 22; Consuelo Araujonoguera, *Lexicón del Valle de Upar: Voces, modismos, giros, interjecciones, locuciones, dichos, refranes, y coplas del habla popular vallenata* (Bogotá: Instituto Caro y Cuervo, 1994), 200.

100. Jacques Delaguerre, "Musician's Guide to the Club System Accordion" (2003), http://www.delaguerre.com/delaguerre/pedagogy/club/ (accessed December 30, 2011).

101. Ibid.; Oñate Martínez, *El ABC del Vallenato*, 26–27, 50; Nereo López, "Photo-

graphs," in Antonio Cruz Cárdenas and Manuel Zapata Olivella, *Homenaje Nacional de Música Popular 1998: Rafael Escalona* (Bogotá: Ministerio de Cultura, 1998). A Victoria Club Model belongs to the private collection of Alberto Murgas, Valledupar.

102. Oñate Martínez, *El ABC del Vallenato*, 58.

103. Spare parts, reeds, and other items are imported directly from Hohner in Trossingen, Germany.

104. Quiroz Otero, *Vallenato hombre y canto*, 203–4; Oñate Martínez, *El ABC del Vallenato*, 28.

105. In 2007 Hohner also launched as anniversary models the Corona II Supreme and the Compadre, equivalent to the El Rey del Vallenato for Mexican and Tex-Mex music. The most-used instrument for these styles is the Corona II Classic.

106. Matt Kerwin, "Hohner Accordion Buying Guide," https://www.musicforall.biz/t-hohneraccordionbuyingguide.aspx (accessed December 30, 2011). "Mussette" tuning, with three sets of medium (M=8') reeds, has set three tuned flat the same amount that set two is sharp with respect to set one. See Hans Palm, "'Wet/Dry' Sound and Tuning," http://www.accordionpage.com/wetdry.html (accessed December 20, 2011).

107. Alberto "Beto" Murgas, personal communication, Valledupar, March 2002. Also reported in Oñate Martínez, *El ABC del Vallenato*, 34. Deviation for Mexican instruments is given by Palm as fifteen cents.

108. As used at http://www.myvallenato.com/ACORDEONES.html.

109. Oñate Martínez, *El ABC del Vallenato*, 30.

110. Alexander Buchner, *Colour Encyclopedia of Musical Instruments* (London: Hamlyn, 1980), 282, 287–89; Marina Frolova-Walker et al., "Russian Federation," in *Grove Music Online/Oxford Music Online*, http://www.oxfordmusiconline.com/subscriber/article/grove/music/40456pg2 (accessed February 9, 2009).

111. Alaina Lemon, "Roma (Gypsies) in the Soviet Union and the Moscow Teatr 'Romen,'" in *Gypsies: An Interdisciplinary Reader*, ed. Diane Tong (New York: Garland Publishing, 1998), 153, 157.

112. Robert Garfias, "Survival of Turkish Characteristics in Romanian Musica Lauterasca," *Yearbook of the International Council for Traditional Music* 13 (1981): 101; and Ekkehard Jost, "Jazz, Mussette, und Cante Flamenco," *Die Musik der Sinti und Roma*, vol. 2, ed. Anita Awosusi (Heidelberg: Dokumentations und Kulturzentrum Deutscher Sinti und Roma, 1997), 14. See also Alain Weber, liner notes to *Road of the Gypsies/L'Epopée Tzigane*, CDs 24-756 (Frankfurt: Network, 1996).

113. I thank Lilio Cristo Gomanovich for his generous information. He presently plays a Hohner International model sent to him by relatives in the United States. See also Ana Dalila Gómez Baos et al., *La Paramici le Rromege kay besen akana and-o Bogotá (Fortalecimiento y recuperación de la tradición oral de la Kumpania de Bogotá a través de cuentos, mitos, leyendas y música)* (Bogotá: Prorrom/Alcaldía Mayor de Bogotá, 2008), 66, 79.

114. Gómez Baos, *La Paramici le Rromege*, 10, 25, 37, 44, 49, 76–77, 118, 129, 144, and 151; and *Ame Le Rom: Música Rom de Colombia*, CD ESP-2155 (Bogotá: Prorrom/Sonotec), tracks 1 and 11.

115. Rafael Escalona, "Los Gitanos," in *El Viejo Pedro: La casa en el Aire* (Bogotá: Xajamaia Editores, 2006), 41–74.

116. José Manuel Izquierdo (Santiago, Chile) and Norberto Pablo Cirio (Buenos Aires, Argentina), personal communications, October 2008. I thank them for their information on the music of the Rom groups of Valdivia (Chile) and Mar del Plata (Argentina). See also J. M. Izquierdo Konig, *Cuando el río suena . . . Una historia de la música en Valvidia, 1840–1970* (Valdivia: Conarte, 2008), 148–49. Unlike the button accordion played by neighboring Rom and the Mapuche Indians, German immigrants and their descendants in southern Chile identified themselves with brass-band music and the piano accordion.

117. "I'ka" is the more common name for this group, along with "Ika," "Ijka," "Iku," and "Arhuaco."

118. Donald Tayler, *The Coming of the Sun: A Prologue to Ika Sacred Narrative* (Oxford: Pitt Rivers Museum, 1997), 38–39. The successful flutes are called *chardu* and *mag'wa'na* (in Torres's version, the guitar and the *caja* are listed as unsuccessful instruments).

119. Fragments of these recordings are included in Jeremy Marre's documentary *Shotguns and Accordions: Music of the Marijuana Growing Regions of Colombia* (1983; reprint, Newton, N.J.: Shanachie, 2001); and Jeremy Marre and Hannah Charlton, *Beats of the Heart* (London: Pluto Press, 1987), 130–32. Luis N. Torres was assassinated along with two other I'ka leaders in late 1990, after being detained in a military checkpoint in southern Cesar by the Colombian army. See "Trois dirigeants Arhuacos assassinés," *Journal de la Sociéte des Americanistes* 77 (1991): 179, and Human Rights Documents and Materials, Human Rights Library, University of Minnesota, http://humanrights.law .monash.edu.au/undocs/612–1995.html (accessed December 30, 2011).

120. Egberto Bermúdez, *Shivaldamán: Música de la Sierra Nevada de Santa Marta*, CD TCOL 002 (Bogotá: Fundación de Musica, 2006), tracks 22 and 23. I thank Saul Tobias Mindiola (Bogotá), an I'ka student at the Universidad Nacional de Colombia, for additional information on the music and present use of the accordion in his community.

121. Lucia de Francisco Zea and Alvaro Chaves Mendoza, *Los Ijka: Reseña etnográfica* (Bogotá: Instituto Colombiano de Antropología, 1977), 50 (fieldwork 1962–63); and Jim Billipp, liner notes to *Sacred and Profane Music of the Ika*, LP FE 4055 (New York: Folkways Records, 1977), 2, 4.

122. Samuel Martí, "Etnomusicología en Colombia," *Revista Colombiana de Folclor* 2.6 (1961): 136. Richard E. Schultes, who studied the use of entheogenic plants (*yagé*) in the area in 1953, photographed the shaman Salvador Chindoy with a harmonica among his ritual paraphernalia. See Wade Davis, *The Lost Amazon: The Photographic Journey of Richard Evans Schultes* (San Francisco: Chronicle Books, 2004), 22, 95. The Kamemtxá are also known as Kamsá, Kamemtzá, Kamsé, Camëntsëä, Coche, or Sibundoy.

123. Egberto Bermúdez, "Del tequila al aguardiente," *Horas: Tiempo Cultural DC* 3 (2004): 38–42, http://www.ebermudezcursos.unal.edu.co/teqaguar.pdf (accessed December 30, 2011).

124. A photograph by Carlos A. Martínez Casas depicts an ensemble of one-row/four-basses button accordion, *tiple*, guitar, and maracas. In Egberto Bermúdez, "La tradición musical de Puente Nacional, Santander," in *Por mi Puente Real de Velez: Música tradicional*

de Puente Nacional, Santander, CD MA-TCOL004 (Bogotá: Fundación de Música, 2000), 11.

125. Juliana Pérez González, "La música mexicana en Colombia: Los corridos prohibidos y el narcomundo," *Anais do V Congresso Latinoamericano da Associação Internacional parao Estudo de Musica Popular IASPM-AL, Rio de Janeiro, 2005*, www.hist.puc.cl/iaspm/rio/Anais2004%20(PDF)/JulianaPerezGonzalez.pdf (accessed December 30, 2011). On the *despecho* repertoire, see Egberto Bermúdez, "Del humor y el amor: Música de parranda y música de despecho en Colombia," *Cátedra de Artes. Universidad Católica de Chile* 3 (2006): 81–111 (part 1), and *Cátedra de Artes* 4 (2007): 63–89 (part 2).

126. For a general view on this subject, see María M. Aguilera Díaz, "Palma africana en la Costa Caribe: Un semillero de empresas solidarias," in *Experiencias exportadoras del Caribe Colombiano*, ed. Adolfo Meisel Roca (Cartagena: Banco de la República, 2002), 102–43; and Joaquín Viloria de la Hoz, "Economía del carbón en el Caribe colombiano," in *Experiencas exportadoras del Caribe Colombiano*, ed. Adolfo Meisel Roca (Cartagena: Banco de la República, 2002), 234–74. See also Fidel Mingorance, Faminia Minelli, and Helene Le Du, *El cultivo de la palma africana en el Chocó: Legalidad ambiental, territorial, y derechos humanos* (Quidbó: Human Rights Everywhere/Diocesis de Quibdó, 2004).

127. Viloria de la Hoz, *Economía del carbón*, 261–63.

128. Salud Hernandez-Mora, "El último botín del imperio," *El Tiempo*, April 25, 2009, http://www.eltiempo.com/archivo/documento/CMS-5066872 (accessed December 31, 2011).

129. This is the case of the "Paz sin fronteras" concert on March 16, 2008, organized—among other enterprises—by Platino Entertainment, part of DMG Holding, whose CEO and owner David Murcia Guzman is in jail accused of money laundering. "Los colados en el concierto: David Murcia colaboró con logística en el evento Paz sin fronteras," *El Espectador*, May 16, 2009, http://www.elespectador.com/impreso/judicial/articuloimpreso141132-los-colados-el-concierto (accessed December 31, 2011).

130. "El gobernador del Cesar, sindicado de nexos con los 'paras,' se entrega ante la justicia," *Semana.com*, May 16, 2007, http://www.semana.com/on-line/gobernador-del-cesar-sindicado-nexos-paras-entrega-ante-justicia/103671-3.aspx (accessed December 31, 2011). The group of indicted politicians includes Governor Hernando Molina and Senator Alvaro Araujo Castro, the former being the son of Consuelo Araujo de Molina (a.k.a Consuelo Araujomolina), the founder, spiritual leader, and theorist of the Festival Vallenato, and the latter his nephew.

131. Gustavo Duncan, *Los señores de la guerra: de paramilitares, mafiosos y autodefensas en Colombia* (Bogotá: Planeta/Fundación Seguridad y Democracia, 2006). See also Holman Morris, "Paramilitarismo en Colombia," *Contravia*, Corporación Arcoiris.TV (2004), http://www.youtube.com/watch?v=ZnuWCx5haMA&feature=related (part 1; accessed December 31, 2011), and http://www.youtube.com/watch?v=TVVmJVWmFXQ&feature=related (part 2; accessed December 31, 2011).

132. Tatiana Najera Cardona, "Influencia de la música vallenata en la política del caribe colombiano," paper presented at 1er Congreso de Ciencia Política, Bogotá, September

30-October 4, 2008, Universidad de los Andes, Departamento de Ciencia Política, http://congresocienciapolitica.uniandes.edu.co (pdf available on Línea 6, Mesa 9)

133. Cesar Flores Maldonado, from PRD (Partido de la Revolución Democrática), qtd. in Elijah Wald, "Corrido Censorship: A Brief History," http://www.elijahwald.com/corcensors.html (accessed December 31, 2011). See also Elijah Wald, "Drug Ballads and Censorship in Mexico" (2002), http://www.elijahwald.com/censorship.html (accessed January 26, 2012).

134. William López qtd. in Cristian Valencia, "Crece la polémica por el retiro de una obra en reciente exposición de colombianos en Gales," *Arcadia*, November 19, 2007. See also "Crece la polémica por el retiro de una obra en reciente exposición de colombianos en Gales," *Semana.com*, http://www.semana.com/wf_InfoArticulo.aspx?idArt=107822 (accessed December 31, 2011).

135. Maria Antonia García de la Torre, "El señor Matanza," *El Espectador*, November 25, 2006, http://cadutadallatorre.blogspot.com/2007/04/el-seor-matanza.html (accessed December 31, 2011), and "Vallenatos 2," http://caidadelatorre.blogspot.com/2006/12/vallenatos-2.html (accessed December 31, 2011); Luis Carlos Manjarrés Ariza, "Política, paramilitarismo, y vallenato," *El Vallenato.com*, November 26, 2006, http://www.elvallenato.com/noticias/1525/Politica,-Paramilitarismo-y-Vallenato.htm (accessed December 31, 2011).

136. Ivan Cepeda and Jorge Rojas, *A las puertas de El Ubérrimo* (Bogotá: Debate/Random House, 2008), 12–15. Peter Manjarrés and Los Hermanos Zuleta Jr. also performed at the celebration.

137. Ibid., 72–73. Estimates of the number of victims of El Salado massacre vary between sixty and one hundred.

138. The Colombian government sponsored this film through its campaign "Colombia es pasión" (Ministry of Commerce and Tourism) and the Fondo de Promoción Cinematográfico (Ministry of Culture); see *El ángel del acordeón*, press book, www.cmoproducciones.com/angel/pressbook.doc (accessed December 31, 2011).

139. Jacques Gilard, "Musique populaire et identité nationale: Aspects d'un débat colombien, 1940–1950," *America: Cahiers du CRICCAL* 1 (1986): 185–96; "Emergence et récupération d'une contre-culture dans la Colombie contemporaine," *Caravelle* 46 (1986): 109–21; "Surgimiento y recuperación de una contra-cultura en el Colombia contemporánea," *Huellas* 18 (1986): 41–46; "Vallenato: ¿Cuál tradición narrativa?" *Huellas* 19 (1987): 60–68; "¿Crescencio o don Toba? Fausses questions et vraies réponses sur le vallenato," *Caravelle* 48 (1987): 69–80; "¿Crescencio o don Toba? Falsos interrogantes y verdaderas respuestas sobre el vallenato," *Huellas* 37 (April 1993): 28–34; and "Le Vallenato: Tradition, identité, et pouvoir en Colombie," in *Musiques et sociétés en Amérique Latine*, ed. Gérard Borras (Rennes: Presses Universitaires de Rennes, 2000), 81–92. On Gilard's writings related to Colombian popular music, and especially vallenato, see Egberto Bermúdez, "Jacques Gilard y la música popular colombiana," *Caravelle* 93 (2009): 19–40.

⨑ **11** ⨒

"A Hellish Instrument"

The Story of the Tango Bandoneón

MARÍA SUSANA AZZI

Argentina's most popular music genre, the tango, had already enjoyed a long history before the *bandoneón* became its quintessential instrument. Known as a danceable music genre, tango involves everything from poetry, song, gesture, and narrative to philosophy and ethical values. During the late nineteenth century, it was a vehicle that accelerated cultural integration, weaving aesthetic and other cultural features from African, South American, and European societies in the Río de la Plata area: mainly the port cities of Buenos Aires, Argentina, and Montevideo, Uruguay. *Gauchos* (fierce and nomadic horsemen of the Pampas of mixed Spanish and Indian descent), *criollos* (native-born "Creole" Argentines), European immigrants, and African Argentines participated in the formation of the genre.

The word *tango* seems to be of Bantu origin, meaning "drums"[1] or "a social gathering with dances."[2] Over the last two hundred years, "tango" has referred to many different forms of dance and music (in chronological order): *tango de negros, tango americano* or *habanera, tango andaluz* or *tango español, tango criollo, tango rioplatense, tango argentino,* and *tango brasileiro.* The dances performed by Africans and African Argentines at the end of the eighteenth and the beginning of the nineteenth centuries, called *candombes, tambos,* and *tangos,* were prohibited by the viceroy and by the *cabildo,* or town council.[3] In all these styles of dances there was no physical contact between the dancers; however, "the" tango of the late nineteenth century, and as we know it today, is a dance of embrace—a pose borrowed from the waltz. This tango style was born in the twin cities of Buenos Aires and Montevideo sometime between 1860 and 1890.

During the period when the tango crystallized as an urban dance in the Río de la Plata area, Argentina was undergoing profound changes in population. In 1778, African Argentines constituted 29.7 percent of the population in Buenos Aires; by 1887 the percentage had declined to 1.8 percent, as the African Argentines were outnumbered by European immigrants.[4] Between 1821 and 1932, Argentina was second only to the United States among nations receiving the largest number of immigrants, followed by Canada in the third place. The total population of Argentina grew from 1.8 million people in 1870 to 8.3 million in 1915.[5] Immigrants came from all over Europe, as well as from Lebanon and Syria, with the largest number coming from Italy and the second largest from Spain. To secure land for ranching and agriculture for the rapidly growing number of newcomers, Argentina's president, Gen. Julio A. Roca, started a campaign to seize the vast plains, which further contributed to the transformation of the Argentine population: by 1879, the majority of the native Araucan people from the Pampas region had been decimated,[6] immigration was strongly encouraged, foreign capital poured in, and the railway network was expanded. In 1880, the port city of Buenos Aires was named the federal capital of the Argentine Republic: "La Gran Aldea," or "The Big Village," would soon become a metropolis.

From the Conquest to the beginning of the nineteenth century, European dances entered the Argentine provinces by way of Lima. After independence in 1816, the port city of Buenos Aires became the center of dissemination. Until the mid-1800s, the European minuet, gavotte, counterdance, and quadrille had dominated Argentine dance floors.[7] With the arrival of the popular waltz, polka, mazurka, and schottische began the decline of the brilliant Criollo choreography of former times.[8]

African Argentine dances and songs had been imitated on stage as early as the 1830s. Between 1856 and 1865, the *compañías españolas de zarzuelas* (Spanish operatic companies) performed *bailes de negros* and sang *habaneras* (*tangos americanos*).[9] The *habanera* is a Cuban dance in 2/2 time with syncopated rhythm, and one of the main influences on the birth of the tango. *Candombes* performed by African Argentines on stage were already frequent during Juan Manuel de Rosas's government (1829–52). As George Andrews notes, "The vitality of African and Afro-Argentine dance could not be repressed by *porteño* [port city] society. . . . Comparsas [musical dance groups], marching and dancing bands, were first permitted in Buenos Aires during the Carnival of 1836. All the African nations fielded themselves to parade through the streets in brilliant costumes, each with its own drum corps and dancers. These black comparsas dominated the Carnival festivities each year (except 1844 and 1852, when Governor Rosas banned Carnival because of the excessive violence) well into the 1870s, when the white comparsas began to take over."[10]

At the same time, in their search for social mobility, African Argentines began to imitate whites, incorporating the mazurka, the polka, and the waltz into their dances. Dance halls or *academias de baile* provided the meeting place for the *candombe*, the *habanera*, the polka, the mazurka, the *milonga*,[11] and the tango. In the late 1870s, African Argentines in Buenos Aires improvised a new dance with some similarities to the *candombe*, which they called "tango." The *compadritos* (young men, often thugs or pimps, from the outskirts of Buenos Aires who imitated the attitudes of the *compadres*, the urbanized *gauchos*), in a spirit of mockery, took elements of this dance, parodied them, and incorporated them in their own favorite dance of the time, the *milonga*. It was the *milonga* that would eventually develop into the tango.[12] The African Argentine dances provided the movement and cadence of the tango and inspired the curves that form the tango poses. The "figure *ocho*" in the tango comes from the *candombe*, which is composed of a succession of *ochos* (eights) drawn by the feet on the floor as a pattern for dance configurations. The figure *ocho* is the base of all movements in the tango, as all other steps pass through it. According to the tango dancer Miguel Ángel Zotto, the typical male dancers in the *academias de baile*, the *compadres* (*gauchos* of the Argentine pampas who moved to the city but maintained their traditional attire and independent attitude), and the *compadritos* imitated and mocked the leg movements of the African Argentines.[13]

The tango was danced in the neighborhoods and *arrabales* (or *orillas*, poor slum areas) on the outskirts of Buenos Aires. It was primarily a dance of the brothels, but it was also danced on the patios of the *conventillos* (tenements), where Italian, Spanish, Polish, and other immigrants shared crowded living quarters. In these early years, the tango was considered a marginal, immoral, and indecent dance, and as such it was rejected by the *porteño*[14] high society. Nevertheless, the *niños bien* (sons of well-to-do families) frequented the brothels, where they would dance and often fight with the *compadritos*.

In 1907, the tango arrived in Paris, and from there it spread to other European capitals and to New York City.[15] In aristocratic ballrooms, the tango was domesticated, leaving aside the *cortes y quebradas* (suggestive contortions followed by a pause). Upon its return to Buenos Aires, the upper class took up this new, "clean" and "decent" tango. The middle class of Buenos Aires also modified the tango in the dance halls of the Italian and Spanish associations, where they danced the *tango liscio* (or just *liso*). Without complicated leg movements, the dancers retained the stamp of elegance and the walk; and they executed the rhythm and tempo with exactitude. This smooth *tango de salón* replaced the *tango canyengue* and the *tango orillero* (both styles full of exaggerated steps and adornments) that could not be easily danced in crowded dance halls. In exhibitions, where there was more space, the dancers continued to use more complicated movements, dancing what was now called the *tango fantasía*.[16] In the 1920s, the tango was as popular in the city center as it was in the lower-class neighborhoods, although the styles remained distinct. While the dance in the center was stylized, the dancers in the *barrios* continued to adorn it with curves. When the great internal migration brought thousands of people from the Argentine provinces to the capital city of Buenos Aires during the 1940s, the tango underwent another transformation. After the midcentury, however, the popularity of the tango declined significantly.[17]

From *Bandonion* to *Bandoneón*

Legend says that in the late nineteenth century, German sailors and immigrants to Argentine shores brought along a free-reed instrument they called "Bandonion." This German Bandonion was a kind of large Konzertina (concertina), related to the diatonic button accordion but without preset chords on the bass side.[18] It was designed and manufactured by Carl Friedrich Zimmermann in the 1840s in Carslfeld, Saxony (Germany), and distributed by the Krefeld (Rheinland) merchant Heinrich Band—hence its name, *Band*onion. To boost sales, Band formed a merchant chain with family members teaching lessons and selling huge numbers of scores and sheet music for Bandonion and chamber music. In 1859 his brother Johann established a shop in Cologne. The Bandonion became so popular that it was even used in churches in the Black Forest as a substitute for the harmonium during religious services, at funerals, and open-air village dances. The Bandonion was at that time considered a sophisticated instrument well suited to be played in church, in contrast to its predecessor, the Konzertina, which remained a "folk instrument."[19]

Ernst Louis Arnold, a former coworker of Zimmermann, bought the original factory in 1864. The great demand for the improved new models allowed Arnold to increase production, making Carlsfeld into the main center for the thriving Bandonion industry. In 1911, one of Arnold's sons founded his own workshop in the same town, competing with his father's company. Both factories produced excellent Bandonions; Arnold Sr. mainly used the more costly aluminum reed plates (to cater to the demand of domestic customers), while his son Alfred continued to built in the heavier and sonorous-sounding zinc reed plates preferred by South American customers. Alfred Arnold proved to be a most effective merchant, particularly in the overseas market. His instruments, known as "A.A." ("double A" or "Doble A") were of the highest quality, yet the two world wars had a negative impact on the production, sale, and image of the popular instrument. During Hitler's regime, the Bandonion—by then regarded a quintessential working-class instrument—fell out of fashion in Germany.[20] Its production continued for export only, but due to fierce competition from other accordion manufacturers such as

Hohner in Trossingen and a restructuring of East German factories after the split from West Germany, Bandonion production eventually came to a halt.[21]

Since around 1880 Argentina imported the German *bandoneón*,[22] as shown by music catalogs of the time—although even before that date, the instrument was known and performed in the River Plate area. In the early 1890s, it had become increasingly popular among *milonga*[23] and tango groups. The *bandoneón* eventually became the key instrument in tango trios, quartets, *orquestas típicas*, and tango orchestras.[24]

In fact, the incorporation of the *bandoneón* into local ensembles can be considered the most important innovation of the first years of the twentieth century: it was the *bandoneón* that, above all other instruments, would give the great tango bands of the next decades their distinctive sonority and marvelous edge; and it was the *bandoneón* players who would become the early "stars" of tango music. The instrument's rich, plaintive, and "serious" sound was vital for the developing tradition of tango music.

Bandoneones exported to Argentina were tuned to the frequency of 440 Hertz (=A), the *orquesta típica* pitch, whereas those manufactured for the German-speaking markets were tuned to the "normal A" (435 Hertz). After Germany joined the International Pitch Convention in 1941, instrument makers switched to the "higher A" for the domestic market as well.[25] The early *bandoneón* was fitted with thirty-two buttons; later models came with fifty-three, sixty-five, or seventy-one buttons (thirty-eight buttons for the upper register, and thirty-three buttons for the lower register—the classic size adopted by *bandoneón* tango players). Since the Bandonion is a diatonic instrument, each button can produce two notes: a seventy-one-button instrument is thus able to produce 142 notes or "voices."[26] The (tango) *bandoneón*'s distinct sound results (aside from the metal amalgamation used for its reeds) from its tuning: when one button is pushed, there are only two reeds sounding. These two reeds are tuned in a pure octave.

With its many buttons, the *bandoneón* is a formidably difficult instrument to learn. Its button arrangements appear incomprehensible at first glance. They seem to have evolved without much rationale as more buttons were added to the earlier models. In Germany in 1924, a commission called for the unification of the different keyboard systems to simplify the edition of sheet music and teaching and to reduce the number of instrument models. The so-called Einheitsbandoneon ("unity *bandoneón*"), with 144 voices, was created. In the Rio Plate area by that time, however, the (tango) *bandoneón* had already taken firm root, and musicians were not inclined to accept a new model.[27]

Nowadays *bandoneones* are manufactured in Argentina (Bandoneones Mariani) and Germany (Hohner Gutjahr II Bandoneon and A.A. replicas manufactured in Klingenthal). Marked with a production number inside the wooden body, age and provenance of an old instrument can often be determined, yet forgery of labels and other dubious practices on the part of dealers and exporters had been common, and even marks of identification made with a branding iron did not protect the valuable instruments from being counterfeited.[28]

Multicultural Beginnings

The rich and volatile cultural commotion of the late nineteenth-century suburban *arrabales* of the River Plate port cities gave birth to the tango. Its music and dance tell the stories of many different people, embracing diversity and accepting nonconformity. Indeed, the tango facilitated and accelerated the assimilation of disparate European immigrant communities and an ethnically mixed array of uprooted native Argentines into a nascent urban Argentine society by generating strong social networks, symbols, and values of cultural identities—from national, urban, and cosmopolitan to *barrio* and gender identities.[29] The melting-pot society of multicultural Argentina is an important key to understanding the history and development of the tango.

The tango not only reflected cultural themes with which Argentines identified themselves; it played a significant role in shaping their very psychology. The tango lyrics were inspired by the daily drama of the newcomers, disillusioned with a burning nostalgia for the homeland left behind and a strong longing to return. In a society of fairly recent immigrants, of masses of dislocated and uprooted people, the tango offered relief and guidance.

Tango lyricists and composers convincingly conveyed the ethos of the *porteños*: nostalgia, fatalism, skepticism, sadness, melancholy, frustration, the inexorable passing of time, lost love, filial love, friendship, and more. The properties that make up the tango experience can not be derived from the elements of the whole, nor can it be considered simply as the sum of these elements. The tango is a complex system of beliefs, norms, concepts, emotions, images, words, sounds, practices, and rituals. The tango encapsulates the pity and suffering of the *porteño* and his peculiar worldview.[30] As Enrique Santos Discépolo, the son of an Italian father and an Argentine mother and one of the finest tango lyricists, once said: "The tango is a *sorrowful thought* that can be danced" (emphasis mine). Dance and music evoke nostalgia and recollections of the past, together with the Weltanschauung that is characteristic of the authentic *tanguero*, the tango aficionado.

Becoming the Quintessential Tango Instrument

At the outset, tango music was simply dance music, mostly improvised. The musical accompaniment of the *milonga-tango* was played in duple meter on violin,

guitar, and flute, with the harp sometimes replacing the guitar. Later, the mandolin, the clarinet, the piano, and sometimes the accordion were added. By the
turn of the century—the peak of European immigration to the port city of Buenos
Aires—the *bandoneón* had largely replaced the flute. As the *bandoneón* produces a
melancholic and nostalgic sound, the tango took on a more solemn character. In
the popular cafés of the waterfront district of La Boca, audiences came to listen
to the tango as music for the first time in 1903. In 1911, the bandleader Vicente
Greco (1888–1924), who had been searching for a suitable sound for the recording
studio, established a sextet with two *bandoneones*, two violins, piano, and flute.
This lineup became the standard format for the tango band, the *orquesta típica*.[31]
The basic tango tempo shifted at this point from 2/4 to 4/4. In the mid-1910s, the
bandleaders Roberto Firpo and Francisco Canaro substituted the double bass for
the flute, giving the *orquesta típica* its unique sonority. Small orchestras may have
included up to four *bandoneones*, a piano, and a string section with violins, violas,
violoncellos, and a double bass. A remarkable number of Italian surnames appear among the musicians of these bands.[32] Hence, the tango, until then strongly
influenced by the *habanera* and the *milonga*, began to assimilate Italian elements,
particularly evident in the changing pathos of the music. While the music's syncopated rhythm still points to Andalusian and African roots, the Italian musicians
left a strong mark on the tango's melody. Argentina's foremost literary figure,
Jorge Luis Borges, with a curious disdain for Italians, acknowledged the Italian
influence on local music:

> The early *milonga* and tango may have been foolish, even harebrained, but they
> were bold and gay. The later tango is like a resentful person who indulges in
> loud self-pity while shamelessly rejoicing at the misfortunes of others. Back in
> 1926 I remember blaming the Italians (particularly the Genoese from the Boca)
> for the denigration of the tango. In this myth or fantasy, of our "native" tango
> perverted by "gringos," I now see a clear symptom of certain nationalistic her-
> esies that later swept the world—under the impetus of the Italians, of course.[33]

In the years around 1920, tango music moved from its formative era, known as
the *guardia vieja* (old guard), into its mature phase—the Golden Age. The 1920s
were marked by the formation of a number of magnificent dance bands, with
bandleaders and instrumentalists paying closer attention to musical quality, its
mass popularity underpinned by the spread of phonographs and radios. Predictably, the tango also became a form of popular song.

The 1930s inaugurated the Golden Age's second great period, which coincided
with the upsurge of nationalism in the Argentine political arena.[34] Radio stations
and recording companies favored Argentine music, so the best tango artists were
broadcasting daily on the radio. The radio was an enormously powerful source at

the time: competing artists began to improve the quality of their bands and change the lineup. The typical sextet was to lose ground as tango bandleaders belonging to both schools expanded their ensembles. The "modern tango" was born with the appearance of Aníbal Troilo (1914–75) and his orchestra in 1937. Troilo symbolized for many the typical port-city man—the *hombre porteño* from the *barrios* of Buenos Aires. He was also simply one of the finest bandoneonists there has ever been or is ever likely to be.[35]

The revival of the tango as a dance in the late 1930s had an unavoidable impact on the structure of tango ensembles, and consequently on orchestration. The larger the orchestras grew, the more need there was for arrangers. The arranger and composer Ismael Spitalnik recalled the changes that became necessary:

> We had to study harmony and counterpoint and apply the new knowledge to enrich the interpretation of the tango. . . . The demand for greater responsibility and the discipline imposed by the music stand—the need to be able to read music—raised the average professional capacity of the musicians. It was very different work from thirty years earlier, when there would be a trio or a quartet *a la parrilla* [to play by ear], with only one score on the piano. The arranger and the music stand disciplined the musicians. From a musical point of view, we stood in opposition to the so-called classical musicians who looked down on us and despised us like rats. But later on the violinists who had mastered the tango played in Symphony Orchestras—the professional quality had improved so much.[36]

The 1950s brought the decline of the tango—its Golden Age came to an end, coinciding with the arrival of rock 'n' roll on the one side, and with the virtual assimilation of the immigrant communities into Argentine society on the other side. This latter process greatly reduced the function of the tango as a means of bringing many disparate nationalities together.[37] The larger orchestras of the 1940s were gradually replaced by smaller ensembles of between three and nine members, and the relationship between the orchestra and audience changed. Whereas in earlier decades the people themselves had been active participants in the tango, the small loyal audience now simply paid the admission price and sat and listened.

A Hellish Macho Instrument

"The *bandoneón* is a hellish instrument," the bandoneonist Rodolfo Mederos once said. "It was made and developed in Germany, at a time when things were meant to last, a time when plastic didn't exist. The materials were noble: wood, metal, leather, mother-of-pearl—they were all used in its construction. For a bandoneonist, the instrument becomes ones's alter ego—it is partly oneself, partly one's wife. There's even a homosexual element to it. One feels possessed and possessor, one caresses it, is aware of its temperature."[38]

Although the *bandoneón* is recognized as the quintessential tango instrument and the tango a national symbol, it has never completely overcome its association with its birthplace—the brothels and cabarets of Buenos Aires's proletarian suburbs—and, hence, the stigma of being low-class, licentious, and lewd. It is no wonder, then, that an Argentine bandoneonist recalled that, in the 1930s, "when we played a tango in family gatherings, if there was a priest in the house or venue, he left the place. . . . I never played [the *bandoneón*] at churches. The priest did not want me to. He told me that the *bandoneón* was born in the brothels." [39] In those days, he emphasized, theology students weren't allowed to listen to tangos in the seminary.

Even half a century later, the church still held an strong antipathy against the *bandoneón*: my request in 1989 to organize a concert with J. S. Bach's music performed by a *bandoneón* octet in a town church was blatantly rejected by the bishop of the diocese. Ironically, the related *bandonika* had been allowed into the Catholic church—it apparently was not associated with city life and did not carry the stigma of "impurity" as the *bandoneón* did. This kind of contradiction recalls the ruling in late nineteenth-century southern Germany to allow the Bandonion—but not the concertina—to substitute for the harmonium during worship. Curiously, the tango *bandoneón* took vengeance in Leipzig, Germany: the Argentine composer and bandoneonist Alejandro Barletta performed Bach's music in the church where Johann Sebastian Bach was buried. Within a different cultural framework, the tango *bandoneón* was thus admitted into church.[40]

While the *bandoneón* was able to transcend some of the socially imposed boundaries, it remained firmly in men's hands. Indeed, bandoneonists, like tango musicians in general, were male—with only a few notable exceptions. When Paquita Bernardo presented her sextet in 1921, the crowd that gathered was so huge that traffic had to be diverted. Paquita was the first professional female *bandoneón* player—the singer Carlos Gardel called her "the only woman who has mastered the *macho character* of the *bandoneón*" (my emphasis).[41] It was certainly more common to see a woman tango singer than a female musician. Even nowadays, a female *bandoneón* player is a rather unusual sight, as Susana Ratcliff recalls her experience in the 1990s:

> When I walk around the city [Buenos Aires] with my *bandoneón* case, when I get on a bus, I can see the surprise in the driver's eyes. The case looks familiar, he knows it's a *bandoneón*, but, in the hands of a woman . . ."No, it can't be." Actually, this reaction makes me feel good. Also, when men look at me, they make

me feel as if I've stolen something. What is a woman doing carrying that case? I like the look on the faces of the ticket collectors, the bus conductors. I put my *bandoneón* to one side, and the bus driver says to me, "I used to play, I played with De Caro's brother. I used to go to his house." He's steering and collecting tickets. . . . There are a lot of *bandoneón*-playing bus drivers.[42]

Tango Nuevo: The New Tango

From its onset, tango music was a blend of many different cultural components, and over the years it has constantly evolved as new elements have been incorporated into the main body of tango. Astor Piazzolla[43] transformed the "traditional tango" of the Golden Age into a new style: *tango nuevo.* A masterly composer and *bandoneón* player, Piazzolla won increasing international fame with his Quintet in the 1980s in Europe, North and South America, and Japan.

Born in Mar del Plata in 1921 and taken by his parents to New York at age four, Piazzolla grew up on the tough streets of the city's Lower East Side. As a teenager he became passionately fond of jazz and classical music, while also learning the *bandoneón.* On his return to Argentina at age sixteen, he quickly found his place in the flourishing tango world, then at its peak in Argentina, joining the most legendary dance band of the period and in 1946 forming his own band. He studied with Alberto Ginastera—Argentina's most important nationalist composer—and tried for a while to establish himself as a classical composer. In 1954 he went to study with Nadia Boulanger in Paris. Boulanger was an outstandingly influential teacher of composition. The list of her pupils is long and includes many distinguished composers, especially North Americans (Copland, Harris, Thomson, Carter, and Piston). She was a frequent visitor to the United States, teaching at Juilliard. It was Boulanger who finally convinced Piazzolla to play the tango rather than classical music. "[Your] music is well written," she told him, "but it lacks *feeling.*" It was a verdict Boulanger handed out to most of her pupils. For a while, Piazzolla was disheartened, walking the streets and pouring out his woes to his friends. Boulanger soon forced him out of his malaise. She asked him what music he played in Argentina. Piazzolla reluctantly admitted that it was the tango. "I love that music!" she exclaimed. "But you don't play the piano . . . to perform tangos. What instrument *do* you play?" Once again Piazzolla could barely bring himself to tell her it was the *bandoneón.* Boulanger reassured him: she had heard the instrument in music by Kurt Weill (Dreigroschenoper), and Stravinsky himself appreciated its qualities. Finally, Boulanger persuaded Piazzolla to play one of his tangos on the piano. He chose "Triunfal." At the eighth bar she stopped him, took him by his hands, and told him firmly: "*This* is Piazzolla! Don't ever leave it!"[44] She told him to develop his own modern tango style, which he did with an extraordinary sequence of works, played by his notable groups—the Octet (1955), the first Quintet (1960), and the Nonet (1971).

Piazzolla's revolutionary experiments with tango music brought him fierce hostility from traditional tango fans. He remained a highly controversial figure in Argentina for the rest of his life. In the mid-1970s, partly in frustration, he based himself in Europe, memorably collaborating with Gerry Mulligan and gradually becoming more widely known. He was briefly drawn into an unsuccessful "electronic" phase (1975–77) before reverting to his true vein with the formation of his second Quintet (1978), which over the next decade sometimes worked with the Italian singer Milva and the jazz-vibraphonist Gary Burton. With the new quintet and its brilliant "contemporary chamber music," Piazzolla won genuine international renown—which has grown still greater since his death in 1992. *Billboard* magazine called him "the hottest composer around."[45]

Piazzolla used to say that he had had three teachers: Alberto Ginastera, Nadia Boulanger, and the city of Buenos Aires. His music reflected and spoke to deep feelings. Although he kept the tango's essential spirit, he made tango to listen to and not for dancers. He did not follow the tango tradition and, as a result, he was rejected by conservative *tangueros.* Piazzolla was as controversial as his audience was heterogeneous: jazz fans, classical-music lovers, rock musicians, university students, and youth. By creating the "new tango," he not only fought the establishment but came to represent a new Argentina with different issues and new sonorities. Buenos Aires has changed dramatically from the *pequeña aldea* to the modern metropolis inserted in the global village.

Piazzolla was an intensely dedicated and disciplined musician. In the years when he played with Troilo at the Tibidabo until four in the morning, he went on three hours later to rehearsals with the Orquesta Filarmónica at the Colón Opera House. Piazzolla had never liked the traditional practice of sitting while playing his instrument. It reminded him too much, he said, of an old woman doing her knitting; it symbolized the world he was trying to reject, or at least renew. Standing up was his declaration of independence.[46]

The qualities of the *bandoneón* have often been recognized outside the tango tradition. "Everything can be played on the *bandoneón,*" the world-famous Spanish cellist Pablo Casals once said.[47] But the finest word-picture stems from a member of the audience who heard one of Piazzolla's concerts in Vienna in the 1980s. It is a description of the onstage Piazzolla in full action:

> He has become one with this instrument. . . . And so, he continues to hold on to it in a double-fisted grip, as if grasping the horns of a bull, digs deep into the music, slams on both sides of the *bandoneón* in spite of its protestations, pulls it apart abruptly, pushing, pressing and oppressing it, hangs on to the keys like

Figure 11.1 Ink drawing
of Astor Piazzolla and
his *bandoneón* by Dedé
Wolff, Piazzolla's first
wife, 1983. María Susana
Azzi Collection.

a race-car driver navigating a hair-pin bend, then lets single notes glide down
his shin—while deftly turning a page with his left hand—then catches them at the
bottom and pulls them to the top with him. He sighs, breathes, whispers, cries
and thinks with the thing, rests in its melodies, dreams himself into it, makes
the bellows tremble by tapping the beat on the black wood, and then looking
down at it all of a sudden in surprise, as if he was holding a screaming, roaring,
irrepressible life-form in his hands. . . . He dances with the instrument, rides
it standing still, and finally jumps up high in the air like a kicking pony let loose
in the springtime. Triumphantly, he pulls apart the bandoneón three feet above

his head, like a brilliant magician showing off his last card trick, like a victorious Laocoön pulling off another defeat of the dragon. . . . Piazzolla really has no choice: he must play.[48]

By nationality, Astor Piazzolla was Argentine. All four of his grandparents were immigrants from Italy—four among the millions of Italians who moved to Argentina in its Golden Age of prosperity and whose mark on Argentine culture remains so vivid today. Deep down, Piazzolla himself was always something of an uprooted, nostalgic migrant. At one time or another he lived in Mar del Plata, New York, Buenos Aires, Rome, Paris, and Punta del Este. Yet although he drew inspiration from several different traditions, his music remained essentially Argentine. As a composer, arranger, bandleader, and performer, his specialty was the music of Buenos Aires: the tango. But although he was thoroughly *tanguero* (i.e., thoroughly imbued with the tango culture), he always played the music of Buenos Aires in his own way. His work brought about something approaching a convergence of the tango, classical music, and jazz. He took tango music (like jazz, a tradition with murky origins) and turned it into a form of contemporary chamber music. He broke with the traditional tango—ossifying in the 1950s after its thirty years of hegemony as Buenos Aires's popular music—and for this, he was never forgiven by traditionalists. The absurd war between *piazzollistas* and anti-*piazzollistas* in Argentina lasted for decades. An agent of deep renewal in tango music, Piazzolla himself constantly evolved, his work reflecting Buenos Aires, the hustle and din of contemporary society, and the whole range of human emotions. Loved and vilified, he died in 1992.

Piazzolla is now regarded as one of the glories of Argentine culture. He always tried to combine his thrust to renew tango music with his own pleasure in experimenting, constantly crossing frontiers and exploring diverse musical cultures and genres. He was a living embodiment of integration and crossover. That does not mean that he ever denied his Argentine roots. But he was also in a real sense a wanderer, always open to new influences. Without ever ceasing to be *tanguero*, he aimed to fashion something more universal. Tolstoy's phrase, "Paint your village, and you paint the world," was one of Piazzolla's favorites. He painted *his* big village with such consummate skill that musicians (and eventually audiences) flocked to him on four continents. He did not live to see the scale of it, but the world has now discovered Astor Piazzolla—Argentine, *tanguero*, and, above all, musician.[49]

His legacy—and the legacy of the many bandoneonists before him—make it impossible to separate the concept of the tango from the sonic properties of the *bandoneón*. The sound of this peculiar instrument has generated cultural memories—emotional memories articulated in music.

Notes

1. Winifred Kellersberger Vass, *The Bantu-Speaking Heritage of the United States* (Los Angeles: University of California, Los Angeles, 1979).

2. George Reid Andrews, *The Afro-Argentines of Buenos Aires, 1800–1900* (Madison: University of Wisconsin Press, 1980), 165–66.

3. Ibid., 65–66.

4. Results of eight censuses of the City of Buenos Aires, 1778–1887 (ibid., 66).

5. Alfredo Irigoin, "La evolución industrial en la Argentina (1870–1940)," in *Libertas* (Buenos Aires: La Escuela Superior de Economía y Administración de Empresas, 1984), 254.

6. During the times of the Spanish conquest, the Araucan people inhabited the central area of Chile and later also the Argentine Pampas.

7. Vicente Gesualdo, *Historia de la Música en la Argentina* (Buenos Aires: Editorial Beta, 1961), 181.

8. A. L. Lloyd, *Dances of Argentina* (London: Max Parrish, n.d.), 5–10. For more information, I highly recommend the excellent introduction of this book.

9. The *zarzuela* is an idiomatic form of opera in which music is intermingled with spoken dialogue. The name comes from entertainments performed in the seventeenth century for Philip IV and his court at the Royal Palace of La Zarzuela near Madrid. The first known composer of *zarzuelas* was Juan Hidalgo, ca. 1644. In the eighteenth century, the popularity of the form was challenged by faster-paced and more satirical *tonadillas*. Despite brief revivals, the *zarzuela* languished until the national movement of the nineteenth century, when desire to create a Spanish opera led to compositions of numerous *zarzuelas*. See, "Zarzuela," in *The Oxford Dictionary of Music*, rev. ed., ed. Michael Kennedy (New York: Oxford University Press, 2006), 978–79.

10. Andrews, *Afro-Argentines*, 160.

11. A form of improvised song to which choreography was added around 1860, the *milonga* was first called the *habanera con cortes y quebradas*, and later, *baile con corte*.

12. Simon Collier, "The Tango is Born," in ¡*Tango! The Dance, the Song, the Story*, ed. Simon Collier, Artemis Cooper, María Susana Azzi, and Richard Martin (London: Thames and Hudson, 1995), 44. See also Andrews, *Afro-Argentines*, chap. 9.

13. Miguel Ángel Zotto, personal communication, Buenos Aires, October 5, 1991.

14. A *porteño* is an inhabitant of the port city of Buenos Aires.

15. Chris Goertzen and María Susana Azzi, "Globalization and the Tango," *Yearbook for Traditional Music* 31 (1999): 67–76; María Susana Azzi, *Antropología del tango: Los protagonistas* (Buenos Aires: Ediciones Olavarría, 1991), 19–57; Sergio Pujol, *Historia del baile* (Buenos Aires: Emecé, 1999), 65–92; Artemis Cooper, "Tangomania in Europe and North America: 1913–1914," in ¡*Tango! The Dance, the Song, the Story*, ed. Simon Collier, Artemis Cooper, María Susana Azzi, and Richard Martin (London: Thames and Hudson, 1995), 66–100.

16. Azzi, *Antropología*, 19–57.

17. María Susana Azzi, "The Golden Age and After: 1920s-1990s," in ¡*Tango! The Dance*,

the Song, the Story, ed. Simon Collier, Artemis Cooper, María Susana Azzi, and Richard Martin (London: Thames and Hudson, 1995), 156–60.

18. The Argentine *bandoneón* belongs to the concertina family. According to Hornbostel-Sachs, the *bandoneón* is a so-called intermittent aerophone (Hornbostel/Sachs no. 412.132). What distinguishes the construction of the *bandoneón* from the concertina is its special combination of air ducts, its long plates, and the layout of its buttons. Although the last few decades have brought some sound improvements based on acoustic research, the *bandoneón* construction has remained the same. See Maria Dunkel, "Bandoneón Pure: Dances of Uruguay," liner notes to *René Marino Rivero,* CD SF 40431 (Washington D.C.: Smithsonian/Folkways Recordings, 1993), 19.

19. A magazine for accordion music established in Leipzig in 1895 was renamed a year later to *Allgemeine Concertina- und Bandonion-Zeitung,* reflecting the growing popularity of the Bandonion in the area: about eighteen Bandonion clubs were registered in Leipzig (but not a single concertina club). Wünsch, the successor of Uhlig, the inventor of the German concertina, wrote in 1890: "This instrument [Bandonion] is becoming more and more known so that all instruments with 88 to 260 voices are now called Bandonions." In the early twentieth century, distinct keyboard systems were developed in different German accordion centers such as the Rheinisch and Chemnitzer/Karlsfelder. See "Music Instruments from Saxony," http://www.inorg.chem.ethz.ch/tango/band/band_node3.html (accessed January 8, 2009).

20. See chapter 1 of this volume.

21. In 1964, the last Bandonion left the Ernst Louis Arnold factory, whose craftsmen began to produce parts for diesel injection pumps ("Music Instruments from Saxony").

22. Originally written with an "i," the Bandonion for the Argentine market changed to "bandoneon"—without accent.

23. The *milonga* is an improvised rural song form that around 1860 added dance steps (strongly influenced by the *habanera* and the mazurka), which mutated into the tango around 1880. The word is also a synonym for "dance gathering" or "cabaret."

24. *Orquesta típica* is the standard term since 1911 for a tango band or orchestra. Tango trios generally included piano or flute, violin, and guitar, with the *bandonéon* replacing the guitar. Tango orchestras may have included up to four *bandoneones,* a sizable string section with violins, a cello and a double bass, and a piano.

25. Dunkel, "Bandoneón Pure," 9.

26. There exist also chromatic, uni-sonic (same note on push and pull) *bandoneones.* Tango musicians, however, prefer the diatonic, bi-sonic *bandoneón.*

27. One of the less-popular models used in Argentina is the nowadays hardly known *bandonika,* commonly called *verdulera-bandoneón* by those who tune or repair it. The term *verdulera* refers to a market woman who sells vegetables and herbs (*verduras* in Spanish). The *bandonika* shares traits with the *bandoneón* and the *verdulera*: it has the square base and keyboards that run parallel to the motion of the bellows of the *bandoneón* and the same number of keys as the eight-bass *verdulera.* See Azzi, *Antropología,* 308.

28. Dunkel, "Bandoneón Pure," 6–8.

29. Goertzen and Azzi, "Globalization and the Tango," 67.

30. The colors grey and blue, mentioned in tango lyrics, are also prevalent in the palette of painters who re-create the ambience of the tango visually.

31. No cylinder recordings with *bandoneón* were made. The first recordings of tangos with *bandoneón* were made by the Orquesta Típica Criolla of Vicente Greco on 78 rpm in 1911.

32. In the period from 1901 to 1910, nearly four thousand European musicians migrated to Argentina. See Jorge Ochoa de Eguileor and Eduardo Valdés, *¿Dónde durmieron nuestros abuelos? Los hoteles de inmigrantes en la ciudad de Buenos Aires* (Buenos Aires: Centro Internacional para la Conservación del Patrimonio en la Argentina, 2000). See also María Susana Azzi, "Multicultural Tango: Italian Immigration and Their Impact on the Tango in Argentina," *International Journal of Musicology* 5 (1997): 437–56.

33. Jorge Luis Borges, "History of the Tango," in *Evaristo Carriego: A Book about Old-Time Buenos Aires*, trans. Norman Thomas Di Giovanni (1930; reprint, New York: E. P. Dutton, 1984), 143–48.

34. María Susana Azzi, "The Tango, Peronism, and Astor Piazzolla during the 1940s and '50s," in *From Tejano to Tango: Latin American Popular Music*, ed. Walter A. Clark (New York: Routledge, 2001), 25–40.

35. Azzi, "Golden Age," 146–47.

36. Ibid., 150–51.

37. Ibid., 156.

38. Qtd. in Cooper, "Tangomania," 113.

39. Roger Lacoste, personal communication, Hinojo, Province of Buenos Aires, June 16, 1989. At the time of the interview, Lacoste was seventy-four years old. The town of Hinojo had a population of 2,600.

40. Azzi, *Antropología*, 307–9.

41. Qtd. in Azzi, "Golden Age," 119–21.

42. Qtd. in Collier, *¡Tango!* 113.

43. This part is based on my co-written book with Simon Collier, *Le Grand Tango: The Life and Music of Astor Piazzolla* (New York: Oxford University Press, 2000).

44. Alberto Speratti, *Con Piazzolla* (Buenos Aires: Editorial Galerna, 1969), 72–73.

45. Joe Goldberg, "Mas que tango," in *Billboard*, September 6, 1997, 52.

46. Ibid., 54.

47. Ibid., 152.

48. Paul Badde, liner notes to *Astor Piazzolla y su Quinteto Tango Nuevo: Tristezas de un Doble A*, trans. Eugene Seidel, CD 15970–2 (Germany: Messidor, 1987).

49. Ibid., xi–xii.

⩗ 12 ⩘

No ma' se oye el fuinfuán

The Noisy Accordion in the
Dominican Republic

SYDNEY HUTCHINSON

Merengue is widely recognized as the national music of the Dominican Republic, its most popular and best-known export. Originally a representative of the country's northern Cibao region, this music and dance became a national symbol, first in reaction to the United States's occupation of the country in 1916–24, and then, more permanently, under the dictatorship of Rafael Trujillo (1930–61). Because of its symbolic centrality, merengue has been the subject of much debate in the public sphere, a debate that seems to grow in intensity whenever migration and/ or economic crises threaten traditional urban class hierarchies or understandings of Dominicanness. This debate is complicated by the fact that in the twentieth century merengue split into different genres, catering to different social groups: the *orquesta* merengue, centered around wind and brass instruments, and the accordion-based *merengue típico*.

By rereading this history and analyzing the discourse surrounding *típico* instruments, one can see that instruments like the accordion represent much more than "things" or even music. They are bearers of cultural meanings and as such often take the brunt of social criticism. The discourse about merengue instruments and the sounds they make is related to social processes such as urbanization, migration, class transformations, and gender construction. In this essay, I examine how the accordion is played in Dominican *merengue típico*, and I outline historical and contemporary meanings of the accordion as related to class, ethnicity, and gender, suggesting that the instrument often embodies Dominicans' changing ideas about themselves. To construct this argument, I rely on newspaper articles, scholarly and lay histories, the visual arts, interviews with practitioners, and my own fieldwork conducted among *típico* musicians in New York City and Santiago, the Dominican Republic's second-largest city and center of the Cibao, since 2001 and 2004, respectively.

The Social Accordion

Class conflict has long been a factor in the production of merengue. It has even been said that Trujillo forced the upper class to dance merengue as a kind of punishment for their earlier rejection of him. Classist views of *merengue típico* are often manifested in descriptions of the accordion's sound as noise rather than music, which date back to the instrument's first appearance on the island in the early 1870s. At that time, journalistic invectives against the accordion included one by a former Dominican president, Ulises Espaillat, who compared the "insipid and hair-raising [*horripilante*]" accordion to stringed instruments like the *cuatro*, "melancholy and so full of majestic harmony."[1] Such opinions helped to push merengue and the accordion out of the cities for nearly fifty years, initiating their conversion into symbols of the rural peasantry.

Under Trujillo, merengue reentered the city by force—but this time without the traditional accordion. In the urban big band or *orquesta* of the 1930s, the button accordion was either replaced by a piano accordion or removed entirely, while the *güira*, similarly considered an instrument of noise rather than music, was reduced to a tangential role. While this new urban style catered to the middle and upper classes in the city centers, rural *merengue típico* remained on the outside. This position is still visible today in Santiago, where most important *típico* sites are located on the outskirts of the city. Yet, perhaps ironically, once the sound had been removed from the button accordion and its "noise" was no longer heard, it seemed to become an acceptable national symbol. Although the instrument was removed from the *orquesta* and barely appeared in folklore scholarship of the time, it appeared centrally in many nationalist paintings and even in nationalist poetry.

I suggest that middle- and upper-class Dominicans rejected the accordion even as merengue rose to the status of national music because the instrument represented a threat. Elites likely perceived the lower classes to be usurping their power and invading city centers. If so, it makes sense that in the wake of the massive urbanization and migration that occurred following Trujillo's death in 1961, polemics resurfaced over the noisy accordion and, implicitly, over those who play it.

In the 1970s, rural migrants brought their accordion music with them to the cities, and debate about the music and the instrument resurfaced on a large scale, often expressed in newspaper columns. *Típico* musicians themselves were not given the chance to speak in these public fora, and their music was generally ignored by the press. Journalists and other commentators, often *orquesta* musicians, referred to the accordion in irate newspaper editorials as a "limited" instrument that "impoverishes," "strangles,"[2] and otherwise does violence to Dominican music and, by extension, to Dominican culture as a whole. Similarly, the migrants who play and support it were later described, rather overdramatically, as "cultural terrorists."[3]

Today, Santiago's long-standing and deeply entrenched two-class structure has been further disrupted by the return of transnational migrants, whose accumulation of wealth puts them on an economic, if not a social, par with the traditional elite. Since the 1990s, some of these *retornados* or "Dominican Yorks" have invested great sums of money in *merengue típico moderno*, acting in the traditional role of patron to this controversial "modern" style defined by its focus on inventive arrangements, expanded instrumentation, tight backing vocals, precise rhythmic breaks, influences from foreign styles like hip-hop and *reggaetón*, and a sectional form organized around riffs called *mambos*. Others work to ensure *merengue típico*'s passage to the next generation by purchasing accordions for relatives back on the island. Many Santiagueros consider both *retornados* and their music to be tacky, even as they also recognize the music's power as a symbol of Cibaeño and Dominican identity. These migrants are the "cultural terrorists" who spark elite fears over the complications they bring to traditional class structures.

Jacques Attali suggests that when sound is discussed in moral terms, it is often divided into the categories of "noise" (disorder) and "music" (order).[4] These categories are often used to maintain existing social hierarchies, even as music may contest them. Indeed, Dominican elites often see musics like *merengue típico* as a kind of noise. Describing it thus is an attempt to maintain an existing social order where *orquestas*, saxophones, and urban elites stay on top, and *típico* groups, accordions, and migrants stay below. Those on the outside of this musical community could never bring themselves to accept the accordion and eschewed it in favor of the instruments one might learn via reading written scores: salon instruments, orchestra instruments, and the instruments of the municipal band. The accordion has thus been associated with the lower classes. Within the *típico*-listening community, however, accordionists are accorded a high status, as the accordionist is typically also the bandleader and gives his or her name to the group as a whole. Accordionists today are often big stars and thus little affected by the views of a wealthy minority, unless these views affect their ability to conduct business.

The title of this essay is taken from a nineteenth-century *décima* by Juan Antonio Alix,[5] where the onomatopoeic "fuinfuán" depicts the sound of the accordion's bellows and reinforces the belief that accordions make noise, not music. In contrast, the recent merengue "Fi-fuá" by the *típico moderno* accordionist Nicol Peña

Figure 12.1 Members of the children's group Tipifrontera practice in the border town
of Dajabón, Dominican Republic, 2007. Photograph by Sydney Hutchinson.

uses the onomatopoeia proudly, noting (or perhaps hoping) that people "all over
the world" are dancing to this music.

The accordion and *merengue típico* therefore have an ambiguous position in
Dominican society today. For instance, the basic trio of core *típico* instruments,
accordion accompanied by the metal *güira* scraper and double-headed *tambora*
drum, is often simply termed a *perico ripiao*. The usage of this term reflects Dominicans' varying evaluations of the music. A *perico ripiao* trio is a nostalgic evo-
cation of the countryside for many Dominicans or, for Cibaeños, even of home
itself; indeed, today such groups can only be heard playing at family get-togethers,
in small towns, or for tourists, since the popular *merengue típico moderno* style
utilizes a much expanded instrumentation. Yet because of the term's association with musicians that can be paid cheaply and with somewhat suspect origins
(the term is sometimes traced to a Santiago brothel of the turn of the twentieth
century), those who today play the music professionally prefer to call it *merengue
típico*. The latter term suggests music that is consciously traditional as well as
rural, and therefore a respectable upholder of traditional values and preserver
of Dominican identity—even though the term and the music in its contemporary

style are a creation of the cities. Struggle over terminology is thus a power play, an attempt to raise or lower the status of this musical genre.

Similarly, newspaper articles tend to avoid the more obviously derogatory tone favored in the past, but the nostalgia that has replaced it is often either patronizing toward modern-day musicians or leaves them out entirely. For example, in an article discussing Rafael Chaljub Mejía's book on *merengue típico* and the CD compilation *Ripiando el Perico*, a noteworthy effort to bring *merengue típico* to the middle classes, Fátima Álvarez writes:

> It is high time for that [traditional] merengue to cease to be the exclusive property of those noble workers of the earth, of the flirtatious mulattas that populate these lands, or of the old men who tell their adventures through the notes of the accordion.
>
> Oh Ñico! If only your mouth could sing today / this song of the people / if your hands could rescue us / and give us comfort![6]

The reporter poetically calls to the foundational accordionist Ñico Lora to return Dominicans to their roots, at the same time as she calls for the removal of *merengue típico* from the hands of peasants like Ñico. Conflicted feelings like these—merengue was better when it was played by peasants, but such "backward" people should not be those who represent the Dominican Republic today; accordionists of the past were noble, while those of today are vulgar—are typical of contemporary middle-class attitudes toward *típico*. Scholarly works, too, tend to leave the accordion out of the discussion because of long-standing views of the instrument and the music as either "simple" or not music at all. Catana Pérez de Cuello, in an otherwise excellent history of merengue, writes the instrument off as nothing more than a "setback" (*atraso*) in merengue's development.[7]

Views of the accordion as noisemaker likely first arose because the sound of these instruments made audible the fact that the lower classes would not stay in their place any longer. This potential threat has in fact become reality with the return of emigrants who now have economic capital to equal those who consider themselves their social "betters." The conflicting attitudes about *típico* that circulate in the Dominican Republic therefore indicate continued discomfort with changing social structures as well as profound uncertainty about Dominican identity in the age of transnational migration, particularly as regards the role of traditional music and its updated variants in creating that identity.

The Ethnic Accordion

The classed meanings of the accordion and the *típico* ensemble are further complicated by the fact that these instruments also have ethnic identities. The conflation of instrument with ethnicity is common throughout Latin America, where "national" musics are often mestizo ones. In the case of the Dominican Republic, the trio of *traditional merengue típico* instruments has been used more than any other symbol, except perhaps the *sancocho* stew, to represent the nation's triethnic makeup.[8] It is said that as *sancocho* combines the indigenous *yuca* root with the African plantain and European beef, so does the merengue combine the European button accordion with African *tambora* drum and supposedly indigenous *güira* scraper.

The assignment of ethnicities to instruments is based less on the histories of the instruments, which in the case of the percussion are hardly known, than it is on a hierarchical ordering of sounds that places melodic instruments at the top and percussive ones at the bottom. In the case of the Dominican Republic, this polarity was also one of class and race: the first group represented Europe and was capable of learning and producing "civilized" music; the second was symbolic of Africa and the unlettered peasantry and thus could produce only "savage" noise. For example, when the Puerto Rican educator Eugenio María de Hostos visited the Dominican Republic in 1892, he wrote of a party he attended in which "the musical instruments are also the agreement and coordination of one instrument of civilization, the accordion, and one instrument of savagery, the bass drum [perhaps *tambora*]."[9]

An outsider to Dominican culture, Hostos gives the expected interpretation: as a recognizably European instrument, the accordion would occupy a higher rung on the social ladder according to the aforementioned hierarchy of sounds. In the Dominican Republic, however, this has not been the case, for three principal reasons. First of all, while within the *típico* community the instrument's origin may give it prestige, outside of it, the accordion's classed meanings seem to have trumped its historical origins. Secondly, the accordion's ties to European colonial powers have made it a suspect source of "national" music for those of a nativist bent. To cite one example, the musician Rafael Ignacio believed that "[merengue] was most denaturalized when the German accordion entered. . . . The foreign influences in our merengue are fixed because the rhythmic basis is African and the melodic basis is Spanish."[10] And finally, Deborah Pacini Hernández suggests that nineteenth-century urban Dominicans reacted strongly against the accordion because the instrument allowed musicians to bring the African-influenced percussive elements of merengue to the fore.[11] Her suggestion gives one possible explanation for the opposition between stringed instruments and the accordion discussed above.

The dialectic between Afrocentric and Eurocentric ways of playing accordion changed over time. During the Trujillo era, Pacini Hernández notes, the *merengue orquestas* had suppressed African-derived rhythmic tendencies, principally by eliminating the *tambora* from their earliest incarnations, and thus highlighted the Hispanic/melodic aspects of the music; but after Trujillo, that trend was reversed.[12] Afro-Americanisms have indeed become more prominent and more accepted in merengue music since the fall of Trujillo, but the accordion has still not improved its status. Ironically, while accordion music may have been too African for nineteenth-century upper-class Dominicans and for twentieth-century Trujillistas, the instrument of German descent was not African enough for post-Trujillo activists. Even Fradique Lizardo, a Dominican folklorist known for his advocacy on behalf of Afro-Dominican traditions, disdained it as a "limited" instrument.[13]

These changes were also related to a change in instruments and the split between *merengue típico* and *merengue de orquesta* initiated in Trujillo's time. Contemporary *merengue orquestas* like that of Luis Alberti, as well as some other groups playing to the middle classes or to immigrants abroad (like Angel Viloria's Conjunto Típico Cibaeño, which was *típico* in name only), changed from button to piano accordion to improve their status and acceptability to the higher classes. The piano accordion symbolized urbanity, cosmopolitanism, and "high" culture, unlike the button accordion of the rural peasantry and urban marginals. Because the button accordion is in many ways better suited to the rapid, staccato, percussively rhythmic playing found in *merengue típico* than the piano accordion, the switch to the latter may have reinforced the shift to more melodic, European-sounding playing in *orquesta merengue* that Pacini Hernández described.

The techniques used to play accordion have had little effect on popular perceptions of the instrument, including its assigned ethnicity. For musicians or ethnomusicologists it may be clear that it is the musician, not the instrument, who ultimately determines what music the instrument will play, and thus it is easy to point out the Afro-Caribbean characteristics of the music Dominicans play on the accordion, in spite of the instrument's culturally distant origins. Yet much Dominican discourse about merengue continues to construe instruments in an essentialized manner in which the instrument itself is apparently the agent who creates music, and origins are thus paramount. The tripartite division of Dominican culture and music remains set.

The Gendered Accordion

Dominican histories of merengue are clear about the ethnic meanings of merengue instruments, and classed meanings become evident through public debate. The instruments' genders are perhaps less obvious but are nevertheless a part of how people construct their relationships with these objects as performers and listeners. Veronica Doubleday has shown how gendered human-instrument relationships assume a variety of forms, from the bullroarer of New Guinean men's cults, protected from women's touch by taboos;[14] to the Indian association of women with *vinas*, established through the goddess Saraswati and the instrument's physical form;[15] to "in-between" instruments like the saxophone, part of both the traditionally masculine brass family and the traditionally feminine woodwinds.[16] The gendered associations of the accordion, *güira*, and *tambora* are likewise not simple, one-to-one relationships in *merengue típico*; in fact, just as *merengue típico* has both high and low status and both African and European associations, each of the instruments in the ensemble seems to embody a kind of gendered doubleness as well.

The most explicit case is that of the *tambora*, which was traditionally made of the skins of goats of two sexes, the female on the right, the male on the left (they can be told apart because the male goat has a stripe down the back that is still visible on the *tambora* skin).[17] Thus, the drum has a dual gender and "sings" in two voices, to paraphrase the poet Manuel del Cabral.[18] Similarly, the *güira* can be considered as dual-gendered through its name and performance practice. This instrument is a metal version of the gourd *güiro* scraper found elsewhere in the Caribbean, and its name is the feminized version of that relative. It is considered the domain of men because of the strength and endurance needed to play it, but is also an instrument frequently taken up by women (at home, if not on the stage).[19]

The accordion, with its focus on upper-arm strength and digital agility, is also typically coded as masculine, but it is commonly performed by women, who themselves frequently enact the partially masculinized role of the *tíguera*, as explained below. The word used for the instrument can itself be either masculine or feminine: *el acordeón* and *la acordeón* are used interchangeably by practitioners of this music. In addition, the construction and tuning of the accordion adds to the gendered meaning of the "noise" it produces. The accordion tuner Berto Reyes explains that once an instrument has been properly retuned for the playing of *merengue típico*, it will sound "hard" and "strong," just as the accordionists themselves wish to appear, and as is appropriate to the kind of urban Dominican masculinity represented by the *tíguere* (or "clever street tough"). The strength of the sound is directly related to the combination of two reeds that must work together, reeds that Reyes describes as "feminine" and "masculine." When he has properly tuned the accordion by adding the smaller, feminine reed sound to the instrument, the accordion produces a strong "mascufeminized" (*machihembriado*) sound in which the feminine reed adds aesthetic appeal and "shine" to the "hard" masculine sound, Reyes says.[20] The *güira* plays a similar role, as the Santiago-based *güira* maker El Buty explains: "The *güira* is what makes the music shine, so if the *güira* sounds bad it will never sound as it should, because the music without the shine is nothing."[21] Together, the masculine and feminine reeds, and the *güira*, *tambora*, and accordion, thus produce a dual-gendered sound.

Figure 12.2   Lidia de La Rosa performs in Queens. Photograph by Alex Perullo.

Atypically for Latin American popular and traditional musics, female instrumentalists play important roles in *merengue típico*. While in related styles like
salsa, women are confined to singing or dancing, or else are segregated into all-
female groups,[22] women in *típico* generally play accordion, thus also serving as
bandleaders in otherwise all-male groups.[23] Female accordionists now form a
significant and growing minority of performers within this musical genre, and
within a culture that has historically been considered *machista*. The fact that
women have not only been accepted in this role but also have been able to make
careers for themselves as performers and bandleaders provides evidence of a
long-standing but little-studied fluidity in Dominican gender construction. In
playing the accordion, women thus take on some masculine characteristics and
help to reconfigure gender roles.

The accordion's sound is associated with the *tíguere*, a Dominican pronuncia-
tion and spelling of the word for tiger. This male role is a masculine ideal for the
lower classes but is considered a useless ruffian among the higher ones. It emerged
as a response to urbanization and changes in the economic system that made it
impossible for most lower-class men to fulfill the obligations of the *hombre serio*,
or serious man, the previously dominant model of rural Dominican masculinity,
a provider and patriarch.[24] The rural migrants most affected by these changes

257

formed the biggest part of *merengue típico*'s audience, as they moved to the cities in the 1960s and 1970s, many of them later moving on to New York. At the same time, the legendary accordionist Tatico Henríquez adeptly negotiated the divide and the overlaps between the *tiguere* and the *hombre serio*, the rural and the urban, helping to establish the music's foothold in its new urban context while providing a role model that young men continue to emulate today.[25]

Women who play accordion today are often termed *tígueras* (female tigers). The use of this word and not the standard Spanish *tigresa* shows that this role is, at least in part, an adaptation of the related Dominican male role. Like a *tiguere*, the *tiguera* is aggressive, a flashy dresser, and unashamed of her sexuality. She knows how to *relajar* (engage in joking wordplay), how to drink, and how to party. If she is a musician, she knows how to play and take control of the stage. She looks like a woman, but she can act like a man when the situation demands it. She can also be found at many *merengue típico* events, on stage and in the audience. Just as male roles evolved over the course of the twentieth century from the *hombre serio* to the *tiguere* as a result of socioeconomic change, so have female roles moved women from the home into the street. While Peter Grant Simonson[26] found no female counterpart to the *tiguere*, I argue that a *tiguera* role has emerged as a specific way of being female over the past two decades, and also that women in *típico* helped to create and define this role.

While feminine *tigueraje* is a new development, it has deep roots in Dominican culture and was made possible by the existence of a number of prior role models. Female accordionists have been documented as far back as the early twentieth century, as in the example of Monguita Peralta, whose name lives on in merengue lyrics.[27] But the most important, perhaps the ultimate, of the *tígueras* is Fefita la Grande, the beloved *grande dame* of Dominican music. She began playing accordion as a child in the 1950s, and one of her earliest performances was for Petán Trujillo, brother of the dictator and director of the state radio and television stations. Fefita's audacity has been an important part of her self-presentation since that time. She explains, "I was a girl who wasn't like the other kids of my time. I was very alert, I had no shame. In that time the great generals trembled to go before those people, Trujillo, Petán. And for me it was like eating a piece of *yuca*."[28] Fefita's embodiment of the *tiguera* can also be seen in her aggressive stage presence, lyrics that unabashedly speak to her freedom of choice in—and enjoyment of—relations with the opposite sex, and in her release, at age sixty, of two calendars featuring herself in a different lingerie ensemble for each month.

In the wake of her success, many other young female accordionists have followed, and Fefita's performance style and strong vocal sound have been widely emulated. Yet the complications surrounding women's professionalization in the *típico* world can be seen in discussions of her accordion playing, which other accordionists often describe as unskilled at best. Certainly, her approach to rhythm is unconventional, and she generally does not play the kind of staccato arpeggiations and ornaments so highly valued in *típico* accordion playing; yet one suspects that what is judged as aberrant in a woman might have been seen as an idiosyncratic personal style in a man. Today's *tígueras* tend therefore to emulate masculine accordion technique as a bid for greater respect.

Tigueraje in both sexes is a function of class—the Dominican middle and upper classes tend to see *tígueres* as worthless street thugs, applying the term only with disdain. Among the lower classes as well as among New York Dominicans, however, young men are often proud to call themselves or their friends *tígueres*—to make a North American analogy, the *tíguere* might be comparable to the *player. Tigueras* tend to come from these same social groups, since lower-class women historically have often been free from many gender-related limitations out of sheer necessity: their families' need for additional income relaxes restrictions on movement in the street and pursuit of economic opportunities. In contrast, the pressure upper-class families exert on women to maintain decorum and propriety at all times serves to constrain the options of otherwise privileged women. The novelist and poet Julia Álvarez, herself from a privileged Dominican family, describes this kind of "entrapment" as "the golden handcuffs."[29] Thus, it is in the margins, the realm of *típico*, that women are best able to make their way into male-dominated or otherwise taboo professions.

Doubleday suggests that to play musical instruments is to wield power, and because "gender is one of the most important parameters in human power relations . . . the power play between humans over musical instruments is often enacted along gender lines."[30] The cross-cultural male dominance of musical instruments, as with other technological realms, is tied up with masculine desires for power and control.[31] Women's experiences in playing *merengue típico* stand out noticeably from this general background of feminine exclusion from instrumental music, forcing us to rethink Dominican gender roles, and indeed the whole concept of Latin American machismo as it is still often presented in academic literature. Nancy López has explained that "Dominican women have a long tradition of engaging in feminist practices through insubordination,"[32] a tradition entirely separate from North American and European feminisms. For some Dominican women, playing accordion is one way of perpetuating this tradition. Yet the gendered meanings of the accordion's sound interact with women's agency as musicians in complicated ways. The dual-gendered nature of the accordion's sound, as well as its association with noise and *tigueraje* in both its feminine and its masculine versions, may relate to the fact that women have succeeded as instrumentalists in this genre more than in any other Latin American popular music. At the same time, they may also contribute to the instrument's devaluation in the larger society.

Building and Playing Accordions

I now turn my focus from beliefs and attitudes about the accordion to the instrument itself, its construction and playing techniques. Such information is not only of use to scholars studying accordion music cross-culturally; it is also a needed intervention within the Dominican Republic itself. In spite of *típico* musicians' attempts at upward mobility, and the economic success of some of them, many members of the educated class persist in viewing them as inferior musicians, when they consider them at all. Scholars have avoided analyzing accordion music because of the belief that the accordion is capable only of playing "simple" music. In addition, I was on various occasions told that *merengue típico* players are not "real musicians" because they can not read music. These persons believe that if an instrument is learned by ear, it is therefore easier to play; similarly, an instrument normally dependent upon written notation is more difficult to play and could not be learned by ear. Naturally, none of these persons had ever attempted to play *merengue típico* or to learn music by ear.

Típico musicians are aware of this disdain, and, turning the tables on literate *orquesta* musicians and their music stands full of scores, they jibe, "If a wind comes up, they're done for." At the same time, many of them buy into the argument they have heard all their lives: that written music is somehow better and more complex. Some believe their own music *cannot* be written down, and that it is therefore fundamentally different from and likely inferior to notated music. A look at techniques used in *merengue típico* today will demonstrate the complexity of this musical style and the impressive abilities of these musicians; it will also help to dispel some of the aforementioned widely circulated Dominican myths about accordion playing.

Mark DeWitt has noted a similar situation with respect to the Cajun one-row button accordion, which has also been viewed as having had a restrictive, simplifying effect on the music.[33] He counteracts this negative view by showing how Cajun musicians have developed complex techniques to expand the capabilities of their instrument or use them to their best advantage. *Merengue típico* musicians have also increased the complexity of their music in its nonmelodic aspects by employing finger and bellows techniques, articulation, and rhythmic elaboration. Prior researchers' perception of *merengue típico* as "simple" is due, I believe, to their focus on the collecting and notating of melodic material only, which has deflected attention from these important areas.

Finger techniques are one area of increased complexity. In *típico*, repeated notes, arpeggiation, and broken chords are a few means used to embellish the melody. The first involves trilling the index and middle fingers quickly on a single button, either to enhance the sound of a single, long note in a melody or as a part of an improvisation. The second involves placing three fingers into a chord position and playing each note separately, creating a fast, rhythmic pattern that often interacts in interesting ways with the meter—for instance, placing a three-note arpeggio over a duple-division pulse. The third typically consists of creating a chord with a third on the bottom, played by the index and middle fingers, and the melody carried by the fourth or fifth finger an octave above the top note. Then rhythmic patterns are created either by alternating the third with the top note or by hammering the whole chord together. Accordion riffs in *típico* are more chordal than melodically based, and these techniques help to increase their interest and difficulty level.

Difficult bellows techniques further increase the level of virtuosity demanded from *típico* accordionists. Many melodies by nature require multiple changes of bellows direction that can be mind-bending for those not accustomed to diatonic instruments. Bellows changes are often emphasized particularly in solos, allowing accordionists to show off strength and speed. In one such riff accordionists play constant sixteenth notes with a bellows change on nearly every note; the rapid movement of the changes adds visual excitement and a slightly nervous quality to the sound that enhances the feeling of speed.

Percussive, staccato playing is generally the preferred style of articulation. Others may be used, as when creating a slur between two notes, but not sustained throughout an entire melodic theme. As is the case with Cajun music, staccato playing keeps bellows movement to a minimum while also providing a rhythmic reference point for musicians and dancers.[34] In the Dominican Republic, it also demonstrates one's strength, agility, and general competence as an accordionist. Staccato playing may be termed *picadito* (chopped) or *picoteao*—also the name of a self-referential song characterized by a particular, precise arpeggiation on the accordion. Along with other strength- or endurance-based techniques like quick bellows changes, staccato playing is often coded as masculine. The accordionist Arsenio de La Rosa traces the current focus on staccato playing to the 1950s, during which time he learned this style from Matoncito, an influential but never recorded accordionist born in Puerto Plata. Tatico Henríquez, considered by many to be the all-time greatest accordionist in the genre, popularized the technique through his playing of "El Picoteao," a tune he learned from Matoncito.[35]

It is likely that some musical aspects of *merengue típico* developed through the application of local aesthetic preferences to the technical possibilities of the button accordion. Examples might include the pointillistic texture created by staccato playing and the focus on rhythmic rather than melodic or harmonic complexity. The enduring nature of such preferences is demonstrated by the fact that they are maintained even when translated to other instruments. For example, in the guitar merengue style that has been developing since the 1960s through the efforts of musicians like Eladio Romero Santos and the growing popularity of *bachata* groups, an accordion-like staccato sound is produced by shortening the strings of the *requinto* or lead guitar to nearly half using a capo. The shortness of the strings produces a more percussive and staccato sound. Arpeggiated riffs, similar to or even borrowed from *típico* accordion playing, are also used in merengue guitar playing.

Left-hand technique is one of the great mysteries of *típico* accordion, and mastering it might be said to be a kind of initiation for beginning accordionists. Its usage is never verbalized or otherwise explained, even in the relatively formal lessons offered by my own teacher, Rafaelito Román. A teenage accordion student told me that at first it was hard for her to learn the bass because of the difficulty in coordinating both hands. "But later you start to get motivated, and . . . you get to feeling the music in your heart, and you can play it [the left-hand part] more easily." Her father also helped her to learn the rhythm, because "[if I learn] to play with the bass . . . I can be a better accordionist." Another parallel with Cajun as well as with Tejano and *norteño* accordion playing can be found in the fact that in neither style are the bass buttons harmonically necessary, having been largely replaced in their function by the electric bass, but in all cases an accordionist who does not use the left hand is considered incompetent.[36] Accordionists employ what DeWitt terms "impossible technique": by barely tapping the left-hand buttons, accordionists suggest an accompaniment using chords the accordion is not actually able to play. Such a practice shows that accordionists often understand harmony differently than a music theorist might. For instance, in "El Diente de Oro," the first merengue I learned in its entirety, I experienced a disorienting kind of harmonic collision: in this merengue, performed in the key of C minor on a B-flat instrument, a minor tonic chord and a major dominant chord were the expected harmonies implied by the melody, but I could only accompany it with a dominant chord and a major mediant, as the tonic was not available. The situation is further complicated by the wide variety of configurations possible and available on the diatonic accordion, meaning that each instrument may have different bass notes and chords available. I was told that it did not matter which chords I actually played, as long as I played them, indicating that rhythm is more important to these musicians than harmony. Thus, when playing alone, only beginning accordionists typically leave the left hand out, and they maintain the practice even when playing with an electric bass, both to convince spectators that they are competent and simply to keep time for themselves.

Dominican accordion technique has changed over the past two decades because of the introduction of the *mambo* section, which may refer either to the latter part of the song where saxophone and accordion unite to play short, catchy, syncopated riffs that serve to motivate dancers, or to the riff itself. The section is also characterized by a driving rhythm where the *güira* plays mostly on the beat, and the *tambora* often plays a controversially truncated pattern called *maco* (toad). Today *merengue con mambo* or *merengue típico moderno* is the most popular style of *merengue típico* among young people.

Accordion playing in the 1950s was relatively tame and unadorned compared to what came after. In the 1970s and 1980s, accordionists like El Ciego de Nagua, Rafaelito Román, and King de La Rosa added new, technically difficult melodies or *pasadas* to their interpretations of traditional songs, as well as prearranged *cortes*, or rhythmic breaks played in unison by the percussion instruments. Some elderly fans complained that such practices distorted the music and interrupted the flow of the dancing.[37] Today, some complain that accordion playing has gone to the opposite extreme—from complexity to oversimplification. The accordionist Lidia de La Rosa, for one, believes that the mambo style has simplified accordion technique: "Right now, merengue is not being played with many notes, as they say—many solos and *picoteos* [rhythmic embellishment using finger techniques]. . . . Right now what is mostly being done is more mambo than anything else. It has changed a lot."[38] However, precisely because some traditionalists were criticizing the new style as too simple, too modern, or even too feminized, many young accordionists, including El Prodigio and Geniswing, are now focused on achieving ever more impressive technique in their performance of Tatico-era merengues with all their *pasadas*.

As the complicated technique used to play *merengue típico* on the accordion was developing, so was the instrument itself undergoing some changes. First of all, over the course of the twentieth century musicians switched from using a one-row to a two-row model of button accordion. The first had ten melody buttons and four for accompaniment and was designed to play in only one key; the second possessed twenty-one right-hand and eight left-hand buttons and could be played in two major keys and, with a little more difficulty, two minor ones (without leading tones). By the 1960s, the latter was widespread, and today the Hohner Erica is by far the most widely used model. The fact that the three-row model used in Mexican and Colombian accordion styles was never adopted may be a result of the association of the two-row instrument with iconic figures like Tatico Henríquez as well as the desire of Dominican musicians to differentiate their tradition from those of other countries.

The change to a two-row instrument not only expanded the accordionists' harmonic and fingering possibilities but also led to a change in finger technique. Before, accordionists had played in a sitting position with the instrument at a distance from the body, the accordion resting on a knee and the right thumb hooked through the leather thumb strap. Later, and particularly with the additional buttons available on the two-row accordion, they desired greater mobility of the right hand and switched to playing with the right thumb resting in a groove beside the keyboard, rather than immobilized in the thumb strap. Because the thumb strap was the only thing enabling the push and pull of the bellows when the accordion rested on the knee, a change in body position and the addition of shoulder straps were necessitated: today's accordions are played standing up with two shoulder straps affixing the instrument to the chest, as with the piano accordion. Chaljub Mejía credits Tatico with having developed the new body position,[39] which facilitated a closer relationship between musician and instrument.

Secondly, while accordions are a factory-built instrument not produced in the Dominican Republic, and local musicians cannot make major changes in the body or construction of the instrument, a specialized class of craftsperson has arisen to keep accordions well tuned and to customize their sound. Their services are required not only by those with old and out-of-tune accordions but by purchasers of new instruments, which usually do not come in the preferred B-flat/E-flat tuning; even those that are in their owner's preferred key may require retuning to achieve a true *típico* sound. To be an accordion tuner requires a good ear, a memory for tones, and a careful hand, and good accordion tuners are highly sought-after. Juan Prieto, the most frequently patronized tuner in Santiago, explains that he has to tune the reeds to satisfy the "noisy" preferences of *típico* musicians. Dominican accordionists, he explains, want their instruments to "sound more alive [*vivo*]. It sounds very lifeless [*apagao*] when it comes from the factory for playing merengue, because the people here who like to hear *merengue típico* like to hear a lot of noise [*escándalo*]." The particular sound he tries to create by ear is one that "has a little more sweetness and a little more tenderness [*cariño*] and liveliness." Interestingly, the sound Juan produces seems to come from an earlier model of accordion that is no longer being made. When he began his career in the 1960s, Juan recalls, the instruments "came prepared from the factory," meaning they needed no alteration. But now, the factory reeds are "all flats," all the same, so Juan explains, "I put a bigger one with a smaller one; that is called a flat and a sharp one on the same note."[40] His Queens-based colleague Berto Reyes terms the two "masculine" and "feminine." Either way, one can see that merengue accordionists prefer a fuller sound than what Hohner provides.

Because of their fairly simple and intuitive construction, accordions are easily and frequently customized. For instance, while the usual factory tuning provides eight out of the twelve possible chromatic pitches in an octave, some accordions have two buttons tuned differently so as to give the missing four pitches. Most young accordionists today add a twenty-second button to their instruments at the top of the keyboard, in its lowest range. The key is often used as a seventh, and Juan Prieto explains that this helps them "to embellish more."[41] Some musicians have added more individual features to their instrument. Juan Prieto's brother

Ernestidio Rodríguez, an accordionist and accordion tuner in East New York, Brooklyn, for example, has added two buttons to the bass side of his accordion to further facilitate the accompaniment of minor keys. The choice of one tuning over another is often related to a musician's choice to play either *merengue con mambo* or traditional *merengue típico*. For example, Rafaelito Román uses the "traditional" factory tuning, while his son Raúl uses the twenty-two-button, twelve-tone accordion to play *típico moderno*.

Two further, though less essential, changes are also made to most accordions. First, a microphone must be added by cutting a round hole into the top of the right-hand side of the instrument and screwing a stripped-down Shure SM58 (when available) into the cavity. Second, customization can also take visual forms, as many accordionists individualize their instrument by adding their names or nicknames to the front of the instrument in paint or rhinestones, and sometimes the bellows are altered, for example, to show the image of the Dominican flag when opened.

While merengue moralists seem to believe that the instrument itself determines what it plays and thus exerts a limiting effect on merengue, the truth lies closer to the opposite of this view. *Típico* musicians stubbornly persist in playing minor-key songs on their button accordions in spite of the critics who insist that this is an impossibility; they add buttons and retune their instrument in order to expand its harmonic possibilities; and they add rather than subtract musical complexity through their finger techniques and rhythmic manipulations.

Conclusions

A U.S. journalist once asked me if people made fun of the fact that I played and studied the accordion. I replied that, if anything, the opposite is true: in the Dominican Republic, many teenagers want to learn accordion like they want to play electric guitar in the United States. The enduring appeal of the accordion and *merengue típico* is due, I believe, to the fact that they symbolize something important—a traditional rural Cibaeño way of life—and that they continue to change with the times. But views of the accordion from inside and from outside the *típico* community differ markedly. To those who subscribe to the *típico* version of Dominican identity, the accordion is a source of prestige and pride. To those who do not, it is an annoyance at best.

The discourse surrounding the accordion has generally had little to do with its actual capabilities; instead, it is a commentary on the values of the times in which each critic was writing. It is to be expected that instruments playing music with a high symbolic value should be used as focal points in debates over identity. At the same time, the forms these discussions have taken are problematic not only in their political dimensions but for the many contradictions they incorporate. *Merengue típico* is simultaneously made to represent the rural and the urban, the masculine and the feminine, highly valued "national patrimony" as well as low-class "noise." The "noisy" accordion raises hackles because it demonstrates that those who play it must be incorporated into Dominican society, and may even determine the form of Dominican identity. Placing musical instruments, in this case the accordion, at the center of ethnographic analysis can thus help researchers uncover existing social hierarchies, while also suggesting how they may be contested.

Notes

1. Carlos Batista Matos, *Historia y evolución del merengue* (Santo Domingo: Editora Cañabrava, 1999), 17.

2. Lizardo qtd. in "Fradique Lizardo: El merengue tiene su origen en Africa," *Ahora!* December 8, 1975, 50–51. See also Rosemary Lora, "Apuntes sobre el origen del merengue," *Ahora!* August 25, 1975, 58–60.

3. Manuel Núñez, *El ocaso de la nación dominicana*, 2d ed. (1990; reprint, Santo Domingo: Editora Alfa y Omega, 2002).

4. Jacques Attali, *Noise: The Political Economy of Music* (1977; reprint, Minneapolis: University of Minnesota Press, 1985), 11.

5. Catana Pérez de Cuello, "Génesis del merengue: Raíces, trayectoria, y difusión en el siglo XIX," in *El merengue: Música y baile de la Republica Dominicana*, ed. Catana Pérez de Cuello and Rafael Solano (Santo Domingo: Verizon, 2005), 328.

6. Fátima Álvarez, "Ripiando el Perico . . . antes de que se vaya," *Hoy*, July 13, 2005.

7. Pérez de Cuello, "Génesis del merengue," 323.

8. See, for example, José del Castillo and Manuel A. García Arévalo, *Antología del merengue* (Santo Domingo: Banco Antillano, 1988), 21–23.

9. Emilio Rodríguez Demorizi, *Música y baile en Santo Domingo* (Santo Domingo: Librería Hispaniola, 1971), 151.

10. Qtd. in Víctor Víctor, "Hablan los maestros," *El Sol*, July 6, 1978.

11. Deborah Pacini Hernández, *Bachata: A Social History of a Dominican Popular Music* (Philadelphia: Temple University Press, 1995), 251.

12. Ibid.

13. Qtd. in "Fradique Lizardo," 50.

14. Veronica Doubleday, "Sounds of Power: An Overview of Musical Instruments and Gender," *Ethnomusicology Forum* 17.1 (2008): 5.

15. Ibid., 7.

16. Ibid., 14.

17. While *típico* musicians generally acknowledge this as the "ideal" case, they also note that it is not always true in reality, nor need it be so. Nonetheless, the fact that this description of the *tambora*'s dual nature is frequently printed and repeated by Dominican scholars and musicians demonstrates its continued relevance for many Dominicans, and thus the importance of including it in my analysis of Dominican gender and music.

18. His line, "Trópico mira tu chivo / después de muerto cantando" (Tropics, look at your goat / singing after death) is often quoted with reference to the *tambora*.

19. Sydney Hutchinson, "Merengue Típico in Transnational Dominican Communities: Gender, Geography, Migration, and Memory in a Traditional Music" (Ph.D. dissertation, New York University, 2008). In chapter 3 I describe in detail the unusual case of a professional female *güira* player in Brooklyn, New York. While she and the one other performing *güirera* I have seen are indeed exceptional cases in the *típico* world today, and she describes her role as one of challenging gendered divisions of musical labor, many Dominican women in fact play *güira* in family contexts.

20. Berto Reyes, personal interview, Corona, N.Y., September 18, 2002.

21. El Buty, personal interview, Santiago, D.R., 2004.

22. See Lise Waxer, "*Las caleñas son como las flores*: The Rise of All-Women Salsa Bands in Cali, Colombia," *Ethnomusicology* 45.2 (2001): 228–59.

23. Sydney Hutchinson, "Becoming the Tíguera: The Female Accordionist in Dominican Merengue Típico," *the world of music* 50.3 (2008): 37–56.

24. Peter Grant Simonson, "Masculinity and Femininity in the Dominican Republic: Historical Change and Contradiction in Notions of Self" (Ph.D. dissertation, University of Michigan, 2004).

25. Hutchinson, "Merengue Típico," 550–604.

26. Simonson, "Masculinity and Femininity."

27. Rafael Chaljub Mejía, *Antes de que te vayas . . . trayectoria del merengue folclórico* (Santiago, D.R.: Grupo León Jimenes, 2002), 317.

28. Manuela Josefa Cabrera Taveras, "Fefita la Grande," personal interview, Santiago, D.R., August 17, 2004.

29. Julia Álvarez, *Something to Declare* (Chapel Hill, N.C.: Algonquin Books of Chapel Hill, 1998), 156.

30. Doubleday, "Sounds of Power," 4.

31. Ibid., 15–16.

32. Nancy López, "Transnational Changing Gender Roles: Second-Generation Dominicans in New York City," in *Dominican Migration: Transnational Perspectives*, ed. Ernesto Sagas and Sintia Molina (Gainesville: University Press of Florida, 2004), 185.

33. Mark F. DeWitt, "The Diatonic Button Accordion in Ethnic Context: Idiom and Style in Cajun Dance Music," *Popular Music and Society* 26.3 (2003): 305.

34. Ibid., 323.

35. Arsenio de La Rosa, personal interview, Bronx, N.Y., July 7, 2006.

36. DeWitt, "Diatonic Button Accordion," 326.

37. See, for example, Miguel Tavárez qtd. in Gloria Moanack, "Los tambores son como hijos," *Listín Diario*, June 3, 1981.

38. Lidia de La Rosa, personal interview, Brooklyn, N.Y., March 26, 2003.

39. Chaljub Mejía, *Antes de que te vayas*, 142.

40. Juan "Prieto" Rodríguez, personal interview, Santiago, D.R., July 10, 2004.

41. "Hacer más dibujos en la música."

13

Between the Folds of
Luiz Gonzaga's Sanfona

Forró *Music in Brazil*

MEGWEN LOVELESS

Though Brazil is perhaps better known for its hot and sultry *samba* rhythms, its sun-kissed beaches, and the delicate swing of its *bossa nova*, it also has a long-standing accordion tradition spanning most of the twentieth century that plays an important role in the story of its popular music and its sense of nationalism. The accordion was brought to Brazilian shores in the last decades of the nineteenth century and soon became a popular instrument on which to interpret foreign *tangos, boleros,* schottisches, waltzes, and mazurkas in the elite salons of the bigger cities.

Still, though popular even through the 1930s (when *samba* began to dominate the national scene), the *acordeom* would have faded into oblivion in Brazil had it not been for the music of Luiz Gonzaga, today remembered as the "godfather" of an entirely new Brazilian music and dance genre, *forró.* Gonzaga truly "rooted" his love for the accordion in his native Brazil by creating and shaping musical "routes" across this increasingly cosmopolitan and diverse country. This essay focuses on the life story of Luiz Gonzaga to elucidate how the accordion has helped to create a sense of identity for present and future generations of Brazilians that is intimately tied to music, space, and tradition.

Luiz Gonzaga, more than any one other person, has carved out a space for traditional rhythms and melodies—as well as for his iconic instrument—in the history of Brazilian popular music; and his music continues to be reinterpreted in countless creative refractions across the nation as well as abroad. As one contemporary has observed, Gonzaga singlehandedly "blazed a trail" for the accordion's musical success in Brazil.[1] I would like to trace that path, analyzing along the way how he shaped Brazilian popular music and how his legacy still ricochets off the walls of dance halls across the nation. This gregarious accordionist arrived on the music scene at a pivotal moment in history, and in this essay I will examine the national musical and political context that enabled Gonzaga's story to speak to an entire nation, as well as future generations of Brazilians.

While *samba* is commonly recognized as the most "pure" representative of Brazilian nationalist expression, other musics can also be argued to represent "the nation" to a wide audience of Brazilians. Increasingly appreciated locally and internationally, *forró* has a special resonance for Brazilians interested in or attached to the rural roots of the nation and is widely popular today in both its original form as well as in various derivative genres.

Forró has been described as "a mixture of ska with polka in overdrive,"[2] and with its hard-hitting beat and memorable hooks, it is a quintessentially Brazilian music. Its infectious sound and exhilarating rhythms form an intimate backdrop for one of Brazil's most popular partner dances, in which couples swivel around one another in sensuous embraces. The faster rhythms of the *forró* complex include *forró*, *xaxado*, and *arrasta-pé*; slightly slower and more romantic rhythms include *baião*, *xote* (a Brazilian-style schottische), and *xamego*; and even slower subgenres such as *aboios* and *toadas* are primarily "listening" music, though some couples may also slow-dance to them. All of these subgenres are direct legacies of Luiz Gonzaga, as during his long career he brought the musics of his youth, spent in the hinterlands, to all of the other regions of Brazil.

During a typical *forró* show, the nonstop twanging of a giant triangle pushes its pulse to a boiling pitch; a large double-headed *zabumba* drum drives its seductive syncopation; and a 120-bass piano accordion pumps out its exaggerated chords. Since the 1990s, there have been increasingly diverse and interesting fusions of *forró*, rock, *lambada*, *axé*, heavy metal, funk, and other regional musics, as generations of musicians continue to tap into the raw potential of Gonzaga's work. To understand the transformative effect of *forró* and *baião* musics on the nation of Brazil, let us go back to the beginning of the story, long before Gonzaga was born, to set the stage for the fanfare he would make with his unwieldy instrument and maniacal grin.

"Os Brasis": Musical Nationalism in Brazil

Since its independence in 1822, Brazil has struggled to create a national identity to unite its diverse regions and ethnic communities. The nation's diversity (or fragmentation, depending on one's perspective) is evident in Brazil's curious tendency to refer to itself in the plural: "os Brasis." With a geographic area larger than the entire European Union, Brazil's territory is truly expansive. It covers half of South America, encompasses a half-dozen climatic regions, and is home to a staggeringly diverse population with phenotypes ranging from Amerindian, Iberian, North African, Mediterranean, Northern European, Middle Eastern, Japanese, South African, to West African, to name only the largest native and immigrant groups. Though it boasts one of the largest economies in the world, it has extreme disparities in terms of wealth,[3] health, and education; and though the official language is Portuguese, hundreds of languages are spoken across its provinces. Brazil has managed to maintain sovereignty as one territory but has historically been plagued by what one scholar called "a tendency toward 'centrifugal dismemberment' that resulted in a disperse, disarticulated, and fluid nation."[4]

Thus, since the early nineteenth century—and increasingly throughout the twentieth century and into the twenty-first century—politicians and intellectuals have been struggling to find a way of defining "Brazilianness" and of conceptualizing a single Brazilian nation coalescing around such divergent peoples, histories, geographies, and cultures. It is largely in the realm of popular culture—and particularly music—that Brazil has found a means of expressing a national culture that might unite its separate parts. As the famous singer/songwriter Caetano Veloso reminds us, popular music is "the Brazilian form of expression par excellence."[5] As we will see, the music of Gonzaga brought the country together in an interesting way—toward its rustic roots—which may provide a new model for conceptualizing Brazil's entrée into the new millennium.

Young Gonzaga: The Early Foundations of *Forró*

Born December 13, 1912, outside of the small Pernambucan town of Exu, where his family scraped out a living as sharecroppers, young Luiz was one of eight children born to Ana Bastista de Jesus and Januário José dos Santos. His name, which he shares with no one in the family, was chosen by the priest who baptized him: Luiz (in honor of Saint Luzia, who shares his date of birth) Gonzaga (the full name of Saint Luzia) Nascimento (in honor of the month both he and Jesus Christ were born). His mother, known by all as Santana, was a devout woman who would sing religious *novenas* to commemorate various saints throughout the year; his father, Januário, was a hard-working man who would spend three days a week working the fields and his remaining time playing and fixing button accordions in the workshop off the main house.

Santana's grandfather had emigrated from Europe, and her family was at first reluctant to marry her to Januário, a poor migrant who had fled to the Araripe, Pernambuco, area after a severe drought elsewhere in the state. Nonetheless,

Santana and Januário were able to start a life together; she sold surplus crops in the weekly market, and he played nighttime parties throughout the region. Having settled in a relatively fertile area, they were able to make ends meet for their growing family, bartering for extra foodstuffs with other local sharecroppers. Santana tended the home and the garden; Januário did what work he could in the field when he wasn't sleeping off a late-night performance. Occasionally another accordion player would come from afar and stay in their home while Januário set to fixing his instrument, but more often the broken contraptions piled up in a back room while Januário waited for parts or simply time to attend to them. As the children grew up, they contributed to the household economy in whatever way they could.

Most young boys born under similar circumstances would have begun working in the fields at twelve years old, and would have gone on to have a family and settle down in the region, but the gregarious Luiz was of a different persuasion. When he was not yet eight months old, a troupe of Gypsies who were passing through took an interest in the baby and pronounced: "He will be worldly . . . he will wander so much and so far that he will walk on calloused feet."[6] The prophecy would come true fewer than eighteen years later, but in the meantime Luiz worked on broadening his horizons locally. Though none of the sharecroppers went to school, he learned the rudiments of reading and writing—even how to eat with a fork and knife—from the daughters of Col. Aires de Alencar, a landholder and local bigwig; he agreed to work as a private vassal for Aires as well, accompanying him on business trips around the area of Araripe, and he joined a local group of Boy Scouts to learn his first lessons in discipline and survival.

More than anything, though, Luiz spent his spare time pawing through the old instruments in his father's atelier and trying his hand at the eight-bass button accordion. Santana would protest, insisting he make an honest man of himself and not get caught up in the bohemian music world like his father—to no avail. Before long, Luiz could hold his own on the *sanfona*, and Januário started to bring him along to accompany him on his paid gigs. That tiny taste of fame whet his appetite, and before long he had saved up enough money from his job as Aires' assistant to purchase a fancy new set of pants and shoes to wear to his weekend performances. Not only that, but Aires agreed to give Luiz an advance on his salary to purchase a brand-new accordion he had seen in a shop window on one of their trips far from home. It was only a question of time—to pay off his debt to the colonel—before Luiz would become a professional musician.

In 1926, when Gonzaga started performing on the local circuit, musical accompaniment was a rustic affair, often with only one button accordion or a pair of fifes and fiddles to keep the dancers moving. John P. Murphy writes that the button accordion, often called *sanfona* or *fole*, was brought to the South of Brazil in 1875 by Italian immigrants to replace the *viola* (Portuguese guitar), as it "was considered easier to learn and more suitable for the performance of the salon dance music that was reaching the rural folk."[7] In what year the accordion made it to the hinterlands of the Pernambuco is unclear, but certainly it had become a mainstay of local entertainment by the turn of the century. Often referred to in the hinterlands as *harmônica* or *concertina*,[8] the button accordion was also called *pé-de-bode*, or "goat's foot," a reference that Murphy believes dates back to the days when even more rudimentary instruments (with only two basses) were played in the region; "the analogy seems to be with the division of the goat's hoof into two parts."[9] Even with its diverse nomenclature, however, one should not confuse the button accordion (*sanfona*) with the keyboard *acordeom*, which was gaining fame in foreign clubs and cabarets in Rio de Janeiro; the latter was considered an elite instrument, while the former was a marker of plebian background. In her biography of Gonzaga, Dominique Dreyfus writes:

> Gonzaga used to love saying . . . that "accordion" and "sanfona" were the same instrument, but when an artist played salon music, he was an accordionist, and when he played popular music, he turned into a "sanfoneiro."[10]

For several years, Gonzaga made a living playing gigs on the weekends and helping out around the house during the week, while flirting with girls he met in town or at his performances. His new profession gave him access to and prestige among the ladies, and Luiz loved them all. At one point, deep in the throes of love with a young girl named Nazarena, Gonzaga was devastated to discover that her father, a white middle-class man, would not accept him—son of a sharecropper, a lower-class accordion player, and dark-skinned as well—as a son-in-law. Gonzaga set out to defy him at knifepoint but instead ended up drunk, humiliated, and whipped into submission by his mother. As Gonzaga tells the story, that episode was the last straw; he was ready for a bigger world than his native Araripe.

With the premise of playing a gig at a faraway ranch, Gonzaga slinked off, his ego still smarting, with his *sanfona* under one arm. He would sell it at the nearest big town to pay for his train ticket to the capital city of Fortaleza, Ceará, where he headed straight for the military camps. Though he wasn't yet of legal age for military service, he was nonetheless accepted, and a decade-long adventure during which he would see a good bit of the country began.

Gonzaga loved life in the military—he loved following orders and getting familiar with all the corners of Brazil where his regiment was sent on various duties. He missed his life as a musician but thoroughly enjoyed the adventure of new assignments and the feeling of independence from the life he was born into. Three years in, he earned a spot as first-seat cornet player for the army, a feat that earned him the nickname "Bico de aço," or "Beak of Steel," but he was not satisfied with the cornet or even with a brief stint of guitar lessons. He tried out for a position as an accordion player in the army orchestra but was turned away at his audition; the maestro asked him to play a "Mi bemol" (E flat) and, having no elite musical training or understanding of music theory, Gonzaga was dismissed unceremoniously.

Gonzaga was determined to succeed musically, however. In 1936 he bought a forty-eight-bass piano accordion and began training on it on his days off military duty—even managing small performances here and there—and in 1938 he picked out a white eighty-bass Hohner from a traveling salesman's catalog and began paying it off in small installments. A year later, when he arrived in São Paulo to pay the last installment and pick up his new instrument, Gonzaga discovered he had been tricked out of his money. Disconsolate, he shared the story with the hotel owner, who "sold" him his own son's accordion—also a white eighty-bass Hohner—for the price of the final installment. That same year Gonzaga would leave the military (Brazil had a maximum cap of ten years, and Gonzaga was already at nine) and go to Rio, where he would await a boat to take him home to Pernambuco. But he never got on that boat.

Rio de Janeiro:
The Burgeoning Capital of Brazilian Sound

During the 1930s, while Gonzaga was traveling around Brazil on military duty, huge changes were afoot across the nation and in Rio de Janeiro, the capital city. *Samba* music was exploding across the brand-new radio networks centered in the capital city. The Revolution of 1930, which brought Getúlio Vargas to power, would also fundamentally change the social and political situation. The Vargas regime set an unprecedented importance on nationalistic art and would set in motion the unification of the nation through the homogenization of culture in a way never before seen in Brazil. Though in large part this "authenticization" of culture was a strategy for consolidating power,[11] it also served to help thwart any cries of racial oppression in a country not yet recovered from centuries of slavery. As Peter Fry writes, "The conversion of ethnic symbols into national symbols masks a situation of racial domination and makes it especially difficult to uncover."[12] Of all the cultural forms encouraged by the Vargas regime, *samba* reigned supreme.

For its proponents, *samba* best represented the Brazilian nation because it was a Brazilian synthesis of foreign and local sound that largely resolved the centuries-old tension between white and black races. Like white rice and black beans (the "national dish"), *samba* was the perfect mixture of captivating African rhythms and catchy European melodic lines, an ideal music/dance genre that arose in the ghettos but eventually found its way into the elite parlors—and onto every radio broadcast for the next ten years.

A New Sound:
Performing with a Pernambucan Accent

After his discharge in 1939, Gonzaga traveled to Rio, where he stayed in the military barracks while awaiting transportation home. Alone and frightened of the massive metropolis (his years of service had all been in much smaller towns), he was averse to exploring the streets of Rio, until a soldier pointed him in the direction of the Mangue—the red-light district of the capital, where the bulk of nightclubs and brothels were located. Musicians positioned themselves up and down the streets as well as inside the bars and restaurants to earn money for their trade. His ticket home forgotten, Gonzaga began his foray into the musical world of Rio.

For months Gonzaga trolled the red-light district with his Hohner eighty-bass accordion, playing the *sambas*, waltzes, *choros*, blues, mazurkas, foxtrots, and tangos that patrons would request—to rather tepid applause. He played on street corners and occasionally was invited to play in a bar (which would bring him slightly more gratuities) but just barely scraped by. His success began to change after he met his first music partner, the guitarist Xavier Pinheiro, with whom he performed as a duo. Gonzaga slowly increased his network of musician friends and his opportunities to play, eventually leaving Xavier to play solo. He upgraded to a 120-bass Scandalli that he bought off of a drunken sailor in the Mangue[13] and booked appearances across the city. Even so, he "massacred" the popular tangos that were always being requested[14] to the extent that he lost one of his gigs and decided to take music lessons from Antenógenes Silva, the most sought-after accordionist in town, famous for his waltzes. He slowly improved his technique and started performing on the *calouros* radio shows, looking for a break.

Created in the mid-thirties, the *calouros* shows were set up by the major radio stations to discover talent; amateur artists were encouraged to showcase their best work live in the studio for a score, the highest of which might earn them a record deal. Gonzaga frequented the two most popular shows: Calouros em Desfile (Freshmen on Parade), with Ary Barroso, and Papel Carbono (Carbon Paper), with Renato Murce. He tried performing tangos, waltzes, *choros*, and *sambas*, and did well—but never brilliantly. As Gonzaga later said in an interview, "When I play, speak, arrange, it's all with my accent. My accent doesn't allow me to sing waltzes, boleros, *samba*. My *sanfona* is just like me."[15]

Gonzaga came to understand his own artistic "accent"—a veritable epiphany—through the intervention of a few law students from Ceará, a state close to his native home of Pernambuco. Six students who heard him performing at their favorite bar caught wind of him speaking and recognized his accent as similar to their own; they pestered him to play a song reminiscent of their homeland. Gonzaga at first declined, but he agreed to return in thirty days after practicing some new material. The subsequent performance of "Pé de Serra," followed by "Vira e Mexe," was a huge hit:

> It was crazy. I breathed deep, gave thanks, and launched into "Vira e Mexe" ... tiiiiiii-tiriririririririririrum, tchan tanran tanran tanran tanran. . . . Ah! It got even crazier. The bar seemed like it was going to catch on fire. It had filled up completely, people at the door, out on the street, trying to get a look at what was happening in the bar. So I grabbed a dish [for tips]. By the time it got to the third table it was full. So I yelled: Gimme a bowl! Then a few moments later the bowl was full. So I asked for a pot! And I thought to myself: *now* we're talking.[16]

Shortly after his great success in the Mangue, Gonzaga returned to Ary Barroso's *calouros* show prepared to play "Vira e Mexe" (Turn and Boogey). Barroso, who recognized Gonzaga as the persistent but not exceptional accordionist of tangos and waltzes, made a sarcastic play on the title: "Well then turn yourself around and do a boogey!"[17] After Gonzaga finished, the stunned audience went wild, and the announcer congratulated Gonzaga on the highest possible score. Luiz had discovered his accent—and it wasn't *samba* or tango. It was Pernambuco. Within a year of his *calouros*-show debut, Gonzaga had made his first solo recording with Victor Music.[18] More than any other, the year 1941 represents the beginning of Gonzaga's rise to fame—as well as the start of an "invented tradition," with Luiz narrating the folklore of his homeland in his familiar and raucous Pernambuco accent.

The first press of Gonzaga's solo work was a two-piece series of 78s: "Véspera de São João" (a mazurka) and "Numa Serenata" (a waltz) on the first release, and the newly popular "Vira e Mexe" (*xamego/choro*) with "Saudades de São João del Rei" (a waltz) on the second record. The release of the exotic "Vira e Mexe" on vinyl was one in a long line of marketing maneuvers that would mark his career and consolidate his sound as that of the "northeast" of Brazil. "Vira e Mexe," the hit that found such success on the *calouros* show, was in fact a *choro*, rhythmically not entirely different from what was already playing on the radio. What set it apart from other *choros* was Gonzaga's performance with an air of rustic folklore. To draw attention to its uniqueness, however, Gonzaga pronounced it not a "choro" but a "xamego," in effect creating a new genre of music—one that was evocative of the sensuality of a backwoods romance. Later, Gonzaga explained that the genre's title was inspired by his brother's reaction to his accordion playing: "Oxente, isso é xamego!"[19] The allusion to the genre as an emotion in and of itself caught on, and his albums disappeared as quickly as they were pressed.

With success finally at his doorstep, Gonzaga remained predictably self-confident, so much so that he began to express an interest in singing. He tried singing a few *boleros* and *sambas* in his live performances but found that his voice did not fit the genres, and so once again he returned to his former success to carve out a space for a future singing career. He paired with Miguel Lima, who wrote lyrics to accompany his "Vira e Mexe," renamed this time "Xamego," and found relative success within his small performance circuit.

His voice, however, had nothing in common with the popular crooners of the day, and he would have to confront great opposition when trying to take his singing career to the radio. José Farias, in his biography of Gonzaga, writes:

> In the musical context of the time, Luiz Gonzaga's voice didn't "match" the vocal aesthetic set forth by Vicente Celestino, Nelson Gonçalves, Orlando Silva, and Francisco Alves . . . the primary vocalists of the golden age of Brazilian radio.[20]

Indeed, Gonzaga's contract with Victor/RCA explicitly stated that he perform instrumentals only—and the director of Tamoio Radio was so outraged with Gonzaga's stubborn insistence upon singing (which was outside of the stipulations of his contract) that he left multiple copies of a memo stapled to the walls around the studio, stating, "Luiz Gonzaga is explicitly prohibited from singing, as he has been contracted as an accordionist."[21] Even as Gonzaga and his new composing partner, Miguel Lima, were able to sell their new songs to Rio's best recording artists, Gonzaga stubbornly maintained his objective. He even dared to give stylistic advice to a Manezinho Araújo, a seasoned vocalist from the North who had reached considerable fame from his recordings of *emboladas* (a newly popularized rhythm from the North). Araújo, furious at Gonzaga's impertinence, retorted that Luiz's voice sounded "like shredded bamboo" and refused to collaborate with him again.[22] Still, Luiz continued to work steadfastly toward his goal: to become a famous accordion player . . . *and* professional singer.

That opportunity came in 1945, with the release of "Dança, Dança Mariquinha," a mild success, followed by "Cortando o Pano," which outsold all expectations, confirming Gonzaga as a singer and "demolishing the last barrier of resistance to his voice on the radio."[23] Shortly after its success, Gonzaga was contracted by Rádio Nacional—evidence that he was an up-and-coming new star with infinite potential.

Rio's *Samba* versus "Música Regional"

In 1945, Rádio Nacional was the place to be. Of the hundreds of radio stations then operating in the country,[24] Rádio Nacional was by far the most popular and housed all of the best performers and producers. It had been acquired by the state five years prior but continued to run as a commercial station, and it not only featured but determined the top talent and top shows in the nation. By 1945, the Brazilian polling organization Instituto Brasileiro de Opinião Pública e Estatística (Brazilian Institute of Public Opinion and Statistics) estimated that 85 percent of the households in Rio and São Paulo owned radios. By 1950, that figure had gone up to

95 percent.[25] Not only that, but residents far away from the capital—in provincial cities all across the Brazilian territory—were tuning in, largely to Rádio Nacional.

At this point, *samba*, still considered the national music, was getting plenty of radio airplay—but its heyday was coming to an end. As Gonzaga's biographer writes,

> Having reached its golden age, samba's popularity was plummeting, as the genre began to transform itself into *samba-canção*, the last stage of a transformation that would ultimately result in *bossa nova*. Alongside this *crooner mania* . . . and every other kind of musical whining, there grew an interest for music with a folkloric taste.[26]

After more than a decade of *samba* dominance, the mid-1940s saw a surge in regional acts. The *sertanejo* duo, or "country twosome," of Alvarenga and Ranchinho as well as Raul Torres from the interior of São Paulo; Dorival Caymmi from Bahia; and Pedro Raimundo from Rio Grande do Sul became regulars on the major radio shows. And Luiz Gonzaga was hardly the only artist hailing from the hinterlands up north; João Pernambuco (who played with Caxangá and, later, the Oito Batutas) and Catulo da Paixão Cearense had paved the way for artists from the North, the likes of Manezinho Araújo (from just outside Recife), Laura Maia from Ceará, and the Turunas Pernambucanas (from which the Jararaca and Ratinho folk duo would form), as well as the Turunas de Mauricéia.[27] Though quite popular, these groups began trafficking regional folklore after *samba* had already been consolidated as the national music. As Fred Moehn explains:

> Folk musics were more often relegated to "regionalist" status. This helps to explain why . . . *música sertaneja* and *música baiana* [music from the state of Bahia], although mass-mediated, are today still not typically associated with national identity, while MPB [*música popular brasileira*, a folk-rock genre], with its roots in Rio de Janeiro's musical traditions, is. In effect, it sets up a hierarchical structure of regional cultures: *carioca* [Rio de Janeiro] culture becomes a synecdoche for "national culture"; other regional cultures, by necessity, are subordinated.[28]

In large part, the regional groups had not been able to break through because they lacked a marketing concept for an increasingly consumerist music industry. With the exception of the *embolada*, which had been popularized in the South by Manezinho Araújo, none of the traditional musics of the North—like the fife bands (*banda de pífanos*) or freestyle poetry jams (*desafio*)—had found an audience in the South. Neither had any of the traditional instruments of the North—the button accordion, the fiddle, the fife, the *zabumba* drum—taken root in the South.[29] Even regional acts at the time used the same instruments popularized by *samba* groups from Rio.[30] The timing was perfect for a new musical sound to take over Rio and its radio networks, and the capital was poised for the next big thing, waiting for an artist with a vision to redirect Brazilian music.

The music that Gonzaga performed was not in itself all that different from other material then available in the capital (recall the *choro* repackaged as *xamego*), but his manner of presenting it was. Dreyfus has called Gonzaga the "first industrial product of the northeast culture";[31] indeed, he nearly singlehandedly invented a tradition of northeastern culture through the iconic performance of his "hymns" about Pernambuco's back-country. Gonzaga's natural talent, however, was not composing: while he was one of the epoch's top performers (and marketing geniuses), he "co-wrote" nearly all of his material, sometimes contributing musical riffs or motifs while other times simply suggesting a theme. His great success—and the foundation for a brand new "northeastern" culture zone—lay in the special alchemy between Gonzaga and his co-authors.

Gonzaga's Baião: Collaborating with Humberto Teixeira

Gonzaga first met Humberto Teixeira through another musician (Lauro Maia, Teixeira's nephew) who had declined an official partnership with Gonzaga, thinking himself far too bohemian for the regimented and intense enterprise that Gonzaga had proposed with his typical enthusiasm. Teixeira, a Ceará-born intellectual who had earned his law degree in Rio two years prior, had already written several popular songs, all of them standard *sambas*, *modinhas*, or waltzes. With Gonzaga, he would break out of the mold and create an entirely new canon of Brazilian music. Their first song, "No Meu Pé de Serra," was a sweet *xote* (a Brazilian-style schottische) in F major that reminisced about the verdant Araripe foothills Gonzaga had left behind in Exu. Today it is a well-known classic, but in 1946 it was eclipsed by Gonzaga/Teixeira's next musical venture: *baião*.

Perhaps the biggest hit of the decade in Brazilian music, Teixeira and Gonzaga's "Baião" had a simple premise: to introduce the music and dance of the northeast to the rest of Brazil. It did so by tutoring its listeners:

> I'm going to show you / how to dance the *baião*
> and whoever wants to learn / please pay attention.[32]

The song served as a manifesto for a new musical movement that brought the traditional musical styles of the backlands to the capital city, where they would be revamped and appreciated anew as urban popular culture with a rustic twist. In fact, the 1946 release of "Baião" by Quatro Ases e Um Coringa (with Gonzaga accompanying on accordion) would spark a new dance craze so popular that Gonzaga had to wait three years to record it himself. The genre is today one of the most important musical trends in twentieth-century Brazilian music, sandwiched historically between *samba* and *bossa nova* and poised to impact greatly a number of popular styles later in the century.

Baião was framed as a traditional rhythm from the hinterlands that Gonzaga had "rescued" and "redressed" for urban consumption, but it was as much invented as it was traditional. Back where he grew up, a *baião*, also called *rojão*, was the plucking of strings as the troubadours prepared their musical poetry duels. As Gonzaga remembered:

> There wasn't really a set music that characterized it [*baião*], with lyrics or any-thing. It was something you would say, like, "Gimme a *baião*. . . ." And someone would sing, "I've got my guitar I tuned the strings . . . nham nham . . . nham nhamm. . . ." It was just to set the mood, a prelude to the singing. It's what the singer does when he starts to strum the guitar, waiting for inspiration.[33]

Many ethnomusicologists have debated the history of the *baião* before Gonzaga brought it to national attention,[34] showing the genre to have matured over more than a hundred years. Certainly, though, all agree that Gonzaga achieved a giant feat, managing with this one musical hit to standardize a genre—by underpinning the traditional syncopations with an accelerated, steady 2/4 pulse[35]—and to intro-duce it via mass media to the nation as a whole. The *baião* was only the first of many rhythms Gonzaga would popularize and the basis for the faster-paced *forró* rhythm that would later become the umbrella category for a variety of regional genres.

The early success of the *baião* was so colossal that it earned Gonzaga his lifelong nickname, Rei do Baião (King of Baião).[36] Indeed, "Baião" could have been the hit of his career, had he and Humberto Teixeira not created an even bigger success less than one year later. "Asa Branca," composed and recorded in 1947, is one of Brazil's most influential songs of all time. It is a veritable hymn of northeastern identity and the most commonly interpreted folk song in the nation.[37] It tells the story of the white-winged dove (*patagioenas picazuro*), the most stalwart and resis-tant of animals, which is finally forced to leave his drought-stricken home in search for a better future. According to local lore, the white-winged dove is the very last creature to flee the parched expanses in time of drought, so its departure means that desperation has truly set in and that the narrator must tear himself away:

> And the white-wing dove has flown now
> far away from these backlands
> So I say now, goodbye, Rosinha
> though in my heart I'll be back again.[38]

One commentator observed that the truly remarkable trait of the *baião* tune was to convey such a melancholy story in a major key. Perhaps more outstand-ing is that "Asa Branca," more than any other song in his repertoire, would help

Gonzaga consolidate an image of Brazil's Northeast—hitherto inexistent—in the imaginations of his listeners.

Gonzaga's *Sertão*:
The *Nordeste* as a Discursive Space

Before 1950, the geographical concept of a Brazilian "Northeast" did not yet exist; it was referred to either as the "North" or as the "interior." Luiz Gonzaga's career was perhaps the culminating factor in creating this new ecological and cultural region in Brazil; in 1946, with the extreme popularity of *baião* and the increased media attention afforded Gonzaga, the nation began to recognize the new trope and to associate it with the imagery contained in his music. The "Northeast" category is, more than anything, a discursive construction[39] that, through regular repetition of its key imagery, has become embedded in the Brazilian imagination as representing a traditional past. The *nordeste*, in this interpretation, becomes the binary opposite of modernity (represented by the capital city), and the *baião* serves as a bridge—building a starting point from a rural "tradition" and simultaneously "translating" it to listeners in the urban destination.

Hobsbawm and others have shown that the "invention of tradition" occurs precisely when modernity forces society to change; the modern transformation of the social order triggers a flurry of nostalgia for a past that may never actually have existed in its imagined form. As Raymond Williams has written, "[P]reoccupation with tradition and interpretation of tradition as an age-old ritual is a distinctly modern phenomenon, born out of anxiety about the vanishing past."[40] And not only is (impending) modernity a push to discover and retain one's roots, but modernity also provides the tools necessary to do so; in the case of *forró*, the mass media available (in the form of radio and, later, television) facilitated the production of the Brazilian *nordeste*, through the music of Gonzaga and countless radio shows that emerged in his shadow.

Lest we get too swept up in wistful reminiscences of the traditional life of the hinterlands, Linda-Anne Rebhun reminds us that

> those parts of the landscape imagined to be backward do not in fact live in the past, nor are the cities building the future. Rather, the entire countryside displays what Garcia Canclini calls "multitemporal heterogeneity" in which "traditions have not yet disappeared and modernity has not completely arrived."[41]

In the case of Luiz Gonzaga, one can be sure that he knew well the impossibility of framing the *nordeste* as entirely backward and the capital city as wholly modern because he himself had lived several lifestyles—and would continue to, throughout his long career—within both of those geographical poles. But the ambiguity of these extremes that Gonzaga would find in his lived experience would not make it into his lyrics and performances, where he would reconstruct, time and again, an age-old rural tradition that was deeply at odds with his modern life in the bustling center of Rio.

The Northeast, or "nordeste," is home to several geographic climatic areas, but none is so deeply entrenched in the Brazilian psyche as the *sertão*, the large expanse of scrublands that spans the states of Pernambuco, Ceará, Bahia, Alagoas, and Sergipe and predominates in Gonzaga's work. As first described in painful detail in the classic tome "Os Sertões" (Rebellion in the Backlands) by Euclides da Cunha, this landscape is regularly decimated by regionwide drought in cycles that are so regular as to be predictable in their timing and swath of destruction.[42] As a result, cyclical migrations are a feature of this area, as poor farmers are forced off the dried-out land and into semi-urban areas to look for work.[43]

Though it has become a key node in Brazilian migrations (in large part from the movement of these *retirantes*, or refugees of various droughts), the *sertão* is framed as an isolated region that was cut off from the rest of Brazil for centuries, allowing the cultural traditions that were brought to Brazil early in its colonization to continue being practiced, impervious to change. Indeed, it is considered home to a medieval social structure that supports rigid hierarchization, family feuds, sanctioned banditry, and unhindered violence—and a rich cultural stew of moorish and gregorian musical influence. Before Gonzaga, the "regionalist" writers of the 1930s and 1940s—José Lins do Rego, Rachel de Queiroz, Jorge Amado, José Américo de Almeida, and, to an extent, Gilberto Freyre—had begun to consolidate the region in their *literatura das secas*, or "drought literature,"[44] which detailed the social and geographical oppressions that kept poverty, violence, and beautiful folk-art traditions so deeply entrenched in the Brazilian *nordeste*.

In his canon of *nordestino* songs, Gonzaga would further reinforce that imagery. Along with the radiating sun, images that are commonly invoked to represent the *sertão* include the sinister black *urubu* vulture, which picks dry the bones of dying animals, the proud *mandacaru* cactus, which holds in an astounding amount of moisture and can survive even the severest of droughts, and various birds (*asa-branca, acauã, sabiá*) whose habitat is disrupted by the arid spells but whose natural migration cycle accommodates the climate, allowing them to return later to verdant fields. In fact, Gonzaga himself seems to epitomize allegorically both the *mandacaru* and the migratory birds—remaining a strong and steadfast telluric force who, in his poetic representations, refuses to "leave" his land, and an itinerant troubadour who travels far to sing the praises of his land yet regularly returns to make it his home. It was from the matrix of an imagined *sertão* community that Gonzaga extracted the "traditions" upon which he based his repertoire, which would come to represent reality for countless Brazilians.

Gonzaga's music told such a compelling story about the *sertão* that Brazilians—and *nordestinos* especially—began to believe in the images as replicas of an ancient and unbroken past. In his 1991 ethnography of percussionists in rural Pernambuco, Larry Crook found that "[w]hether or not the older style has remained virtually unchanged for hundreds of years is not the main issue here. More importantly, musicians and audiences *believe* that it has and believe that the old style is the tradition of their forefathers. This imbues the style with a certain amount of authority which is unchallenged and legitimizes it."[45] Between 1946 and 1952, also known as the "*baião* epoch," Gonzaga built upon this story—and further entrenched its legitimacy—by adopting a performance style all his own.

Gonzaga's Performance:
Staging a "Country Bumpkin" Identity

Having left his hometown nearly a decade earlier, Gonzaga had already started assimilating "southern" cultural standards when he first arrived in Rio. As he asserts in an interview with Dreyfus: "Nobody knew I was a *nordestino*. I was a wily guy, I had thrown myself in with the mulattoes, I dressed the same as they did, I even sang *samba* in the downtown clubs. I wanted to absorb the Rio accent. The northeastern accent . . . I had long since lost."[46] Still, we know from his experience in the Mangue that his accent *was* apparent, albeit faint—apparent enough that the law students from Ceará could hear his northern homeland in his voice. After the success of "Vira e Mexe," Gonzaga must have found that an exaggerated backwoods accent to accompany his "campy" style of playing was received enthusiastically, and so he encouraged his native sound to surface. Gonzaga used the raw nasality of his voice, combined with exaggerated pronunciations, linguistic puns, long spoken passages, midsong exclamations, and onomatopoeia to create an onstage persona. Certainly he had discovered a niche market, since other singers at the time exemplified suave and sophisticated vocals, while "his shouts of exhortation exuded unrehearsed, backwoods charisma."[47] Indeed, Gonzaga's vocals often "bent a half-note below the melodic line,"[48] and his lyrics walked a line between standard Portuguese and regional dialect. Often, his puns featured double meanings not entirely clear in standard Portuguese but riotously funny in northern slang—and his very comfort in switching between official and nonstandard dialects shows his linguistic expertise. Though he made constant references to himself as "semiliterate," his artistic wit showed that he was able to skillfully yet mischievously play various roles, including "the rube," the polished heartthrob, and the shrewd businessman.

Several scholars have noted that, in addition to the linguistic markers he used to classify himself as a backwoods *matuto*, or country bumpkin, Gonzaga also used his accordion as another symbol of his rustic flair. Bryan McCann notes that his accordion work "was deliberately choppy and shaded with flat notes," and Durval Albuquerque writes that he had an innovative manner of playing that approximated the *sanfona* to an "instrument of percussion, being joggled, opened and closed quickly, unlike the traditional manner of playing waltzes, when it was opened and closed slowly."[49] Gonzaga threw his accordion around on stage with unequaled zeal, and at times it looked like he and his *sanfona* were engaged in a rowdy couple dance, spinning around the stage, enraptured in the music and the moment.[50] Indeed, Gonzaga's performances turned good songs into phenomenal hits. As Dreyfus writes, "[T]he music came to him with lyrics and melodies. But it arrived naked, silent! It was Gonzaga, then, who would clothe it, decorate it, give it shine, sensuality, personality."[51]

An interesting chapter in Gonzaga's performance life is his decision to create an attire all his own in which to perform. By 1948, his *baiãos* were playing all day, every day on every radio station in the nation, and he had begun to fine-tune his stage show. The sophisticated suit that he wore for his auditorium (live) recordings was certainly stylish, but it didn't reflect his performance persona. At the time, other regional acts were circulating, and Gonzaga took a piece of inspiration from their outfits: Pedro Raimundo dressed in the *gaúcho* style of the southern pampas; Jararaca and Ratinho wore straw hats from the interior; the carioca *sambistas* had their own uniform of striped button-down shirts; Bob Nelson dressed like a North American cowboy . . . so Gonzaga wrote home to his mother and asked her to send a leather hat in the style of Lampião. A bandit who had terrorized the northern states for nearly two decades with a unique and perverse form of violence, Lampião was the most famous *cangaceiro* in Brazilian history. He and his band of outlaws wore large leather hats turned up on two sides, with the turned-up brim facing forward and backward. Generally, the brim featured ornate leather- and metal-work and came to be an iconic symbol of the *cangaço* (banditry) of the Northeast. It was a brilliant marketing moment: the juxtaposition of the "Rei do Baião" with the "Rei do Sertão."

Gonzaga, who as a child had reveled in stories of Lampião's bravery, added the hat as a way of redressing a typical image of the Northeast.[52] To the unusual hat he added the leather gear of the cowboys who traversed the spine-ridden countryside, all elaborately worked by hand. That the new uniforms commanded attention, no one doubted. But the artistic director at Rádio Nacional was furious and prohibited the costume: "Oh, no *cangaceiro* here at the National, no way! You can put your hat away."[53] Thanks to Gonzaga's stubborn streak, though, the hat remained a fixture in every single interview and performance outside of Rádio Nacional—until it became such an iconic element of his persona that Rádio Nacional conceded to allow him wear it, after all. This episode shows not only typical persistence on the part of Gonzaga but also his creativity: he literally turned a stylized "costume" into a uniform,[54] creating a style that to this day is reflected on nearly every *forró* stage in the nation.

Shortly after developing his signature fashion, Gonzaga further fortified his performance iconicity by standardizing his stage presentation into a three-piece band made up of the accordion, the *zabumba* drum, and oversized triangle—the very instrumentalization used today in *forró* performances. A great debate arose over whether or not Gonzaga was the first person to put together this *trio conjunto* (as he had proclaimed on more than one occasion); in fact, as he admitted later, the triangle-*zabumba*-*safona* (sometimes substituted with the fiddle) combination dated back to precolonial Portugal, where *chula* music boasted the three instruments.[55] Still, Gonzaga should be credited with bringing this instrumentation into the national limelight and consolidating a playing style for generations of *nordestino* bands. Certainly, a considerable element to the driving rhythm of *forró* is the syncopated peal of the thick metal beater clanging up and down between two triangle sides—and the extreme popularity of this triangle-playing style even sixty years later is a tribute to Gonzaga's ingenuity.

Unearthing a Soundtrack to Migration:
Zé Dantas Delivers Saudade

By 1950, Gonzaga had established the *baião* as one of the most popular musics of Brazil; he was the most successful recording artist in the nation; he had married Helena das Neves Cavalcanti (a difficult relationship that would be fraught with tension for the rest of his adult life) and brought his entire family from Pernambuco to settle in and around Rio, often accompanying Gonzaga for performances and recordings (four of his siblings would also become accordionists in the capital city, specializing in northeastern styles). His partnership with Humberto Teixeira had its ups and downs, as did his relationships with most of his friends and family, but he had just finished recording a big hit, "Vem Morena," with a new partner, Zé Dantas.

Zé Dantas would enhance Gonzaga's work even beyond the richness of the Gonzaga-Teixeira collaborations by adding elements of synesthesia and a true intimacy of the *sertão* to his lyrics and melodies. Having spent his childhood on a ranch in the Pernambuco backlands, he was infinitely comfortable and in tune with the natural environment; his music sketched the northeastern scrublands in language that was palpable and visceral while highly poetic. One can sense his love for the *sertão*. Gonzaga used to joke that he could "smell the stink of goat" on Zé Dantas, a good-natured reference to his deeply rooted telluric talent.

Zé Dantas had made a life for himself in Rio as a distinguished obstetrician, and he continued to work as a doctor, even while writing with Gonzaga and occasionally collaborating with Humberto Teixeira. He had "hopped aboard the tram midway," Gonzaga would say, "but boy, could he drive!"[56] For a few years, Gonzaga worked closely with both Humberto Teixeira and Zé Dantas—even coproducing a live radio show with them—but, like most of his collaborators, Teixeira and Zé Dantas would eventually part ways with Gonzaga, largely over contractual issues. While all three were performing on the "No Mundo do Baião," they struck on a synergy of their personas that was highly popular: Teixeira would play the part of the pedantic professor, espousing truths about the *sertão* while Zé Dantas would impersonate animals, people, and institutions of the backlands, and Gonzaga would tie it all together with another one of his larger-than-life grins and accompanying expansive chords on the accordion.

More than anything else, the music of Zé Dantas has come to stand out as an anthem to *nordestino* culture and people; the relatively few songs of protest from Gonzaga's collection are mostly the work of Zé Dantas, whose heart longed for a simple and healthy life for the oppressed peons of the Northeast. In his classic "Vozes da Seca" (Voices of the Drought), Gonzaga sings mournfully:

Kind Sir, the *nordestinos* are very grateful
for the assistance of the southerners during the great drought,
but Sir, a handout to a healthy man will either kill him or turn him to vice
and that's why we ask you for your protection.[57]

While geographic, economic, political, and social conditions have always made the Northeast an area of cyclical migrations, the twentieth century saw unprecedented migration out of the area, due mainly to an acute series of droughts, asymmetrical and irregular land development, an age-old landed oligarchy, and burgeoning industrial centers (mainly in São Paulo, Rio, and Brasília) that beckoned unskilled laborers with few other options. The capital city, in particular, doubled its population between 1920 and 1950, in large part due to the influx of migrants from the north, and São Paulo grew even faster (with additional immigrants arriving from abroad).[58] While research has shown that only a small minority of the migrants from the North came from the *sertão*,[59] its vast deserts of scrub brush and cacti became iconic of the plight of the *retirantes* (refugees). These downtrodden men and women, exiled from their homeland, would travel south on the backs of rickety trucks; called *pau-de-araras*, or parrot perches, the truck cargoes packed so tightly that the refugees looked like tiny birds stuck in a cage. As hundreds of thousands of these *retirantes* flooded the cities of the south looking for work, the tunes of Luiz Gonzaga spoke to them and consoled them during their homesick anguish. Gonzaga came to symbolize everything that they had left home and everything they longed for in return.

Portuguese has a special word for nostalgic longing: *saudade*. Often *saudade* is said to be untranslatable, impossible to express or emote in another language,[60] but, in a pinch, it can be conveyed as *nostalgic longing*. Nostalgia (from *nostos*: return home; and *algia*: longing) is a perfect descriptive for the plight of the *retirantes*: a longing for a home that no longer exists or *has never existed*.[61] Nostalgia is an important step in the invention of tradition, as it must be evoked along with repetitive imagery to establish a yearning, in the present, for an imagined past; and yet its impossibility confounds. As Svetlana Boym writes, "Nostalgia tantalizes us with its fundamental ambivalence; it is about the repetition of the unrepeatable, materialization of the immaterial."[62]

The evocative tunes of Zé Dantas and Luiz Gonzaga brought forth the sensations, tastes, smells, and sounds that hundreds of thousands of *nordestinos* felt for their native land. As one *nordestino* ethnographer wrote, "Gonzaga's Northeast is created to nourish the migrants' memory."[63] There is a certain pleasure in prolonging one's pain; and Gonzaga's tunes beg the listener to recall his or her native soil, to bask in the searing *sertão* sun, to visualize the sad departure of the last white-winged dove.

Gonzaga's Midlife Crisis: The "Ostracism" Years

Gonzaga's music remained wildly popular throughout the early 1950s, particularly with his *nordestino* audience, but the political climate began to change in 1956, with the transition to Kubitschek's presidency and the move to modernize Brazil with "fifty years of progress in five," and Gonzaga's music no longer appealed to the broad middle-class and elite audience he had once charmed. As José Farias dos Santos writes, "The musical moment as lived by the urban crowd wasn't a good fit for Luiz Gonzaga and his *baião* . . . the leather [*cangaceiro*] hat was switched out for leather jackets, his sandals for moccasins, and his accordion . . . replaced by the guitar and the electric guitar."[64]

Though his shows were canceled and media presence squashed in all of the big cities, Gonzaga continued to enjoy extraordinary success in the small towns of the interior. So he set off on a series of national tours that would keep him away from home for months at a time, playing on traveling stages set up in the plaza of various municipalities to a modest but enthusiastic rural public—the only public that continued to adore him.

A populist at heart, Gonzaga had always made music *of* the people and *for* the people. Though he socialized liberally with Rio's elite, even at his peak he preferred to leave the fancy club performances to other, more sophisticated artists.

Throughout his career, he had struggled with music executives to continue producing 78s, then LPs, even after more advanced technology had become available,
to keep costs down for his fans with humble origins like his own. Following with
this attitude, he set out to make his national tour and his individual shows free;
he found companies and/or politicians to underwrite his shows, and he signed
on to hundreds of advertising contracts, which would subsidize additional tour
costs. Writes Dreyfus:

> With the same tone, the same vigor with which he sang his music, Gonzaga pro-
> moted liquor, coffee, tobacco, wine, appliance warehouses, shoe stores, phar-
> macies, medicines, cleaning products.[65]

Often, Gonzaga would record or perform jingles for his various sponsors to
the tune of his most popular hits, changing a word or two to fit in an advertisement where necessary. He even backed opposing political candidates, each with
his own version of his publicity. For over a decade, Gonzaga peddled his wares in
a constant musical peregrination across Brazil. He continued to collaborate with
veteran lyricists, he sponsored up-and-coming musicians, he created countless
more *forró* classics—and, amazingly, three decades after he was first discovered
as a young *nordestino*, Gonzaga, the Rei do Baião, had a professional resurgence
with his urban audiences.

Resurgence: *Forró* Comes Full Circle

After the frenzied years of tackling modernity under Kubitschek, Brazil underwent
a violent and oppressive regime change, resulting in the military dictatorship
that ruled the nation until 1985. Though certain phases of the regime were more
repressive than others, students and intellectuals began to speak out against the
regime soon after the coup. Gonzaga, though he had publicly protested the plight
of the *nordestino retirantes* from early in his career, was famously ignorant about
politics—he appalled even his biggest supporters when he retorted that the claims
of torture under the Castelo Branco military regime were bogus. Nonetheless, a
generation of left-wing sympathizers had grown up with Gonzaga's music as a
backdrop to their youth, and these young musicians would welcome Gonzaga back
to his throne at the head of Brazilian popular music.

In 1965, Geraldo Vandré was a young up-and-coming singer-songwriter from
Paraíba who had not yet consolidated his fame as a protest singer. He performed
a version of "Asa Branca" on his second album—only a few years before he had to
exile himself for fear of repercussions from the increasingly severe regime—and
gave a new social legitimacy to the message of the music of Luiz Gonzaga. Then,
in 1971, Caetano Veloso produced an album from exile that also featured "Asa

Branca." Notably, Veloso included "Asa Branca" as the *only* Portuguese-language song on the record, embedding it with multiple layers of meaning: though prior interpretations of "Asa Branca" cited only the pain of being expelled from one's homeland *in the Northeast*, Veloso repackaged the music to address political exile as well, helping the song to become an anthem not only of the plight of the *retirantes* but of all Brazilians far from home.

Along with the enhanced significations of Gonzaga's music, the young generation of protest singers also heralded a new appreciation of folkloric roots. The *tropicália* movement of the late 1960s, driven most famously by the work of Caetano Veloso and Gilberto Gil, would reformulate the "cannibalist" project of Oswald de Andrade from the 1920s, encouraging a new Brazilian art that would "gorge" itself on folk traditions as well as modern sounds and recording techniques to create, through the anthropophagy of foreign and local elements, a truly Brazilian aesthetic.

Not only did the *tropicalists* inspire interest in Brazilian folklore; they also referred directly to Luiz Gonzaga as one of their earliest and most prominent influences. In one interview, Gilberto Gil compared Gonzaga to the great Pelé, saying that Gonzaga

> [was] among the five most important influences on Brazilian popular music. . . .
> All of us architects of *tropicália* . . . had, in our infancy and adolescence, huge
> influence from *nordestino* songs, especially the music of Luiz Gonzaga. If you
> take the first album of *tropicália*, you'll find there a variety of compositions, all
> of them derived from the *baião* style.[66]

Later Gil would call Luiz Gonzaga "the first musical phenomenon that had a great impact on me" and cite Gonzaga as "the first really significant thing to happen in the realm of mass culture in Brazil."[67] Caetano would also name Gonzaga as one of his strongest influences, even mentioning in his memoir that the first song he ever composed was a *baião* in C minor.[68] While short-lived, the *tropicália* movement influenced hundreds of artists across the nation, many of whom would also come to admire and emulate Luiz Gonzaga's work. In the coming years, Alceu Valença, Morais Moreira, Geraldo Azevedo, Zé Ramalho, and Raimundo Fagner (the so-called hippy-haired ones), as well as Elba Ramalho, would carry the torch of *nordestino* musical identity alongside Gonzaga.

With this new surge of interest in *nordestino* identity and culture, Gonzaga would continue touring throughout the 1970s and 1980s—this time, including the bigger cities in his journeys—and would even record with the younger talent, embracing different genres like rock. In turn, the young performers would record his classic hits. Gonzaga became, on many levels, a paternal figure of Brazilian popular music, sharing his expertise and his good-natured laughter and friendship with subsequent generations of artists. Even while afflicted with a slowly growing prostate cancer, Gonzaga continued touring and recording; he brought in additional accordionists when the weight of the instrument became too much for him and would still sing his timeless pieces, to the thrill of his always enthusiastic audiences. He succumbed to the cancer in August of 1989 but lives on through his classic recordings and the new generations of *forró*, which continue to flourish in Brazil.

Gonzaga's "Roots" Discourse Takes "Route"

The discourse created within the *forró* genre—as it is typically narrated—re-creates the dichotomies that Brazilian society has been reinforcing since the onset of modernity. As the standard story goes, the accordion represents the antithesis of progress; one pole of what Martín-Barbero calls a "schizophrenic" process, in which Brazilians combine a fevered push for "progress" with a renewed populist "return to roots." In this interpretation, an increasingly globalized Brazil compels the populace to begin looking to cultural products such as *forró* that might represent a rural and bucolic past, an imagined place and time untouched by modernity that might somehow better reflect an "authentic" Brazilian experience.

Luiz Gonzaga himself is complicit in this construction; he played up these oppositions through his performance style, lyrical content, and interviews, emphasizing the dualisms of Northeast versus South, rural versus urban, uneducated versus highly literate, poor versus elite, underdeveloped versus industrialized, and so forth. Gonzaga narrated the *forró* musical tradition as one exoticized extreme of the Brazilian culture spectrum. By positioning himself thus, he helped to develop and consolidate a region that, until the 1920s, never existed as such. Gonzaga (along with other well-known artists, politicians, and intellectuals who also built up the discourse) is a primary agent of the construction of the Northeast. This region, dressed as it is in novel nomenclature, is discursively and politically restricted in its development.

However, an alternative analysis of Gonzaga's music and career, as a cyclical and peripetetic invented tradition, may instead bring us one step closer toward bringing the age-old dialectic (of modernity versus tradition) to resolution and toward finally understanding Brazilian music through a different paradigm.

From its conception, *forró* has been tied to migration. It was not only created from but continues to be consumed because of an ever-growing cycle of Brazilian migration. The troubadours of Brazil brought European, African, Latin, indigenous, and Middle Eastern melodies and rhythms to the furthest corners of Brazil, where they evolved over time; Luiz Gonzaga brought the tunes he remembered from his youth to the capital city of Rio; he then created a career based on iterative musical tours crisscrossing the nation. Instead of interpreting Gonzaga's life as one between two opposing poles, we should conceptualize his career as an intricate network: a root system, or a migratory pattern. Indeed, Gonzaga "blazed a trail" for the success of the accordion in Brazil, but he also created thousands of diverging "routes" for new creative refractions of the *sanfona*.

The trope of peregrination and, ultimately, return to one's homeland is one treated again and again in the lyrics of *forró*. Few songs exist in the *forró* canon that don't somehow hail or reference *saudades* or nostalgia for one's home, as well as reiterate the suffering of an itinerant community. The emphasis of Gonzaga's music on nature (recall the *mandacaru* cactus, the white-winged dove, the countless descriptions of the *sertão* and drought . . .) invokes the very cyclical quality of seasonal changes, and of life itself.

Gonzaga's music doesn't simply "bridge" the tension between Brazilian poles; it functions as its dialectical resolution. Albuquerque writes:

> Though his song lyrics showed a traditional, antimodern, antiurban *nordeste*, his rhythm and harmony were a modern urban invention. At the same time that he spoke of a space that rejected bourgeois mercantile relations, [his music] was highly commercial . . . the *baião* was the perfect expression of a conciliation between modern forms and traditional content.[69]

Gonzaga himself was a *retirante*, of sorts, whose continued commercial success allowed him to return to his native land, lyrically and literally, over a lifelong musical journey.

Notes

1. Gildson Oliveira, *Luiz Gonzaga: O matuto que conquistou o mundo* (Brasília: Letraviva, 2000), 37.

2. By the musician and record producer David Byrne, who has specialized in producing and distributing world music (particularly Brazilian) artists under his label Luaka Bop.

3. Brazil is infamous for its income inequality. The UNDP's Human Development Report in 2003 found that Brazil had the greatest inequality among middle-income countries and was surpassed on the global level only by Sierra Leone. The data show that the poorest 10 percent of the population receives only 0.7 percent of total income, while the richest 10 percent receives almost half (Amanda Cassel and Raj Patel, "Agricultural Trade Liberalization and Brazil's Rural Poor: Consolidating Inequality," Global Policy Forum, August 2003, http://www.globalpolicy.org/globaliz/econ/2003/08agribrazil.htm (accessed May 12, 2004).

4. Raimundo Faoro qtd. in Hermano Vianna, *The Mystery of Samba: Popular Music and National Identity in Brazil* (Chapel Hill: University of North Carolina Press, 1999), 37.

5. Caetano Veloso, *Tropical Truth: A Story of Music and Revolution in Brazil.* (New York: Alfred A. Knopf, distributed by Random House, 2002), 87.

6. Qtd. in Oliveira, *Luiz Gonzaga*, 25.

7. Maria Elizabeth Lucas, "Gaucho Musical Regionalism," *British Journal of Musicology* 9.1 (2000): 53–56; John P. Murphy, *Music in Brazil: Experiencing Music, Expressing Culture* (New York: Oxford University Press, 2006), 127. In Rio Grande do Sul (in the south of Brazil), the same instrument is referred to as *gaita*.

8. Dominique Dreyfus, *A vida do viajante: A saga de Luiz Gonzaga* (São Paulo: Editora 34, 1997), 35.

9. Murphy, *Music in Brazil*, 104. As Helena Simonett notes in the introduction to this volume, local nomenclature of the accordion often betrays social conceptions of the instrument: likening it to a goat hoof clearly "locates" the *sanfona* as a lower-class instrument in a rural context.

10. Dreyfus, *A vida do viajante*, 79 (all translations mine).

11. See Bermúdez's essay in chapter 10 of this volume for a more careful examination of this phenomenon, as it occurred in Colombia with the musical genre of *vallenato*.

12. Peter Fry, "Feijoada and Soul Food," qtd. in Vianna, *Mystery of Samba*, 13.

13. Dreyfus, *A vida do viajante*, 79.

14. Ibid.

15. Qtd. in ibid., 80–81.

16. "Foi uma loucura. Respirei fundo, agradeci e joguei o 'Vira e Mexe' . . . Tiiiiiii-tiririririririririririririrum, tchan tanran tanran tanran tanran. . . . Ah! Foi mais loucura ainda. Parecia que o bar ia pegar fogo. O bar tinha lotado, gente na porta, na rua, tentando ver o que estava acontecendo no bar. Aí peguei o pires. Na terceira mesa já estava cheio. Aí eu gritei: 'Me dá um prato!' Daqui há pouco o prato estava cheio. Aí pedi uma bandeja. E pensei: agora a coisa vai" (qtd. in Dreyfus, *A vida do viajante*, 82–83).

17. "Então arrevire e mexe ai!" Qtd. in Dreyfus, *A vida do viajante*, 85.

18. Victor was one of two major multinational companies running the music business in Brazil; it later changed names to RCA Victor, then RCA, and currently BMG. The other multinational was Odeon, later called EMI (Dreyfus, *A vida do viajante*, 88).

19. I might translate this as, "Whoo—that is sweet lovin'!"

20. José Farias dos Santos, *Luiz Gonzaga: A música como expressão do nordeste* (São Paulo: Instituto Brasileira de Difusão Cultural, 2002), 40.

21. Qtd. in Dreyfus, *A vida do viajante*, 98.

22. Qtd. in Oliveira, *Luiz Gonzaga*, 45.

23. Dreyfus, *A vida do viajante*, 102.

24. Between 1941 and 1950, Brazil's radio stations burgeoned from one hundred to three hundred. Bryan McCann, *Hello, Hello Brazil: Popular Music in the Making of Modern Brazil* (Durham, North Carolina: Duke University Press, 2004), 24; Mário de Andrade, *Cartas de Mário de Andrade a Luís da Câmara Cascudo* (Belo Horizonte: Villa Rica, 1991), 149.

25. McCann, *Hello, Hello Brazil*, 23.

26. Dreyfus, *A vida do viajante*, 112.

27. Mundicarmo Maria Rocha Ferretti, *Baião dos dois: Zedantas e Luiz Gonzaga* (Recife: Fundação Joaquim Nabuco, Editora Massangana, 1988), 59.

28. Frederick Moehn, "Mixing MPB: Cannibals and Cosmopolitans in Brazilian Popular Music" (Ph.D. dissertation, New York University, 2001), 113–14.

29. Dreyfus claims that the rudimentary nature of *sertão* instruments (like the button accordion) made accompanying vocalizations difficult (Dreyfus, *A vida do viajante*, 106).

30. Ibid., 150.

31. Ibid., 158.

32. "Eu vou mostrar pra vocês / como se dança o baião / e quem quiser aprender / é favor prestar atenção."

33. Roberta Lana de Alencastre Ceva, "Na batida da zabumba: uma análise antropológica do forró universitário" (Master's thesis, Universidade Federal do Rio de Janeiro [Antopologia Social do Museu Nacional], 2001), 17.

34. On the etymology of *baião/abaianada/baiano* styles, see Larry N. Crook, "Zabumba Music from Caruaru, Pernambuco: Musical Style, Gender, and the Interpenetration of Rural and Urban Worlds" (Ph.D. dissertation, University of Texas at Austin, 1991), 235–36; José Ramos Tinhorão, *Os sons dos negros no Brasil: cantos, danças, folguedos, origens* (São Paulo: Art Editora, 1988); Oneyda Alvarenga, *Música popular brasileira* (São Paulo: Duas Cidades, 1982), 177; Mário de Andrade, *Danças dramáticas do Brasil* (Belo Horizonte: Editora Itatiaia, 1982).

35. Suzel Ana Reily, "Forró for all: Saldanha Rolim," *British Journal of Ethnomusicology* 4 (1995): 181–82.

36. Dreyfus writes that Gonzaga's crown was his leather hat (see below) and his scepter, his accordion (Dreyfus, *A vida do viajante*, 145). Along with the King of Baião arose the designations "Queen" (Carmélia Alves), "Prince" (Luiz Vieira), "Princess" (Claudete Soares), and "Baron" (Jair Alves). The media attention and "baptism" out of his control of so many artists irritated Gonzaga, who said, "Que é isso, agora tem dinastia do baiao?" (What is this, now there's a dynasty of *baião*?). Qtd. in Dreyfus, *A vida do viajante*, 172.

37. To hear a recent rendition by David Byrne and New York–based Forró in the Dark, see http://www.youtube.com/watch?v=v8OWpeF8jyo (accessed January 6, 2012).

38. "Até mesmo a asa-branca / bateu asas do sertão / entonces eu disse, adeus Rosinha / guarda contigo meu coração."

39. See also Edward Said, *Orientalism* (New York: Pantheon Books, 1978).

40. Qtd. in Svetlana Boym, *The Future of Nostalgia* (New York: Basic Books, 2001), 19.

41. Qtd. in Linda-Anne Rebhun, *The Heart Is Unknown Country: Love in the Changing Economy of Northeast Brazil* (Stanford, Calif.: Stanford University Press, 1999), 2–3.

42. The key distinguishing characteristic of the Northeast's climate is not the low rainfall per se, but rather the high degree of rainfall variability. The fact that the droughts are unpredictable, that there may be ten or twelve rainy years and suddenly a profound and long-lasting drought, makes life and livelihood precarious. Kampton Webb, *The Changing Face of Northeast Brazil* (New York: Columbia University Press, 1974), 44.

43. The fact that there is a *coincidental* relationship between the drought area of northeastern Brazil and the area of greatest poverty does not mean that there is a *causal* relationship between them. The actual causes of poverty have more to do with antiquated land-tax structures, inheritance patterns, types of land tenure, and the ideas of the

socio-economic-political elite groups than they do with climatic drought and soil infertility. Webb, *Changing Face*, 178.

44. "Literatura das secas" was first coined by Tristão de Ataide to designate what he calls this peculiar species of *sertanismo regional*. See D. Barreira, *Historia da Literatura Cearense* (Fortaleza: Ed. Do Instituto do Ceara, 1986).

45. Crook, *Zabumba Music*, 212.

46. Qtd. in Dreyfus, *A vida do viajante*, 8.

47. McCann, *Hello, Hello Brazil*, 114–15.

48. Ibid., 114–15.

49. Durval Muniz de Albuquerque Jr., *A invenção do nordeste e outras artes* (Recife: Fundação Joaquim Nabuco, Editora Massangana, 1999), 163; McCann, *Hello, Hello Brazil*, 114–15.

50. Readers may find it easy to compare Gonzaga's performance style with that of the Italian American Guido Deiro; see Zinni's essay in chapter 8 of this volume.

51. Dreyfus, *A vida do viajante*, 167.

52. Vianna reports that Gonzaga was not the first performer to use *cangaceiro* costumes for performance; in 1913 the Grupo de Caxangá dressed as bandit followers of the famous outlaw Antonio Silvino (a predecessor of Lampião). Vianna, *Mystery of Samba*, 28.

53. Dreyfus, *A vida do viajante*, 136; see also Oliveira, *Luiz Gonzaga*, 55.

54. For more on the dialectic of costume versus uniform, see Roberto Da Matta, *O que faz, o Brasil, Brasil?* (Rio de Janeiro: Rocco, 1989), 74.

55. Mário de Andrade had noted the use of accordion with triangle in Pernambuco as early as 1928 (in his "Ensaio Sobre a Música Brasileira"). Furthermore, the leading music historian José Ramos Tinhorão calls attention to a photo published in 1929 showing a young boy playing a triangle alongside a band of *pífano* (fife), snare, *zabumba*, and fiddle players, and there is ample evidence showing that the trio concept had been employed in the *nordeste* since early in the twentieth century. See José Ramos Tinhorão, *Pequena História da Música Brasileira* (São Paulo: Art Editora, 1986), 220–21.

56. Qtd. in Dreyfus, *A vida do viajante*, 149–50.

57. "Seu doutô os nordestino têm muita gratidão / pelo auxílio dos sulista nessa seca do sertão. / Mas doutô uma esmola a um homem qui é são / ou lhe mata de vergonha ou vicia o cidadão / É por isso que pidimo proteção a vosmicê."

58. McCann, *Hello, Hello Brazil*, 97.

59. The largest number originated in the sugarcane area of Pernambuco, with the "agreste" temperate zone accounting for only 35 percent and the *sertão* with only 4 percent. Gilberto Osório de Andrade, *Migrações internas e o Recife* (Recife: Ministério da Educação e Cultura, Insituto Joaquim Nabuco de Pesquisas Sociais, 1979), 39.

60. Boym points out that "[c]uriously, intellectuals and poets from different antigonal traditions began to claim that they had a special word for homesickness that was radically untranslatable." She goes on to list: "German *heimweh*, French *maladie du pays*, Spanish *mal de corazón*, Czech *litost*, Russian *toska*, Polish *tesknota*, and Romanian *dor*" (Boym, *Future of Nostalgia*, 12–13).

61. Ibid., xiii.

62. Ibid., xvii–xviii.

63. Albuquerque, *A invenção do nordeste*, 159.

64. Santos, *Luiz Gonzaga*, 63.

65. Dreyfus, *A vida do viajante*, 210.

66. Qtd. in Oliveira, *Luiz Gonzaga*, 81–82.

67. Qtd. in Augusto de Campos, *O Balanço da Bossa e Outras Bossas* (São Paulo: Perspectiva, 1978); Dreyfus, *A vida do viajante*, 244.

68. Veloso, *Tropical Truth*, 13.

69. Albuquerque, *A invenção do nordeste*, 162–63.

⚛14⚛

The Accordion in New Scores

Paradigms of Authorship and Identity in William Schimmel's Musical "Realities"

MARION S. JACOBSON

The American composer and accordionist William Schimmel (b. 1946) has composed four thousand works over a twenty-year period, none of them original. In fact, all of them are based, thematically and structurally, on the works of other composers. Works that reference other composers—*A Rossini Reality*, *Bizet's Carmen Fantasy*, *Fantasy in Long Hair*, and *Tantric Bartok*—are not transcriptions or fantasies in the conventional romantic sense of that term, nor do they represent conventionally modernist techniques of collage.[1] Rather, as Schimmel has explained them, they constitute "musical realities" that do not depend principally on conventional relationships between the original and the "new" composer.[2] In exploring relationships between different musical traditions and practices, Schimmel relies on an instrument that is somewhat unusual in the postmodern world of contemporary composition: the piano accordion. Schimmel, a childhood "accordion prodigy," exploits the instrument's unique tonalities, textures, and what Raymond Williams might recognize as a "structure of feeling"[3]—to entice the audience into imaginary worlds of memory, tradition, and community. As Schimmel has said, "The accordion offers its own Diaspora. It has a hidden memory bank inside it. There is something in the marrow of it that when people hear it, it reminds them of something—a nostalgic moment, a flavor. It could evoke a taste, a memory. No matter how abstract—it can sound like Webern!—the accordion can evoke something that plays on a person's memory."[4]

Schimmel's "realities" for accordion unfold on multiple creative levels—modernist explorations of selfhood, otherness, angst, and the search for a usable past—and his compositional process evokes Bakhtinian relationships; that is, he does not treat his sources as fixed, self-contained entities, but as fluid matter.[5] Another Bakhtinian principle evident in his work is the dialogics of compositional control and intertextuality. In historical terms, collage is a modernist tool, but it can also be seen as a postmodernist strategy, for trading authorial control for intertextual references and eclecticism are themes that run through the history of twentieth-century accordion music. Indeed, it is these tensions that make Schimmel's work so fascinating. Each work has its own musical "world," evocative of particular places, spaces, and ethnographic moments, subject to a particular moment of music history and reworked through experience, memory, and self-reflection. Moreover, they resonate with Schimmel's search for a fitting role and identity in the contemporary musical world, both as an accordionist and as a composer—or, as he prefers to describe himself, a "practitioner of musical realities."[6]

The different sites, periods, and ethnographic traditions of his works like *Variations in Search of a Theme for Accordion, Holbein in New York—A Seantic Drama, The Dolls: A Medieval Cantata, Fantasy in Long Hair, A Rossini Reality*, and *A Portrait of Harry Lime* are reflections of Schimmel's trajectory as a composer and working musician in New York City in the 1970s and 1980s. The concepts of space, place, and disaffection in Schimmel's music are more than personal experiences and events; they also embody tropes recurring in postmodern musical composition—of being, exile, and the resulting discovery of the emergent self and the Other. Says Schimmel about these works, "They occupy their own space."[7] As Kevin McNeilly has written about John Zorn's musical works, it is useful to think about Schimmel's uses of other composers' themes and forms as a "subversive process from which the music emerges remade, having reshaped the fundamental ways in which we listen, both to each other and to the world around us."[8] As Roland Barthes has suggested, "[T]o give a text an Author is to impose a limit on that text, to furnish it with a final signified, to close the writing."[9] Schimmel contends that by "opening up the writing," we can come to define meaning and patterns of coherence in music. This essay explores paradigms of composition and identity in Schimmel's music, with a view to linking these critical theoretical discourses to ideas developing around the accordion in the American musical scene in the twentieth century, and the composer's intellectual and creative motivations in these works.

My first interactions with Schimmel took place in a musical context in which the accordion plays a unique role—the national membership organization for accordion players and enthusiasts, the American Accordionists Association (AAA). Its governing board, of which Schimmel is a member, consists of prominent accordion teachers, concert artists, and industry representatives. Each year in July,

Schimmel presides over the AAA-sponsored Accordion Seminars in New York City.[10] Compared to the rigid formality and buttoned-up concert-recital norms of AAA concerts, Schimmel's two-day series of master classes and miniconcerts is an informal and festive event. The repertoire presents the cutting edge of the accordion, showcasing multimedia and theatrical works for accordion and works of younger accordion artist-composers, many of them his students. As Schimmel's creative experiences are directly linked to his work as an accordionist and as an accordion "activist," in and outside of the AAA, I will explore some of these in this essay. Schimmel has been quite reflexive about the types of musical relationships engendered in the "accordion world," as well as the roles and identity they have attempted to cast for the accordion. There are frequently multiple, and often subtle, linkages among Schimmel's life experiences, his compositional creativity, and his use of the accordion.

Prestige Value of the Piano Accordion

The accordion can mean many things. As the contributors to this volume have demonstrated, the accordion functions and is valued variously in different musical communities. It may facilitate musical participation and sociability, propel the physical motions of dance, serve as a status icon, stand as a manifestation of Old World "tradition," and so on. Within some communities, there exists a hierarchy among musical discourses that attributes more prestige to some of these functions than others. The systematic discrediting of the accordion at midcentury, reflected in some of the accordion jokes Richard March relates in chapter 2 of this volume, was a product of the divisions of the musical world and the erosion of prestige for the folk and ethnic traditions with which the accordion was associated.

In 1938, a rear guard of accordionists and teachers, represented by its founding accordion luminaries (Anthony Galla-Rini, Charles Magnante, and Pietro Deiro, the reputed "Daddy of the Accordion") drafted its stated mission to "stimulate an increasing knowledge of, and appreciation for, the accordion."[11] They aimed to enhance the prestige value of the accordion within the academy and the mainstream classical-musical world, while resisting the influences of folk and popular-music styles. This position was not invented in the twentieth century. It is an outgrowth of the late nineteenth-century notion that the accordion, marketed initially as an affordable, portable, one-man-band instrument, could serve to make the great classics of Western art music more accessible to everyday listeners and consumers of music (the bourgeoisie). The motivation for this position could be traced in part to the development of a profitable, global accordion-manufacturing industry in the late 1800s, and the success of accordion makers to appeal to a new audience in the United States—particularly, the waves of immigrants to America who had encountered the instrument earlier, at some point during Europe's late nineteenth-century accordion craze. Within the context of postwar capitalist America, as the accordion reached its peak in popularity, two mutually exclusive economies of the accordion developed: one aimed at the instrument's popular and commercial success, and another aimed at defending the accordion against pluralism. They were present to oversee proper pedagogy, technique, and to remind us not to enjoy ethnic music too much. One of their aims was to disassociate the accordion from the heritage musics with which the instrument had been associated since its early development. Their castigations of "vulgar" folk music appeared in the official publications of the AAA, as well as in music trade magazines. In an article entitled "The Accordion in the Field of Serious Music," Anthony Galla-Rini wrote, "[G]ood musical taste having been of a deplorably low standard in the past, such banalities as 'Sharp-shooters March' and 'Beer Barrel Polka' should not be played in public, or given as lesson assignments."[12] Accordion teachers turned against folk and traditional music, unless it was arranged in formal compositions, which were presented in graded exercises for the beginning player and competition pieces for the advanced player. Galla-Rini and Deiro set the groundwork for the Great Accordion Canon that remains the mainstay of accordion competitions and the concert and festival audience. By condemning "Beer Barrel Polka"—based on a Czech popular song—Galla-Rini articulated a position that would ultimately lead to the self-alienation of accordionists from their working-class immigrant constituency.[13]

Although tinged with ethnocentrism and elitism, the work of the accordion luminaries like Deiro, Galla-Rini, and Magnante is to some extent motivated by the social idealism that marked American culture in the 1930s and 1940s—a desire to wean the indiscriminate middle class from the empty banalities of commercialized popular culture such as Lawrence Welk's "Champagne Music" and Dick Contino's endless repetitions of "Lady of Spain," which had contributed to the instrument's visibility and popularity on television and radio; and to instill what they regarded as the proper habits of listening and reception. Students of accordion were steered toward "proper methods"—Charles Nunzio's *Wizard Accordionist*, based on Hanon exercises, and transcriptions and arrangements of the complex music of serious composers. Because the piano accordion's arrangement of bass notes had been standardized for most of the time it had been present in the United States (since the 1900s), some of the accordion's self-appointed protectors feared that the instrument would never develop and improve unless they intervened.[14] Willard Palmer, a noted teacher of the accordion and the developer of a series of method books (the Palmer method), launched an attack against the piano accordion's traditional layout of bass tones and chords, known as the Stradella system.[15] Another concert accordionist wrote about the Stradella bass system, "[T]he bass side of the instrument is a stumbling block to the true and conscientious artist but a boon to the mediocre performer for [it] enables him to play certain forms of hackneyed and inferior music with greatest of ease and a minimum of effort."[16] Since the Stradella system was originally designed as a shortcut for easily reaching I, IV, and V chords in the most common major keys (C, F, and G), and these chord-bass patterns are used in many traditional styles of music, we can easily interpret these statements to mean that accordion pedagogs feared that inferior folk music would remain a hindrance to the acceptance of the instrument in mainstream musical culture, unless they did something about it. One of the most famous results of their efforts, designed to remove the limitations imposed by the Stradella system, was to develop a new system for playing single bass tones, known as the "free bass" accordion. Schimmel, initially involved in this effort as a spokesman for Titano, one of the most preeminent American manufacturers of free-bass accordions, faced pressure to abandon the Stradella system, to which he felt deeply attached. The free-bass advocates' argument against the Stradella bass—that the fixed chords handcuffed the player to the conventions of European folk music—pinpointed what Schimmel loved about the accordion. He held out against the free-bass accordion. Later, Schimmel adopted a "compromise," the quint converter system, based on mechanics of the Stradella system.[17] Most of Schimmel's accordion scores, including the musical "realities" discussed in this chapter, indicate that the music can be played on either the free-bass or traditional accordion, or "adapted for any kind of accordion."[18]

Another major initiative of the organized accordion world was to encourage compositions for accordion by recognized composers and to provide funds for commissioned works. The commissioning committee of the AAA, headed by the legendary accordionist/activist Elsie M. Bennett, resulted in a modest repertoire of "serious" compositions for accordion (written by nonaccordionist composers and highlighting, primarily, neoclassical and romantic musical idioms). The AAA premiered these works in major venues such as Carnegie Hall, where the accordion was first featured in 1947, when the accordionist Toralf Tollefifson presented Pietro Deiro's *Accordion Concerto in E.* Schimmel's connections with the AAA benefited him at a moment when he was attempting to build his reputation as a composer and earn tenure at Brooklyn College, where he taught composition and theory. His *Variations in Search of a Theme for Accordion* (1967–76) and *The Spring Street Ritual* (1979, dedicated to Igor Stravinsky) were commissioned by the AAA (the latter work was a test piece for the 1979 Coupe Mondiale world accordion competition in Cannes).

It could be argued that all of the official projects of the AAA—arrangements of serious music, establishment of competitions, and efforts to improve the technical sophistication of the accordion—served to reinscribe the very divisions they thought to transcend. High-mindedness easily turns to contempt. In the decades following World War II, and especially the 1960s, the serious accordionist could feel beleaguered by the reified, invariably modernist and romantic classical-music repertoire for accordion, as well as by the AAA, which controlled discourses about the accordion and shaped its reputation on radio, recordings, and television. In the 1960s, the AAA's leaders worked as hard to resist the encroaching popular-musical influences of the 1950s as they did other vernacular musics, urging teachers not to give in to their students' urge to play rock 'n' roll on the accordion. By regarding the popularity of the accordion as a problem and a nuisance, Nunzio, Magnante, and Palmer promoted a "siege mentality" that shaped the creative trajectory we are about to see emerging in Schimmel's work. Schimmel had plenty of motivation to align himself with the accordion rear guard and accept their commissions and opportunities to enhance his prestige in the accordion world. But taking up composition in New York in the 1960s required him to adopt a different perspective and a different set of values to sustain his academic career and his emotionally satisfying (and profitable) ties to the accordion and its folk and ethnic repertoire. The rhetoric of identity and survival runs through all the experiences Schimmel relates about his education and creative development in New York City.

Schimmel's Background

As a composer, musician, writer, and teacher, William Schimmel has been a prominent figure in the New York City music world for more than three decades, since his arrival in 1967 to study composition at the Juilliard School. Born in 1946 in Philadelphia, Schimmel was orphaned as an infant and adopted by German-speaking parents. He first learned the accordion from his three uncles, skilled "weekend musicians" who performed at local weddings and parties. Their unrestrained performances of German polkas, waltzes, and popular songs at family gatherings gave Schimmel his first glimpse of the accordion's ludic, transgressive pleasures: "My uncles would arrive with their accordions, and all hell would break loose: dancing, eating, drinking, cigar smoking, poker playing—real fun!"[19] Through the Frankie Yankovic albums the family collected with a passion, Schimmel enjoyed early exposure to Slovenian-style polka and a wide variety of accordion-based popular dance forms.

In 1960, Schimmel enrolled in a Philadelphia Catholic high school known for strict discipline. There Schimmel was subjected to, and witnessed, a variety of physical punishments. "If you passed through the cafeteria on your way home and saw the students in detention, with hands on top of their heads, hands folded behind their backs, kneeling with their hands on top of their heads, kneeling with their hands folded behind their backs, you were reminded of Dante's *Inferno* and the various degrees of punishment leading to eternal punishment."[20] For Schimmel, adolescence was a lesson in endurance, compassion, patience, and learning to live with shame and fear. His school experiences intensified his musical aspirations and, in particular, his desire to play the accordion. As a child, Schimmel received lessons at the Jacob C. Neupauer Conservatory of Music. A full-service music school, offering lessons in all the major orchestral instruments and in theory, Neupauer was in the heyday of the accordion school and studio movement in the 1940s and 1950s, known as an "accordion conservatory." This implies an oxymoron, because few mainstream American music schools recognized the accordion, or even offered formal instruction. Neupauer aimed to not only offer a comprehensive curriculum that would focus on Western classical pedagogy, performance, and theory, but to prepare the student for a career as a professional accordionist, "entertaining at elegant dances, shows, and concerts," as Jacob Neupauer's own ballroom orchestra certainly did. "My personal escape plan was through my accordion. It was, and still is, a reality unto itself. I could leave high school and go to the Conservatory and be in a whole other place, mentally as well as physically, with people different from me, yet centered on the accordion and its culture."[21] After graduating high school, Schimmel enrolled in the conservatory as a full-time student for two years, receiving the accordionist's equivalent of a trade-school diploma and racking up numerous competition prizes, the official evidence of recognition in the accordion world.[22] Later, Schimmel himself became codirector of the Neupauer Conservatory, a title he shared with Jacob Neupauer until 2011 when Neupauer died. Today, Schimmel offers the Neupauer Conservatory curriculum through his own independent study program in New York City.

Schimmel's experiences at Neupauer and his exposure to the masterworks of the Western musical canon through the accordion fortified him emotionally and intellectually. His classical training on the accordion helped gain him admission to Juilliard—not as an accordionist but as a pianist. Well aware of the accordion's "outsider" status, Schimmel knew that "you didn't walk into Juilliard wearing an accordion." To study with, and gain the favor of, such musical luminaries as Paul Creston, Elliott Carter, Luciano Berio, and Hugo Weisgall, composers with whom Schimmel studied and regards as mentors, one needed to minor in piano, which Schimmel also did.[23]

To earn extra income while at Juilliard, Schimmel would return home to Philadelphia on weekends and play Italian and Polish wedding gigs. A number of his classmates and teachers learned about Schimmel's background as an accordionist and expressed curiosity about the instrument. An accordion piece written by Schimmel's roommate, presented in Stanley Wolfe's class, landed him a teaching fellowship. Berio tapped him for a recording of Kurt Weill songs that Berio himself had arranged for soprano the Cathy Berberian. Adding to Schimmel's revenue was a contract with Mercury to arrange two popular songs weekly—"one of the last Tin Pan Alley gigs."[24] After teaching at Juilliard, Schimmel would change out of his preppy blazer and into a fringed suede vest before heading downtown to Mercury's offices, but not before hearing a barrage of comments ("You whore!" was one he particularly remembers from a classmate). Schimmel notes that in those days at Juilliard, writing popular music was something you "just didn't do."

Schimmel's expanding network of friends and mentors within and beyond the academy landed him a number of musical and theatrical collaborations. In 1979, at a production of Aristophanes's *The Birds* at La Mama, he met Micki Goodman, a Juilliard-trained dancer to whom he has been married for twenty-nine years and who has collaborated with him on many dance, theatrical, and video works. In 1981 Schimmel joined the pianist Michael Sahl and violinist Stan Kurtis to record classic Argentine tangos. The Nonesuch producer Eric Salzman expressed enthusiasm about Schimmel's "tango project," and the trio released its first *Tango Project* albums that year. It rose to the number-one position on the *Billboard* charts and won the *Stereo Review* Album of the Year award. The Tango Project Trio (with the violinist Mary Rowell replacing Kurtis) went on to produce three follow-up albums. Schimmel focused his early compositional works on serialism and postmodern musical vocabularies. Influenced by his primary composition mentor Hugo Weisgall, Schimmel's *Concerto for Three* is written in a highly dramatic musical style.[25] His *Variations in Search of a Theme*, notes Schimmel, reflects some of the serialist procedures later explored in Berio's own *Sequenza 13*. In 1971, working with Elliott Carter, Schimmel wrote *Parousia: the coming of CHRIST*, which functioned as a bridge from the avant-garde style to tonality. In 1976, denied tenure at Brooklyn College, Schimmel made his exit from the academic world and launched his career as a "missionary/mercenary"—an independent composer and a musician for hire. He also began writing about music, and he posts all of his articles—more like mini-performance-art projects with images and words—on his website.[26]

Schimmel emphasizes that many of his ideas about writing music—and his justification for composing—indend to reveal sounds that are manifest in the structure and timbre of the accordion. Attached to the body with straps, the accordion has been seen as one of the world's most "embodied" instruments. Its distinctive bellows action (initiated by the left arm and shoulder) requires dynamic whole-body, dancelike movements—a phenomenon explored in the works of other accordionist-composers who have written for the instrument, like Schimmel's contemporary Pauline Oliveros, also a childhood accordionist.[27] As his first instrument—if not his primary instrument in the music world—the accordion played an important role in engendering and realizing his musical compositions. Schimmel recalls that the first time he put on an accordion, attempting to reproduce Clementi and Mozart piano sonatas, he felt as if he were "composing" his own music (he had no idea at the time that he may have been "transcribing" these works from memory). For Schimmel, the accordion is a "culture." He became aware of this idea

Figure 14.1 William Schimmel performs at the Accordion Seminars at Tenri Cultural Institute, Manhattan. Photo courtesy William Schimmel.

early on, living in the cultural divide between parochial school and the Neupauer Conservatory and, later, in the divide between the Philadelphia ethnic communities whose weddings he played and New York City's academic musical community. Because much of the classical literature he played at Neupauer consisted of other composers' transcriptions of the classics, Schimmel (like other accordionists in the 1950s) was keenly aware of the paucity of serious musical works for the instrument. Witnessing the advent of rock 'n' roll as an accordion-playing teen in Philadelphia, Schimmel became keenly aware of the instrument's "outsider" status, and he was willing to embrace it himself—as a personal mission and a way of enhancing his career. Schimmel continues to enjoy the challenge of explaining the accordion to fellow musicians and composers and making the instrument more visible. Being an accordionist in a conservatory environment forced him to be cognizant of his purpose in life, and he came to consider being an accordionist as an integral part of his creative process. The structure of the accordion forms an intellectual scaffolding for the music and represents important linkages to understanding Schimmel's compositions and works for the accordion. After graduation, Schimmel enjoyed a fifteen-year period of substantial compositional output, including instrumental solo and chamber music, solo compositions, and multimedia pieces. His stylistic idioms are diverse, spanning atonality, neoclassicism, dodecaphony, and neoromanticism.

In 1984, Schimmel endured a personally devastating experience that nearly cost him his will to compose. The *New York Times'* music critic, Bernard Holland, dismissed his latest work, *Tarrytown Concerto* for accordion, violin, and orchestra, as "some warmed-over nineteenth-century European hokum."[28] Immediately following the review's appearance, Schimmel's opportunities for commissions and collaborations dried up overnight. His wife Micki advised Schimmel, depressed and despondent over his career, to move in a new direction; she commanded him to "watch MTV and learn how to become a rock star."[29] Shortly after, the opportunity came to make rock 'n' roll music with Tom Waits, with whom he appeared on the *Late Show with David Letterman* and released several recordings, including a rendition of Kurt Weill's *Lost in the Stars*.[30] Observing Waits's methods of collaboration suggested a different approach to composition as "creating music that was not original."[31] The result was Schimmel's "musical realities." Discussion of two of these works, *A Rossini Reality* and *A Portrait of Harry Lime*, will provide insight into Schimmel's compositional process and his use of the accordion.

A Rossini Reality

In the early 1980s, Schimmel heard some recordings of Argentine tango dating as far back as 1901. Researching the history of tango music, a style brought to Argentina by Italian immigrants and popularized in working-class milieus such as cafes and dance halls, Schimmel perceived tango as the Argentine counterpart to the blues, music he had come to admire while growing up in Philadelphia. Through the tango, he began to experience, in a fresh light, the idea of otherness—his own as well as that of the people whose violent lives, sufferings, and struggles are represented in this music. He was deeply impressed and moved, noting at the time that "the tango is reminiscent of romantic failure and existential despair. The tango expects all of that, but the trick is that you go down and out, but you do it in style. It's the ultimate 'screw you.'"[32]

Another absorbing element of the project was the challenge of reworking the tangos, traditionally played on the *bandoneón*, for the piano accordion. Like other diatonic free-reed instruments, the *bandoneón* produces different tones on the press and draw of the bellows. The chromatic piano accordion, however, produces the same pitch on the press and the draw, requiring a different bellows technique—one that is smoother and less percussive.[33] To fully capture what he felt was the essence of Argentine tango, Schimmel avoided overt references to stylistic conventions of the newly emerging *tango nuevo* phenomenon, ignited by Astor Piazzolla's second visit to the United States in 1985.[34] Maria Susana Azzi describes Piazzolla's style as a "fusion of jazz and classical music with sounds and musical practices that come from traditional tango and the lower classes."[35] Like Piazzolla's, Schimmel's tangos are compositions for instruments, not vocal ensembles. Schimmel focuses his efforts on capturing, without the presence of lyrics, the tango's storytelling tradition and the tragic, violent images and feelings reflected in its lyrics. The Argentine tango theme presented in Schimmel's composition *A Rossini Reality* presents the overarching themes of displacement, violence, and conflict in Schimmel's works, themes that recur in various guises in his other compositions for accordion.

Referred to as a "musical reality," *A Rossini Reality*[36] is a set of stylized snapshots that seem to suggest various relationships, confrontations, and emotions surrounding the juxtaposition of a classic Argentine tango tune and snippets of two Rossini opera overtures. Schimmel first heard this particular tango, "Ole Guapa," in Luis Buñuel and Salvador Dali's revolutionary film *Un Chien Andalou*. The tango was played live on a phonograph by the directors at its first Paris screening in 1929 and added to the score in 1960.[37] The tango accompanies the film's iconic opening moment, and one of the most shocking moments in film history, when a man (actually Buñuel himself) slices the eye of a young girl with a straight razor—in close-up. The 1960 score combines the sounds of the French accordion with Wagner's music; *A Rossini Reality* juxtaposes snippets from "Ole Guapa" with musical fragments taken from the overtures to Rossini's *La Gazza Ladra* and *The Barber of Seville*. Schimmel first encountered these overtures not in their operatic context but as transcriptions for accordion. Later, listening to the originals, he found, "I liked the transcriptions better than the originals, because the accordion heightens the music's folk dimensions."[38]

The seven-minute-long *Rossini Reality* opens by reproducing the *Barber* overture's famous two-chord fanfare, played in F major, and about one minute of the familiar thematic material apparently borrowed directly from the accordion transcription. It functions here as an "overture" to the tango theme in E minor, played in the classic 4/4 tango meter, with almost grotesquely heavy accents on the first beat of the measure, which is typically accented in the tango. This material (about ten seconds' worth) reveals itself to be no more than a second introduction, this time to the march theme from Barber, played much faster than the "original." Schimmel then introduces the *Gazza Ladra* waltz theme, with several variations that, seemingly appropriate for Rossini's early romantic idiom, might slip by a listener unfamiliar with the score. Following this, Schimmel adds a flourish that leads into a more extended version of the tango theme before returning to the *Gazza Ladra* waltz—or is it the *Barber* material? The two Rossini overtures blur into what Schimmel calls "perverse, grotesque, nasty, and punky adaptations."[39] These feature dissonances, abrupt bellows/breath changes, muddy-sounding glissandi, and erratic use of rubato at the beginnings and ends of phrases. It is as if Schimmel himself (or the player) is pulled between two opposing desires for the pretty, lighthearted tunes of Rossini and the lewd rhythmic distortions of the tango—both expressed in the 4/4 march tempo.

This tensely dramatic and multilayered work ends with a bright, quirky cadenza and returns to the initial F-major key, representing a feeling of relief or "return to normalcy" after the end of the turmoil. This piece provides an effective sonic expression of Schimmel's identity as a hard-working accordion virtuoso, giving way to his interest in modernist and avant-garde music and the intellectual and emotional challenges he faced in the tango genre. With *A Rossini Reality*'s exploration of the accordion as a dramatic instrument of the nineteenth century, its operatic and orchestral references, and its multivocality, Schimmel follows new creative pathways that, consciously or unconsciously, parallel his travels through different musical worlds (the ethnographic world of the tango, popular music, and bel canto). Indeed, *A Rossini Reality* is about Schimmel's personal journeys and rites of passage: Schimmel's voyage from accordion virtuoso to modernist to "rock star."

In its original stylistic dimensions and its historical/ethnographic references, *A Rossini Reality* contributes to a small but significant repertoire of musical works that highlight surrealist writing techniques, such as Andre Breton's automatic writing, in the composition of music.[40] *A Rossini Reality* seems to reflect Buñuel's famous commentary on his *Chien Andalou*: "Nothing in the film symbolizes anything."[41] In terms of aesthetics, the juxtapositions created by the encounters of opera, tango, and "punky" sounds for the sake of sounds evokes a self-referential audio collague, a creative process described by Rene T. A. Lysoff (after John Oswald) as "plunderphonics."[42] These "authorized" juxtapositions produce a sense of displacement and difference in the listener.

A Portrait of Harry Lime
(After Carol Reed's Film *The Third Man*)

In his 2006 solo work for accordion, *A Portrait of Harry Lime*,[43] Schimmel continues his explorations of "filmic reality," in which his music takes on a cinematic dimension inspired by the Soviet auteur Sergei Eisenstein. Schimmel writes in his introduction to the score that he aims to allow the listener to experience the work in the overtones of the montage, like the segments that comprise it.[44] Schimmel likens the role of the solo accordionist performing this piece to that of a method actor interpreting the character of Harry Lime, the shadowy, villainous character famously played by Orson Welles in the 1949 film *The Third Man*, making the piece a "three-way collaboration between composer, performer, and listener."[45]

Extending his practice of "musical realities" based on other composers' works, Schimmel derives most of his material from the dotted-quarter-plus-eighth-note chromatic-scale motifs that not only comprise Anton Karas's haunting *Third Man* score, originally played on the zither, but "much of European cabaret music." Schimmel presents this motif in a succession of dance rhythms indicated in the score: reggae/shimmy, tarantella, foxtrot, tango, and *fado*, wandering from one to the other without closure, as if the accordion had a "mind of its own."

Each of these rhythms is based on ideas and experiences underlying not only the West's popular dance rhythms but the conventional repertoire of the club-dating accordionist (Schimmel himself has played hundreds of club dates). In *A Portrait of Harry Lime*, Schimmel steps outside the conventions associated with these forms, shattering their familiar and pleasurable associations with pretty background music to explore their dark, sinister dimensions. Each of these dance sections, ranging in length from thirty seconds to one minute, is rudely interrupted by a cluster of dissonant notes or an abrupt change in rhythm. The sections marked "slow shimmy/reggae" and the tarantella themes are truncated by the addition of new unmetered material marked as "senza misura" (without barlines). Throughout the work, "smeared" tones, dissonant chords, and eerie sustained high notes seem to violently "attack" the lyrical melodies and regular rhythmic accompaniments, gradually unraveling the piece's fabric of Western tonality and shattering its elegant society-ballroom mood.

Schimmel appears to have been motivated to write this piece by certain aspects of social realities as he encountered them in his musical career: "accordion gig-itis,"[46] brought on by endless repetitions of familiar songs at club dates, the commodification of the arts (i.e. popular music and the movies), and the obsession with compositional procedure. Schimmel indicates each section's tempo markings with precision but blurs them with exaggerated *rubati*. In conjunction with his references to European dance music and contemporary popular culture, Schimmel suggests a connection between folk traditions and compositional practices in contemporary music. Schimmel's juxtaposition of such forms as the tango, Portuguese *fado*, and reggae parallels his own observations likening the accordion to a world unto itself, a diasporan landscape.

The link between old and new, past and present, is represented in the parallel worlds evoked by the piece: the hedonistic, amoral, pleasure-seeking world of postwar Vienna (represented in the film by theater and café scenes) and the decay of Imperial Vienna, represented in the film by piles of postwar rubble and lonely statues of composers in the Burggarten. Invoking Bakhtin's "chronotope" concept in relation to other of his compositions, *A Portrait of Harry Lime* has a metaphorical dimension in that Schimmel is using cinematic time (the film) and this place (Vienna) as a means of probing into the subconscious of contemporary culture. As the setting for *The Third Man*, Vienna appears as a place where musical performance and its accompanying pleasures (cabarets, theater scenes) are mixed with fear, deceit, and an uncertain, anxious energy.

The Harry Lime theme presented in this piece is made up in part by Schimmel's recollections of Anton Karas's music, and in part from what he recalls from the cinematic performance by Orson Welles, to whom the work is dedicated. His own major impetus in "creating" this piece was his desire to bring to life the ambivalence and anticipation surrounding Harry Lime's character. Harry Lime's presence in the film is significant: he engages the other characters (his girlfriend Anna Schmidt and an American friend Holly Martins, the film's protagonist) and the viewer on different levels, drawing them into his world and casting his spell. Schimmel has created his own musical version of Lime—an ambivalent symbol of evil, banality, disillusionment, and the existential dilemma.[47] As Harry Lime's "theme" appears, it clearly becomes Schimmel's creation in the way that it references European cabaret music, while suggesting the character's world-weariness and dissipation.

The introduction of each new rhythm is followed by an abrupt dissolution of that rhythm: the tango is followed by an agitated "listesso" section; the tarantella and foxtrot sections are both followed by faint scattered murmurings in an unmetered "senza misura" section. The violent disruptions of the pleasant dance rhythms underline the idea that the routines of pleasure are not implacable.

The piece concludes with a dramatic thinning of the texture: sustained low bass tones punctuated by shuddering eighth-note figures. With some carefully calculated pushes on the bellows, Schimmel creates eerie tone-bending distortions in the low bass notes (D and C), evoking the sinister mood of the film's final scene in which Lime is "hunted down in the sewers of Vienna, where he dies like a rat."[48]

The treatment of thematic material in *A Portait of Harry Lime* suggests that Schimmel is aiming to create dramatic situations through the performance of the accordion, both with and without the specific visual and textual references. In emphasizing the imaginative response of the composer to the mood of the film score, and the listener's response to the sound, and moving in and out of the film score as its author/composer, this work can be linked to Schimmel's other musical realities, including *A Rossini Reality*. Unlike *A Rossini Reality*, *Harry Lime* features the fictional figure of Harry Lime and his milieu, which invites depiction in a subjectively apposite and creative fashion. We are more than listeners or viewers but partners in the creation of William Schimmel himself, entering our own world through his world and Harry Lime's.

Final Reflections

Schimmel's musical realities present a decentralizing movement toward alternative modes of dramatic expression and performance on the accordion, expressed in textual and musical tropes that become increasingly personalized and intense, following his abandonment of traditional romantic and modernist compositional techniques. Underlying all of these "realities" is what one could call a mission, which is connected to the selection of the works' themes, contexts, and the central role played by the accordion in his composition. This mission can be seen as parallel to the crusading efforts of Schimmel's contemporaries in the "accordion world" to legitimize the accordion and call attention to its "place" in the world of composition. Although Schimmel has likened the accordion to a diaspora on the margins of the more "central" classical and romantic idioms, I believe that the musical landscape he creates offers a slice of the global ecumene described by Ulf Hannerz, a metaphorical "place" where different cultural traditions, vocabularies, and sounds can find common ground.[49] Placing the accordion "outside" the mainstream of European music does not tell the whole story; the instrument reflects a dense layering of social relationships and the flow of culture.

Returning to Bakhtin's idea of the "chronotope," we might say that Schimmel's searches for the past are also searches for the present. Stories and films from the past are also stories about now. Different landscapes merge, and the accordion becomes a metaphor for exploring and feeling rather than self-knowledge and mastery. Underlying his realities is another creative trajectory, a progression in which the composer moves from two sites of learning: from his classical training and adopted ethnic "heritage," the tango, to a third, more abstract, autobiographical place, a site that is rooted in the present moment, the imaginary spaces of his musical realities. A sense of adventure and discovery, as well as pleasant security, after finding a safe "home" following his dual exile from academe and the accordion world is mingled with an anxious, uncertain rootlessness. Given the importance Schimmel attaches to the listener's response, real or imagined, to his music, this trajectory took on a special significance in the uncertainty that an accordionist faced in the world of Juilliard and the compositional world of New York City, in which Schimmel lived and worked.

We might consider Barthes's idea of the "modern scriptor"—a collaborator born "simultaneously with the text" rather than as a father of the text.[50] Composing a text (music) is more like a set of encounters or conversations—or travel—than the creation of a fixed work. "Writing can no longer designate an operation of re-cording, notation, representation, 'depiction'; rather it designates exactly what linguists call the performative, a rare verbal form (exclusively given in the first person and in the present tense) in which the enunciation has no other content (contains no other proposition than the act by which it is uttered)."[51]

Schimmel's "realities" challenge us to respond to his music, and all musical composition, not only as performative but as means to understanding identity processes. At the same time, they remind us of the vital themes of otherness and displacement in his work. Schimmel came to be himself as an artist—and as a person—through processes of rupture and displacement.[52] As a volume dedi-cated to the idea of the "accordion on new shores" has revealed, the accordion has become a symbol of and metaphor for migration, displacement, and renewal. The instrument is not a fixed entity but is always contingent on local structures of race, culture, gender, sexuality, and history. These structures often overlap, making the identity realities surrounding the accordion not so much about ori-gins and homelands, chosen or forced, but as sites of creativity, authorship, and travel. Studying Schimmel's "new scores" for piano accordion not only reveals the instrument's rich layers of musical signification and the deeply variegated roots of his compositional practices; it can also help us to extrapolate rich stories about the historical, cultural, and social construction of the accordion's identity as a compositional tool and the reasons for its universal embrace (at least in the Western world) as a symbol of the human experience.

Notes

I would like to thank William Schimmel for his neverending availability and generos-ity in the preparation of this essay. Bill's comments on my analysis of his music and career were invaluable, as were all of the manuscripts, scores, writings, and recordings he cheerfully provided. In that sense, this essay is more representative of collaboration than the work of a single author. However, Jacobson, not Schimmel, must answer for any inaccuracies that may appear in this essay.

1. See Björn Heile's discussion of modernist and postmodernist musical collage tech-niques, "Collage vs. Compositional Control," in *Postmodern Music/Postmodern Thought*, ed. Judith Lochhead and Joseph Auner (New York: Routledge, 2002), 288; see also Glenn Watkins, *Pyramids at the Louvre: Music, Culture, and Collage from Stravinsky to the Postmod-ernists* (Cambridge, Mass.: Harvard University Press, 1994).

2. William Schimmel, personal interview, New York, August 8, 2008.

3. Raymond Williams, *The Sociology of Culture* (1981; reprint, Chicago: University of Chicago Press, 1995), viii.

4. William Schimmel, personal interview, New York, August 8, 2008.

5. Mikhail Bakhtin, *The Dialogic Imagination: Four Essays*, ed. Michael Holquist, trans. Caryl Emerson and Michael Holquist (Austin: University of Texas Press, 1981).

6. William Schimmel, personal interview, New York, August 8, 2008.

7. Ibid.

8. Kevin McNeilly, "Ugly Beauty: John Zorn and the Politics of Postmodern Music," *Postmodern Culture* 5.2 (2005), http://muse.jhu.edu/login?uri=/journals/postmodern_culture/voo5/5.2mcneilly.html (accessed January 23, 2012).

9. Roland Barthes, "Death of the Author," in *Image, Music, Text* (New York: Hill and Wang, 1977), 147.

10. The annual event is held at the Tenri Cultural Center in Manhattan. Schimmel posts the information on his website, http://www.billschimmel.com.

11. American Accordionists Association membership information, http://www.ameraccord.com, (accessed January 25, 2009).

12. Anthoy Gallarini, "The Accordion in the Field of Serious Music," *Musical Merchandise Magazine* (1948): 1.

13. This idea of ethnic self-alienation is expressed in James Periconi's insightful memoir of playing (and abandoning) the accordion as a self-conscious Italian American: "*Vergogna e Risorgimento*: The Secret Life of an Italian-American Accordionist," *Free-Reed Journal* 4 (2002): 48.

14. Marion Jacobson, "Searching for Rockordion: The Changing Image of the Accordion in American Popular Music," *American Music* 25 (2007): 219.

15. Known as such because it was developed by the pioneering Dallapé firm in Stradella, Italy, and adopted as the "industry standard" by all of the major European accordion manufacturers as early as 1900. The Stradella system is seen as the key to the piano accordion's popularity because it is simple and intuitive.

16. Willard Palmer, "Should Accordionists Play Bach?" *Accordion World* (1949): 17–18.

17. Willaim Schimmel, personal communication, February 4, 2009. Schimmel also wrote about his fondness for the Stradella system in *Learning from Lawrence Welk* (New York: Studio Muse Productions, 1987).

18. William Schimmel, introductory notes to "A Portrait of Harry Lime" (unpublished ms. in the author's possession, provided by the composer, 2006), 1.

19. William Schimmel, personal interview, New York, June 17, 2003.

20. William Schimmel, *Accordion Culture: Time, Space, and High School* (New York: Studio Muse Press, 2007), 3. Available from the author's website: www.billschimmel.com (accessed January 25, 2012).

21. Ibid.

22. William Schimmel, personal interview, New York, August 8, 2008.

23. His piano teacher was Frances S. Goldstein, whom he describes as "kind yet demanding" (personal communication, February 3, 2008).

24. Ibid.

25. Daniel Binder, "A Formal and Stylistic Analysis of Selected Compositions for Solo Accordion, with Accompanying Ensembles by Twentieth-Century American Composers,

with Implications of their Impact upon the Place of Accordion in the World of Serious Music" (Ph.D. dissertation, Ball State University, 1981).

26. See http://www.billschimmel.com.

27. Marion Jacobson, rev. of Pauline Oliveros, *The Wanderer: Works for Accordion and Voice, Journal of the Society for American Music* 3.1 (2009): 120–21. Although Oliveros's reputation is expanding in the new music field, not much has been written about the accordion's influence on her avant-garde and postmodern compositions.

28. Bernard Holland, "Summer Concert: Hudson River Backdrop," *New York Times*, July 1, 1984, http://query.nytimes.com/gst/fullpage.html?res=9B04E5D81539F932A3 5754C0A962948260&sec=&spon=&emc=eta1 (accessed January 6, 2012).

29. William Schimmel, personal interview, New York, August 8, 2008.

30. Schimmel's recordings with Waits include *Raindogs* (RCA Ariola, 1987), *Frank's Wild Years* (New York: Island, 1987), *Lost in the Stars* (Ocean, N.J.: MusicMasters, 1993), and *Beautiful Maladies* (New York: Island, 1998 [Distributed by PolyGram]).

31. William Schimmel, personal interview, New York, August 8, 2008.

32. William Schimmel, personal interview, New York, June 17, 2003.

33. Some scholars have noted, as do María Susana Azzi and Sydney Hutchinson in this volume, that diatonic accordions such as those used in tango and *merengue típico* engender a more physical, percussive playing style. The piano accordion, with its fluid bellowsing dynamic, lends itself to a smoother playing style and sonic aesthetic, which has been encouraged by its advocates. My book, *Squeeze This! A Cultural History of the Accordion in America* (Urbana: University of Illinois Press, 2012), discusses the different playing techniques, aesthetics, and contexts of diatonic and chromatic accordions and how these distinctions reflect cultural differences in the communities that play them.

34. Schimmel likes to emphasize that he was one of the first American musicians and scholars to become interested in Argentine tango and Piazzolla's work, "four years before Piazzolla's second coming in '85." (According to María Susana Azzi, Piazzolla had been living in New York City from 1925–37, and again from 1958–59; he visited the United States in 1976 and in 1985.) Schimmel's pronouncement that "we [the Tango Project] ushered in the tango revival in America, which made it very good for Piazzolla" (personal communication, February 5, 2009), should be taken with a grain of salt.

35. María Susana Azzi, "Tango, Peronism, and Astor Piazzolla," in *From Tejano to Tango: Latin American Popular Music*, ed. Walter Aaron Clark (New York: Routledge, 2002), 38.

36. Schimmel recorded this work live in 1998, at a concert at Our Savior's Atonement Lutheran Church in New York.

37. Luis Buñuel and Salvador Dali, dirs., *Un Chien Andalou*, DVD (Les Grands Films Classiques, 2004).

38. William Schimmel, personal interview, New York, August 8, 2008.

39. Ibid.

40. Anne LeBaron, "Reflections of Surrealism in Postmodern Musics," in *Postmodern Music/Postmodern Thought*, ed. Judith Lochhead and Joseph Auner (New York: Routledge, 2002), 29.

41. "Mystery of Cinema," abridged transcript of speech given by Luis Buñuel in 1953, included on the DVD of *Un Chien Andalou*.

42. Rene T. A. Lysoff, "Mozart in Mirrorshades: Music, Technology, and Ethnomusicological Anxiety," *Ethnomusicology* 41.2 (1997): 212–15; LeBaron, "Reflections of Surrealism in Postmodern Musics," 28–30; John Oswald, "Creatigality," in *Sounding Off: Music as Subversion/Resistance/Revolution*, ed. Ron Sakosky and Fred Wei-han Ho (New York: Autonomedia, 1995), 87–90.

43. Schimmel, "Portrait of Harry Lime," 1.

44. Ibid.

45. Ibid.

46. Schimmel's latest recording project, *Duality Wrecks*, is a series of musical realities inspired by his baby-boomer audiences at club dates (personal communication, February 5, 2009).

47. Ibid.

48. Schimmel, "Portrait of Harry Lime," 1.

49. Ulf Hannerz, *Transnational Connections: Culture, People, Places* (New York: Routledge, 1996), 3.

50. Barthes, "Death of the Author," 145.

51. Ibid., 148.

52. These processes keep surfacing in his stories about his creative life and career, such as being denied tenure at Brooklyn College in 1976, which cut short his academic career at age twenty-seven.

[blank page 314]

Glossary

Accordion: Refers to a variety of bellows-driven portable *free-reed* instruments with different physical and musical characteristics. The accordion belongs to the aerophone family—its sound is produced by air flowing past a flexible reed in a frame, causing it to vibrate. Air pressure is generated with a bellows that is operated manually by pushing and pulling. In a free-reed instrument, the physical characteristics of the reed itself, such as material, mass, length, and stiffness, primarily determine the pitch or frequency of the musical note produced. The pitch is further affected by the physical dimensions of the chamber in which the reed is fitted and by the airflow. The instrument's name reflects its unique feature by which through the handing of one key or button, a full chord resounds (derived from the older German word *Accord,* meaning "chord").

Bandonion: The diatonic German (Chemnitz) concertina distributed by Heinrich Band (Krefeld) in the 1840s, which—unlike its English counterpart—works on the same two-pitch (push/pull) principle as the *diatonic accordion.* This type of concertina, in Spanish called *bandoneón*, is traditionally featured in tango music due to the instrument's popularity in Argentina in the late nineteenth century, when tango developed from the various dance styles in the River Plate area (Argentina and Uruguay). The Argentine musician Astor Piazzolla (1921–92) is considered one of the most famous exponents of this instrument.

Chromatic button accordion: A type of button accordion whose treble (melody) keys are arranged chromatically. The bass-side keyboard is usually arranged in the Stradella system (a button board layout that features rows of single-note buttons of related key tonalities) or in one of the various free-bass systems (a button board of single-note buttons). The best-known types of chromatic button accordions are the Russian *bayan*, the French *musette*, and the Viennese Schrammel accordion. The first chromatic button accordion was built by the Viennese musician Franz Walther in 1850.

Concertina: A free-reed instrument similar to the accordion but with buttons parallel to the bellows on both sides (the buttons or keys of an accordion are perpendicular to the bellows). Concertinas come in square, hexagonal, and octagonal shapes.

The English (or Wheatstone English) concertina is a fully chromatic instrument on which a single button produces one pitch regardless of the push/pull direction of the bellows. The instrument was developed by the physicist Sir Charles Wheatstone in the late 1820s; he filed a patent for an improved version (a hexagonal double action, forty-eight key instrument) in 1844.

The square-shaped German Konzertina (or Chemnitz concertina), with single notes on the bass side, was developed in Chemnitz by Carl Friedrich Uhlig in the early 1830s. The various German concertina types share common construction features and core button layout. In the American Midwest, the term "concertina" often refers to the Chemnitz concertina.

The hexagon-shaped Anglo (or Anglo-German) concertina is the British adaptation of the Chemnitz concertina.

Diatonic accordion: A type of button accordion whose treble (melody) keys are limited to the notes of diatonic scales. "Diatonic" refers to the arrangement of the seven natural pitches within an octave without altering the established pattern of a key or mode (such as the major and minor scales). The available notes on the melody side of a diatonic button accordion are based on different keys. Most diatonic accordions are "single action" (they produce two different sounds on one button when the bellows change direction). Left-hand buttons are usually "double action" (they produce the same pitch on push and pull) and play bass notes and chords for accompaniment.

Other diatonic members of the accordion family include the German Konzertina (or Chemnitz concertina) and its derivatives, the Anglo (or Anglo-German) concertina, and the Argentine *bandoneón*.

Free reed: The term refers to the sound production in a variety of instruments, such as harmonicas, reed organs, and accordions, as well as the Chinese *sheng* and the Japanese *sho*. The reed is fixed by one end in a close-fitting frame—the optimal distance between reed and frame is 0.03 millimeter (less than the width of a hair). Airflow over one side of the reed creates an area of low pressure on that side, causing the reed to flex toward the low-pressure side. The reed frame is constructed so that the flexing of the reed obstructs the airflow, which reduces or eliminates the low-pressure area and allows the reed to flex back. Each time the reed passes through the frame, it interrupts airflow. These rapid, periodic interruptions of the airflow create the audible vibrations perceived by the listener.

Uni-sonority, bi-sonority: The free reeds used in accordions are usually steel tongues, riveted to a metal reed-plate with two slots of the same size of the reeds. One reed is attached on each side of the plate, and a leather tap covers the opposite side to each reed to prevent air from entering and actuating the reed. If the pair of reeds is identical, the same pitch will sound on either push or pull; this principle is called "uni-sonor" (used in the piano accordion and certain concertinas). If the reeds are of different size or thickness, each button actuates two different pitches—one on bellows push, and the other on pull; this is called "bi-sonor" (used in diatonic accordions). The three basic models with combinations of fixed chords and single notes that were either uni- or bi-sonor existed as early as 1834.

Piano accordion: A chromatic accordion with a piano-type keyboard on the treble side and a bass-button keyboard on the left-hand side. Although accordions are technically related to the reed organ, the accordion equipped with a right-hand keyboard is called "piano accordion." With the development of the Stradella bass system (a standardized button-board layout that features rows of single-note buttons of related key tonalities), the piano accordion became the first standardized accordion. Multiple reed blocks combined with switches provide the piano accordion with a huge range of notes and sounds. Various free-bass systems have been designed, which consist of single-note buttons with a range of up to five octaves. "Converter" accordions are capable of switching from standard bass to free bass.

The Viennese instrument maker Matthäus Bauer exhibited a three-octave "Clavierharmonika" (piano harmonica) at a trade fair in Munich in 1854. The Parisian manufacturer M. Busson's instrument, variously known as *accordéon-orgue, flûtina,* or *harmoniflûte,* featured a piano-type keyboard for the right hand; it was shown at the World Exhibition in Paris in 1855.

Squeezebox: Pulling and pushing (squeezing) the bellows generates airflow that is directed on reeds by depressing buttons or keys that raise palettes, hence this popular name for the box-shaped diatonic accordion or concertina.

Tuning: The tuning of the individual reeds is a crucial component of eliciting particular tone colors. For the common button accordion, the number of reeds per pitch for the right-hand buttons varies between one and four. Multiple reeds may be tuned in different combinations of the fundamental note and its upper and lower one or two octaves, and from "dry" (with reeds in unison and no acoustic beating) to various degrees of "wetness." For the latter, some of the reeds that sound together are slightly detuned relative to the other(s) to produce a "beating"—an interference between sound waves of slightly differing wavelengths. This "beating" results in a tremolo or shimmering effect.

Contributors

MARÍA SUSANA AZZI is a cultural anthropologist who, through the tango, looks at the history of multiculturalism in Argentina and the recovery of social networks, symbols, and values of cultural identity (national, metropolitan, barrio, and gender identities). She has widely published on various aspects of the tango, including *Le Grand Tango: The Life and Music of Astor Piazzolla* (with Simon Collier), *¡Tango! The Dance, the Song, the Story* (with Simon Collier, Artemis Cooper, and Richard Martin), and *Antropología del Tango* (1991). Azzi has presented papers and lectures throughout Latin America, the United States, and Europe. She served as a consultant for several documentaries on the tango, sound recordings, the Metropolitan Museum of Art in New York, the National Geographic Society, the British Library Sound Archive, and the Smithsonian Institution.

EGBERTO BERMÚDEZ studied early music-performance practice and musicology at the Guildhall School of Music and King's College, University of London. Currently he is a professor at the Instituto de Investigaciones Estéticas of the National University in Bogotá, Colombia. He has published a number of works on Latin American and Colombian music history, traditional and popular musics, and musical instruments. In 1984 he founded, and since then directed, Canto, an ensemble that specializes in Spanish and Latin American Renaissance and Baroque repertoire. In 1992, he established (with Juan Luis Restrepo) the Fundación de Música, an institution dedicated to disseminating the products of research on the Latin American musical past among scholars and the general public. He served as president of the Historical Harp Society from 1998 to 2001.

MARK F. DeWITT received his doctorate in ethnomusicology from the University of California, Berkeley. He holds the Dr. Tommy Comeaux Endowed Chair in Traditional Music at the University of Louisiana at Lafayette, where he is a professor of music. He is also the author of *Cajun and Zydeco Dance Music in Northern California: Modern Pleasures in a Postmodern World* (2008). In 2004, the Society for Ethnomusicology awarded him the Klaus P. Wachsmann Prize for Advanced and Critical Essays in Organology for his 2003 essay, "The Diatonic Button Accordion in Ethnic Context: Idiom and Style in Cajun Dance Music."

JOSHUA HOROWITZ received his M.A. in composition and music theory from the Academy of Music in Graz, Austria, where he taught music theory and served as research fellow and director of the Klezmer Music Research Project for eight years. Horowitz plays *tsimbl*, nineteenth-century button accordion, and piano. He is the founder and director of the ensemble Budowitz and a founding member of Veretski Pass. He has performed with the Vienna Chamber Orchestra, Theodore Bikel, the late Adrienne Cooper, Joel Rubin, and Brave Old World. He taught advanced jazz theory at Stanford University with the late saxophonist Stan Getz and is a regular teacher at KlezKamp, the Albuquerque Academy, and Klez Kanada. His musicological work is published in *The Sephardic Songbook* (with Aron Saltiel) and *The Ultimate Klezmer*. In addition to his work as a musician, he led the first post–World War II music therapy group at the pioneering Beratungszentrum (Counseling Center) in Graz, Austria.

SYDNEY HUTCHINSON received her Ph.D. in ethnomusicology from New York University and is assistant professor of ethnomusicology at Syracuse University. While a Humboldt Fellow at the Berlin Phonogramm-Archiv of the Ethnological Museum in Berlin, she conducted field research that focused on masculinity and movement in competitive air guitar. Hutchinson is the author of *From Quebradita Of Duranguense: Dance in Mexican American Youth Culture* (2007), as well as articles on topics such as Latin American dance, music and the body, public folklore, salsa dancing, and *merengue típico* in *Ethnomusicology, Journal of American Folklore, Folklore Forum, the world of music,* and *Centro: The Journal of the Center for Puerto Rican Studies,* as well as several edited volumes. She is working on a book on the performance of gender in Dominican *merengue típico,* and she still plays accordion and yodels in her spare time.

MARION S. JACOBSON is an ethnomusicologist, author and freelance writer who has written hundreds of reviews and features of live concerts and events of all the major world music traditions from Indian ragas to Cajun/Zydeco for the *Washington Post, Stereo Review,* and dozens of music magazines and blogs. Jacobson earned her PhD in music from New York University in 2003. She began digging for the fossilized remains of lost American accordion cultures in New York City. Grants from the American Philosophical Society and the Mellon Foundation allowed her to continue excavations in the accordion centers of Houston, San Antonio, the Twin Cities, and the San Francisco Bay Area, leading to *Squeeze This: a Cultural History of the Accordion* (2012), the first comprehensive scholarly book on the piano accordion. Jacobson has been involved with arts councils and community arts since 1997. She was the first staff folklorist at New York State's largest arts council, Arts Westchester, staff folklorist at the Staten Island Council on the Arts, and consulting folklorist for the Brooklyn Arts Council, the Bronx Council on the Arts, and CityLore.

JAMES P. LEARY is a professor of folklore and Scandinavian studies at the University of Wisconsin at Madison, where he also serves as director of the folklore program and is a cofounder of the Center for the Study of Upper Midwestern Cultures. A native of northern Wisconsin, he has conducted field research on the traditional music of America's Upper Midwest since the mid-1970s, resulting in such documentary recordings as *Accordions in the Cutover: Field Recordings of Ethnic Music from Lake Superior's South Shore, Ach Ya! Traditional German-American Music from Wisconsin* (with Philip Martin), *Minnesota Polka, Midwest Ramblin,'* and *Down Home Dairyland* (with Richard March); and in books that include *Yodeling in Dairyland: A History of Swiss Music in Wisconsin* (1991), *Wisconsin Folklore* (1998), and *Polkabilly: How the Goose Island Ramblers Redefined American Folk Music* (2006).

MEGWEN LOVELESS completed her Ph.D. in cultural anthropology at Harvard University. Her research in ethnomusicology focuses on music and dance from the Northeast of Brazil as well as regional/national migrations and the juxtaposition of modernity and tradition in Brazilian popular music. Her work in second-language acquisition focuses on the use of music and new media in the language classroom. She teaches in the Spanish and Portuguese department of Princeton University, where she is currently acting director of the Portuguese language program.

RICHARD MARCH holds a Ph.D. in folklore from Indiana University. He is a folk and community-arts specialist for the Wisconsin Arts Board, responsible for planning and implementing a statewide folk-arts program for Wisconsin, as well as a research associate at the Institute of Ethnology and Folklore Research in Zagreb. He has carried out field and archival research on the traditions of the South Slavs in Europe and in American ethnic communities. Having widely written on German/Eastern European polka and Balkan Slavic music from the Upper Midwest, he is currently finishing a book on *tamburitza* music that will be published in Croatia. March plays the Slovenian button accordion.

CATHY RAGLAND is assistant professor of ethnomusicology and director of the Masters of Music program in ethnomusicology in the Department of Music and Dance at the University of Texas, Pan American. Her research centers on music and the politics of migration and global networks. She is the author of *Música Norteña: Mexican Migrants Creating a Nation between Nations* (2009) as well as articles and reviews in *Ethnomusicology, Yearbook for Traditional Music, Journal of American Folklore, Free-Reed Journal,* and others. A native of San Antonio, Texas, she has been a music critic and columnist at the *San Antonio Express-News,* the

Seattle Times, the *Seattle Weekly*, and the *Austin American-Statesman*. She is also committed to community-based education and advocacy through music, having produced radio programs, festivals, workshops, seminars, and exhibits as a folklorist and program director at the Center for Traditional Music and Dance in New York, Texas Folklife Resources in Austin, and Northwest Folklife in Seattle.

HELENA SIMONETT received her doctoral degree in ethnomusicology at the University of California, Los Angeles, and is a faculty member of the Center for Latin American Studies and Blair School of Music, Vanderbilt University, Nashville. She is the author of *Banda: Mexican Musical Life across Borders* (2001) and *En Sinaloa nací: Historia de la música de banda* (2004). Her current research focuses on ceremonial music making/dancing among indigenous people of northwestern Mexico. She grew up listening to her grandpa playing the Swiss button accordion and is fond of many kinds of accordion music.

JARED SNYDER is an independent music researcher living in Rochester, Washington. He is a graduate of Boston University with a B.A. in anthropology. His articles have been published in *American Music, Black Music Research Journal, Free-Reed Journal, Encyclopedia of the Blues, Concertina and Squeezebox, Musical Performance*, and *SingOut!* He is an accordionist and guitarist.

JANET L. STURMAN earned her Ph.D. at Columbia University. She is professor of music in the School of Music at the University of Arizona and served on the board of directors of the Society for Ethnomusicology and the College Music Society. She is the author of *Zarzuela: Spanish Operetta, American Stage* (2000). Her research focuses on Latin American and southwestern U.S. traditions and addresses the relationship between musical performance, politics, ethnicity, and class. She has published on intercultural performance practice in music and theater as well as on the impact of technology and transnational economic policies on musical practice.

CHRISTINE F. ZINNI holds a Ph.D. in American studies from the State University of New York at Buffalo. Her master's thesis, an oral-history video project accomplished under the direction of the ethnomusicologist Charles Keil, focuses on the performances and interconnected stories of Italian American accordionists in the immigrant community where she grew up. Zinni's research into the legacy of Italian Americans has been published in *Voices: The New York Journal of Folklore, Oral History, Oral Culture, and Italian Americans* (2009), and *Uncertainty and Insecurity in the New Age: Studies in Italian Americana* (2009). Zinni teaches in the anthropology department at the State University of New York at Brockport and also works as a consultant/videographer on the New York Folks Arts programming. Along with documentaries and traveling exhibits about Italian Americans, she has organized public folklore projects on the regional traditions of Native Americans and Polish Americans.

Index

324

MUSIC IN AMERICAN LIFE

The University of Illinois Press
is a founding member of the
Association of American University Presses.

Designed by Jim Proefrock
Composed in 10.5/13 Filosofia
at the University of Illinois Press
Manufactured by Sheridan Books, Inc.

University of Illinois Press
1325 South Oak Street
Champaign, IL 61820-6903
www.press.uillinois.edu